The Future of the Biblical Past

Society of Biblical Literature

Semeia Studies

Number 66
The Future of the Biblical Past:
Envisioning Biblical Studies on a Global Key

edited by
Roland Boer and Fernando F. Segovia

THE FUTURE OF THE BIBLICAL PAST
ENVISIONING BIBLICAL STUDIES ON A GLOBAL KEY

Edited by

Roland Boer and Fernando F. Segovia

Society of Biblical Literature
Atlanta

THE FUTURE OF THE BIBLICAL PAST:
ENVISIONING BIBLICAL STUDIES ON A GLOBAL KEY

Copyright © 2012 by the Society of Biblical Literature

Library of Congress Cataloging-in-Publication Data

The future of the biblical past : envisioning biblical studies on a global key / edited by Roland Boer and Fernando F. Segovia.

    p. cm. — (Society of Biblical Literature semeia studies ; no. 66)

Includes bibliographical references (p.   ) and index.

ISBN 978-1-58983-703-4 (paper binding : alk. paper) — ISBN 978-1-58983-704-1 (electronic format)

1. Bible—Criticism, interpretation, etc. I. Boer, Roland, 1961- II. Segovia, Fernando F.

BS511.3.F88 2012

220.07—dc23

2012041816

Printed on acid-free, recycled paper
conforming to ANSI/NISO Z39.48-1992 (R1997) and ISO 9706:1994
standards for paper permanence.

Contents

Acknowledgements

This volume has been made possible due to the assistance and support of a good number of people, to whom we are deeply indebted and most thankful. First and foremost, to all those who took part in the project, for their gracious acceptance of our invitation and fine contributions. Second, to Mr. Luis Menéndez Antuña for his superb editing of the manuscript, who, as a doctoral student in New Testament and Early Christianity in the Graduate Department of Religion at Vanderbilt University, served as editorial assistant for the project. Third, to the editorial board of Semeia Studies for their kind acceptance of the volume for publication in the series and to its editor, Gerald O. West for his work in shepherding the volume toward publication. Finally, to the entire publications staff of the Society of Biblical Literature for its impeccable assistance throughout the process of publication.

ABBREVIATIONS

ABD: Anchor Bible Dictionary
ACHEI/UBCHEA: Asian Christian Higher Education Institute of the United
Board for Christian Higher Education in Asia
ADRA: Adventist Development and Relief Agency
AJT: *Asia Journal of Theology*
ANZABS: The Aotearoa-New Zealand Association of Biblical Studies
ANZATS: Australia and New Zealand Association of Theological Schools
ATF: Australian Theological Forum
AThR: *Anglican Theological Review*
BiBh: *Bible Bhashyam*
BibInt: *Biblical Interpretation*
BMRC: Biblical Manuscript Research Centre
BTESSC/CDSS: Board of Theological Education, Senate of Serampore College/
Centre for Dalit /Subaltern Studies
BThZ: *Berliner Theologische Zeitschrift*
CARICOM: Caribbean Community
CBS: Contextual Bible Study
CCC: Caribbean Council of Churches
CEBI: Centro de Estudos Biblicos
CELADEC: Comisión Ecuménica Latino Americana de Educación Cristiana
CEP Centro de Estudios y Publicaciones, Perú
CETA: Caribbean Evangelical Theological Association
CEV: Contemporary English Version
CGST: Caribbean Graduate School of Theology
CLAR: Conferencia Latinoamericana de Religiosos
CMS: Christian Missionary Society
CTP-CMI: Centro de Teología Popular, Bolivia
CTQ: *Concordia Theological Quarterly*
CUPSA: Casa Unida de Publicaciones Sociedad Anónima
DEI: Departamento Ecuménico de Investigaciones
EST: Escola Superior de Teologia de São Leopoldo
ExpTim: *Expository Times*
FAT: Forschungen zum Alten Testament

FBBS: Facet Books Biblical Series
HB: Hebrew Bible
HB/OT: Hebrew Bible/Old Testament
HSRC: Human Sciences Research Council (in South Africa)
HvTSt: Hervormde Teologiese Studies
IDB: Interpreter's Dictionary of the Bible
IJT: Indian Journal of Theology
ISEDET: Instituto Superior Evangélico de Estudios Teológicos
JAAR: Journal of the American Academy of Religion
JBL: Journal of Biblical Literature
JRT: Journal of Religion and Theology
JSNT: Journal for the Study of the New Testament
JSNTSup: Journal for the Study of the New Testament Supplement Series
JSOT: Journal for the Study of the Old Testament
JSOTSup: Journal for the Study of the Old Testament Supplement Series
JTS: Jamaica Theological Seminary
JTSA: Journal of Theology for South Africa
LHBOTS: Library of Hebrew Bible/Old Testament Studies
MAI: Multilateral Agreement on Investment
NCU: Northern Caribbean University
Neot: Neotestamentica
NIV: New International Version
NT: New Testament
NTT: Norsk Teologisk Tidsskrift
NTSSA: New Testament Society of Southern Africa
NZQA: New Zealand Qualifications Authority
OECD: Organization for Economic Cooperation and Development
OTE: Old Testament Essays
PBRF: Performance Based Research Fund
PMLA: Proceedings of the Modern Language Association
PUC: Pontifícia Universidade Católica de Rio de Janeiro
REBILAC: Rede Biblica Latino-Americana e Caribenha
RIBLA: Revista de Interpretación Bíblica Latino Americana
ROK: Republic of Korea
SARS: Severe Acute Respiratory Syndrome
SBL: Society of Biblical Literature
SDA: Seventh-day Adventist
SEÅ: Svensk Exegetisk Årsbok
SEBILA: Seminario Bíblico Latino Americano
SJOT: Scandinavian Journal of the Old Testament
SNTS: Studiorum Novi Testamenti Societas
SNVAO: Skrifter/Norske videnskaps-akademi Oslo
SPCK: Society for the Promotion of Christian Knowledge

SR: *Studies in Religion/Sciences Religieuses*
ST: *Studia Theologica*
STK: *Svensk Teologisk Kvartalskrift*
TEC: Tertiary Education Committee
TRu N.F.: *Theologische Rundschau, Neue Folge*
TS: *Theological Studies*
TZ: *Theologische Zeitung*
UBL: Universidad Biblica Latinoamericana
UBS: United Bible Societies
UMESP: Universidad Metodista de São Paulo
USAID: United States Agency of International Development
USAMGIK: United States Army Military Government in Korea
USQR: *Union Seminary Quarterly Review*
USSR: Union of Soviet Socialist Republics
UTC/ISPCK: United Theological College/International Society for the
Promotion of Christian Knowledge
UTCWI: United Theological College of the West Indies
UWI: University of the West Indies
WUNT: Wissenschaftliche Untersuchungen zum Neuen Testament
WW: *Word and World*
YDP-UIM: Yong Dong Po Urban Industrial Mission

Introduction: The Futures of Biblical Pasts

Roland Boer and Fernando F. Segovia

This volume has been so long in the making that between the time when the book was first conceived and its eventual completion the world began one of its accelerated periods of irruptive change. However, given the significance of the mandate we have undertaken here, this collection of essays has required more energy than most. We asked contributors to answer the following twofold question: what does global biblical studies look like in the early decades of the twenty-first century, and what new directions may be espied? The last time such a comprehensive task was undertaken was well over twenty years ago. In 1985 *The Hebrew Bible and Its Modern Interpreters* appeared, edited by Douglas Knight and Gene M. Tucker. A few years later, in 1989, it was followed by *The New Testament and Its Modern Interpreters*, now edited by E. Jay Epp and G. W. MacRae. The third volume of this series was *Early Judaism and Its Modern Interpreters* (Kraft and Nickelsburg 1986). All three works soon become widely referenced and significant resources for students and scholars, so much so that they continue to be in print with SBL Publications. To find an earlier effort along the same lines, we must go back to 1951 and H. H. Rowley's *The Old Testament and Modern Study*, a staple of studies well into the 1970s. If the former volumes reflected the dominance of U.S. based biblical studies since the Second World War, then Rowley's was the last gasp of yet an earlier economic and intellectual empire.

Much has changed since these earlier and authoritative works were produced. Even though they appear different from one another, with Rowley's volume still assuming the dominance of historical criticism and those by Knight and Tucker, Epp and MacRae, and Kraft and Nickelsburg celebrating the host of new directions in biblical criticism from the 1970s, they have far more in common: the scholars writing are overwhelmingly white and male, and they assume the North Atlantic dominance of biblical scholarship. Since the late 1980s a good deal has changed, not least of which is the breakdown in the North Atlantic dominance of biblical scholarship or the severe downturn of those economies since 2008 and the seismic economic shift to Asia. Voices from the majority of the globe have begun and continue to speak in ways that are reshaping biblical studies, relativizing the absolute claims that have been made and continue to be made by some of the discipline's practitioners. In the process, it has also become clear that biblical criticism does not have one agreed-upon past. It has multiple pasts, depending as much upon your conversation partner as her or his provenance. The futures that spring from these pasts are equally multiple.

How does this situation influence the organization of contributors to this volume and their essays? Instead of focusing on various slices of the Bible, (ancient) historical periods, or different methodologies, we have opted to differentiate in terms of geopolitics and culture. The reason: a concern with biblical books or methods obscures matters such as the global division of labor, patterns of exploitation, and issues related to gender and race. Thus we have gathered essays from all parts of the world, the contributors of which seek to map biblical studies in their area of expertise through a combination of retrospection, synopsis, and peering into the future. Coming from Africa, Asia, the Pacific, Europe, Latin America, the Caribbean and finally North America, the essayists offer a rich panoply of analyses and proposals, among which may be included: the relationship between traditional and innovative scholarship; the way study of the Bible is both tied to religious institutions and has a life of its own; the hindrances and promises of the institutional contexts of biblical studies; the effect of colonial histories of missions on study of the Bible; and the depth of engagement—culturally, politically, economically, and religiously—that global picture provides. Above all, the volume as a whole showcases the changing patterns and fascinating diversity of biblical scholarship throughout the world.

Of course, such divisions into global regions have their own limits, as they focus on identified and fixed regions that actually have their own myriad and fluid diversities. Notably, one ocean and one sea appear among the land masses that our species prefers to inhabit, and perhaps more fluid categories might have been used, enabling a greater sense of inbetweenness. However, the strength of the current format is that it seeks to highlight rather than conceal global patterns of political and economic power, especially in light of significant changes under way.

Two factors require additional comment. First, Western Europe is absent from the collection. This is not through want of trying; but because one contributor after another was unable to complete the task, we agreed in the end to leave Western Europe blank. Is this not a significant omission, given the crucial role that Western European and Protestant biblical scholarship has played in the development of modern biblical scholarship? We do not think so. For in many ways the point of imperial "origin" has long since lost its leadership role. Or rather, the only contributor from Western Europe, Elisabeth Schüssler Fiorenza (born as an ethnic German in Romania), migrated many decades ago from Germany to the United States, because women were not allowed to teach in universities at the time (due to a concord between the Roman Catholic Church and the Third Reich). But what about the place to which she went, the United States? The reader will note that the United States is significantly represented in this volume. Yet the reader will note as well that nearly all contributors from the United States hail from diaspora minorities, a situation that illustrates both the fact that empires attract those from the margins and the fact that such minorities serve as thorns in the flesh in the heart of the beast.

Introductions such as this usually offer the obligatory survey of contributions. This one is no exception, for it offers readers the opportunity to gain a sense of the whole and dip in where interest may take them. The volume begins with Africa and the pieces by Israel Kamudzandu, Sarojini Nadar and Jeremy Punt. In the multitude of challenges within that context, Kamudzandu argues for a community-oriented and crosscultural approach to biblical criticism. As with so many contributions to the volume, this approach is deeply engaged, fully aware of the faith and spirituality of the millions who read the Bible in Africa, rather than arguing for a disengaged, objective or "scientific" approach so characteristic of those zones in the world that produced the era of massive colonial competition. Given that the Bible is neither a product of African culture nor, indeed, of Western culture, Kamudzandu suggests an approach that is characterized by full awareness of its specific conditioning in time and place and a profound sense of curiosity and humility when entering the world of the Bible as Africans. The reason: one encounters cultural, theological, and spiritual shock in that alien world, which enables one to engage across cultures in the sheer diversity of Africa and the rest of the world.

Sarojini Nadar draws on empirical data gathered at contextual Bible studies (a method of Bible study that attempts to work at the interface between faith communities and the academy around issues of social transformation) she facilitated in order to push the boundaries of what is meant by the roles of the "ordinary" reader and the intellectual. Nadar's contribution draws on postcolonial and feminist theories to analyze the dynamics of contextual Bible studies in the South African context. Her essay argues that if transformation is the goal of contextual Bible studies, then the critical resources which the intellectual brings to the process will have to be far more nuanced than they have been in the past; that the effects of globalization, particularly as reflected in the ubiquitous term "biblical values," which comes up often in contextual Bible studies, will have to be addressed; and the identity of the intellectual (particularly if the intellectual is not an organic scholar) will have to be unmasked. The paper argues that promoting "community wisdom" or "hidden transcripts" on the one hand or promoting the "all-powerful" intellectual on the other are both unhelpful for understanding the dynamics of contextual Bible study. Rather, a more nuanced and honest unmasking of the identities and functions of the intellectual and the "ordinary" reader are needed.

With a synoptic reading that sweeps over past, present, and future, Jeremy Punt stresses the reality of transition in Africa, especially in South Africa, in light of the political, social, and cultural shifts associated with the move from white minority to black majority power. He urges a complex engagement between cultural and postcolonial approaches with specific focus on the way the Bible has been interwoven with disproportionate power relationships at all levels, ranging from global geopolitical levels to interpersonal relations. And like Kamudzandu and Nadar, Punt recognizes that his approach to biblical criticism is anything but disinvested, for it remains engaged, negatively and positively, in all manner of complex patterns.

A move eastward brings us to Asia, where Monica Melanchthon offers us the first of three contributions. Melanchthon focuses not on ruling class biblical interpretation, not on the discourse of the powerful, but on *Dalit* biblical interpretation. She argues that as India's Dalits gain confidence, and as their experience of suffering and humiliation for millennia under the tyranny of caste is exposed, their reading of the Bible, using "pollution" and "untouchability" as key criteria, offers us alternative readings of the text. These readings, she suggests, unleash the power inherent in the Bible, subdued until now by casteist interpretations, and thereby empower those discriminated by the evil of caste. Biblical interpretation for Dalits is informed by the bodily experience of pain and prejudice, of being discriminated against, marginalized, and excluded. This approach may be described as a hermeneutical strategy from below, which is in many ways similar to and yet distinct from those inspired by sexism, racism, and classism. In particular, Dalits deploy their oral culture, their creative art forms, their religious rituals and expressions, the rich symbolism inherent in their culture, their holistic approach to life, their experiences, their strong will and resilience to survive amidst pain, and their faith in a God who will liberate. Melanchthon seeks to explore and utilize these gifts for the purposes of identifying new and effective methods of reading the Bible, especially those methods that aid in their struggle for liberation, for both men (who have dominated Dalit biblical and theological reflection until now) and women.

Next, Yong-Sung Ahn reflects on the nature of biblical criticism when its practitioner has moved from study in the United States back to Korea in order to teach—an extremely common pattern. Through his changing perspectives on Luke, empire, and the passion narrative (the topic of his doctoral work), Ahn has found himself being recontextualized in a rapidly changing Korea. Before he left Korea some years before, Korean intellectuals still understood their country as "neo-colonized" or "peripherized" by the power nations, especially by the United States. Now, however, neither "empire" nor "colonialism" is a matter of concern to Koreans, who are self-confident enough to be actors in a globalized world. During the military regime that continued for more than thirty years until the early 1990s, the Korean church declared itself "apolitical." In recent years, however, the church has become so political that conservative churches and pastors are on the frontline of anti-government demonstrations. Reconsidered in this context, neither the theme of empire nor the political dimension of the passion narrative appears effective or timely as a cultural discourse. Rather than imperial politics, it is the central role of the religious leaders in the crucifixion of Jesus that seems more relevant to biblical interpretation in present-day Korea, particularly because Korean churches wield tremendous power. Church membership is typically concentrated in urban, not rural, areas and predominates among the rich rather than the poor. Compared to the overall population, Christians are also overrepresented among politicians and entrepreneurs. That is, the Korean church is of the rich and the powerful. Church leaders possess political influence, just as the religious authorities did in the early first century. So Ahn sets out to analyze anew the text of the passion narrative in Luke with a focus on the political initiative of the religious leaders, concerned specifically with how the "conservative" discourse of the church has supported the church's conservative politics.

Closing out the section on Asia, Philip Chia's focus is a rising Asia, especially China, which has once again become a world power. Initially written before the Western economic crash of 2008, it now reads with even more relevance. Being the largest of the seven continents, Asia has long been "the East" (Far East and/or Middle East, depending where "the center" may be presumed to be), living under the shadow of "the West" and its "project of modernity." Modern biblical criticism has been inextricably tied up with that project, expanding with that culture and gaining global reach. In response, Chia's essay attempts to map out the role and relevance of biblical studies among Asian people within such a global context. The study consists of three parts. The first attempts to map out the highly diversified and pluralistic nature of Asia. The second traces the short history of biblical studies in Asia, focusing on issues of tradition, methodology, and community. The third part asks what the potential orientation of biblical studies will be within the living realities of Asian people, particularly in light of the juxtapositions of Chinese economic-political power and a Western-based political ideology of liberalism.

The third part of the collection moves to the source of the much-discussed Western culture. However, the contributions here—from Milena Kirova and

Hanna Stenström—come from the periphery of the Western European project, one from the east in Bulgaria and the other from the far north. And both are written by women, who were traditionally excluded from European biblical scholarship until relatively recently.

Milena Kirova points out that biblical studies has been problematic in Bulgaria since Christianity was violently imposed for political reasons upon a pagan population in the mid tenth century. The dominating proximity of the mighty Byzantine tradition, the bloom of heretical trends, five hundred years of Muslim oppression, and, finally, half a century of communist secularism have all impeded progress. In spite of (or perhaps also because of) that history, Bulgarian culture is experiencing a wave of interest in the Bible. This is particularly so since the beginning of the new century and has emerged in secular academic research and literature. Kirova surveys these fascinating, rather nontraditional developments, and analyzes their background and fruits with an eye for possible future developments. In many respects, her contribution may be seen as a microcosm of what is happening in Eastern Europe.

Hanna Stenström surveys biblical scholarship in Scandinavia (Iceland, Denmark, Greenland, the Faeroe Islands, Norway, Finland, and Sweden) from the beginning of the twentieth century and into the future. Due to the diversity of biblical scholarship in Scandinavia, she focuses on Swedish New Testament scholarship in the twentieth century. This enables her to analyze a specific case in depth, searching for similarities and points of contact between biblical scholars in those five countries. It also allows her to look at the whole landscape from this specific place, drawing parallels, showing similarities and differences. The key questions for Stenström include: 1) the relation of biblical scholarship with the churches (in practice often the Lutheran national or state churches), the academy at large (especially in terms of current ideals of scholarship), and the general public (biblical scholars write also for the general public and are they active in different debates in society); 2) the reception in Scandinavian countries of various new approaches that widen the understanding of historical-critical scholarship or challenge it, with a specific focus on feminist exegesis and other methods that raise issues concerning the ethical and political dimensions of biblical scholarship; 3) the place of exegesis in contemporary state universities, as well as the possible consequences of the establishing a number of university colleges that have a formal connection to a church; 4) which trends may prove to be more than temporary fads. Is there a new Scandinavian school in sight, or perhaps a number of Scandinavian schools?

In our zigzag path around the globe, we move to Latin America and the Caribbean. Pablo R. Andiñach arranges "Liberation in Latin American Biblical Hermeneutics" in four parts. First, he provides a brief overview of Latin American biblical hermeneutics from 1960 through 1990. Here he traces the path one may observe in the work of Jorge Pixley, J. Severino Croatto, Carlos Mesters, and others from their initial intuitions to their mature proposals. Second, he lays out a variety of contemporary models of Latin American hermeneutics (feminist, indigenist, ecological, and so forth), bringing out the distinctive characteristics of each but emphasizing their common elements. Third, he explores the theological grounds shared by all such models, as well as the differences among them. Lastly, he pursues the question of the future of present-day hermeneutics in Latin America, its perspectives and possibilities.

Nancy Cardoso Pereira follows with a judicious assessment of both the negative and positive dimensions of the Bible's checkered history in Latin America. It must be seen as both wound and salve, as instrument of colonization to be resisted and tool of resistance to appropriate. The key to moving from the former to the latter is allowing the absolute, conquering role of the Bible to give way to a profound sense of relativization: rather than a singular voice, the Bible becomes one voice among many. In the process, the Bible reveals its multitude of perspectives: "the peripheral peasantry, imperialism and its abuses of power, the daily character of poverty (hunger, insanity, illness), the marginality and abandonment of women and children, the reinvention of ways of living together and sharing."

Jorge Pixley follows by defining liberation-theological readings as the emancipation of the Bible from its entrapment in a dogmatic cage that is hurtful to real people of flesh and blood. His essay is a survey of the interface between the liberation theology pastoral movement and its academic allies and supporters. In particular, it focuses on the difficulties of the interface between popular and academic Bible study. Pixley also offers an overview of key moments in the history of liberation biblical interpretation, closing with a consideration of the major issues that face such interpretation in the future: the study of scriptures and texts beyond the Bible; alliances with sociologists in order to study the massive demographic changes taking place in Latin America; exploration of the option for the poor among the early church fathers, including Origen; the effect of changing patterns of biblical interpretation, especially those historical issues relating to the liberation from slavery in Egypt; and the tie between pastoral practice and academic biblical scholarship.

From the Caribbean (now living in South Africa) is Gosnell Yorke's study of this region with its kaleidoscope of linguistic, religious, and cultural traditions. Consciously focusing on the Anglo-Caribbean, Yorke sounds a note similar to that of Pereira. The Bible has been and remains profoundly ambivalent: on the one hand, it has enabled colonial powers to justify their conquest and genocide of the Caribbean (in the name of God, gold, and glory); on the other hand, it has provided deep incentives to resistance and revolt. Yorke traces in detail the growth of academically trained biblical scholars, the fact that these scholars are invariably grounded in the denominational traditions (including but not limited to Anglican, Baptist, Church of God, Disciples of Christ, Methodist, Moravian, Presbyterian, and Seventh-day Adventist), and come from different linguistic and postcolonial backgrounds (Anglophone, Francophone, Hispanophone, and Netherlanderphone. In light of this sheer diversity, the main challenge is working across and through these myriad patterns of difference within a postcolonial situation.

Now we sail out over the Pacific and find Jione Havea's contribution. He begins with the point that *Pasifika* (Pacific Islander) people continue to move away from the islands. As they do so, their sense of belonging and meaning is adrift. Pasifika people and customs are drifting, and the islands are eroding because of global warming. Reading the Bible in such situations requires one to confront the displacement of the Bible. In Pasifika, the Bible is in diaspora; because of the Bible, Pasifika is in diaspora. Havea's essay adds a Pasifika flag to those that call for the decolonization of the Bible and its interpretation. It focuses on some of the drifting-home stories that bob on the watery surface of the Bible…if you get his drift!

Still on the Pacific, Judith McKinlay's focus is Aotearoa/New Zealand. She begins by considering the arrival of the Bible within the colonial past, including its impact and subsequent reinterpretation within certain Maori groupings. Yet the gradual emergence of biblical studies as a discipline preserved its European roots, as McKinlay illustrates. The present state of biblical criticism in Aotearoa/ New Zealand is diverse, with scholars variously looking for connections and inspiration to Europe, the United States, Asia, and Africa. One finds many Australian connections, with scholars sharing and collaborating in an Australasian perspective. The result is a plethora of different approaches and methodologies in a very small scholarly world. As for the future, the essay concludes by offering one view, seasoned with both hope and fear.

Roland Boer argues that biblical criticism in Australia has always been in a curious situation: it has hung on to the idea that it is an outpost of Western scholarship while it exists at the intersection between the Pacific and Asia. The complexities of this background, marked not least by the fact that more than two hundred languages are spoken in Australia (including more than sixty Aboriginal and Torres Strait Islander languages), have generated a range of responses in biblical scholarship: the past British and Irish influence (a mix of colonial overlords and deported political agitators) on biblical scholarship; the drive for "secular" universities that has led to biblical scholars finding room in all manner of strange places; the tension between former intellectual subservience first to "Great" Britain and then the United States on the one hand and the advantage of being outside such contexts on the other; the history of Aboriginal missions and claiming of the Bible by indigenous peoples in their own ways; and the increasing awareness of Australia's fading "Western" identity and the reality of its context within Asia and the Pacific. The result has been a tenuous hold of traditional scholarship, whether theological or historical-critical, or both, and a far greater interest in all manner of new approaches. The future, Boer suggests, lies in pushing the advantages of the Pacific and Asian contexts and making the most of the current reality, in which biblical scholars are in conversation with a host of other disciplines.

Finally we turn to North America, including both Canada and the United States. From Canada, Fiona Black investigates the migrational realities of biblical studies in that part of the world. Black's paper explores the state of the discipline in Canada, which includes an investigation of the origins and developments of the Canadian Society for Biblical Studies, the discipline's eighty year old governess. Canada is a New World country yet, like many similar nations, remains still firmly grounded in its Commonwealth identity. Consequently, Black investigates the interaction of critical study of the Bible with the country's colonial roots, its indigenous cultures, and its current self-identification as a secular nation (notwithstanding its reluctance officially to separate church and state). Of greater interest to the paper, however, is the presence of the Bible in a country that describes itself proudly as composite and multicultural, and that, on a popular level at least, seems united largely by its fixation to differentiate itself from its neighbor to the south. If, as the government maintains, a good many Canadians are immigrants or of immigrant extraction, the paper inquires as to the impact of national identity on the discipline when that identity seems impossible to pin down. Indeed, what is Canadian about biblical studies in Canada? Black explores this question by reflecting on what it might mean to do biblical studies under the auspices of her own hybrid identity as a Caribbean-Canadian.

Across the border lies the fading superpower from where five voices speak: George Aichele (postmodern), Tat-Siong Benny Liew (Asian American), Elisabeth Schüssler Fiorenza (feminist), Fernando Segovia (Cuban American), and Vincent Wimbush (African American). In "The Virtual Bible," George Aichele explores the impact of "electronic culture" and the "digital revolution" on the Bible, especially in relation to the question of whether "biblical studies" retains any meaning in a postmodern world where "the Bible" as a discrete object (the printed codex) no longer has any privilege of place. Just as the computer and internet dissolve the Bible into streams of binary code, so poststructuralism deconstructs the play of biblical intertextuality and semiosis. Meanwhile, popular culture rewrites and redistributes the canon. Yet, just as the World Wide Web finally transforms the Bible into a global phenomenon (and thereby liberates it from the church), its inevitable virtuality keeps it local and partial, fragmentary, perpetually incomplete, and thus subversive. The Bible has always been virtual, but only now are we becoming aware of it, and thus we have not yet thoroughly or systematically examined the implications of that concept.

Tat-Siong Benny Liew explores the paradox of an imperial center that is increasingly defined by its racial/ethnic minorities. As with many of the other contributors to this volume, Liew stresses the way these readings are thoroughly engaged, deriving their impetus in the United States from theological movements (Black, liberation, story, *minjung*) that blow apart and reconfigure the (imperial) separations of theology and biblical criticism, let alone the relations between biblical criticism and other academic disciplines. Liew usefully points out that ethnic readings of the Bible began in conflict—between slaves and masters who read the Bible in opposing ways, or by those who sought answers to "ethnic" threats, such as the "yellow peril," in the Bible itself. Very different eyes read the same common text, and ethnic readings function as a "thorn in the flesh" of dominant interpretations. In mapping three stages of scholarly minority readings since the 1970s, Liew espies the beginnings of a new stage in which inter-communal readings happen across minorities. Even more, he urges greater engagements between minorities and indigenous peoples in the United States, calling them to mine the tradition to locate sidelined voices, and a transglobal engagement with minority readers across national boundaries.

Elisabeth Schüssler Fiorenza, having moved to the United States with a profound experience of post-Third Reich Germany, focuses on feminist biblical criticism. As an academic area of study, feminist criticism has its roots in the nineteenth and twentieth-century wo/men's movements, but has become established as an academic field of research only in the past thirty years or so. Her essay reflects on the situation of mainstream biblical studies when this new field of study emerged, traces its beginnings and development, articulates the different theoretical and methodological approaches that characterize the field, looks at its relations to other areas of critical emancipatory studies, and articulates important questions for its future not only in the academy but also in wo/men's movements for change and transformation. Fiorenza's thesis is that the biblical past and biblical studies have no future if they continue to disregard wo/men, the majority of biblical readers, as subjects of interpretation.

The penultimate study of the collection comes from Fernando Segovia. He bases his contribution on earlier work that presents the path of biblical studies as an academic discipline, from its inception in the early nineteenth century to its position at the turn of the twentieth century, in terms of three paradigms of interpretation: an extended period of exclusive dominance by historical criticism through the 1970s; an irruption of rapid diversification in the mid 1970s, with the emergence of literary criticism and sociocultural criticism from within, as well as feminist criticism and materialist criticism from without; and a subsequent period of competing paradigms, marked by the consolidation of the literary and sociocultural paradigms and the expansion of the ideological paradigm through minority, postcolonial, and queer criticisms. As Segovia notes, this earlier formulation is an archaeological narrative developed from within the discipline itself. In this study he advances this narrative of origins and development by bringing two discursive frameworks into dialogue with one another: biblical studies and cultural studies. In so doing, he proposes a vision for the future of the biblical past, not only in terms of conceptualization and practice but also in terms of pedagogical impartation and social-cultural pursuit. Toward this end, he addresses such issues as the incorporation of traditions of interpretation besides the academic/scholarly one; the interdisciplinary character of the enterprise as a whole in critical dialogue with any number of fields of studies; the responsibilities and aims of the critical task as such; and the vision of intersectionality in the pursuit of ideological criticism.

The final essay comes from Vincent Wimbush, who makes the case for a new and ongoing critical orientation that has as its focus not the content-meaning or aesthetic arrangements of texts but the social textures, gestures (or performances), and psychological and power dynamics that are found to be in complex relationships to texts—especially those texts ("scriptures") accorded special status. As part of an ongoing project, Wimbush continues to arrogate to himself the right and privilege to think with that "fluid and haunting formation called the Black Atlantic," with a specific concern with African Americans. In this essay, his point of entry is the figure Olaudah Equiano, notably his work from 1789, *The Interesting Narrative of the Life of Olaudah Equiano or Gustavus Vassa, the African. Written by Himself.* For Wimbush, this complex negotiation of the fetishizing of the dominant culture's book, the Bible, becomes a means for reflecting on the need to engage with the structural power relations of the modern world by "placing focus not on texts but on the social textures of the peoples, their consciousness of and responses to such structures."

This is a rich and full collection that points to ways biblical criticism negotiates its troubled past and highlights the creative subversions, redeployments, and reengagements with that past that generate distinctly new futures. One can only wonder what a book like this might look like in another twenty years.

Part 1
Africa

1

Biblical Interpretation and Criticism in Neocolonial Africa: Challenges, Conceptualizations, and Needs in the Twenty-First Century

Israel Kamudzandu

Biblical criticism, unwittingly commemorating liberation in Africa, can become an alibi unless it is situated within the parameters of African culture—past, present, and future. It is no accident that, in spite of Western oppression and apartheid, Christianity has become one of the native religions of Africa to an extent that people in Africa have renamed it "African Christianity." While the presence of Christianity has deep historical roots that go back to apostolic times, the interpretation of the Bible faces a complex and a daunting challenge. This challenge is motivated by the hunger for an appropriation of the gospel in ways that are pragmatic and existential in nature.

Therefore, biblical criticism in Africa must, first and foremost, acknowledge the rich mosaic of the African worldview. In other words, biblical methods urgently needed in Africa must be community oriented. During and after colonization, African Christianity reestablished itself anew and exploded geographically. The motive for this explosion of Christianity was newfound independence from the British and, in the case of South Africa, from apartheid. Statistically, Southern and central Africa is considered 100 percent African Christian, while Northern Africa is largely Muslim. In this wide spread of African-Christianity, biblical criticism faces a multitude of challenges, such as culture, HIV/AIDS, famine, abject poverty, neocolonial dictators, ecclesial conflicts, economic downturns, closure of healthcare facilities, mortality, as well as a fast decline in life expectancy for both female and male. Thus the challenges biblical interpretation and criticism face arise from the geopolitical legacies and cultural context of Africa. With all the competing critical methods advocated by biblical scholars, the question that remains is which method will allow people to hear God addressing them in the midst of all these life threatening issues? African biblical interpreters and theologians need to develop creative methods that serve the present neopolitical African context. As I write this essay, I am conscious of my diaspora context as a professor of New Testament Studies in the United States of America. However, my reflections on the needs and challenges, the conceptualizations and methods, of biblical criticism are in conversation with other African scholars, both in and outside of Africa. The method that I propose and that I shall address in this essay can be characterized as a crosscultural approach.[1]

The world of the Bible and the world of African traditional religion overlap and dovetail at many important points, yet Africa itself continues to grapple with issues of identity. Africa continues to wrestle with the issues of demonization imposed on her by missionaries and colonialists. No continent or nation has been associated with heathenism more than Africa; indeed most history books refer to Africa as a "Dark Continent" or as a continent behind God's face (Kurewa 1997, 37–50). Africa finds itself at a crossroad: searching and longing for a salvation that addresses not only the soul but also culture at its deepest level. Thus, first and foremost, Africa needs to address the issue of renaissance, especially in this age of globalization and financial downturns.[2] Although Africa blames the West for the reality and experience of colonization, the urgent need is for African biblical scholars to assist people in defining who they are and where they are heading in the global community and to formulate practical strategies and solutions for future action that will benefit the African church. Together, the Bible and the rich mosaic of religious heritages strongly affect methods of biblical criticism taking shape in the present.

While the historical-critical method has been of value, new and indigenous methods are needed in order to address and engage the issues currently faced by African Christians. Mimicry is not an option in this regard. Here I have in mind a formative concept of the postcolonial critic Homi Bhabha, for whom mimicry represents the adoption, adaptation, and alteration of the culture of the colonizer by the colonized.[3] Africa simply cannot continue to imitate the missionary interpretations of the Bible. While the historical-critical method is oriented

1. Crosscultural, prophetic, and political readings share a common agenda: (1) respect for and value of African culture(s); (2) exposing and critiquing neocolonial systems that have paralyzed Africa for the last six decades.

2. I use the word "renaissance" in this study to refer to the ways in which Africa defines itself before and after the colonial-missionary encounters.

3. For an in-depth explanation of mimicry, see Bhaba 1994, 121–31.

toward discovering the past, the urgent need in Africa is for ways to appropriate the gospel in an existential manner. African biblical interpretation needs to be authentic to an authentic culture. This calls for authentic critical dialogue between the Bible and the African culture (Grant and Tracy 1984, 168–80).

The word culture points beyond such components as music, tribal boundaries, artifacts, and heritages. Culture has to do with the worldview of a people, that is, their identity, their origins, their purpose, and their way of worship. It is, therefore, for biblical interpretation to become indigenized in a manner that assists Africans in being true to the gospel of Jesus Christ. The Bible has become part of the heritage of the African continent, but interpreters continue to use Euro-American methods of biblical criticism. In so doing, people have failed to connect the message of the Bible with their culture. Therefore, the need for a crosscultural method is urgent.

Cross-Cultural Interpretations

The Christian gospel cannot be seen apart from the socioeconomic status of the people. Thus, first of all, a crosscultural methodology has to address the present status of poverty, hunger, disease, and political instability in the continent. In this sense, salvation for an African must no longer be approached as an issue of life after death but rather as lived-out experience. Second, a crosscultural methodology must have a holistic and ethical agenda capable of bringing into being a new person and a qualitatively different society (see Sugirtharajah 2005, 65). Consequently, the socioeconomic reality of Africa can only be properly addressed by a methodology that takes the biblical text seriously, because the God of the exodus as well as the prophetic writings of the Old Testament was focused on overthrowing the oppressive status quo. The Magna Carta of the historical Jesus is an example of liberative praxis, and the apologetic literature of the New Testament carries a message of practical life (Sugirtharah 2005, 66; see, e.g., Luke 4:16–19). Thus, biblical interpretation in Africa needs to be politically and culturally relevant.

The call for crosscultural interpretation was first put forth by Richard Rohrbaugh, who, based on his study of the Bible as a product of the Mediterranean world, argued, "Cross-cultural reading of the Bible is not a matter of choice. This means that for all non- Mediterraneans, including all Americans, reading the Bible is always an exercise in cross-cultural communication. It is only a question of doing it poorly or doing it well" (1996, 1–2). The truth of such a statement cannot be doubted, for it points to the ambivalent nature of the Bible as it crosses cultural and ethnic boundaries of the world. This truth needs to be received by African critics as prophetic words in the twenty-first century world. Since the Bible is not a product of ours, our approach is in many cases ideological, and, as such, the misunderstanding that results is enormous and pervasive. Thus, crosscultural readings belong to a more comprehensive line of approach known as social-scientific criticism (Rohrbaugh 1996, 1–2). Consequently, a cultural-sensitive reading is needed, especially in today's Africa where the majority of people practice African-Christianity. The Euro-American readings need to be challenged because, despite their claim to superiority, such readings do not constitute a standard for all humanity. The Bible has crossed cultures, so it must be read through cultural lenses.[4]

A fundamental factor to be taken into account in this regard is that, before the 1890s, missionaries had scant respect for traditional African culture. Yet culture is the life-center of meaning-making for tribal nations. However, missionary contact with African religion resulted in new perspectives among some missionaries, especially the Catholics, who, after experiencing the healing power of African medicine, began to have a new understanding of African spiritual ways. A crosscultural methodology must seek to bring traditional and ritual practices into African Christian worship. This is crucial, because Africans regard therapy as the means through which God speaks and meets their needs.

Today we experience African-Christianity as having embraced both Western and traditional healing methods. The way African converts to Christianity understand the new religion is conditioned by their long-established traditional beliefs and values. While a crosscultural methodology can be given prominence, the historical-critical method need not be forgotten in light of its complementary role, since its focus is on the past character of the text as well as on illuminating the present.

Related to therapy is the notion of "causality" or power, which is believed by Africans to constitute an inherent aspect of the created universe and which is a vital energy that pervades the world and is responsible for everything that happens.[5] Western biblical interpretation has never taken this concept into account, yet it forms part of an African's relationship with God. African Christians have a deep thirst and hunger to understand ways through which they can encounter this power, not just in abstract terms but also in concrete ways. For an African, nothing happens without a cause, and therefore any form of good life as well as bad fortune has to be addressed on the basis of this power, believed to be God. This power is like electricity, in that it too is ubiquitous, occurring in some degree

---

4. A number of such readings are mapped out in Sugirtharajah 2000.
5. The concept of causality is described well in Kearney 1984, 148.

in all things, but unevenly (Kearney 1984, 148–49). The approach that I have characterized as crosscultural interpretation has uttermost value in allowing Africans to see themselves not as individuals but as community-oriented people. Historical criticism and its rival methods, as part of the project of the Enlightenment, are steeped in individualism and advocate for individual salvation. Thus, crosscultural readings encounter the older methods with the question of community. In this sense, biblical interpretation is not the result of a stand-alone exercise; rather, it forms part and parcel of the social location of a people.

It is a known fact that Africans are keen to know their past, their present, and their future. These three perspectives point to what Africans refer to as community. It is a community that brings together the "Living Dead," the physically living, and the unborn (Mbiti 1969, 22–25). Africans are notoriously obsessed with the world of ancestors—a world that is still opaque to most Western biblical readers and interpreters. This world cannot be opened by the historical-critical method, but it can be accessed through the perspective of Africans. It must be added that cross-cultural readings value pluralism and respect diversity. My call for cross-cultural biblical criticism is not an attack on other methods, and neither is it an attack on the Bible. My aim is to remind twenty-first century readers about the ambivalent nature of the Bible, especially given its use by missionaries and colonizers to promote an ideology of power and dominance.

A crosscultural hermeneutic has, among other things, the liberative effect of the word of Jesus. In other words, this methodology seeks to contextualize Jesus within the worldview of Africans. Theologically speaking, there will be no incarnation of Jesus in Africa unless scholars and clergy interpreters make an effort to read the Bible contextually. The words of Canaan Banana are relevant here: "Jesus Christ is not a product of the Bible. He existed before the Bible; the Bible is a product of Jesus Christ" (Banana 1991). In other words, what Banana is arguing for is a contextualization of Jesus among the liberated people of Zimbabwe—a notion that is pertinent to all African-Christians. A methodology that refuses to become indigenous runs the risk of being rejected by the people. For Africa, crosscultural reading is not an option but a required practice. While Africans did not know Jesus prior to the coming of missionaries, their encounter with God cannot be doubted (Bourdillon 1977). The young African-Christian breed are searching for a new image or a new face in consonance with their culture. They want to know how Christianity relates to Africa on matters of culture, religion, political and economic development, modern technology, business ethics, and many such other issues (Kurewa 2000, 31). Young African Christians continue to dream of a contextualized church where the gospel will be authentically African.

All that I have said so far leads to one fundamental question: Has the Gospel been truly contextualized in Africa, or does it continue to struggle? The answer to this question can be addressed on two fronts. First, African traditional religion responded well to the gospel of Jesus Christ, and credit for this should be given to the monotheistic nature of African faith. Second, it should also be mentioned that African religion prepared people to be receptive of Jesus Christ, without naming him in the way the writings of the New Testament do. Therefore, the African Jesus is known by a variety of names which I will not discuss in this study. Thus, African religion has certainly played a complementary role in the spread of the Jesus movement. At the same time, it has gone a step further by allowing Jesus to find home in the African worldview. Hence, we need a methodology that speaks to the way Jesus has been contextualized in Africa. It should be added that the world of the Bible and that of African Christianity have overlapped and dovetailed in many important aspects. Together the two have strongly affected the Christianity that is emerging today. In the same manner, the emerging Christology bears the marks of African religion, similar to those found in the New Testament writings.

Biblical interpretation in Africa must assist Christians in restoring their self-esteem, so that their voices cease to be private and become public. At the same time, African Christians must take responsibility for deciding whether they want to adopt Western modes of Christianity or develop their own local interpretations. Here issues of sexuality, gender, and patriarchal modes of thinking, as well as socioreligious and sociopolitical issues must be taken into account when reading the Bible. In effect, any meaningful and life-giving interpretation must be sensitive to local culture.

CHALLENGES AND CONCEPTIONS

Having argued for a crosscultural methodology, I want to briefly discuss the challenges faced by both biblical interpreters and lay people together. I want to designate these challenges under three categories; poverty, the political realm, and globalization. All one needs to do is to Google African problems and one will see a kaleidoscope of challenges haunting Africa today. Without mentioning HIV/AIDS, Africa is on the brink of cultural, economic, and political collapse. As African readers and interpreters of the Bible, we are not just mere spectators but must play a crucial role in assisting people to navigate through these daunting scenarios. The question facing critical readers of the Bible is, What does it mean to interpret and read the Bible in a state of emergency? My contention is that, as critical exegetes and interpreters of the Bible, we have to speak prophetically, on the basis of scripture, to both neocolonial African political leaders and ecclesial leaders, holding them accountable for the dilemmas facing the African continent.

Indeed, the challenges are daunting and cannot be ignored. They beckon us to search for a hermeneutic that is relevant to the state of emergency in which the masses of people are trapped. This hermeneutic must be a way of entering into the struggle for justice, reconciliation, and peace. My focus in what follows is to suggest ways rather than offer solutions.

REVISITING AFRICAN STORIES

As an exegete of the New Testament, I am fully aware that the Bible is a book of stories of people who responded to Christianity in their own way. In other words, early Christians were able to place their stories within the larger story of God's salvation. The people of Africa are a story people, and therefore they must be given a platform to tell their own stories and be able to place these stories within the context of God's workings. The function of the Bible is to unite Christians against those things that hurt and divide them. Africa is a tribal continent, and these tribes need to seek ways of working together to remove barriers that have separated them even before the arrival of the missionaries. It must be added that Africa needs to view itself as part of a larger global context within which it has major contributions to make in terms of biblical interpretation. It has always been assumed that the roots of the exegetical tradition are sunk deeply in ecclesial tradition, and thus the dominant view continues to be that historical criticism of the New Testament exists to serve the faith and life of the Church.[6]

However, this view does not give credit to the people who form the ecclesial community; it treats people as objects rather than subjects. What crosscultural hermeneutic does is give various tribes a voice and allow them to have a meaningful dialogue. In other words, there is no interpretation without a critical engagement with "real flesh and blood" readers. In the same manner, there is no world peace without ecclesial and religious peace. The horizon of our critical readings is now larger and ecumenical. It must involve those who are suffering daily from lack of food, medicine, freedom, and who struggle to live meaningful lives. Both public intellectuals and laity must become partners in the interpretation of the Bible and think together to conceive road maps to end Africa's ills (see West 1999c).

---

6. See, e.g., Ernst Käsemann: "The history and exegesis of the New Testament exercise a function in the life of the Church and relate to the Community within which Christians live.... New Testament theology gives an overall direction to all specialist skill and puts this discipline of ours, whatever the tensions, in relation to the Church" (1972, 236).

In our engagement with lay people, we must remember that we have been called to be a critical intelligentsia, individuals who are not comfortable with the status quo in our societies. Our call is to afflict the comfortable and transform the uncomfortable.[7] The problem with African ecclesial leaders and biblical interpreters is that they have to some extent aligned themselves with the status quo and become comfortable in their individual settings. Justin Ukpong, a Nigerian New Testament scholar, has argued that "critical scholars must not be comfortable with the status quo of oppression and domination of the poor" (2001, 152–53). While faith has played a major role in New Testament Studies, the world of the twenty-first century calls us to grow beyond the naïve faith of the past—a faith that has proved to be an illusion.

Biblical interpretation in Africa must be done in the spirit of mutual respect, which means that all cultures must be allowed to define God in their own terms. The New Testament is a record of peoples whose lives and faith responses to God provide a window of lessons for the present generation. All cultures have a record of such people or heroes. Zimbabwe is a special case, as it has its own heroes of faith, such as Nehanda, Chaminuka, and Mkwati, as well as other tribal religious leaders (Needham 1984, 128–29). These heroes are similar to figures such as Abraham, Sarah, Jacob, and Isaac, insofar as they point people to ethical and spiritual ways of living; yet, they are not talked about in the field of biblical interpretation. This way of allowing religious and spiritual voices should shape the ethos of African cultural readings of the Bible.

Language and Cultural Diversity: Its Impact on Reading Strategy

The diversity of the African context calls for a reading strategy that is different from that of our former Euro-American masters. In light of the appropriation of Christianity in Africa, indigenous faith practitioners need to ask themselves certain fundamental questions: Do we, as African Christians, understand who we are and where we are going in this increasingly globalized world, where conformity to technological pressures seems to be the norm? Africa is diverse ethnically and racially, and thus in matters of culture one cannot talk of a common language, a common race, or even a single nation. While the translation of the Bible into a multitude of African languages represents a major accomplishment, we still need a methodology that will respect and honor all these diverse languages.

---

7. See Thompson 1981, 9–14.

Within these cultures we find that the majority of people are controlled by those in power, especially the ones who succeeded the colonial masters. Thus our exegesis has to aim at elevating all marginalized voices—especially those of women, youth, and children.

The rich diversity in Africa pushes all exegetes to think of an approach that is holistic, inclusive, ethical, and pluralistic. Holistic thinking means that we see every tribe and culture as of value in matters of biblical interpretation. Every interpretation must be ethically relevant so as to contextualize Jesus within the culture of a people. Failure to respect and value each culture will lead to failure in addressing the issues facing Africa today, and our interpretations will be rendered useless as a result. As Christians and as professional interpreters of the Bible, our readings must be part of our faith as well as our witness in the spread of the gospel. I must add that life-situation exegesis is a must for all biblical interpreters. Life-situation exegesis has the agenda of lifting up biblical themes such as the all encompassing parenthood of God, the brotherhood and sisterhood of humankind, peace and justice, reconciliation, and many other aspects that are part of our common bond as a human family. From this perspective, ideological readings must be challenged because they do not accord a safe platform to all cultures.

African diversity means that our exegetical practices must be African in nature and in approach. They must not be an imitation of Western readings but must endeavor to open new vistas in biblical interpretation. Rather than viewing the Bible as a site of struggle, the Bible should be approached as a tool that helps us value diversity and see a God who is genderless and impartial to all nations, peoples, and races. To borrow Gerald West's terminology, we must read "with" other cultures in mind. Reading "with" all cultures means creating critical readings for the masses and building communities of crosscultural faith that find their ground of being in God's voice (West 1999c, 15–45).

The challenges, methodology, and suggestions I have outlined above challenge us on two fronts. First, we must endeavor to do our interpretation in full awareness of other cultures. In the case of Africa, we must realize that the days of demonizing the West are over and that it is time to redefine ourselves in relation with other global contexts. Africa must be relevant, first and foremost, to its own indigenized faith and practices, but also to the entire world. Second, Africa needs to make its contribution to the world by being a partner in spreading the gospel of Jesus Christ. This entails creativity and originality on the part of our reading methods. In fact, what makes African Christianity distinctive is its existential approach to Christianity—a practice born out of years of oppression and dehumanization by colonizers.

Conclusion

In this study I have attempted to highlight the fundamental challenges facing contemporary Africa, challenges that face all biblical interpreters both within and outside of the continent. I have argued for a crosscultural approach, given the ambivalence of the Bible and the fact that it is not a product of our culture, or of Western culture either. What such an approach entails is, on the one hand, a view of the Bible as conditioned by the time and place in which it was written and, on the other hand, a sense of great humility and curiosity in entering its world as Africans. Through such immersion in strange Mediterranean readings of the Bible, we risk cultural as well as theological and spiritual shock. While a variety of critical methods has been applied in the study of the Bible, the truth of the matter is that they are not enough; we need a new and creative ways of reading the text. Our crosscultural methods must make a new contribution to a global world hungry and thirsty for practical Christianity. Africa, alongside other "Third World Christian Faiths," has offered the world an example of practical and lived-out faith. I want to further emphasize that Africa must endeavor to be in partnership with the rest of the globalized world or else the consequences will be regrettable. I am convinced that organizations such as the Society of Biblical Literature and the American Academy of Religion must address Africa, Asia, and Latin America as venues in which to deliberate the future role of the Bible in the global world.

2

Beyond the "Ordinary Reader" and the "Invisible Intellectual": Pushing the Boundaries of Contextual Bible Study Discourses

Sarojini Nadar

At the World Forum on Liberation and Theology in Belem, Brazil, January 2009, I was asked to respond to a panel of presentations that dealt with the topic of liberation and embodiment.[1] Chung Hyung Kung, the eminent Korean feminist theologian, began her reflections praising liberation theology for saving her from destruction—physical, mental, and spiritual—but lamented at length about the question one of her Korean students at Union Theological Seminary, New York, had posed to her. It seemed that this student earnestly and seriously wanted to know why, after forty-odd years of liberation theology, the world still faced so many problems and so many injustices. And she was right: Too many years after liberation theology, violence against women has not ended, we still have the pro-verbial "poor among us," and racism and ethnic wars rear their ugly heads over and over again, as can be seen by the current catastrophe in the Gaza Strip.

At the same forum, Mary Hunt, an equally eminent white American feminist theologian, urged us to consider that our bodies do not lie. The bodies of Palestinian children on the Gaza Strip do not lie, she reminded us. They tell a story of real suffering. Bodies do not lie and bodies are imbued with names and identities and characteristics. For example, my name is Sarojini. It is an Indian name which means the lotus flower. The interesting thing about the lotus is that it is a flower that grows on the surface of a river or a lake. Its roots grow deep in the muddy waters, but the flower remains untouched by it. It is a symbol of strength and

---

1. This chapter first appeared as an article, "Beyond the 'Ordinary Reader' and the 'Invisible Intellectual': Shifting Contextual Bible Study fromLiberation Discourse to Liberation Pedagogy," *Old Testament Essays* 22 (2009) 384–403.

endurance and beauty in many of the Eastern religions, including Hinduism and Buddhism, because, although it is *untouched* by the murky and muddy waters, it is also ironically *sustained* by them. It is beyond the scope of this essay to go into all the details here, but this muddy, murky, story is the story of my life.[2] It is this murky experience that makes me the biblical scholar I am, that makes me attentive to the cry of the oppressed, and that makes me passionate about liberation hermeneutics and Contextual Bible Study (CBS).

These embodied experiences can be described variously as follows: being the youngest of seven children and growing up in apartheid South Africa; experiencing sexual violence as a child; experiencing post-Apartheid South Africa, including the ambiguity of the fact that the next president of our country might be someone who said in his rape trial that the complainant had been asking for sex because she was wearing a skirt[3]; experiencing being a fourth-generation South African of Indian descent, sometimes feeling like an outsider to South Africa and yet being refused a visa to go to India in 2002! These are the embodied experiences that make me so passionate about the work I do and about the cause of liberation and transformation to which I am committed. Yet how does this answer the question Chung's student posed about why, after years and years of liberation theology, we still have so many problems and injustices in the world, and what does all this talk of embodiment have to do with CBS?

With regard to the first question, the answer is that it is precisely in the problems, in the lived (and embodied) experiences, in the mud as it were, that liberation theology and hermeneutics—like the lotus flower—finds its impetus, its meaning, its existence. In other words, I would argue that, after forty-odd years of liberation theology, we still have problems because this is exactly where liberation theology starts and belongs—with the problems, at the heart of injustice, in the mud. This assertion, however, should not be interpreted as a glorification of the mud, or the problems, or the injustice—not by any means. I am simply making the point that it is the experience of injustice that provides us with a reason to work for justice.

In his foreword to the English edition of Paulo Freire's classical book *Pedagogy of the Oppressed*, Richard Shaull highlights the fact that it was Freire's experience of starvation and real hunger pangs that made him make a vow at the age of eleven, "to dedicate his life to the struggle against hunger, so that children would not have to know the agony he was then experiencing" (1996, 12). Shaull goes on to say:

---

2. I have documented part of this story in an earlier essay (Nadar 2000, 15–32).

3. The ambiguity lies in the fact that the man who was once a struggle-hero against racism could also make some of the most sexist and misogynistic statements in his rape trial (see Nadar 2009).

His early sharing of the life of the poor also led him to the discovery of what he describes as the "culture of silence" of the dispossessed. He came to realise that their ignorance and lethargy were the direct product of the whole situation of economic, social, and political domination—*and of the paternalism* [emphasis mine] of which they were victims.

Inherent in Shaull's assessment of Freire's motivation for his work are two points: (1) Freire's commitment to the cause of justice stems from his own *experience* of not just injustice but also its subsequent effect, hunger; but (2) this experience caused him to want to work toward liberating the oppressed by conscientizing them to the reasons for their oppression in the first place. In other words, liberation could only be achieved when people were so conscientized of not only their own oppression but also that of others that they became inspired and motivated to take steps to change the situation, to step out of the mud.

With respect to the second question, the answer is that CBS similarly works within this hermeneutical spiral—the "see, judge and act" method (De Gruchy, nd; West 1995). It begins with the context and experience, analyzes the context (in dialogue with the biblical text), and then attempts communally to find ways of engaging in the struggle to overcome oppression and suffering. CBS was a response to liberation theologies, which urged scholars to take context seriously. It was a post-enlightenment development that eschewed the "objective" historical-critical method of reading the bible in favor of a method that argued that "objective certitude" (Keegan 1995, 1) was a virtual impossibility and that all interpretation is motivated and ideological.

Proponents of CBS have claimed that the end goal of CBS is transformation, liberation, and change. My own definition of CBS, which I have used in training workshops and university classes on the subject, is that Contextual Bible Study is an interactive study of particular texts in the Bible, which brings the perspectives of both the context of the reader and the context of the Bible into dialogue for the purpose of transformation. Hence, the main purpose of CBS, it can be said, is transformation and change. This is perhaps one of the things that both the original proponents in Latin America and those who have followed in this liberative tradition, like many in South Africa, can agree on. However, in response to the call of liberation theology to be connected to the context and to "the people," as it were, the question we can rightly ask is: has CBS as a method been able to help us toward our goal of overcoming injustice—of getting us out of the mud?

The question Chung's student asked is pertinent. Of course, it is easy to reject the claim that liberation theology has not helped the world with its problems. After all, we have witnessed lotuses flourish all over the world: Barack Obama's presidency; the fall of the Berlin wall; and, closer to home, the demise of apartheid. Liberation theology has certainly had a hand in these events. Yet the student's assessment cannot, and must not, be so easily dismissed because, as Mary Hunt pointed out, bodies do not lie. The bodies of children in Gaza, and the bodies of American soldiers in Iraq, and the bodies of women raped in war-torn countries like the Sudan and the Democratic Republic of the Congo do not lie. The world still faces the problems that liberation theology has worked so hard to overcome. We have not been able to overcome all the problems, and we never will. Such an expectation is unrealistic.

However, what we can and must do, as Tinyiko Maluleke urged us to do already in 1996, is to "critically examine the methods used to establish or claim connection to 'the people' as well as to evaluate the objectives of that connection" (21). Taking Maluleke's challenge seriously, this is what I will do in this essay. I want to push our understanding of the methods of connection we have to "the people" and to evaluate the objectives of that connection so we can begin to per- haps truthfully answer Chung's student question—Is liberation theology and hermeneutics achieving what it claims to or what it wants to achieve?

The answer is complicated and has to do not with the formulation of the method itself but with its focus and its end goal. What is of concern for me, after years of working in this field, is that in most academic reflections and analyses of CBS in South Africa, the focus is not on *how* participants are challenged to change and transform their interpretations of the Bible or their analysis of the social context in which they find themselves. Rather, the preoccupation is on a rather bland and, dare I say, romantic description of both the participants in the Bible study and the intellectual. On the one hand, descriptions of the participants range variously from "oppressed," "poor and marginalised," "other," "ordinary," to "sur- vivors." On the other hand, descriptions of the intellectual range from "trained reader" to "socially engaged biblical scholar" to "activist-intellectual (Cochrane 1999; Philpott 1993; Petersen 1995; Haddad 2000; West 1999).

At the time when these epithets were coined, which was mostly during the period when South Africa was "burning," as it were, on the brink of the demise of apartheid or in the infancy of post-Apartheid South Africa, it was clear who the "ordinary" readers were and who the "trained readers" were: the "ordinary" readers were black, poor, and marginalized; the "trained" readers were white, middle-class intellectuals. CBS was important because it was a tool that could be used to engage people and convince them of the injustice of apartheid, especially in a context in which apartheid was religiously sanctioned. CBS was only one such tool among others.[4]

---

4. De Gruchy with Ellis (2008, 1) points to some of the other programs, tools, and activities that were being formulated to oppose apartheid: "From the time of the Cottesloe Consultation of the South African members of the World Council of Churches in 1961, following the Sharpeville

However, the objective of liberation that CBS claims to have had as an end goal seems to have gotten lost in the academy. The hermeneutics of liberation, which was born in the academy, seemed to stay within the academy, with a proliferation of new and more fashionable liberation hermeneutics being born at a consistent rate. Feminist, womanist, Bosadi, inculturation, divination, and postcolonial hermeneutics are just some examples of the plethora of innovative and perhaps even "exotic" methods that flooded the biblical scholarly guild. The academy was taking seriously the call of liberation scholars such as Gerald West to experience a "conversion from below," to be "partially constituted" (1999c, 44–54) as it were, by the real experiences of those who are "poor and marginalised." Out of this desire to take the muddy experiences seriously was also born a series of empirical research projects into Bible reading practices of grassroots communities. Consequently, a series of critical analyses of the praxis of CBS in communities began to be reflected on in the academy (the most notable of these are: Phillpott 1993; Cochrane 1999; Haddad 2000; Dube 1996; West 1996, 1999a, 1999b, 1999c, 2001; Ukpong 1996).

It is in academic reflection on the process of CBS that my concern lies, and perhaps where we might find an answer to the question of why liberation theology has not been that effective.[5] In a sense, liberation discourses force biblical scholars to use their skills of interpretation not just for the sake of scholarly debate but in service of the project of liberation in the wider society. CBS, as an offshoot of liberation hermeneutics, is an attempt at doing precisely that. But if what is being represented and reflected back to the academy about this process is anything to go by, then I am afraid that the assessment of Chung's student is correct: we are not succeeding in the cause of liberation toward which we are working, however noble those attempts may be.

Hence, in this study I will, as Maluleke has urged us, critically reflect on the method and the objectives of CBS, so that perhaps the contours of the discourse can be adjusted or reshaped to suit the changing realities of the world in which we find ourselves. Drawing on my varied experiences of facilitating contextual

---

massacre of the previous year, the relationship of Christianity to apartheid dominated public debate. It shaped the work of para-church organisations that took a strong anti-apartheid stand such as the Christian Institute, the South African Council of Churches, the Institute for Contextual Theology, and the regular conferences of all the major Church dominations; and it was expressed in documents and programmes such as the Message to the People of South Africa, the Programme to Combat Racism, the Black Theology Project, the Belhar Confession and the Kairos Document."

5. Again, I must emphasize that this is not to deny the gains made by this method. It is simply to push us to consider that a more interventionist method and an honest exploration of the nature of CBS will help us better evaluate our attempts at liberation.

Bible studies, I will push the boundaries of the understanding of the roles of the "ordinary" or "untrained" reader and the intellectual in the process of Contextual Bible Study—a method to which I am deeply committed, because I still think that it is one of the few viable ways to work at the interface between faith communities and the academy around issues of social transformation. I will argue that, if transformation and liberation are the end goal of Contextual Bible Study, the critical resources the intellectual brings to the process will have to be far more emphasized and nuanced than in the past, that the effects of globalization—particularly as reflected in the ubiquitous term "biblical values," which comes up often in contextual Bible studies—will have to be addressed, and that the identity of the intellectual will have to be more fully explored than simply declaring one's social location and then carrying on with business as usual. I want to argue that neither an understanding that promotes "community wisdom" or "hidden transcripts" nor an understanding of the "all-powerful" intellectual is helpful for understanding the dynamics of Contextual Bible Study. What is needed is a more nuanced and honest exploration of the identities and functions of the intellectual and the "ordinary" reader.

THE FIVE CS OF CONTEXTUAL BIBLE STUDY

In order to facilitate this discussion, it would be helpful to elucidate some of the characteristic features of CBS, so that we can begin to engage some of the concerns raised above. I will do this through a discussion of what I have called the Five Cs of CBS. This list is by no means exhaustive, but it is helpful for sketching the contours of the method of CBS. It is based on how I define CBS in the training workshops I have been asked to facilitate over the years, and it may be helpful to restate this here: "Contextual Bible Study is an *interactive* study of particular texts in the Bible, which brings the perspectives of both the *context of the reader* and the *context of the Bible* into *critical dialogue*, for the purpose of *raising awareness and promoting transformation*." The five key words which correspond to the five Cs in the above definition are: interactive (Community), context of the reader (Context), context of the Bible (Criticality), critical dialogue and raising awareness (Concientization), and transformation (Change).

COMMUNITY

As I have already said, CBS takes its cue from liberation theology, and one of the central tenets of liberation theology is a focus on the community as opposed to the individual. The method of CBS takes community very seriously, and hence a

CBS is always interactive and participatory in nature. It is not "taught"; it is facilitated. CBS requires the voices and opinions of all who participate in the study. This means that questions are engaged with and debated, not simply answered by the facilitator. This is not to downplay the role of the facilitator but to help participants draw conclusions through logical and critical argument, rather than to have a simple return to the all-powerful pastor or intellectual who says "the Bible says" or, worse still, "God says."

In the process of doing the Bible study, all answers provided by the participants are put up on newsprint or on a board. In one Bible study group, I overheard a woman pointing to the newsprint proudly and declaring to another participant that she had provided that particular answer. Thus, this tool empowers those who are not often given spaces within a church setting to articulate their views.

Although all answers provided are written up, the method is not a way of validating what Kelly Brown Douglas calls "vulgar relativism" (1)—anything goes. During the discussion, for example, on what the theme of a text is, heated debate ensues among the participants themselves. An example will help at this point. Over the years, I have facilitated several Bible studies on the book of Esther, and the participants usually have a very spirited discussion about whether the king in the story actually rapes the virgins or whether they are willing participants in the act. In one group, some male pastors who were very resistant to feminist interpretations of the text even went as far as to suggest that saying that the king was drunk was a "feminist distortion" of the text. They debated whether the phrase "merry with wine" meant drunk (Nadar 2003, 278)! However, putting up participants' responses to questions makes other participants react, creating a discussion that often even goes beyond the text. As facilitator, I have to choose the level of intervention. As a feminist scholar, I often find it more important to engage the group on the issue of the rape of the virgins rather than on whether the king was drunk or not. Some interpretations are not necessarily life-denying and so do not require as much intervention as others do.

Unfortunately, the academic discourse on community engagement and popular usage of the Bible does not often capture the fierce debates that can go on between participants, but also between the facilitator and the participants. In other words, "community wisdom," like culture, is not a monolith. It is fiercely contested, legitimized, and defended. Yet all academic discourse has done with this is to valorize the interpretations of the community and raise them to a level of community wisdom. Such a *modus operandi* can sometimes actually be counter productive to the goal of transformation we seek.

Although not an analysis of CBS, Gerald West's article on Isaiah Shembe and Jephthah's daughter (2007b, 489–509) is an example of how liberation (of women, in this case) can be sacrificed on the altar of "community wisdom." So engrossed is West in the notion of community that is created in the Shembe community with the Bible that he devotes almost the entire article to simply describing how the Bible is appropriated by Shembe, who "steals" the story of Jephtah's daughter and reshapes it for the sake of the *AmaNazaretha* community, along with the rituals that were supposed to be observed by the virgins in honour of Jepthah's daughter. It is clear from West's descriptions of the liturgical and hermeneutical practices of Shembe that there were clear "hierarchies of compliance," in West's own words (2007b, 502). Yet Shembe's hermeneutic is valorized simply because he reads and appropriates the Bible over and against the ways the missionaries did. This is a concern when it comes to the discourse of liberation that focuses on community and indigenous knowledge. There is uncritical acceptance of indigenous knowledge as almost sacrosanct, without an acknowledgement that the community itself can be in possession of destructive and life-denying interpretations which need to be exposed, interrogated, and ultimately transformed.

Of course, this may be because the community has simply "internalised" its oppression, or because of some romantic attachment to outdated forms of culture and tradition, or even because the community has an "incipient theology" that is yet to be articulated (West 2005, 23–35). Whatever the reason may be, the fact is that after eight years of experience of working in communities of faith with the Bible, I have discovered from the participants shocking and disturbing interpretations of biblical and social contexts, more life-denying than life-promoting. I have documented elsewhere how this is made even worse because of globalized forms of religion, such as the increasing charismatization of churches in the Global South, which promote "biblical values" as a universalizing standard for how people should live their lives (forthcoming).

From my experience—and many of my weekends are taken up doing this in different contexts—facilitating Bible studies in communities that are both poor and middle class, black and white, educated and uneducated, male and female, and with people from across the world, from India to Canada, I can honestly say that, in all of these interactions, I have struggled to find "incipient theologies" (Cochrane 1999) and "hidden transcripts" (Scott in West 2005). Most times during the course of such Bible studies, I have wanted to do nothing more than shake people out of their complacent "survival" mode (Haddad 2000) and bring them to a point of realising that it is not "God's will" that they suffer or that oppression of women, for example, is not acceptable just because "it is part of my culture!" In other words, what I am expressing here is my frustration at the "exoticizing" discourse that permeates the discussion around CBS. Of course, there are lotuses, but these cannot be cheap plastic flowers that say "made in China" when turned over. The lotuses must be acknowledged *with* and *because of* but also *in spite of* the mud from which it emerges and grows.

As facilitator, I have often had to challenge participants particularly when their interpretations have been sexist. This is what it means to read the Bible in community and not individually. It is understood that there is a wider spectrum of interpretation which exists beyond the individual and often pious interpretations that are peddled from the pulpit. Reading in community helps overcome the challenge of the power imbalance that is created when interpretation is left in the hands of one all-powerful individual. Even so, "reading in community" must not be mistaken for a valorization of "community wisdom" when such wisdom is not always life-giving or liberationist.

Context

A second feature of CBS is its focus on context. Inspired by Liberation Theology, CBS always begins with context and experience. However, in the discourse around CBS, which is reflected back to the academy, "context" is used to describe the contexts of those who are more often than not poor, women, or black. For example, in Mary Hunt's paper on embodiment, to which I referred at the beginning of this essay, she urges us to consider that we find suffering bodies across the world, and yet most of her examples take us to Palestine, Zimbabwe, and Cambodia—which, of course, begs the question if suffering occurs in the United States. Context is the starting point for CBS, but I ask whether that context always has to be that of the poor and marginalised. Is it easier for the poor to pass through the eye of the CBS needle than it is for the rich?

Let me illustrate this point. In 2008 I was one of four biblical scholars invited by the Church of Sweden to facilitate training workshops on CBS. After facilitating a Bible study on Esth 2:1–18, one of the insights that was shared by the group was that they found it difficult to identify with the text of Esther because, they said, sexual violence was not as big a problem in their context as perhaps it was in mine. However, when pushed to consider further how the text did apply in their context, they revealed that beauty standards set by glossy magazines was increasing the prevalence of eating disorders such as bulimia and anorexia in the Swedish context. It became very clear as the week progressed that context was not "out there," but at hand. We are all embodied. We are all in the mud. Everybody has a context. So CBS cannot be only for the poor and the marginalized. I am concerned that when we talk about context and embodiment in our academic discourses, we talk about women's bodies and women's contexts only—or black bodies, or bodies with disability, or bodies with HIV. What about the bodies of men? What about white bodies? Is there not a context for this? Can CBS be done among white, middle-class communities, or is it only a tool for the "poor and marginalized," as our discourses have tirelessly revealed?

Anders Hagman, the Swedish photographer and journalist at the "Bible Days" in Sweden, captured this tension very clearly in a beautiful reflection on the process which was sent out to the participants and the four facilitators:

> After 20 years of visits by fantastic individuals that come to inspire us with their theology I must ask: are you more than Esters [sic] more unfortunate sisters to us? Passive representations of "the other" that come one by one called by the King in the North, to spend a night with us before we send you off as not quite exotic, thrilling, or beautiful enough to satisfy more than our most urgent desires. Are we able to fall in love with the message you bring; are we prepared to invite you to our dinner table. Are we able to show that commitment?

He was also able, very insightfully, to put his finger on the problem of contextuality as restricted to the "other" or the exotic and on the difficulty of making context more real at home:

> The space for contextual theology that we offer, I'm afraid, mainly fills a representative role; representations of colour of ski[n], of other faiths and cultures. We are driven by feelings of bad conscience, of ambitions to be worldwide and open, of a longing for someone to save us, but we do not really open any channels into the heart of our churches that could transform us in any deeper sense, or on a bigger scale.

Hagman's reflections hit the nail on the head in terms of the failure of our academic discourse to see the benefit of CBS beyond simply servicing the "other," to see it also as in service of the cause of transformation—whether that is in a white middle-class church in Hillcrest, South Africa, or a rural community church in Inanda, KwaZulu-Natal, South Africa. CBS has the potential to transform us, if we are committed to addressing the challenges we face in our particular contexts. These contexts cannot continue to be named in the abstract. As Freire has argued, "The oppressor is solidary [sic] with the oppressed only when he [sic] stops regarding the oppressed as an abstract category and sees them as persons ... to affirm that men and women are persons and as person should be free, and yet do nothing tangible to make this affirmation a reality, is a farce" (1996, 32–33).

CRITICALITY

A third feature of CBS is its focus on the critical. This is where the role of the intellectual is crucial, not just in employing the tools of biblical studies tools but also in making it contextually applicable to the participants. While the context of the reader is important, particularly in an increasingly globalized world that tends to make ubiquitous phrases such as "biblical values" universalized givens, this feature of CBS cannot be downplayed. Contrary to the misperception of those in the academy who are beholden to the historical-critical method, and who think that CBS is "uncritical," I would point out that, actually, respect for the text in its own context is an important characteristic of CBS. As I say in my training workshops, this facet of CBS is to understand that reading "the Bible is like reading someone else's mail"—it was not written to us, but we nevertheless are trying to derive meaning from it. It is here that critical tools are employed to attempt to understand the text in its own context.

Most of the time, the easiest way into the text is through a literary methodology—asking questions regarding character, story, plot, and so forth. However, depending on the context and the ability of the participants to engage in historical discussion, the facilitator may also introduce some sociohistorical information regarding the text. For example, in the Bible studies on Esther, although I employ a literary method for the CBS, questions of empire often come up, since Esther is a text set in exile. Easing into a sociohistorical discussion of the text helps participants realize that, notwithstanding the sacred nature of the Bible, it was written, read, translated, and interpreted in a time different from our own.

The critical nature of CBS also means that participants are sometimes enthused to ask general theological and hermeneutical questions that are beyond the text. For example, at the end of a Bible studiy on Esther with a group of middle-class, Indian Pentecostal women, one participant asked, "Why did God choose the Israelites to be His [sic] chosen people and not anyone else, for example the Indians?" (quoted in Nadar 2003, 303). The participants learn very quickly that a good interpreter does not only know all the right answers but learns the skills to ask the right questions.

Again, in the academic discourse on CBS, the role of the intellectual has been downplayed and to a certain extent underestimated. In wanting to foreground "community wisdom," CBS discourse has failed to recognize the yearning of participants in CBS for the professional biblical scholar to provide insights to which they would have otherwise been blind. Colleagues who have facilitated Bible studies often share their experiences, as one person put it, of the participants' eyes going as "wide as saucers" when confronted, for example, with the idea that there are two creation stories in the Bible. I think that the problem in academic discourse is that the phrase "reading with" (West 1996, 26) has obscured the power imbalance between facilitator and participant. My experience has been that participants want to hear from the "expert" and that the critical skills and tools gained through the academic study of biblical texts prove crucial in order to meet this need.

CONSCIENTIZATION

Another important aspect of CBS, and one that is related to its critical and intellectual dimensions, is the question of conscientization. This implies a particular interventionist strategy on the part of the intellectual. However, not all intellectuals agree on conscientization as a goal of CBS. West, for example, has the following to say about the process:

> The socially engaged Biblical scholar is called to read the Bible with them ["ordinary readers"], but not because they need to be conscientized and given interpretations relevant to their context. No, socially engaged Biblical scholars are called to collaborate with them because they bring with them additional interpretative resources which may be of use to the community group.

Later, in another article, he elaborates on why he makes such an argument against conscientization: "I realise that in making this argument I may simply be exhibiting my own identity dilemmas as a white, male South African. For who am I to intervene in breaking the culture of silence of blacks or women? So instead of naming false-consciousness for what it is, I call it something else, so assigning myself a less problematic role" (2008). Haddad makes a similar admission when she describes how her attempts at intervention were met with silence in a Bible study group made up of black women:

> I now recognize that my role is not to conscientize but to enter into mutual dialogue and collaborative work with those I work with.... I am less bold or hasty than I used to be about what action I think should be taken against the many gendered injustices I see around me. I listen more, speak less and do not rush into any prescribed solutions to these evils.... At times in discussions with women of Sweetwaters and Nxamalala, I have not been able to be quiet and found myself speaking out my perspective on their oppression. Instead of having the desired effect of moving them into unanimous agreement, it has more often than not elicited silence. (2000, 49)

Notwithstanding that both West and Haddad admit that they choose not to conscientize because of their identity as white and privileged, their admission does little to help Chung's student, who asks why liberation theology has not fully succeeded in its aim to liberate. Yet this is precisely where the answer lies. Perhaps instead of only attempting to bring the poor into the academy, we should be taking the academy to the poor. It seems as though the purpose of CBS reflection in the academy has been to use it as a research tool, to allow scholars to be peeping toms into the lives of the poor. Although West has outright rejected the use of CBS as a research tool, in a sense this is exactly what his and other similar scholarly work has done.[6] Although claiming to bring the "resources of biblical scholarship to the community," West nevertheless admits that he also intends to "take the questions of the community into the field of biblical scholarship" (2006, 325). It is the latter intention of bringing the voices of the community into the academy that is foregrounded in the discourse rather than the former intention of education and conscientization of the community. There is nothing wrong with doing this, provided that we are overt about it, rather than claiming liberation and transformation as our only goal. Again, Maluleke has already urged us to consider this matter: "More reflection on the evaluatory process within grassroots research must be done. My impression is that apart from blindness to biases, some researchers tend to fail to differentiate between the tools used in evaluating on the one hand, and the data unearthed in the investigation, on the other" (1996, 42).

Having said this, it must also be said that the tendency to valorize community interpretations, or to use CBS as a research tool, has not only been restricted to white intellectuals; it has been present among black intellectuals, as well. Madipoane Masenya's Bosadi hermeneutics and Musa Dube's divination hermeneutics and Semoya readings have also come under scrutiny for attempting to simply replace the "lost figure of the colonised" in academic discourse without being critical of the inherent inequalities and even injustices that may be present in such grassroots approaches. The attempts to bring the voices of the marginalized into the academy have been done through a valorization of the survival methods of the oppressed rather than through a critique of why survival is needed in the first place. As Maluleke has argued, "Survival is necessary but it is not subversive activity. Survival theologies and hermeneutics may valorise the agency of women in oppressive situations, but it does not change the systems" (2001, 245). And it is changing the systems, not glorifying the mud, which will help to answer the question from Chung's student.

Almost five years ago, Tinyiko Maluleke and I asked some difficult questions in an article, which stirred up much debate in the South African academy but which has yet to be fully taken up. One such question was "whether the academy ought to see its role in relation to the poor and marginalized as that of conscientization, education, and the imparting of skills" (2004, 7). We argued that "for some, the fact that the poor and marginalized are and can be agents

---

6. West (2006, 324) emphazises: "It must be stressed that this collaborative reading process is not research. It is part of the praxis of the Ujamaa Centre—a process of action and reflection.... We reflect on the process, among other reasons, primarily in order to reconceptualize our action."

of survival and transformation, implies all intellectual interventions should be dialogical (reading with, for example) rather than pedagogical and kerygmatic" (2004, 7). My experience of facilitating CBSs over the years has taught me that it must of necessity be both, lest we be judged that the only people who are ever transformed through our hermeneutical practices are those within the academy. Besides, while we carry on talking to ourselves, people of faith continue to live and die by the very texts over which we spend our lives arguing. In a global-ized world, where the Bible is being increasingly deified and used as a "textbook" rather than as a "sourcebook," it has never been more urgent to rouse people out of their "false consciousness" (Bretter 2007, 7).

A precursor to this concientization must of necessity be critical thinking, which we have outlined above. As Freire describes it, "True dialogue cannot exist unless the dialoguers engage in critical thinking— ... thinking which perceives reality as process, as transformation, rather than as a static entity—thinking which does not separate itself from action, but constantly immerses itself in tem-porality without fear of the risks involved" (1996, 69).

CHANGE

The fifth and final characteristic of CBS is its focus on change. This is grounded in the "Action Plan" which ends a CBS. Inasmuch as it is the muddy experiences which ground us and make us more attentive to the cry of the oppressed, our task is, nevertheless, still to ask whether our liberation discourses can help us transcend the mud. Has it only ever succeeded in valorizing, or perhaps even venerating, the mud? We have to ask the critical questions that will ultimately help us transcend suffering, but then we also have to do something about the suffering.

Change and transformation must be a constant goal. Transformation hap-pens on various levels. On the one hand, the ways in which we read the Bible are transformed. In other words, we learn how to read the Bible in a way that is liberating and inclusive and in a way that stays faithful to who we are in our con-texts. On the other hand, it is also transformative in that it is hoped that the Bible study can transform us to such an extent that it spurs us to action for change and justice in a world that is often unjust and unwilling to change. Bishop Dom Helder Camara captures some of the hermeneutical moves of CBS: "When I give food to the poor, I am called a saint. When I ask why the poor are poor they call me a communist." Criticality and conscientization—asking why the poor are poor—must lead to some change, whether that means actually being challenged enough to give food to the poor or whether that means protesting at the unequal neoliberal economic policies of successive U.S. governments. CBS ends with an

Action Plan, where participants are required to say how the CBS has challenged them and what measurable difference they can make in response to the CBS.

CONCLUSION

After forty years of liberation theology and over twenty years of CBS, are we making a real difference in the lives of the oppressed, as Chung's student prompted us to ask. Or have the oppressed simply become "raw data" for us to write our papers—pretty lotuses to put into our vases? Have we simply placed them in our academic discourses to remind ourselves that we need to be mindful of the poor, while our hermeneutics of liberation have actually failed to become a hermeneutics of transformation and change in their lives? Who are the oppressed and the poor and marginalized? Can men and white, middle-class people be oppressed too? All of these questions need to be honestly addressed and engaged if we are serious about the end goal of CBS. This does not mean we have to polarize the debate and come up with an either/or answer. Perhaps, as Alissa Jones Nelson has recently argued, our answer lies in "contrapuntal hermeneutics." This she describes as a hermeneutics that "seeks to embrace outsider voices without falling prey to either assimilation or segregation. It points towards integration, which attempts to avoid both the elision and the overstatement of differences" (2009).

Due to the constraints of space, I am not able fully to explore the above idea, but what I want to stress is that finding this middle ground is more important than ever in this globalized age of rising religious fundamentalism and conservatism. What I have done in this article is attempt to engage with some of these difficult questions, to try to negotiate that difficult in-between space between discourses of agency and oppression, hegemony and freedom—between the lotus and the mud.

3

Dealing (with) the Past and Future of Biblical Studies: A *New* South African Perspective

Jeremy Punt

This contribution proceeds from the southern African context as its specific social location for reflecting on some aspects of the future of the biblical studies enterprise in light of its past. Cognizant of important changes in the region since the dawn of the post-Apartheid era, the study takes its point of departure from and interacts with the complex settings and legacies of South Africa, given its rich human diversity as a former Dutch settlement, a British colony, and an Apartheid state. In so doing, it attempts to understand the future of biblical studies while recognizing that it does so amid the current post-liberation, democratic dispensation that has brought about many changes, of which the transfer of power from a white minority to a black majority has been the most telling element. However, beset by many problems of various kinds, the new dispensation in South Africa has thus far not brought about the expected significant improvement in the lives of the majority of its citizens, even while it has developed more of a global profile. Attempts to enhance this profile, especially at the level of economics, often further complicates an already complex situation—a postcolonial setting in many ways.

In all of the twists and turns of what constitutes contemporary South Africa, or the *New* South Africa in local parlance, the Bible and its interpretation have remained important concerns. On the one hand, amid the recent changes, and notwithstanding *both* a secularizing trend *and* a swing toward Pentecostal evangelicalism (even if their juxtaposition may at times sound like an anomaly), perceptions about the Bible are constantly shifting in South Africa. Still, the presence of the Bible and its invocation, even from political and other public platforms, continue unabated (Punt 2006, 2007, 2009). On the other hand, conscious attempts to account for practices of biblical interpretation within and as part of particular social locations already ring in a first important concern for considering the future of biblical studies in South Africa: until recently, the region has been characterized as much by prolific research on the Bible and related fields of study as by the apparent obliviousness of biblical studies to its contemporary social location.[1]

Identifying the social location of biblical interpretation as neglected emphasis could be understood against the background of past South African biblical scholarship. Whereas a fair amount of energy was expended in the past on discussion of method (Punt 1998) to the detriment of investigating the social role of the Bible and particularly its use and abuse in national politics,[2] serious contemplation of theory largely stayed out. Such absence of, or at best shortcomings in, the discussion of theory was characteristic of South Africa for its own specific and probably altogether different reasons. However, the theoretical deficit was until recently—and some would claim, still is—largely characteristic of biblical interpretation globally, as well. In fact, it has been argued that biblical scholarship in general has remained less interested in discussing theory and more in using theory as the means to achieve a larger goal, namely generating particular interpretations, explanations, or understandings of texts in the Bible.

While one contribution can hardly undo the theory deficit in biblical studies, at least the deficit can be pointed out as part of the larger parameters of any attempt to survey and size up the field of biblical studies, to account for biblical studies, however brief, incomplete and (necessarily) perspectival such an endeavour will inevitably be. To be sure, this contribution does not aim in any way to exhaustively discuss the current field of biblical hermeneutics, in theory and/or practice, in terms of approach or methodology—the temptation to consider and evaluate specific methodologies is avoided as far as possible, concentrating rather on larger trends in biblical studies and hermeneutics. With a rather narrower aim, this article interacts with some trends in biblical studies and hermeneutics from a

---

1. Two caveats: First, the study will concern itself largely with South Africa, but much of it will be applicable to the broader Southern Africa region, too, including countries such as Lesotho, Swaziland, Namibia, Zimbabwe, Angola, Mozambique, Zambia, and Malawi, and to some extent even countries further afield like Tanzania, Kenya, and the Democratic Republic of Congo. Second, the study will focus largely on debates in academic circles, but not to the detriment or exclusion of biblical interpretation in either ecclesial or public environments for reasons that will become clear below.

2. Although not reflecting in the first place on *methodolomania* in South African New Testament Studies, the systematic theologian and ethicist, Piet Naude (2005, 339–258) did reflect, in a paper in the journal of the SA New Testament Society, *Neotestamentica*, on how New Testament scholars were slow in leaving behind a past in which NT studies disengaged from sociopolitical issues in SA.

specific South African perspective, without claiming to be representative of South African biblical scholarship.

Interpretative Frameworks, Paradigms, and Schemes: Beyond the Communication Model?

The dearth of reflection on theory in biblical interpretation has not meant the absence of theoretical reflection about hermeneutical approaches and exegetical strategies. Without denying the connections between such reflections, they, of course, neither share the same focus nor address the same concerns and issues. In fact, recent years have seen a proliferation of new hermeneutical methodologies and theories of interpretation.[3] While there is little agreement whether the current plethora of and diversity in methodologies in biblical interpretation is cause or effect of what constitutes an interpretive crisis for many, one scholar insists that "the only reason I can think of for denying that there is *a* crisis in biblical interpretation today is that there are so many of them" (Westphal 1997, 58). Some scholars understand the search for the meanings of texts as simply part of "the predicament of our modern situation" (Ricoeur 1991, 286). Others make a connection on the one hand between the inability of historical-critical approaches to accomplish an interpretation that can adequately address interpretative needs and concerns and one the other hand a perceived current hermeneutical crisis (Luz 1994, 12).

Since every discussion of New Testament interpretation is grounded in a particular chronologically and socially determined moment (Green 1995, 6), it has become important within the last decade or so to overtly account for contemporary contexts, of both individual interpreters and interpretative schools and trends. This is why this astonishing diversity in models of interpretation attracts most attention, a phenomenon that is often attributed to the challenges directed at the historical-critical model during the last three decades, as will be explained below (e.g., Segovia 1995a, 1; Caldwell 1987, 315–316; Harrisville 1995, 206; Schneiders 1999, 23; Soards 1996, 93–106; and Yee 1995, 109–11).

In the past, a number of useful frameworks, paradigms, or taxonomies of the biblical hermeneutics endeavour were construed in order to address the three focal points that have dominated in the (theory of the) interpretation of the Bible

---

3. The vast number of textbooks and other material on hermeneutics, mostly on methodology and practice, underscore this trend; for a small sample of a vast field of literature, see Barton 1998b; Green 1995; Hayes and Holladay 1987; McKenzie and Heynes 1999; Schüssler-Fiorenza; Schneiders 1999; Tate 2008; Tuckett 1987.

for a long time. However, since they naturally also show more than the obvious categorization of methodology, taxonomies betray perceptions about hermeneutics in general and interpretative processes in particular, so that the taxonomies are illuminating in more than one way. Phrased in a different way but from mostly a communication perspective, as author-text-reader or history-structure-theology (e.g., Lategan 1988; recently, Gooder 2008) or the worlds behind/in/in front of the text (e.g., Ricoeur 1975; Schneiders 1999; Tate 2008), these taxonomies were primarily intended to provide some background for biblical hermeneutics, as grids to plot the enterprise, as it were. The taxonomies have made a helpful contribution in two ways: (1) providing a grip on or interpretative framework for the array of hermeneutical approaches and methodologies; and (2) identifying underlying theoretical and ideological concerns, specific points of entry as exegetical starting points, or foci within scholarly research.

Like any heuristic device, a taxonomy of hermeneutical methodology is not only illuminating but also tends to reflect the social location and vested interests of those who subscribe to it, even to create and authenticate certain structures and their accompanying vested interests. However, with the democratization of biblical studies (broadly conceived), taking social location as primary marker for thinking about and analyzing biblical hermeneutics may prove to be more than simply an alternative to the communication model in biblical hermeneutics and, in fact, may amount to more than an equally fruitful endeavour. Notwithstanding such tensions in conceptualizing biblical scholarship, the emphasis on the importance of social location in biblical studies—the social location of the contemporary interpreter or scholar but also, more generally, of the texts and their fore- and afterlives—has indeed meant a renewed historical awareness and, to some extent, even a reframed historiography.

Value of History: Something(s) Old, Something(s) New

While some scholars have invested in redefining or reconceptualizing historical criticism in biblical studies (Barton 1998, 9–20; Collins 2004, 196–198; Collins 2005; Fitzmyer 2008), others have pointed out serious challenges in the approach. Speaking generally, the following underlying principles characterize the historical-critical model of biblical interpretation: its strong positivistic foundation and orientation; its claims to neutrality, objectivity, and universalism; and its focus on methodological rigour to the neglect of the social positions of readers.[4]

---

4. In the end, even if not necessarily exclusively so, it is a modernist notion that history entails access to events of the past and their chronological sequencing—in short, seeing history

The emphasis on methodological expertise had, however, a number of salient weaknesses, including lack of training in literary criticism, scant attention to sociological or anthropological models, and an overriding concern for the theological content and message of the texts. In addition, the call for and negation of the partiality of biblical critics has mostly been more apparent than real (Segovia 1995, 278–80).

The historical-critical model revealed a serious tension between aim and praxis since, its claims notwithstanding, it rendered no univocal or objective meaning(s). The model was exceedingly naïve, with personal and social constructions of the texts often presented as scholarly retrievals and reconstructions. Historical criticism was inherently colonialist and imperialist, since the bracketed, male Eurocentric identity was unreflectively universalized. In the end the historical-critical method and its dominance in the field of biblical studies collapsed[5] because of both internal factors (its own methodological development could no longer effectively address emerging new questions, concerns, and challenges) and external factors (the focus on theory as perspective with its own ideological and social foundations; Segovia 1995c, 281–85).

Amid ongoing attempts to relaunch the historical-critical boat, scholars have never disputed the importance of a historical consciousness in biblical studies. Nevertheless, many circles promote of necessity a different approach to and understanding of history and historical enquiry.[6] It is important to emphasize that, amid the serious challenges posed to traditional historical criticism, there is in many circles of biblical scholars a keen sense of the revaluation of history, of a new sense of historiography (Partner 2008, 1), of what some have called a new historicism (Henz-Piazza 2002). According to Carroll, "New Historicism is essentially a turn away from theory and a movement in the direction of culture, history, politics, society and institutions as the social contexts of the production of texts" (1998b, 52). A new historicism approach acknowledges that access to a full and authentic past in the sense of a lived material existence is impossible (Schüssler Fiorenza 1989, 23).

---

as intelligible structure populated by accumulated facts. So also is it a modernist idea that the historian is neutral, without bias or presupposition, merely recording facts in the sense of objective reality.

5. On the other hand, historical criticism in many universities of the West tends to remain a rather dominant mode of biblical scholarship (see Carroll 1998b, 51).

6. Three important aspects of the study of historical narrative include: the writing of history is always more and less than the past; historiography accounts for the present to which the past has led, hence it is a powerful implement of community legitimation, identity formation, and instruction; and, in writing history events acquire narrative form (Green 2005, 61–62).

A word of caution is in order here. With all the benefits a poststructural approach to history has brought about in the sense of offering a different understanding of and format for historiography, poststructuralism not only has challenged modernist positions but also has given new life to reactionary theological values with animosity toward the Enlightenment and historical-critical scholarship, with postmodernism and fundamentalism ending up as unlikely bedfellows (e.g., Carroll 1998b, 51). Nevertheless, the important contribution to biblical studies of the many diverse historical approaches that can be encapsulated under the new historicism rubric is situated in their concern for the material conditions of the texts' production and accompanied by a serious examination of possible omissions, alternative explanations, and the incorporation of other relevant material. A further contribution is found in its retaining a historical focus while, at the same time and in the guise of cultural poetics (à la Greenblatt), respecting history as literature without textualizing history, and so avoiding the poststructuralist trap of treating the Bible as simply text. Finally, a new historicism approach demands recognition that texts do not reflect events of the past impartially but also have a formative relationship to their own and later times, including our own.

CULTURAL STUDIES AND THE BIBLE: A USEFUL VANTAGE POINT

On the one hand, then, the significance of dealing with the historical dimensions of biblical texts and their interpretation has not decreased in importance. In fact, the scope, breadth, and depth of endeavors aimed to address such dimensions—not to mention the spectrum of methodologies and concerns addressed in and through such endeavors—have increased in range, importance, and often in relevance. However, given the longstanding dominance of historical criticism and the general tendency of scholarship to adhere to (its) conventions steadfastly—even when the benefits of doing so may no longer be immediately evident or when continued loyalty becomes counterproductive—the question is whether a viable alternative can be suggested for the historical-critical approach in biblical studies and hermeneutics without relinquishing the gains of past scholarship or giving up on the importance of matters such as historical work, linguistic and textual concerns, and attention to readers and their interpretative communities and histories. On the other hand, given the newer approaches to history, translating their impact and effect on biblical studies while taking the social location of scholars and scholarship into account, the question is also how to include a proper and adequate historical consciousness in scholarship that takes the social embeddedness of biblical studies as its point of departure and frame of understanding.

One particularly fruitful avenue is cultural studies, admittedly an epithet used for a broader field of academic work and research. It is an area that increasingly intersects with and impacts biblical studies and can be employed as a cultural-critical model of biblical interpretation. Cultural criticism allows for the inclusion of other voices in society in biblical interpretation, as it favors and supports a "polyphonic hermeneutics" (Glancy 1998, 461). While various scholars have voiced support for a cultural studies approach in biblical work (e.g., Exum and Moore 1998b and Moore 1998b), Fernando F. Segovia has probably most cogently argued for the necessity of "intercultural criticism" as a viable hermeneutical approach to the biblical texts (Segovia 1998b, 35 and 35n3; c.f. Blount 1995). He characterizes this approach as one in which the text is viewed as "construction." Segovia wants to express the notion that interpretation and meaning are the result of an interactive process between reader and text, but never in a neutral way since the text is "filtered by and through the reader" (1995c, 296; see 1995a, 28–31 and 1995b, 7–17).

Three basic dimensions of using cultural studies in biblical hermeneutics could be considered. First, the text is regarded, like any contemporary social group, as a socially and culturally conditioned "other," since texts are never disconnected from specific settings in time and location; they are never "atemporal, asocial, ahistorical, speaking uniformly across time and culture." Second, the reader is equally regarded as socially and culturally conditioned, an "other" to the text and other readers. The reader is taken seriously, but not in the first place and probably not at all as a unique or independent individual. Rather, he or she is regarded as a member of a distinct and identifiable social configuration, that is, from a social location. Third, the interaction between the text and the reader cannot be taken as a neutral encounter but as the filtering of the text through (the world of) the reader.[7] Added to the otherness of the reader and text, the interaction between the text and reader (reading) should be understood in terms of both construction and engagement. All attempts at reconstructing the text, even as the "other"—regardless of how well-informed or self-conscious it may be—are nothing but construction.[8] Further, as far as engagement with the text is concerned, perceiving the text as "other" requires *critical* engagement with it, with "liberation" as goal. In addition, engagement with the text as "other" requires the

---

7. Since conventional scholarship is rather reluctant to reflect upon its relationship to society generally (Horsley 1995), the social engagement presupposed and required by postcolonial criticism, among others, is at times considered ideologically laden and thus either irrelevant for or a threat to traditional and established approaches.

8. As Vincent Wimbush argues, the "cultural worlds of readers" determine which texts are to be read, how they are to be read, what they mean—even the meaning of "text" itself (1991, 129).

effort to understand how the text has been interpreted by others (Segovia 1995c, 297–98).

In a cultural studies approach, both the value and authenticity of popular readings are acknowledged without necessarily assuming the legitimacy or condoning the effects of any particular reading. On the one hand, romanticizing popular readings should be avoided, since, as with other forms of readings, they also are not without liabilities, relying as they often do on common sense, which is "an uneven mix of insights, prejudices, contradictions, and images imposed by hegemonic discourse" (Glancy 1998, 476). Popular readings are not necessarily innovative and liberating, nor do they in all instances challenge the "great tradition" of the particular (oppressive) society (so Draper 1996, 2); in fact, they are at times tied into particular (established) traditions or histories of interpretation.[9] On the other hand, popular readings have not only come to stay but also address the needs of many communities, as they often arise because conventional readings are found inadequate. Consequently, the integrity of popular readings should not be denied from the outset (Segovia 1995c, 285). Indeed, rather than presupposing a chasm between the scholarly and popular readings or being oblivious to the nature of unequal power relationships, one should see scholarly readings as serving in conjunction with popular readings, as, for example, in addressing the needs of the poor (Rowland 1993, 239, 241).

Cultural studies can be pursued in different guises within biblical studies. But it is postcolonial theory that has consistently aided the interpretation of biblical texts in recent years.

POSTCOLONIAL BIBLICAL CRITICISM:
PUNTING A CONTEXTUAL FAVORITE

Postcolonial biblical criticism constitutes a shift in focus. It is a reading strategy that attempts to accomplish two goals at the same time: to point out what was missing in previous analyses, and to rewrite and correct. A postcolonial approach therefore involves restoration and transformation as well as uncovering and disclosure.[10]

---

9. Not romanticizing or idealizing the disenfranchised or the poor should not lead to a situation where the victims are blamed. Cultural studies, and postcolonial studies, are rather concerned with such social or other structures and institutions which foster and contribute to victimhood (Sugirtharajah 1998, 22–23).

10. A postcolonial perspective acknowledges the complexity of cultural and political configurations and structures that form boundaries between the opposing sides of the powerful

Postcolonial criticism understands the postcolonial as a psychological or social term related to consciousness rather than as a descriptive reference to historical conditions (Segovia 2005, 67). It is not a specific methodology; in fact, employing a postcolonial approach is everything but a monolithic enterprise. Sugirtharajah states, "It must be stressed that it [postcolonialism] is not a homogenous project, but a hermeneutical salmagundi, consisting of extremely varied methods, materials, historical entanglements, geographical locations, political affiliations, cultural identities, and economic predicaments" (1998, 15). A postcolonial hermeneutic is interdisciplinary in nature and, therefore, capable of accommodating a diversity of criticisms, approaches, and methods, even if as mode of critical inquiry it is strongly aligned with ideological criticism.

Space does not allow extensive discussion of postcolonial biblical criticism, but a number of its benefits should be registered.[11] It should come as no surprise that, at the level of hermeneutical *orientation*, postcolonial biblical studies has a twofold effect: On the one hand, it challenges the totalizing forms of Western interpretation, exposing its co-optation by imperial interests and destabilizing its frame of meaning. On the other hand, it forms a counter-hegemonic discourse, paying special attention to hidden and neglected voices (Kwok 1998b, 110) as well as to voices of protest or opposition in the texts (Sugirtharajah 1998b, 21). It therefore encourages and welcomes contributions from marginalized groups neglected in the past: Dalits; indigenous peoples; migrants; people in diaspora and in borderlands; and, above all, women in these communities (Kwok 1998b, 105–11). In the end, a postcolonial reading posture has as its aim a twofold exposé: (1) the relationship between ideas and power, language and power, and knowledge and power, and (2) how these relationships prop up Western (read: hegemonic) texts, theories, and learning (Sugirtharajah 1998b, 16–17).[12]

---

and the marginalized within a hegemonic context (Bhabha 1994, 173). As such, it provides a useful approach to the hegemonic context of the first century of the Common Era, given the power imbalance imposed and maintained by the Roman Empire, supported by and coexisting with various other social configurations such as patriarchalism and slavery.

11. Useful and informed overviews—involving the scoping and mapping of important criteria, characteristics, and areas of research—of the postcolonial approach in biblical studies may be found in, e.g., Kwok (1998b, 105–12), Segovia (2005, 23–78, esp. 64–70), and Sugirtharajah (1998, 15–24).

12. Postcolonial hermeneutics also highlights the acquisition and propagation of a *new identity*, realising the importance of hybridity, a concept popularized by Bhabha, as "a doubling, dissembling image of being in at least two places at once", and so colonial otherness is situated in separateness—between the colonialist Self and colonized Other—and not in a particular (essentialist) identity of either colonizer or colonized (Wan 2000, 110). Identity is understood as hyphenated, fractured, multiple, and multiplying—"a complex web of cultural negotiation

As hermeneutical *approach*, postcolonial interpretation addresses disproportionate power relationships at the geopolitical as well as subsidiary levels—the
relationship between the imperial and the colonial, between the powerful ruler
and the subaltern, between the center and the periphery—while investigating the
interrelationship and debunking the apparent distinctions and contrasts between
the two.[13] This focus on relationships of power and hegemony—on domination
and subordination—is particularly useful for investigating the wide-ranging and
often interconnected areas of gender, race, sexuality, and economics in biblical
texts, as well as in later and current interpretations of biblical texts and their orig-
inators (Segovia 2005, 24).

At the level of hermeneutical *practice*, a further valuable contribution of
postcolonial theory to biblical hermeneutics is found in the role it plays in efforts
to account for the contexts of origin of biblical and related contemporary texts
and documents, particularly in accounting for the extent to which these texts
were influenced by imperialist, sociocultural, and economic-political powers
past and present. In the case of New Testament studies in particular, postcolonial theory is increasingly seen to be a viable theoretical position for interpreting
texts that originated in an imperial setting dominated by the Roman Empire
and its collaborators. A postcolonial reading goes beyond an anti-imperial(ist)
reading,[14] since the understanding of what constitutes the postcolonial, and even
the imperial, requires consideration. In picking up on surface level and underlying tensions in texts, postcolonial biblical criticism is useful *and* effective in
studying Empire not only as material setting but also as heuristic grid for biblical
interpretation (Punt 2010).[15]

---

and interaction, forged by imaginatively redeploying the local and the imported elements"
(Sugirtharajah 1998, 16–17; see n. 40).

13. The scope (or range of the field) of postcolonial studies, as far as operative breadth is
concerned, covers the wide range of imperial-colonial formations, since the empires of antiquity
up to the present reach of global capitalism. As for underlying framework or foundational
contexts, both economic and political environments are included, up to and including capitalism
and modernity (Segovia 2005, 70–72).

14. This is partly a problem with terminology: should all forms of political rule and/or
government in the Bible simply be posed as "empire," as some scholars appear to do (Bryan
2005)? Greater sensitivity is needed for the most plausible sociohistorical settings as well as
for (as gleaned from social and political sciences) the intricacies and involved in the nature of
empire: attraction/allure, mimicry, hybridity, and so forth.

15. While the importance of a historical perspective, and a critical one at that, is important
in postcolonial studies, it is doubtful whether the claim that "postcolonial criticism does not
reject the insights of historical criticism" (Kwok 2005, 80) is altogether appropriate; see, e.g.,
Segovia (1995c, 278–85; 2000, 39). On the danger of "promiscuous marriages" of theoretical
frameworks of perspective, see Schüssler Fiorenza (1999, 38–39). On the other hand, this is

The interpretation of biblical texts in the complex and often tension-filled situations and relationships between people and communities in the wake of the end of colonization in Africa, and the fall of the South Africa Apartheid regime in 1994—and in the face of the lingering effects and influence of these systems in the former colonies and "new South Africa"—can greatly benefit from postcolonial criticism. Given the ability of postcolonial theory to avoid strong and exclusivist binaries, through its focus on mimesis and hybridity in the postcolonial setting, it makes available theoretical perspectives with which to address pressing and lingering tensions without the predisposed tendency to simply reverse alienation, marginalization, and disenfranchisement.

Naturally, cultural studies is not without potential danger. One particular danger associated with a cultural turn is the balkanization of knowledge, especially when (for want of better terms) conservative or traditional scholars withdraw to their "bounded communities" away from the public realm, or when more liberal scholars engage in uncritical celebration of popular culture, or simply when social location and identity replace rational explanation as the source of legitimation for or disallowance of certain positions (Davaney 2001,10).

Nevertheless, cultural and postcolonial studies are deliberately not disciplinary but rather are inquisitive activities that question the inherent problems of disciplinary studies and are intent on disciplining the disciplines (Gugelberger 1994, 582). Cultural studies and analysis, with its value for work on the New Testament,[16] and sustained investigations of the theoretical stance(s) of postcolonial theory in particular, can have great value for the post-Apartheid South African context. In short, cultural studies allows for a responsible position in and an accountable framing for biblical studies. It also shows the significance of postcolonial hermeneutics in biblical interpretation, not only for explaining the texts in their historical, imperial settings but also for understanding and appropriating such texts in South Africa, which is affected by its colonial past and enduring legacies and increasingly influenced by our global (post)modern and often neocolonialist world.

---

not to deny historical criticism's suspicious and against-the-grain readings of ecclesial authorized readings of the Bible (see Barton 1998, 16–19).

16. The effect of the cultural turn for theology, Davaney claims (2001, 12–13), is twofold: first, a rejection of the study of religion as *sui generis*, yielding to its study as one dimension of human culture; second, the inclusion of theology as an integral part of the study of religion.

Shifting Focus: Another Triad for Biblical Hermeneutics?

When the focus shifts from a singular *sach*-critical interest in the meaning of individual texts in the Bible to the broader scope and setting of biblical studies and hermeneutics, then other, different taxonomies are required to make sense of the lay of the land of biblical studies. Rather than only a restricted or all-absorbing emphasis on textual meaning, what would a concern for the context in which and the use to which such meanings are put imply for how biblical studies is or could be perceived in the future? This is a particularly important question in the South African context, where the presence of the Bible is pervasive and not limited to either academy or church but is very much present in both. In fact, the Bible is the book with the widest circulation figures in Africa, as one scholar has remarked: "There is no doubt that the Bible is the most influential, most widely translated and the most widely read set of documents in contemporary Africa" (Mugambi 1997, 78). At the same time, the extent to which the academy plays a significant role in how the Bible is read and appropriated is debatable, because in South Africa—and maybe this is not unique to the subcontinent (see, e.g., Wimbush 2008)—the Bible is publicly claimed, particularly in ecclesial, political, and cultural settings.

Claims regarding the ownership of the Bible are neither new nor surprising (see Punt 2004). Since the earliest days of the Christian Bible, and in no small way because of the insistence upon its translatability, various communities have laid claim to these texts. Whereas religious formations in their particular settings, in the form of different groups within the early Christian church and particularly in North Africa, were the initial impetus for translations of the Bible,[17] since the rise of sixteenth-century Protestantism, with its focus on vernacular Bibles, Bible translations have probably done more both to spread *and* fragment Christianity than any other single factor. More recently, the translatability and transportability of the Bible have reached even beyond its commodification in various formats of popular culture to include its deployment on political platforms (see Carroll 1998a, 46–69). I would propose, therefore, that another triad or taxonomy

---

17. Such has been the case going all the way back to the translation of the Hebrew Bible into Greek on African soil in Alexandria, ostensibly during the latter half of the third century (ca. 280–260) b.c.e., commissioned by Ptolemy II Philadelphus. Other early Bible translations in Africa include: the Old Latin version from Carthage in the third century; the Sahidic (Upper Egypt Coptic) Bible from the end of that century; or soon thereafter, the Bohairic and Bashmuric Bibles. The Ethiopian Bible, in Geʿez, might be dated as early as the fourth century (Schaaf 1994, 12, 14, 21). For a taxonomy of Bible translations in African languages by 1885, see Schaaf 1994, 91–93); for a more recent picture, see Schaaf 1994, 132–44).

for making sense of biblical studies in the future could focus on those spheres beyond the academy where the Bible is visibly present and actively used. In fact, will the work of biblical studies in the academy of the future not increasingly be directed toward church, politics, and culture?

Church's Bible: Bible and Spirituality or Back to Prooftexting?

The particular importance of the Bible for the church has never been in doubt. However, it is important to frame the concern with the use of the Bible in the church in South Africa within three varying yet important trends: (1) the rapid rise of Pentecostalism in Africa south of the Sahara, to such an extent that some scholars contend that the centre of Christianity has shifted to the African continent; (2) the range and diversity of "back to God" or "the return of God" movements, with renewed interest in spirituality inside (but certainly also outside) organized religion and the church; and (3) a seemingly growing ecclesial anti-intellectualism, complete with calls for the simplicity of faith, including appeals to literal, commonsense biblical interpretation.

Strong appeals for a theological reading, for rediscovering the Bible in the church, for reading the Bible as Scripture, for reading Scripture with the church, and various other formulations thereof, are all solid indications of the renewed interest—at least among some scholars—in asking about appropriate, and mostly also responsible and accountable, ways of framing the relationship of the Christian churches with the Bible and biblical hermeneutics (Adam et al. 2006; Bockmuehl 2006; Schneiders 1999; and Treier 2008). Such concerns are not limited to the South African subcontinent; recently a North American scholar remarked that the crisis of hermeneutics is "a crisis affecting the conception of the theological task and the very nature of theology" (Schüssler Fiorenza 1991b, 118). In South Africa, references to the Bible Wars, particularly inside the church or ecclesial communities, are not uncommon.

On the one hand, however, the reclaiming of the Bible on behalf of the church or theology can amount to a reactionary plea for retaining a theological status quo (see, e.g., Donfried 2006), and the espousal of a decidedly theological hermeneutic is too often inclined to gloss over the historical and social location of texts and (certainly) of contemporary readers.[18] Interpretative frameworks,

---

18. A theological interpretation is constructed in different ways. For Donfried, it consists of a "Trinitarian hermeneutic" and an insistence on what at least at one level amounts to harmonizing all texts in support of a canonical approach (2006, 11–14, 20–31). See Kraft (2009, 10–18) on the "tyranny of canonical assumptions" that forces the variety of what constitutes the Bible into one homogenous whole.

enduring scholarly hermeneutical frameworks and positions, and the influence and legacy of all these on current interpretation are often ignored in the interest of pursuing a theological interpretation. In the end, the argument for a theological reading tends to favor establishing maintaining set, fixed, and predetermined theological positions and ecclesial policy, often including an appeal to the long-established teaching of the church.[19] On the other hand, moving beyond the notion of the Bible as ultimate, final, and authoritative source within the church requires a different understanding of the role of the Bible and its responsible use in the church.[20]

Politicians' Bible: Bible in the Public Square or Toward Instrumentalism?

The Bible has probably never *not* been part of South African politics, and so its invocation in various spheres of everyday life in South Africa is not too difficult to explain. Ostensibly used as reference and with clear legitimating purposes by the colonial masters, its influence on legislative and other processes in the Apartheid years and its use by liberation movements in the political struggle against apartheid have meant a prolific presence of the Bible in South African politics. The Bible's prevalence, and continuing appeals to it in political discourse, attract attention and require further investigation. Questions need to be asked, such as the following: To what degree has the Bible become politicized? Has its politicization been maintained or heightened? What are the implications of using religious documents to validate political positions and decisions and, in some cases, to ratify perceived political gains? The list could go on (see Punt 2007, 206–33).

---

19. Donfried applied his Trinitarian hermeneutic, which amounts largely to canonical criticism à la Childs, on homosexuality as a test case. The mantra represented by the claim that "an ethical application or claim of the gospel made by the authors of the New Testament, whether contingent or not, can only be revised or modified when Scripture itself provides such a justification" contradicts the appeal to historical interpretation, which necessarily requires investigation of the sociohistorical contexts of the texts. Similar concerns can be expressed for the remarks about divorce, women leadership, slavery, and the inclusion of Gentiles offered here in support of rejecting the use of the Bible in arguing a theological case for homosexuality (2006, 118–53).

20. Cultural studies and postcolonial hermeneutics are not intent on either protecting or salvaging the authority of the Bible. They investigate, rather, its content and reception history for ambiguity and contradiction (Sugirtharajah 2002, 101), understanding the Bible as archetype, as "a site of struggle over meaning and biblical interpretation as debate and argument, rather than as transcript of the unchanging, inerrant Word of G*d" (Schüssler Fiorenza 2008, 169–70).

Old habits die hard, and the danger lurks that past practices of claiming biblical justification in state-authored, national political discourse in many decades of colonial and later Apartheid-minority rule may yet again come to be seen as politically expedient. While a new South African concern for a "rainbow nation of God" may be worlds apart from the Apartheid government's attempts to spike their propaganda with ostensible biblical support for a racially segregated society, the dangers in appeals to the Bible in public political discourse are not altogether absent. Indeed, the new South Africa's constitution is considered novel and groundbreaking in many ways. It underwrites nondiscrimination at many levels, in particular with regard to religious conviction and persuasion, even in the face of the fact that an overwhelming majority of South Africans claim allegiance to Christianity. In this context, the presence of biblical rhetoric is perhaps not so difficult to explain, but the prevalence of explicit quotes from and references to biblical material require further investigation.[21]

CULTURAL BIBLE: DEMOCRATIZATION OR TOWARD ENTITLEMENT?

In South Africa, as in many other parts of the world, the Bible has become a cultural legacy (Brenner 2000, 7–12; Sugirtharajah 2003b, 81), sometimes achieving iconic, if not idolized, proportions. Sometimes the pervasive presence of the Bible in culture today is ascribed to modernity. Here Sugirtharajah is to the point:

> "The Bible," as David Jasper once remarked, "simply swarms us." Western culture and literature are saturated with its language and imageries. It has invaded colonies and has intruded into the political and social and cultural life of peoples who were not necessarily part of the biblical heritage which is infused with Semitic and Greek and Hellenistic imageries and concepts." (2002, 204)

Northrop Frye has referred to the Bible as the "great code" that underwrites Western civilization (1982; see Kwok 2005, 82).

Many indications of the Bible's presence and even popularity can be found in various cultural expressions over the centuries, with current and probably future use particularly in films, music, and other forms of art (Moore 1998b). Various suggestions can be offered for the popularity of film in (post)modern

---

21. The political Bible in increasingly becoming apparent at a broader level than national politics, since important new developments such as ecological criticism (see the contribution of Wainwright and others in Habel and Trudinger 2008), anticipate, without claiming the political as either representative or exhaustive of such approaches, the global, political setting of Bible use.

life, among others its ability to convey shared values and concerns, the way in which movies address and (sometimes) challenge the collective memory, and the fact that movies often prove a reference point for many people in terms of norms and values, worldview and ideology, convictions and aspirations. Movies reflect the worthwhile symbols and values of society and yet, at the same time, also shape them. "In the new century," Robert Kysar states, "the media are likely to become the most decisive factor in shaping human consciousness and reshaping language" (2005, 223).

The study of the Bible in film, art, music, and other areas points in various directions: (1) the extent to which the Bible's influence is constantly extended, or the broadening out of biblical scholars' horizons and interests; (2) the impossibility of fencing in the Bible for the purposes of any specific community, notwithstanding (strong) claims on the Bible or appeals to historical practices; (3) a process of democratization of the Bible, given the presence of the Bible beyond the control of academics and theologians and the church, not totally unlike what has happened since the nineteenth century, when the academic study of the Bible wrestled it from the total control exercised over it by clerics.

Finally, given the increasing acknowledgement that impartial, disinterested, and noncommitted academic work and research are at best a well-intentioned but never achieved goal and at worst a subterfuge for protecting vested interests, power, and control, is it not important to work toward two goals? One is to relinquish claims on impartiality, disinterest, and nonpartisanship and to expose the interests that underlie such claims. The second, rather than investing ever more time in denying the former claims, is to enlist a greater effort for analyzing and trying to understand the social location of biblical studies, trying to explain the vested interests, the driving forces, and the bigger social projects of which all biblical studies, research and scholarship represent an inevitable part (e.g., Kwok 2004, 135–54; Hess 2004, 207–24).

CONCLUSION: NEW ROLES FOR BIBLICAL STUDIES AND INTERPRETERS? OR MORE OF THE SAME?

The laconic remark of Robert Carroll from more than a decade ago still applies to South African biblical scholarship: "The future of biblical studies looks bright but rather confusing" (1998b, 62). In the South African context, where biblical interpretation "matters" (sometimes in very tangible ways, when the invocation of the Bible in political, moral, and other areas, besides its prominence in ecclesial settings, is considered), concerns about the ethics and politics of biblical interpretation are evident, important, and unavoidable. As Glancy has stated,

"Interpretation is political. This is true of all interpretation, regardless of its location: classroom, conference, journal" (1998, 461; see also Collins 2004, 195–211; and Buell and Hodge 2004, 235–51). What the future of biblical studies in South Africa will be, of course, depends largely on who the future biblical interpreters will be as well as on which concerns they will pursue and by what methodologies. It will also depend on how biblical scholars will perceive their role in terms of ethical and political positions and responsibilities.

My argument is not a plea for scholars to become uninvested, whether from a historical consciousness, a literary engagement, or reception-historical concerns (to reenact the well-worn taxonomy): such work will and should continue, even if with different hermeneutical and ethical lenses. My plea is rather for reinvesting, for reconceptualizing of what happens while historical, textual, and reception work is carried out. It is a call for reframing the larger enterprise of biblical studies in an effort to understand the venture as a whole and, in that way, to be able to address the social location of biblical studies and to make sense of the increasing variety in biblical studies as far as scholars and areas of concerns, methods, and interests are concerned.[22] Of course, such reorientation and self-conceptualization of biblical studies and hermeneutics, is—as much as an argument for maintaining the status quo or an insistence on "business as usual"—anything but innocent or neutral.

---

22. Some scholars see hermeneutics as the vehicle for change in biblical studies. For example, Schüssler Fiorenza argues that the combination of a rhetorical emphasis with feminist theory will enable the "full-turn" of biblical studies, since a paradigm shift in biblical studies has so far failed to take place due to the inability of rhetoric to link up with feminist, liberationist and postcolonial studies (1999, 13).

PART 2
ASIA

4

Unleashing the Power Within: The Bible and Dalits

Monica Jyotsna Melanchthon

India can legitimately be described as one of the earliest recipients of the Bible (Sugirtharajah 2001, 15–22), and yet Indian biblical scholarship has had little impact if any on biblical studies worldwide. I thus welcome this opportunity to participate in *The Future of the Biblical Past*, while aware of the problematic roles that are thrust upon the nonWestern individual when she and her work enter the orbit of certain kinds of academic concerns and discursive practices pursued supposedly and predominantly only in the West. However, biblical study and interpretation are not a project of the West alone. Third World individuals should be recognized as crucial partners of mainstream Western voices engaged in biblical criticism, as critical interlocutors of strategies at work in versions of academic multiculturalism or international cooperation as initiated by the Society of Biblical Literature.

Improving the range of texts we attend to and the issues we take seriously, as well as including a range of marginalized voices into academic institutions and public debates, are important social and political tasks. Yet I hope that this project, diverse and multicultural as it is, is not seen simply as a way to reduce the parochialism and enlarge the understandings of mainstream Western subjects, since the stakes of nonWesterners go far beyond a simple "inclusion." We seek to make critical interventions not only into the perspective of mainstream Western culture itself but also into our Third World discourses about our contexts and communities. We have experienced that our interventions have not always been considered "scholarship," of appropriate "method" and "relevant interpretation."

Hence *The Future of the Biblical Past* project is an opportunity for those involved in biblical study and interpretation to be self-reflective about the project of appreciating the "voices from the majority of the globe" that are contributing to the "breakdown of the North Atlantic dominance of biblical studies." However, I think that we need to be cautious that the views of an elite social group at a particular historical moment do not become the defining components of the worldview of the context represented. It is essential that we reflect on how the actual religious practices, spiritual understandings, and scriptural interpretations of various groups of women, oppressed castes, and groups variously socially and culturally marginalized, might challenge and subvert rather than endorse the views found in such essays. An uncritical appreciation may obstruct an understanding of the place of these "cultural positions" within the moral and political fabric of their social contexts and obscure their ideological functions as justifications for practices or institutions that were unjust and exclusionary and that worked to disempower and marginalize a great many of the inhabitants of these cultural contexts.

This could occur particularly with a culture such as India's, which considers itself to be deeply, internally religious and is very hierarchical and stratified. The diversity of culture, language, religion, and caste makes India an almost undefinable entity, one that cannot be encompassed with a single approach or perspective.[1] Well-known studies that have so far showcased biblical studies and biblical methodology or described the reception of the Bible in India have paid some attention to interpretations from the perspective of caste (Sugirtharajah 1998a, 283–89; 2001, 15–22; 2005a, 73–84; Prabhu 1980, 151–70). This essay is an attempt to survey and reflect critically on the following areas: (1) the reception of the Bible by the *Dalit* Christian community in India; (2) the hermeneutics and methods, as well as the function of the Bible, in the struggle for Dalit emancipation; and (3) the future prospects for biblical scholarship and reflection from the perspective of caste in India.

THE SCRIPTURALISM OF CASTE DISCRIMINATION

The caste, or *Varna*, system in India is a comprehensive sociocultural system, traditionally stratified and hierarchical, that developed in ancient India. It is characterized by *exclusion* (rules governing marriage and physical/social contact based on a system of purity and pollution), *hierarchy* (order, rank, and status according to caste and subcaste status), and *interdependence* (division of labor; each caste is assigned an occupation). Caste is the most visible, pervasive, and

---

1. I say this aware of my own limitations as a Dalit woman whose life was in many ways a privileged one and that what I present in this essay cannot encompass the thoughts and positions of the diversity that exists within the Dalit community.

powerful expression of Indian culture and society and the operating principle in all social interactions and relationships. As a religio-cultural ideology of social inequality, it allows and justifies hierarchies and discrimination, yielding a social order peculiar to India, "a land of the most inviolable organization by birth and text book example of hierarchical society" (Beteille 1981, 32 and 49).

According to current statistics, the "scheduled caste" population comprises over sixteen percent of India's total population. Therefore, more than 200 million people in India are considered "Untouchable"—people tainted by their birth into a system that deems them impure, less than human. The Untouchables of India, now called "Dalits,"[2] are relegated to the lowest jobs, such as scavenging, cleaning, sweeping, leather tanning, weaving, fishing, and so forth, and live in constant fear of being publicly humiliated, paraded naked, beaten, and raped with impunity by dominant-caste groups seeking to keep them in their place. Wearing shoes or merely walking through an upper-caste neighborhood, drinking water from a pot or well reserved for the upper caste, or visiting an upper-caste temple are life threatening offenses. Having been relegated to a segregated position character-ized by poverty and misery for nearly three millennia, they continue to be the most disadvantaged of the Indian population.

It is almost impossible to ignore the caste question today, since the prob-lems of Dalits figure in every agenda. The social sciences, practical politics, artistic expressions, journalistic writings—all pay attention to Dalits. This has not occurred because of any sudden and miraculous changes in perception or con-sciousness that the upper-caste intelligentsia have come about on their own. The struggles of the Dalit masses in all fields of life—religious, social, cultural, ideo-logical, and political—have forced this realization on the rest of society. The caste struggle has quite some time ago crossed the boundaries of mere opposition or resistance to upper-caste power and dominance or of attempts at upward social mobility. It is a movement that is challenging the very existence of the system in India and is calling for the total annihilation of caste. It is seeking to harness even the living religions of India, including Scripture/s, for the purposes of the struggle.

This is essential because caste derives its legitimacy and strength from the dominant Brahminical Hinduism whose ancient Hindu Scriptures hold that the four castes, called *varnas*, came out of the primordial man, the *Adi Purusha*: the *Brahmin* (priest) from his head; the *Kshatriya* (ruler) from the shoulders; the

---

2. The term "Dalit" is a descriptive term, for it portrays the conditions under which Dalit find themselves—oppressed, broken, subordinated, crushed, split, and the like. It is a name that they have given themselves to counter names given by others, such as "untouchables," "*harijans*," "scheduled classes," and "backward classes."

Vysya (trader) from the torso; and the *Sudra* (laborer) from the thighs (*Rig Veda* 10.90). This scriptural rhetoric is based on concepts of purity and pollution and the resolve of the upper castes to surmount through the forces of *Hindutva*.[3] This "scripturalism" is used to emphasize unity and continuity in Indian culture. The Hindu Scriptures influence deep-seated convictions about the nature of Indian reality and the survival of its customs and mores. They solidify a national identity forged by the Hindu rhetoric of Brahmanical or caste supremacy.

Hence an examination of the Bible and Dalit experience should take place keeping in mind this "scripturality" of the Dalit experience, the pervasiveness of scriptural legitimation of upper caste consciousness by Hindu scriptural mandates. Dalits have had to read and study any Scripture, including the Bible, in such a context. That reading and study have been contested, and for centuries Dalits have been involved in a struggle for access to Hindu Scriptures, which sanctify and justify the hierarchical and discriminatory system of caste and fuel the hegemony of the dominant caste groups through interpretation, religious rituals, symbols, and myths. Dalits have also had limited access and authority to interpret Christian Scriptures.

Dalit Reception of the Bible: A Brief Overview

Sugirtharajah speaks of the tolerance with which the Bible was received in pre-colonial India: it was revered as an icon with mystical and magical powers and privileged because of its holiness and transcendental properties (2001, 16–18).[4] The language of the Bible (Syriac) used by the St. Thomas and other Christians in the Malabar region made it inaccessible to the common populace, who were predominately illiterate. Translations were discouraged; hence, the contents of the

---

3. The concept of *hindutva* (Hindu-ness), basic to the ideals of Hindu Culture, or *rashtra* (nation), is a combination of acknowledging the land of *Bharat* from Indus to the Seas as one's Fatherland as well as his/her Holy Land, i.e., the cradle land of one's religion.

4. It is also imperative that we do not forget that this much celebrated Hindu tolerance stands exposed in the extensive and ruthless displacement, encroachment, and erosion of religions such as Buddhism in India and the death of other "little" traditions within Hinduism which seemed to counter the Hindu ideology of caste and hierarchy by mainstream Hinduism (Sharma 1993, 8). Tolerance was a principle incorporated into Brahminic Hinduism but never fundamental to it. Tolerance of diversity in religion was in some ways possible by the majority Hindu populace partly because the caste identity subsumed all other identities and hence conversion to other religions was not met with any opposition. Caste, a highly intolerant hierarchical structure which permeates the entire fabric of Indian society, contributed to the maintenance of a forced tolerance between diverse religious faiths!

Bible were made familiar through various nontextual means, such as sermons, liturgy, the veneration of saints, pilgrimages, and festivals. The Bible presented as a book in harmony with the tenets of other faiths found a place alongside these scriptural traditions (Sugirtharajah 2001, 37–40). Control over interpretation and transmission of the Bible, its contents and message, was very much in the hands of the priests. What Sugirtharajah does not address is the issue of caste in precolonial India. If the first converts to Christianity were the dominant castes (Brahmins), as is popularly maintained, then is it possible that they did not want it translated or circulated? Would Hebrew or Syriac have acquired a status similar to that of Sanskrit as a holy language among these new converts and as a language of Scripture restricted to only those who could read and interpret? Would these early custodians of the Christian Scriptures, given their caste identity, intentionally shelter the Bible from being "polluted" by the so-called "Untouchables?"

In colonial India, however, the missionary focus shifted to the lower caste groups, and the Bible was translated and printed into vernacular languages. With its availability in English made possible by the work of the British and Foreign Bible Society, more and more people began reading and meditating on the Bible, despite its use to stem any resistance to colonial occupation and oppression (Sugirtharajah 2001, 45–73). The Bible became polyvalent in use: as a colonizing book, a metasymbol of the colonialists, to inculcate European manners, values and symbols; as a medium through which education and literacy became available; and as an icon in a culture with a history of iconizing material objects (Clarke, 2002a, 245–66). Yet it was popular among the "newly converted," because it was accessible to all who could read irrespective of caste or gender. It became an instrument of emancipation for the colonized. The gospel was a godsend, because it *seemed* to weaken the caste system. Given the Dalits' exceptional need for acceptance, the possibility of liberation—from physical slavery, serfdom, social stigma, and almost total degradation—promised through salvation in Jesus Christ and participation in the life of the Christian church came as good news. Many Dalits responded accordingly and accepted the Bible as their Book of Faith and Scripture. The offer of a new self-image as a person God in fact loves and has already forgiven, as well as the offer of hope—primarily for eternal life, but also for a life free from cringing fear and terrorized subservience here and now, all of which were denied Dalits by all parties in their existing circumstances—were further reasons to accept Christianity and its Scriptures. Yet, at the very same time, their culture and identity as Dalits were also being eroded.

At a time when missionaries were trying to utilize the Bible as a strategic resource to demarcate familiar colonial binaries (Christian and heathen, saved and damned), many Indian philosophers and thinkers began to familiarize themselves with the Christian Scriptures and to engage them in dialogue with the

Indian Scriptures (Boyd 1973, 141–62; John 1965, 43–51). These early thinkers, Christian and nonChristian, belonged mostly to the privileged and literate caste groups; hence, their interpretations and reflections paid little attention to the needs and aspirations of the Dalits.[5] They used traditional brahmanical philosophical concepts and esoteric theories as interpretive keys to unlock the biblical message for India, one which had little significance for the millions suffering caste tyranny (cf. Sugirtharajah and Hargreaves, 1993).[6]

Dalits and Biblical Studies: Impediments

Postcolonial India is still addressing the issue of caste and, although by constitution all Indians are equal, caste continues to function in all spheres of life, including the church and theological education. It is important to view Dalit contributions to biblical studies in the light of this historical background and recognize that such study is inhibited by three major factors.

First, since all fields of intellectual activity were barred to them, about 80 percent of Dalits, even today, remain illiterate. Their cultural and creative activity was denied or considered debased and vulgar. This large scale illiteracy among Dalits leads Maria Arul Raja to remark, "It is an irony to think of a Dalit interpretation of the written text of the Bible, when a vast majority of them are kept as illiterates" (1997, 336). There are just too few biblical scholars/theologians from the Dalit community who are equipped with the formal tools of biblical study and interpretation. Even then, those few have been trained within a Western system with methodological tools that are not always appropriate or helpful in the Indian context. Hence they struggle trying to be sensitive to the needs of the context and be faithful to method (read: Western).

---

5. A. P. Nirmal (1990, 142) "Whether it is the traditional Indian Christian theology or the more recent third world theology, they failed to see in the struggle of Indian dalits for liberation a subject matter appropriate for doing theology in India. What is amazing is the fact that Indian theologians ignored the reality of the Indian church. While estimates vary, between 50% and 80% of all the Christians in India today are of scheduled-caste origin. This is the most important commonality cutting across the various diversities of the Indian Church that would have provided an authentic liberation motif for Indian Christian theology. If our theologians failed to see this in the past, there is all the more reason for our waking up to this reality today and for applying ourselves seriously to the 'task of doing theology.'"

6. The legacy of these thinkers is their questioning of the biblical text and the setting of the Christian Scriptures within the larger textual tradition of India, the intertextual nature of texts, which set for us a direction for an interpretative process that is Indian and that takes seriously the multiscriptural context of India.

Second, for a community that had no scriptures of its own, or scriptures that have been erased or incorporated into the dominant tradition, the Bible became an alternate canon, the Christian "Veda," filling a void and supplying the Dalits with a framework for knowledge which they did not have to begin with and which they desired (Thangaraj 1999, 138–39). The Bible is "Scripture," the revealed Word of God; as talisman, an icon with sacred power, it contributes to the notion that the Word of God is found in the letter of Scripture. Yet Scripture in its status as "Word of God" inhibits the Dalit reader from reading the Bible as a historical document open to critical inquiry. This is further exacerbated by similarities in the cultures of the Bible and India. Scripture and culture collude to reinforce hierarchy, particularly in matters pertaining to women. Questioning scripture is considered redundant.

Third, flawed or biased interpretations of the Bible have hindered Dalits from playing a more active role in church and theological education. While the authority of the Bible has not been used to legitimate the enslavement of Dalits, unlike apartheid, it has not been utilized to address the issue of caste. Even though the good news for Dalits was still presented in terms of a new self-image (a new community granting Dalits greater equality, respect, and caring) and a new hope (defined primarily in terms of enhanced opportunities for individual and family), mobility was/is still a distant dream. Social transformation is confined to social reform, and Indian Christian theology has failed to come to terms with Dalit political aspirations. The church has therefore remained casteist, as though caste were not contrary to the message of the Gospel.

Dalit Interpretations: A Sampler

Over the last three decades, alternate interpretations of the Bible have been rendered by Dalit Christians, who are often at the risk of being considered "untutored exegetes." These interpretations were unmistakably shaped by the status of the interpreters as outsiders.[7] It is still the case that the social, political, economic, and aesthetic marginalization of Dalits—their dislocation both within society and church—conditions their approach to and use of biblical imagery, precepts, and motifs. The Bible holds a central place in Dalit theological discourse, and it is emphatically declared that Dalit theology is biblical (Carr n.d., 71–84; Devasahayam, 1992; Arul Raja 1997, 336–45). Bible study is recognized as an important method for forging Dalit identity and mobilizing Dalit struggle

---

7. Many of these interpreters are not recognized as "scholars" in the field. Most belong to departments of theology and hence pay little attention to biblical methodology.

and resistance. Dalit readings and interpretations of Christian Scriptures use the concepts of "pollution," "untouchability," and poverty—all derived from their stigmatized experience as key criteria.[8] These alternate readings are part of an effort to unleash the power inherent in the sacred text, a power that has been subdued heretofore by casteist interpretations in an attempt to empower those discriminated by the evil of caste. In what follows I offer a few examples of Dalit interpretations of select biblical texts.

Genesis 4:1-10. Veeramani Devasahayam uplifts Abel as the first Dalit martyr, whose heirs are the Dalits (1992, 8–12). Cain the vegetarian assumes privilege and strength by virtue of being the firstborn, a status understood as "God-given," and expects Abel as the "meat eater" to assume the weaker and secondary role (on grounds of pollution). Devasahayam draws parallels between the caste system and Cain's actions, which begin at the altar (read: religion) and are taken into the field (read: sociopolitical and cultural life of Dalits). Unlike the God of the Hindus, however, the biblical God refutes the dominant values of Cain (dominant caste groups) by listening to the cry of the blood of Abel (Dalits). This God does not destroy the dominant ones but warns them, and the same warning comes to all who entertain caste prejudices and practice discrimination.

Mark 5:24-34. Devasahayam lays emphasis on what he calls the subversive faith of the woman (1992, 28–35; see here for other biblical studies). She mingles in the crowd fully aware of her unclean and ritual status; thus, "She dares to pollute others in order to become clean. The irony of this subversive faith is that she wants to break the laws precisely through channels that were created to remind people of the law and seek its compliance." It is a faith that "dares to act when it appears feasible by daring obstacles." By seeking to know who touched him and then commending her in public, Jesus exposes the sin of the oppressor. Devasahayam therefore reminds us, "Theology has the prophetic task of pronouncing judgment on the oppressor and the structures in order to call them to repentance." It needs to expose the sin of the oppressor in order to induce confidence in the oppressed, promote their full humanity, and release them from any fear even after being healed.

Mark 5:21-45. Philip Peacock focuses on the pollution that is passed on by touching (2007, 56–58). Jesus overcomes untouchability by touching—blood and death are considered to be polluting but, by being touched by the woman and by touching the dead girl, Jesus brings healing to both. Rather than becoming polluted, he heals. The christological import of this text lies in its message that

---

8. Untouchability for the person from the dominant social group is a marginal issue, viewed as something that Dalits have brought upon themselves through their occupations, whereas Dalits view untouchability as a creation of the Brahmins.

the blood and death of Jesus are the means of salvation. That which is polluting (read: Dalit) becomes the means of salvation. The touch of men, Dalit and non-Dalit, on Dalit women's bodies is an act of accumulating power, to exert power over, but Jesus relinquished power in order to empower.

Luke 15:11-32. George Zachariah reads the parable of the Prodigal Son from the perspective of the prostituted women and wonders if the text mentions these women only to enhance the sinfulness of the young man and to emphasize the intensity of the forgiveness that the father has granted to his son (2007, 65–72). He notes that the text exhibits excitement over the *metanoia* of the son but says little about the system that dehumanizes him. Similarly, the prostituted women are those who are, like Dalit women, socially ostracized and prostituted by a colonial system of hierarchical power relations as well as by its morality and religiosity. He asks whether "salvation is a rescue operation of young rich men from 'sinful' women." He further inquires, "Is there a Father [*sic*] who is concerned with systems that make women prostitutes and is committed to redeeming those systems and its victims?"

Mark 7:24-31. Surekha Nelavala, in her treatment of the Syrophoenician woman, celebrates the success of the woman seeking healing for her daughter (2006, 64–69). By employing the methods of a trickster, with wisdom and intelligence, the woman challenges Jesus on his exclusionary views. Nelavala's reading emphasizes the need for the oppressor and the oppressed to work together for liberation and transformation to be complete. Anshi Zachariah reads the same text and challenges the reader to recognize the fact that we see people at the boundaries as objects of charity and never stop to ask, "Why they are where they are?" (2007, 59–61). She sees this text as a call to listen to people at the periphery and to re-articulate our faith and redefine our ministry in the light of their claims of the divine. Jesus' presence at the boundaries and amidst the boundaries is not to legitimize boundaries but to manifest God's preferential option for the poor.

Jesus in Mark. Maria Arul Raja reads the Markan Jesus alongside the legend of the martyred Madurai Veeran, who is upheld as a protector god by the Dalit *Arundhathiar* community in Tamilnadu (2002, 264). He poses the question: "How are the cruel death and defeat of the murdered heroes to be transformed into the weapon of the weak community?" By analyzing both texts and their impact on the communities that these heroes represent, Arul Raja concludes that by divinizing these murdered heroes, the communities venerating them "seek to deliberately denounce all forms of dehumanization promoted in the name of religious Puritanism (Jewish authorities) and orderly harmony ('casteist' hegemony)." He further claims, "the pronounced and executed punishment meted out to these heroes itself is transformed into the springboard from which the communities evolve new ethical alternatives."

John 4. The Samaritan woman is also particularly significant for Dalit interpreters on two grounds: first, because her ostracized experience as both a Samaritan and a woman resonates with the Dalit experience of rejection and isolation; second, because the narrative locates this encounter between Jesus and the woman at a well. The focus of the conversation is water, which is a primeval issue for rural Indian women and a crucial issue for Dalits (Dietrich 2001, 106). What is significant is that the woman exhibits signs of having transcended gender norms, transgressed cultural taboos, and subverted cultural expectations—all norms which need to be emulated by Dalits as well. "Living water" here is understood as the capacity for physical emancipation from the drudgery and pain of caste labor, violence, discrimination, and suffering. It is understood as the empowerment that comes with being equipped with the mechanisms and the mindset to resist and overcome caste and other forms of oppression (Melanchthon 2007, 50).

Exodus. Sathianathan Clarke examines the Exodus narrative as a paradigm of liberation and reflects on its significance for Dalits, who no longer see or experience any "mighty acts of God" delivering God's chosen oppressed ones from the clutches of their oppressors (2002b, 285–86). Instead, they experience "an apparent reversal of direction of the mighty acts of God." In fact, there are "no miraculous signs clearly disrupting the hierarchical and unequal social order in India." Clarke therefore calls for rethinking the nature of God and God's involvement with the poor and the oppressed in terms of the way in which Dalits work for their own liberation. God must be found, he says, "in the process of funding and sustaining the non-violent and repetitive acts of 'chipping away' at the conventional order."

DALIT INTERPRETATIONS: METHODOLOGICAL INDICATORS

The Bible holds a central place in Dalit theologizing because it is seen as a source of power and comfort and because it provides Christian identity and continuity with the Christian tradition (Devasahayam 1992, 4). The potential of biblical texts for liberation, negotiated and renegotiated in the light of Dalit experience, makes possible the discovery of God within the Dalit social and cultural milieu and their liberation from oppressive forces.

What identifies the method employed by Dalit biblical interpretation? This question has been repeated often, and Dalit interpreters have been challenged to name the unique characteristics of Dalit biblical methodology. Actually, Dalit biblical interrogation employs a variety of methods. It has definitely found helpful the insights gained from traditional historical-critical methods as well as from literary methods. However, the heart of Dalit biblical methodology is found in the post modern reader-oriented methods.[9]

There is also growing awareness among Dalit theologians that, in addition to the biblical text, there are in the lives of Dalits other texts that need to be studied and interpreted (Arul Raja 2006, 103–11; Clarke 1998, 35–53; Dietrich 2001, 244–49). These include folktales, songs, dances, art, and other cultural productions of the Dalits—namely, literary works and other writings by Dalit authors; Dalit experiences of revolt, protest, and revival; and Dalit living stories that are told and retold. These are often juxtaposed and brought into conversation with the biblical text and woven together with the use of imagination and the wealth of experience (intertextual, crosstextual, contrapuntal, reading in juxtaposition). It is to be noted that these other texts are not restricted to the written but are, in a majority of cases, oral, and are by their very nature fluid and flexible and do not alway originate in the written word. They provide new and fresh insights into the meaning of the biblical text, and hence the biblical text is seen as one among other texts that has to be read.

Whatever the method, Dalit interpretation pays attention to the context and experience of the interpreter (autobiographical, experiential). The context, therefore, becomes the means through which the text becomes available and is read. The historical nature of the text (the background of the text) is also important. Crucial also is the generation of faith and action for resistance and transformation. It is a very subjective approach to the biblical text. Arul Raja points out, "The Dalit reading of the bible [*sic*], like any other contextual reading, does not indulge in the rhetorics of claiming value-neutrality, a historical point of view, scientific objectivism, presuppositionless exegesis, a-political [*sic*] detachment and universal meaning" (1996, 31). This subjectivity is justified on the grounds that, "The real objectivity starts with the declaration of the subjectivity. If one's subjectivity is in tune with the subjectivities of majority [*sic*], then only it becomes objective one [*sic*]" (Appavo 1993, 4).

The Context as Medium for Reading and Interpreting the Text

The many convergences in the matrices of the biblical and the Dalit worlds are an important methodological consideration, as in the case, for example, of the

---

9. Arul Raja writes, "The bible [*sic*] is … oriented towards 'performing' a transformation.… Any method that claims to facilitate a genuine dialogue between the 'performative' Dalit consciousness and the 'performative' biblical text, has to be necessarily performative.… Such a method of the Dalit reading of the bible [*sic*] is oriented towards concrete historical commitment transforming the present reality into a new liberative one" (1996, 30–31).

biblical dictum of a preferential option toward the poor and the Dalit struggle for equality (Jesurathnam 2002, 2–3). Therefore, both the exegetical starting point for Dalit biblical interpretation and the material force that grips the Dalit are grounded in a materialistic epistemology that is characterized, among other things, by its location of truth not in a world beyond history but indeed within the crucible of historical struggles. The social, cultural, economic, and political world of Dalits and their denied humanity constitutes the valid hermeneutical staring point for reading Scripture for liberation. This emphasis on context requires attention to what is particular, concrete, and experiential. Paying serious attention to the context is one way of exhibiting responsibility to the faith community on behalf of whom the text is being interpreted.

The Historical Nature of the Text

While Dalit interpreters claim in theory to take the context of the text seriously, published Bible studies by Dalit authors reveal that this is not always the case. One gets the impression that historical-critical issues and the sociohistorical foundations of the text are not as important unless they touch on Dalit experience; such is also the case with the inherent and varied ideologies and agendas of the text. Yet some trained Dalit readers emphasize that it is imperative that the Bible is received as a text, a result of human effort (Arul Raja 1996, 30). In other words, there is awareness that the Bible should not be seen as divinely inspired but rather as becoming the "Word" when read in community and in the light of the community's experience. Such an approach, according to Peacock, has various effects: (1) it enables a questioning of the text and facilitates a dialogical approach that gives room for multiple meanings; (2) it eliminates the necessity of and dependency on a priestly class (read: Brahmin) to be the "expert" interpreters of the text; (3) it frees the text from the mysticism attributed to it, which has often been used to oppress the marginalized, to legitimize their oppression, and to stress the notion that the text cannot be argued with; and (4) it brings about the realization that the biblical text, as all other texts, is ideological and that it either justifies a particular status quo or challenges it. Dalit readers of the Bible see the Bible as a book of liberation. Yet they realize that not all biblical texts are liberative; indeed several texts actually legitimize hierarchies and the status quo (Peacock 2005, 3–4).

The Text as Praxis Generating

The effectiveness and relevance of a reading is measured by the extent to which it has touched upon the life of the individual and the community. There is, therefore, a special sensitivity to the practical implications of the reading for the reader. New interpretations are futile unless they motivate and provoke the community into action. The move from their particular experience to the Bible, from the Bible to action, and then back again to the Bible is emphasized, requiring a process of mutual validation between experience and text. Only then can one envision the liberation of Dalits, the renewal of the church, and the transformation of society.

DALIT HERMENEUTICAL MARKERS

What seems more important than a fixation on method is the hermeneutical lens through which the text is read and interpreted. Perspective and approach are crucial to Dalit readings. Dalit readings, therefore, criticize that which is merely theoretical; they validate the experiential, the lived, and the ambiguous. There is a consciousness regarding modes of knowing that may be considered ambiguous, disruptive, and even chaotic, but which are closer to actualities than those offered by verbal authorities. The overarching perspective adopted by Dalit interpreters of the Bible is one of *resistance and liberation*. It is a perspective that is influenced by *Dalit consciousness*, a mindset informed by the Dalit experience not only of suffering and rejection but also of overcoming the same. The term "Dalit" is a result of this new consciousness and determination (Manchala n.d., 4). The name bears witness to their awakening and their awareness of subjugation and of their oppressors. It affirms their determination to annihilate slavery, both internal and external, and their visions for an egalitarian, casteless society. It asserts that their new identity is shaped by shared visions and formed as a counter to imposed oppressive identities (Manchala n.d., 4). This desire to surmount repression makes their experience a legitimate and creative theological resource. It is within such experience that the affirmation of God's liberating power also takes place.

A. P. Nirmal, a pioneering Dalit theologian, while comparing the Dalit struggle for liberation with that of the slaves in Egypt, identifies five important features of the struggle within the Deuteronomic creed (Deut 26:5–12). These are: the affirmation of one's roots; collective struggle; the experience of suffering, as well as the experience of liberation; and the vision of liberation and restoration (Nirmal n.d., 65–69). These features present in the historic struggle of the Dalits are also the ingredients of Dalit consciousness. Such consciousness is a prerequisite for reading and interpreting the text for Dalit liberation. Dalit readings of Scripture are not unbiased; they are readings that are committed to the cause of justice and holistic life for all people and for the entire earth. Hence, the ultimate goal of Dalit readings is to instill in the community the impetus to strive for political and social liberation and to provide the community with possible blueprints for action towards liberation, a new identity, and fullness of life (Manchala n.d., 4).

Dalit biblical hermeneutics are closely bound up with their direct involvement in the process of production and hard physical labor. By their physical exertion they contribute to the maintenance of life, and not just of themselves but of the entire society. Without their services the entire social structure would collapse. Dalits have, therefore, been likened to the "thumb" on a hand. This life needs to be protected when it is threatened, and hence they are "skeptical and suspicious of religious sources that do not vibrate with their daily lives, instead seem to contain ideological legitimization of their subjugated condition and bondage" (Wilfred 2005, 150). The lack of fulfillment of their basic material needs for a dignified life makes the Dalit reader very sensitive to the present moment (Wilfred 2005, 150). They challenge the theological and social determination of the dominant castes to keep Dalits in subservient roles by finding ways either to revise or reject both scriptural and social dictums that have imposed on them a life of drudgery. Through openly performed rituals,[10] through song, dance, and act,[11] they read, enact, or revise oppressive traditions and thereby equip themselves and the community with strength and hope to address and cope with the predicament of exclusion, discrimination, and exploitation.

Indian tradition affirms that "no hermeneutic by itself will yield truth in its fullness without purification of the mind, transformation of the heart and discipline of the body" (Samartha 1991, 307). Faith is both a starting point and the end result of Dalit interrogation of Scripture. Faith is considered an effective hermeneutic because it helps the interpreter to be cautious in his/her use of tools used to sift the text of the Bible for meaning, irrespective of the method employed. The study of the Bible for the Dalit is a matter of faith, and biblical research is not merely an intellectual exercise but ultimately a means to respond

---

10. Charsely (citing Gluckman 1954) identifies these performances as "rituals of rebellion" (Charsely 2004, 287n11).

11. Through his study of the Madiga community in Andhra Pradesh, Charsely (2004) shows how they undermine the claimed superiority of the dominant Brahman by calling on cosmogonic traditions that emphasize the female *Shakti* and by making secondary and junior the great male gods of contemporary Hinduism. The practical importance of this community—traditionally assigned to work with leather and hence considered polluting—to others is emphasized, and an embraceable caste identity at odds with sheerly negative conceptions of "the Untouchable" is constructed. The problematic aspects of their identity as untouchable, polluted, and excluded are also accounted for within contextualized positive elements. For example, "The ability to move and skin dead cattle is given a forcefully positive evaluation. The eating of beef is not represented as a mistake" (285).

to God and God's demands. This provides both the motivation and goal in all aspects of biblical research. The faith of the Dalit cannot be equated with the intellect alone. Rather, it is characterized and defined by its "earthliness" (Wilfred 1996).[12] It indicates urgency, immediacy, and directness; it is bound up with the material and physical realities and needs of life (Wilfred 1996, 58).

FUTURE POSSIBILITIES IN DALIT BIBLICAL INTERPRETATION

The future of Dalit biblical interpretation lies certainly in addressing the impediments listed above. Further, the possibilities for Dalit interpretation would be immense if biblical studies in India were more open to the following resources and strategies: the voices of Dalit women; informal and creative learning and interpretative strategies and methodologies; reading the many oral resources (stories, rituals, songs, poetry) alongside the biblical text; and reading and interpreting in community.

Despite the radical and liberative rhetoric of inclusion, Dalit theologians (read: male) have not given due respect to the voices of Dalit women. Gender is very much an ignored lens within Dalit theologizing and biblical interpretation. Far more serious efforts need to be made to encourage and include the reflections arising from among Dalit women and their experience of being thrice marginalized (gender, class, and caste) from all movements of social change, including the women's and the Dalit movements, and alienated from all sources of society. Patriarchy and caste collude to keep women in a servile position to men both within and outside their caste grouping. Thus, Devahasayam writes, "The concern for humanity in the Indian context should start from concern for Dalit women, where humanity is most disgraced. It is only a Dalit women's perspective that would be adequate to serve the liberative struggles" (1997, 33).

Dalit women live lives of pathos, protest, and indefeatable will to survive. Their voices, if given attention, will restore the mark of this exiled "other" on

---

12. In his discussion of those Dalits who converted to Christianity in exchange for rice and who are therefore called "rice Christians," Wilfred writes, "The seeds of a subaltern hermeneutics were present in the acts of the subaltern peoples in their quest for a religious affiliation which would respond to their needs for rice, wheat, security and other material necessities. Today this hermeneutic is unfolding itself with greater incisiveness and force. The growing critique by the subalterns of the religious traditions for denying equality of treatment, freedom and dignity is a further elaboration of their hermeneutics of religion through "rice"—a symbol of all that a human being requires to live and to live with dignity. This critical earthliness forces the religious traditions to find their true bearings in a politically, socially and culturally situated praxis" (1996, 59).

the many institutions—familial, psychic, ethical, ecclesial—that ground their personal and political lives. Their voices will renew the understanding of patriarchy and the various oppressive systems that sustain it. The questions raised by women are frightening and yet full of promise, and thus the inclusion of the Dalit woman's perspective in Dalit biblical hermeneutics and interpretation would fill a serious historical gap by documenting the relationship of Dalit women with God and would bring fresh insights to the reading of Scripture.

Wilfred emphasizes in his writing the "primacy of the oral" in Dalit culture, made evident in their mode of communication, interaction, and transmission. Because it is oral, performance takes center stage in their religious experience and expression. Through performance, one can more easily communicate emotion, mood, feeling, and the like—all of which may not be as effectively communicated through the written word (1996, 60). The oral tradition is by nature collective, hence knowledge, including knowledge of Scripture, is acquired through participation in the collective, in the community of faith. The oral traditions of the Dalits, their rituals, and symbols, and the manner in which the Bible is presented—all of which are interpretations of life and faith—are still very much untapped sources. Placing these oral and performative reflections alongside the biblical text could result in new and exciting interpretations. Just allowing the community to perform the biblical text in context would provide for some fresh insights. The hermeneutics employed to interpret these oral reflections may need to be different from those used to decipher and interpret the written text (Wilfred 1996, 61).

Sophisticated and complex methods of biblical interpretation are a challenge in a community that is illiterate and functions orally. The Bible is known to these masses not as a written text but as one that is heard and seen. Orality provides for the use of imaginative, informal learning and reading strategies. However, since there is an obvious bias in favor of academic learning, many Dalits from poor rural and urban areas of India continue to feel incapable of doing biblical interpretation, given their lack of access to the written text. Thus an emphasis on informal methods of Bible study that enable illiterate Dalits to participate in the articulation of theology and biblical interpretation would prove beneficial. Storytelling, role play, and other traditional forms of telling and retelling need to be identified and kept alive in a world that stresses textual modes of knowledge. Such methods enable the community to release itself and the text from traditional interpretive processes. Dalits are known to act out their rebellion and their conflict with the environment or the status quo through many traditional art forms. Learning to act out the biblical text and reflect on it from one's inner being and instinctual center would elicit a response that is powerful and congruent with knowledge derived from faith and experience.

Conclusion

Every Dalit reading of the Bible forcefully claims an approach that is vested in the experience of pain and prejudice, of being discriminated against, marginalized, and excluded. It employs a hermeneutical strategy from below that is in many ways similar to, and yet different from, those used in struggles against sexism, racism, and classism. Dalits bring to the table a multitude of gifts: their oral culture; their creative art forms; their religious rituals and expressions; the rich symbolism inherent in their culture; their holistic approach to life; their experiences, both liberative and burdensome; their strong will and resilience to survive amidst pain; and their faith in a God who will liberate. These gifts need to be explored and utilized for the purpose of identifying new and effective methods of reading the biblical text that would aid them in their struggle for liberation. A critical solidarity between conscientized Dalit intellectuals and the unlettered, untutored Dalit members would provide for engaged and meaningful conversation and reflection on the biblical text. This along with the resilience, the energy, and the Dalit desire for change, liberation, and transformation could contribute to an interpretation of the text that would result in new meanings and stimulate new ideas for conversion of self and community (Melanchthon 2005, 64).

> We have washed away
> Your dirt from our eyes.
> We have removed the locks
> You clamped over our mouths.
> Now it is your duty
> To hear what we speak.
> Scratch it on your brains.
> Liberation is ours, at first.[13]

---

13. From a poem entitled "At First It Is Ours" by Azhagiya Periyavan. Trans. Meera Kandasamy. Online: www.museindia.com/showconnew.asp?id=363.

5

FOR A BETTER FUTURE IN KOREAN BIBLICAL STUDIES: DIALOGUING WITH MYSELF IN A DIFFERENT CONTEXT

Yong-Sung Ahn

Korean Christianity has been marked by two features in particular: on the one hand, astonishing church growth, especially among Protestant churches, which has generated megachurches of more than ten thousand members; on the other hand, minjung theology and the active participation of theologians in politics. Both aspects can be understood as responses to the same social phenomenon— miraculous economic growth alongside political suppression, or what has often been referred to as "the tyranny of development." The majority of Korean churches have supported the side of "development," strengthening the significance of economic success with their Christian teachings of blessings, while a considerable number of other churches have struggled against the side of "tyranny," demonstrating the prophetic and liberating voices of the Bible. These two elements, however, do not represent Korean Christianity today. Church growth is no longer a current phenomenon, while minjung theology[1] is no longer a subject of frequent discussion, not even in progressive circles.

These recent changes in Korean Christianity can be related to changes in society. The country, a member of the Organization for Economic Cooperation and Development (OECD) since 1996, no longer ranks among the rapidly "developing" countries. Along with the country's accomplishments in terms of material wealth, the swelling of churches has stopped and has even receded. Statistics show that the number of Protestants, which had amounted to 19.7 percent of the population in 1995, had decreased by 2005 to 18.3 percent (The Korea National

---

1. Minjung theology was formed in the process of the struggles for democratization, that is, against the "tyranny." The Korean word, "minjung," means people who are oppressed, exploited, and marginalized.

Statistical Office). While such a development needs further scientific analysis, a decrease of church membership in economically prosperous societies can be seen in other developed countries, as well. The regression of minjung theology can be more clearly connected to the development of civil society. Among progressives in Korea, the problem of the minjung, along with the issues of class and nation, is no longer privileged as the dominant grand narrative. It is now considered just one of many issues, including women, the environment, food, education, the disabled, the political system, and foreign migrants.

Personally, I have experienced these changes very keenly in both society and the church, given my absence from the country for a period of eight years beginning in the mid 1990s. At that time, while drastic changes were occurring in Korea, I was pursuing graduate studies in the United States. When I came back home in the summer of 2005, I found Korea, especially Seoul and other large cities, extensively changed in almost every respect. Rather than pretend to be objective, I want to describe these changes in Korean church and theology—a context of biblical interpretation—through the lens of my own personal experience. Thus, rather than providing a statistical report about biblical scholars and their interests, I will focus on the context of interpretation, because I consider this the best way to explain recent changes and developments in Korean biblical studies. In so doing, I will show that the present context of biblical interpretation in Korea is different not only from that of the West but also from those of other Asian societies. After such proposed retrospection and analysis by way of personal story, I will attempt to peer into the future of biblical studies.

READJUSTING MYSELF TO MY OWN CONTEXT

My first book, a revision of my doctoral dissertation titled *The Reign of God and Rome in Luke's Passion Narrative: An East Asian Global Perspective* (2006), was written while I was residing in the United States. This volume explored the theme of "empire," which had been a hot issue in American cultural studies since the events of 9/11. Focusing on the colonial-political dimension of the passion narrative in Luke, I set out to show how the Jewish authorities in the narrative do not act on their own but as minions of and collaborators with the Roman Empire. Toward this end, I drew on theoretical perspectives and analytical tools of cultural studies, including postcolonial theory, for the analysis of both my reading context and the biblical text.

With regard to the text, I showed how the author of Luke-Acts is ambivalent toward empire, moving between pro-Roman and anti-Roman postures. Luke is hardly explicit in his criticism against the empire, and sometimes even blames those involved in the anti-Roman struggles (e.g., Luke 23:18–19, 39). Nevertheless, Luke denounces Rome indirectly but clearly through criticism against the Jewish authorities, who are aligned with the empire instead of God. Luke describes the Jewish leadership, along with the Roman officials, as the "power of darkness" (Luke 22:53).

With regard to my context, I focused on recent history in Korea, from the end of Japanese colonial occupation through the present, and attempted to show how the colonial legacy had continued and how the succeeding American influence had operated through the use of imperial discourses and ideologies. I described the present condition of Korea as hybrid, as both profiteer and victim of the global economy of neoliberalism. I characterized the Korean context as an "East Asian global" space, where unequal global relations have operated in the peninsula through its history. This concern with geography was prompted by postcolonial theorists, especially Edward Said (1979, 1983, 1993), and was sharpened by the notion of "the spatial" used by critical geographers. Doreen Massey, among them, understands "space" as a geometry of power relations that is imbued with time (2001). Thus the spatial is always understood as space-time. A spatial understanding of the East Asian global context provided me with an insight into the interpretation of Luke as a text written in colonial relations. In particular, I demonstrated how Luke constructs two narrative spaces in conflict: the temple as the space of Jesus, and the city of Jerusalem as the spae of the empire.

My understanding of East Asian space in terms of unequal power relations was affected by the situation that I had encountered in the United States. While I was staying in the country, often characterized as "the neo-empire," my reading context was that of the ethnic minorities, many of whom have come to the United States from formerly colonized worlds. My interpretation of the Bible was thus regarded as a "voice from the margin," to borrow the title of the groundbreaking volume edited by R. S. Sugirtharajah (1991). That marginal space is also the place in which most postcolonial theorists work. This is an exiled interstitial site, which Homi Bhabha calls "the third space." With that peripheral voice, I attempted to persuade Western scholars in academia. I combined several scholarly theories and methods in my study: the aesthetics of reception as a hermeneutics; narrative criticism as a reading method; and cultural studies, including postcolonial criticism and theory, as a way of contextual analysis. I was talking to the academic center from the social and cultural margin.

When I returned home, I asked myself whether my thesis was pertinent to the Korean context of that time. Although my volume was intended to have a Korean framework and thrust, I found that I had to re-contextualize myself within that context, which not only was very different from where I had been in the United States, but which also had undergone considerable changes while I was abroad. First of all, I found myself no longer in the margins; I was now located at the center. In effect, I teach at a denominational seminary, the Presbyterian College and Theological Seminary in Seoul, that stands as the central institution among several theological schools within the denomination. Although my position is a temporary one, I am expected to teach and train pastors on their way to service on behalf of the church. While in the United States as a minority student, I never wrestled with ways in which I could change the American church; I merely sought to make a contribution with my distinct voice. Now, however, I find myself trying less to make my own academic voice heard and seeking more to forge a new way for the Korean church as a whole. At present, therefore, I talk to the churches from the academic center.

Although the change in location is personal, it is not peculiar to me, since the majority of Korean theologians are not independent from their respective denominations. The church constitutes the major context of Korean theology. The country has a number of theological schools and university departments, but most belong to church denominations. The majority of professors in theology are ordained pastors. Even nondenominational schools rely on the denominational churches for monetary support. Support from secular institutions, such as the Korea Research Foundation, are limited. While there are academic societies in every area of theology, including the New Testament Society of Korea and the Korea Old Testament Society, the members of these societies usually speak and write more for their own denominations than for other scholars. The societies themselves are supported mainly by the churches.

Such a strong influence on the part of the church may be seen as both a crisis and an opportunity for theologians. The dimension of crisis is clear. Theologians are expected and requested to work for the "needs" of the church, which are mostly conservative in nature. As is often said, there is no progressive church in Korea: there are only less conservative and very conservative churches. At present, the slogan "Theology Serving the Church" can be readily heard throughout, but the "service" in question is frequently identified more with being traditional and less with being theological. Sometimes the slogan is used politically to increase the influence of the churches upon the theological schools. New and diverse voices are kept in check thereby, under the pretext of the needs of the church. At the same time, the dimension of opportunity is no less clear. Theologians could make use of this situation to their advantage, if they could find a way to secure an audience within the church with fresh and genuinely helpful ideas.

THE TIME OF MINJUNG THEOLOGY

The predominance of church over theology is not new to Korea. The number of theologians was much smaller a few decades ago while the church was growing rapidly. Most theological journals and many theological schools in the country began only recently. Nevertheless, in those days theological discussions were involved in social and political issues outside the church more than now. The struggles of the people against the political dictatorship represented a good context for minjung theology. Some theological institutions were supported by Western churches and/or world ecumenical organizations, so that they could be relatively independent from the Korean church. Theological journals like *Gi-dok-gyo Sa-sang* (*Christian Thought*) and *Shin-hak Sa-sang* (*Theological Thought*) provided leadership in such discussions and commanded a wide readership. With the support of the German church, a center of minjung theology and one of the most popular publishing companies, the Korea Theological Study Institute, were established by the late Byung-Mu Ahn, the first generation minjung theologian. The works of minjung theologians were read even outside Christian circles; in return, the mood of intellectuals in general was supportive of such progressive theological endeavors.

Minjung theologians formed part of a large circle of minjung intellectuals, which included artists, sociologists, political scientists, economists, poets, historians, philosophers, and performers. While they worked in different areas, they shared common ideas and goals and sometimes joined with other groups to struggle against the dictators. Most of them were not themselves minjung but "organic intellectuals," in Gramsci's sense, who attempted to apply principles and problems raised by the subaltern classes to their own intellectual activities and struggles. They not only publicized their opinions but also organized minjung groups, which included laborers, peasants, and the urban poor. Such organizers and leaders of the struggles were found mostly among students. Having graduated from or even dropped out of college, the student activists found employment as manual workers in companies and educated the laborers to organize strikes and political movements. Among them were Christian pastors in urban and rural ministries, including those of Yong Dong Po Urban Industrial Mission, founded in 1957 (YDP-UIM).

At the end of the 1980s, the initiative within the minjung movements shifted from the organic intellectuals to the minjung themselves, and the laborers in particular. The turning point was the June Uprising of 1987, which was initiated by student groups, supported by a wide range of people, including white-collar workers, and finally led to the amendment of the constitution for direct presidential elections.[2] After the success of these struggles, the political scene

---

2. The June Uprising forms a watershed in the Korean history of democratization, serving as a decisive moment for the termination of the military dictatorship. The movement started on June 10 and lasted until June 29 of 1987.

changed drastically. While the movement for political democracy weakened, the labor movement surged until the early 1990s. Those on the front line were no longer intellectuals but laborers. In turn, this change was followed by the rise of the civil society movement in the early 1990s. The middle class, rather than the subaltern, began to be the focus of social change. In addition, social issues became specialized, reflecting diverse voices within civil society.

These social changes, along with the spread of postmodern modes of analysis and thinking, began to relativize and even problematize some basic premises of the minjung movements. The discourse on social class, a significant factor of minjung theology, was not dominant anymore; it was now discussed together with other problems raised by diverse sectors of society. In addition, minjung intellectuals had been basically nationalists, identifying the whole Korean nation as a suppressed people, who had experienced Japanese colonialism and who were still subordinated to the neo-empire, the United States. They understood "minjung nationalism" as resistance against the power-wielding states. However, the country's enhanced position in the hierarchy of corporate globalization made it hard to identify the nationalistic sentiments of Koreans as resistance. Korea now occupies, as stated earlier, a hybrid position as both profiteer and victim within the globalized neoliberal economy. Major transnational corporations based in Korea, the so-called *Jaebols*, are among those who gain from globalization, while peasants and stockbreeders are among the losers. Migrants from other Two-Third World countries now reside in Korea as low-wage workers of manufacturing companies, as domestic women workers, and as wives of peasants. Although postnationalism is not yet widely discussed in the country, the pitfalls involved in an essentialist understanding of the concept of "nation" are acknowledged more than before.

In terms of biblical hermeneutics, minjung theologians, for the most part, made use of historical criticism, along with an orientation toward social scientific interpretation. Sociological approaches were effective in illuminating the political and economic dimensions of the Bible. Historical criticism was also useful for these theologians, because they wanted to release the Bible from the control of church tradition. However, the historical-critical approach fell short in elaborating the relationship between text and reader. Because historical criticism locates meaning in the past, as the meaning that the historical author intended for his/her contemporary audience, the interpreter needs to fill the gap between the ancient text and the present reader in order for the text to be meaningful to those living now. Minjung biblical scholars did not fully take account of this gap of interpretation; they tended rather to identify the people of the Bible—for example, the *ochlos* or crowd in Mark—simply with the contemporary people of Korea. This hermeneutical need was pointed out by Chang-Rak Kim (1997, 87,

91–92), a leading minjung theologian and New Testament scholar who succeeded Byung-Mu Ahn in the movement.

While minjung theology was neither the only Korean theology in the last decades of the twentieth century nor a dominant factor in Korean Christianity, its influence was significant. Its perspective and arguments had both ardent supporters and harsh opponents. At one pole, progressives praised it as a distinctive Korean voice and a unique way of doing theology. At the opposite pole, conservatives denounced it for the idealization of minding and even argued that it was not a theology at all but a political theory. The books of minjung theologians were included in the government lists of "banned books." Such severe criticism shows that minjung theology did provoke responses even from the conservatives. Nevertheless, the noble idea of the minjung could not find enough supporters within the churches. Although the active participation of the theologians in the world became an exemplary model for organic intellectuals, and although their distinctive theological ideas drew the attention of the Western scholarly community, minjung theologians lacked rhetorical persuasiveness among the congregations at large in the Korean church.

Some arguments of the minjung theologians proved unacceptable to ordinary Christians, such as, for instance, the radical claim that the minjung was the Messiah. However, the church and conservative theologians have also neglected many ideas in minjung theology that uncovered the liberating aspects of the Bible. If minjung theologians had tried to find a greater audience within the church, they could have done so. Understandably, minjung theology proved too restricted to be rhetorically effective. At the same time, there were some high hurdles to jump. For example, in the years that followed the Korean War (1950–1953), strong anti-communist sentiments came to the fore in both Korean society and Christian teachings. Thus minjung theologians had to defend themselves against those opponents with a "red complex," who accused them of drawing on Marxism. For conservative Christians, who had been taught that religion and politics should be separated, minjung theology proved "too political." However, the conservatives themselves were political as well, insofar as they implicitly participated in politics by way of tacit consent regarding the status quo.

The Overtly Political Church

When I came back home in 2005, I found that the Korean church had turned explicitly and excessively political. During the five years of the government of President Roh Moo-Hyun (2003–2008), the megachurches of Korea were on the front line of anti-government and pro-U.S. demonstrations. It was not rare to

hear preachers criticizing the president from the pulpit. These Christian leaders frequently associated the government's progressive policies with socialism.
Combined with the church's traditional identification of religious faith with anti-
communism, their anti-government political stance was easily looked upon as
"Christian." In contrast, since the incumbent president, Lee Myung-bak, took
office (2008), the Korean churches have been ardent supporters of his government. This is not only because the president is an elder of a Christian church,
but also because church leaders view his policies as representing their own
concerns—for the rich rather than the poor, for the powerful rather than the
powerless. The church's active participation in politics is very different now from
what it was a decade ago. During the time of the military regime in particular,
which lasted for more than thirty years until the early 1990s, the mainline Korean
church declared itself "apolitical." Ironically, the allegedly apolitical conservative
churches are now at the front line of politics.

In this context of an overtly political church, an emphasis on the political
aspect of the Bible would be pointless. Since the theme of my aforementioned
volume was the Roman Empire, its focus was on the social/cultural/political
dimension of the Lukan text. I argued that the modern division between religions and politics was not pertinent to the ancient text and proceeded to show
the political aspects of Luke. In the same vein, I demonstrated that the Jewish
"religious" authorities are not only religious but also political. Since they are not
simply the leaders of the Jewish people but also collaborators of Rome, I argued,
Luke's description of the Jewish authorities needed to be understood from the
perspective of imperial politics.

Contending with the claim that Luke exculpates Rome of the crucifixion of
Jesus by inculpating the Jewish leaders, I showed that both the Jews and Rome
work together for the crucifixion. It is the empire that brings Jesus to death, in
which process the Jerusalem leaders function simply as faithful servants. Such
a reading of the Gospel was prompted by the historical experience of Japanese
colonialism in Korea. History shows that colonial domination would not have
been possible without the collaboration of the colonized. Inferring that such
must have been the case as well with Roman imperial rule of Rome over Palestine, I argued that Luke acknowledges and narrates just such a collaboration. In
the passion narrative, for example, the Jewish collaborators are presented as loyal
participants of the empire (e.g., Luke 20:20).

Reading Luke again in the context of contemporary Korean churches, my
focus moves from the system of empire to the active role of the Jewish religious
leaders. I see in the passion narrative a direct conflict taking place between Jesus
and the religious leaders, who initiate the process of his crucifixion. Seeking
the security of the empire, upon which their own power is based, the Jerusalem

leadership levels the charge of an anti-Roman crime on Jesus. However, they in essence believe that Jesus is undermining their own established domestic power. It is the religious leaders who drive Jesus to death. Such a shift in reading focus is prompted by present reality, in which the Korean church wields tremendous power. Church membership is typically concentrated in urban, not rural areas, and found predominantly among the rich, rather than the poor. Compared to the overall population, Christians are also overrepresented among politicians—including the president—and entrepreneurs. In effect, the Korean church has become the church of the rich and the powerful. Church leaders are certainly influential enough to wield political initiative, just as the Jewish religious authorities did in the early first century, according to the Gospel of Luke.

The Withdrawal of the Empire

This shift of focus away from Rome also corresponds to the downplaying of the theme of "empire/imperialism" or "colonialism" in Korea. Until recently, studies of Korean history prior to and following the liberation from Japanese colonialism, whose aim it was to examine the founding process of the Republic of Korea (ROK), had constituted a major area of scholarly interest. In addition, Korean intellectuals had understood their country as "neo-colonized" or "peripherized" by the power-wielding nations, especially the United States. These days, however, the terms "empire" and "colonialism" have all but disappeared from scholarly discussions and civil movements. This lapse of memory has been promoted by the status quo. Yet even among progressives, the past history of colonialism in Korea is discussed less than before.

A short historical survey would be useful to understand the present situation. The reestablishment of Korea after liberation was not initiated by Koreans themselves but by the occupying forces of the United States. The southern part of Korea was occupied by the United States Army Military Government in Korea (USAMGIK), while the northern part was under the influence of the Union of Socialist Soviet Republics (USSR). Korea was liberated from Japan on August 15, 1945, and the Republic of Korea was founded just three years later, on August 15, 1948. The three years of U.S. occupation did not destroy the colonial foundation in Korea but rather solidified it. Influence of the United States on South Korea was simply established over the pre-existing structure of Japanese colonialism, which power structure has lasted now for more than sixty years. Although the liquidation of Japanese colonial legacy was considered an important task of the nation, it was not easy, even for the progressive government of President Roh, to carry out such a project, given the tough resistance from the establishment.

Recently the debate around the liberation and foundation of Korea has been reactivated due to the attempt by conservatives to change the title of August 15 from Independence Day to National Foundation Day. It is the New Right that has initiated this debate with implicit support of the government. In so doing, they praise the contributions of both Rhee Syng-man, the first president of the ROK (1948–1960), and Park Chung-hee, the first ex-military president (1961–1979), who initiated the era of miraculous economic development. However, Korea had existed even before the Republic of Korea was founded. The progressives suspect that the conservatives are conspiring to distort history in order to legitimize the present establishment. Thus, for example, there were ongoing struggles for independence on the part of nationalists during the Japanese colonial occupation. In the process of founding the ROK, the nationalist groups, including the Korea Provisional Government and the Committee for Preparation of Korean Independence, were not acknowledged by the USAMGIK but were crushed in order to sustain U.S. influence in the country. As a result, the pro-American Rhee was elected as the first president of the Republic. Subsequently, under Park's "tyranny of development," the people's yearning for democracy was cruelly suppressed. Protesters were arrested and even murdered.

In a sense, the candlelight demonstrations that took place in the summer of 2008, which lasted for several months, may be understood as a sign that the topic of "empire" does remain in the memory of popular consciousness. These demonstrations were sparked by opposition to the resumption of negotiations with the United States regarding beef imports, after suspension in 2003 following a case of Mad Cow Disease in the state of Washington. At the time, the people were facing a less independent government, after ten years of progressive administrations, and had to contend with its policy of servitude to the United States. However, these demonstrations, which took place in and around City Hall Plaza in Seoul, may be better understood as an expression of growing self-confidence on the part of the people rather than of resistance to the empire. In effect, while the conservatives continue to live in a time of subordination, the younger generation is experiencing a totally new world. In the course of the last few decades, Korea has achieved remarkable development in every sector of society, not only in terms of the economy but also in terms of democracy and foreign affairs. While American influence does remain strong, the people no longer take it seriously into account.

Two Paradigms in Conflict

The conflict that played out around City Hall Plaza does not simply concern the ostensible issue of beef importation from the United States. Rather, it symbolizes at a more fundamental level a contest between two unique cultural paradigms: the future-oriented Internet generation and the status quo newspaper generation.

At one pole, then, there is a new generation of people who supported the candle demonstrations. In the two decades that followed the termination of military rule, they have enjoyed freedom of expression and have advanced a new type of political culture. This new culture, which some refer to as "democracy: version 2.0," a designation borrowed from the term "web 2.0," emphasizes interaction, participation, and the mass population. Their venue is the Internet. They do not trust the traditional newspapers, represented by three mammoth press companies, the so-called *Cho-Joong-Dong* (a combination of the acronyms of the three companies: the *Chosun Daily*, the *JoongAng Daily*, and the *DongA Daily*). The generation of democracy 2.0 wants future-oriented ways of thinking. The somber term, "postcolonial," which privileges the Western history of colonialism, would find hardly any supporters in such a setting.

At the opposite pole, one finds the conservative status quo, which supports the administration of President Lee. They are mostly newspaper readers, so the *Cho-Joong-Dong* have a powerful influence on them. They usually have no trust in information provided through the Internet; they even denounce it as "info-demics," a combination of "information" and "epidemic." Using this newly-coined term in his address to the Opening Ceremony of the National Assembly in July of 2008, while the candlelight demonstrations were going on, President Lee characterized the situation in terms of "a society rampant with excessive emotional behavior, disorderliness and rudeness." According to his definition, "infodemics" is "a phenomenon in which inaccurate, false information is disseminated, prompting social unrest that spread like epidemics."[3]

Such conflict between these two paradigms of culture constitutes a significant feature of contemporary Korea. Church and theology, in their role as guide of the world, need to provide a channel of communication between these paradigms. At present, however, church leaders represent for the most part the pole of the conservative status quo. They are viewed as uncommunicative and stubborn, not as facilitators of communication. Although a number of Christian laity and pastors were to be found in City Hall Plaza, their presence was not enough to change the popular impression of the Korean church as incorrigibly conservative. Church leaders do not communicate because they already have all they need. The church is rich and powerful. Those who criticize the church, the Protestant church in particular, say that the church is arrogant, because it is not open to

---

3. The abridged text of the Presidential address can be found at http://www.koreatimes. co.kr/www/news/nation/2009/07/116_27445.html.

dialogue. In reality, the church is very worldly, insofar as its leaders are deeply involved in political issues. Yet, ironically, the church is secluded from the world. It is reluctant to communicate.

For a Better Future

The present context of biblical interpretation in Korea is thus one in which the majority of theologians are located within church denominations, which have become overtly political while having lost communication with the world. As theologians serving the church, biblical scholars are expected to contribute, through their interpretation of the Bible, to the promotion of communication between the church and the outside world. Looking toward the future, I see two ways in which such an endeavor can be undertaken and promoted.

More concretely, the hermeneutical task needs to be carried out in sustained interdisciplinary fashion, so that all the various aspects of the contemporary world can be duly taken into account. Above all, biblical studies should be in closer communication with the other theological disciplines. As long as biblical studies remains oriented toward historical criticism, deeply engaged as it is in historical questions of Jewish and Christian origins, it is very hard for the other disciplines to find relevance in biblical studies for their own contemporary questions. In addition, biblical studies should be in dialogue with such disciplines as literary criticism, given its attention to the role of readers in the process of interpretation, and rhetorical criticism, given its focus on the strategies and techniques of persuasion. More generally, the hermeneutical task needs to persuade church audiences, in their communication with the world, to be humble and to serve those outside. The church should be urged to "sell all that it has and distribute to the poor" in order to follow Jesus. While the kings of the empire lord it over the people, the church, as the disciples of Jesus, should become those who serve, following the paradigm of the master who serves.

I cannot foretell the future of theology and biblical interpretation in Korea. I can only imagine and yearn for a better future, when both theologians and churches find the right track. The church in Korea exercises great influence on theological institutions, and theologians are asked to "serve the church." Since the church holds the leverage of power in this relationship, this service frequently deviates from the ideal way. Without checks and balances, service can easily become servitude. The peculiar context of theology and biblical interpretation in Korea requires both church and theology to reconsider their relationship and to find a better way of cooperation. Reconfiguring their relationship is imperative for a better future for Korean theology and criticism, given the role of the church as the major context of theology and biblical interpretation in Korea. A theology in genuine service of the church—not simply a traditional or conservative theology, but a theology open to discussion and communication—could become the characteristic "Korean theology" of the future.

6

BIBLICAL STUDIES IN A RISING ASIA: AN ASIAN PERSPECTIVE ON THE FUTURE OF THE BIBLICAL PAST

Philip Chia

The rise of modern biblical studies as a discipline has been, since the heyday of the Enlightenment and the Reformation, a predominantly Western institutional-academic phenomenon closely associated with the modern development of Western culture and the academic enterprise. With the expansion of Western civilization and Christianity in the modern world, biblical scholarship gained access into nonWestern cultures. Western imperial/colonial power spread globally via sea and land, fleets and gunpowder, under the *Geist* and project of the Enlightenment and modernity. It brought with it the biblical text, which it readily made available to nonWestern peoples, together with modern tools of interpretation and a variety of other products of modernity—all in the name of human "advancement" toward global civilization.

As a result, the institutionally established and widely followed historical-critical mode of investigation and interpretation of the biblical texts became, like so much of Western culture, a universal standard for academia throughout the world. Within this scientific-positivist paradigm, neither differences in culture and ideology nor issues of locality and identity required consideration as vital elements in the process of meaning production with regard to the biblical texts. Biblical scholarship thus became a discipline reserved for professional scholars, intellectuals, and well-informed readers and clergy.

Recent scientific advancements, especially the availability of common telecommunication technology since the 1980s, have contributed to the current reality of globalization. Such interconnectivity has favored the possibility of inter-subjectivity rather than the subject-object relation between nations and people. Consequently, intertextuality has become a process of mutual recognition and interaction, in which all readers negotiate meaningful and relevant interpretations of the biblical texts, each advancing their own textual meaning. Acknowledgment, if not confession, of Western domination in establishing the allegedly universal and objective standard of interpretation—now recognized as distinctly Eurocentric and androcentric—may be seen in such publications as Daniel Patte's *The Ethics of Biblical Interpretation* (1995), which called for "repentance from our sins" on the part of European and Euro-American critics, and Fernando Segovia and Mary Ann Tolbert's *Reading from This Place* series (1995), which foregrounded and applied elements of locality and identity in the production of textual meaning. This acknowledgment has contributed to the possibility of a reading of the biblical texts that is conscious of culture and identity without having to worry much about the issue of legitimacy in interpretation. Since the 1980s, modes of investigating the biblical texts have become more multidimensional and pluralistic. Such readings have proved more human than the previous scientific mode of reading, given their sensitivity to the living contexts of human beings and their commitment to ethical responsibility and accountability in interpretation.

With the rise of Latin American and African biblical scholarship now firmly established, with wide academic recognition and legitimacy bestowed on the contextual character of their biblical interpretation, social locations and cultural identities can no longer be ignored in biblical criticism. In turn, Christianity in both Latin America and Africa has played an important role in the recent history of economic and political transformation in these continents. On the other side of the globe, Asia, a geographically vast and culturally multidimensional continent, has also become increasingly active in biblical scholarship.In July 2008, for example, the newly-formed Society of Asian Biblical Studies held its first conference in Seoul, Korea, on the theme of "Mapping and Engaging the Bible in Asian Cultures," where many issues pertinent to Asia, such as "Peace and Conflict in Asia," were addressed.

At the same time, the world has changed so dramatically in the last decade that the characterization of "runaway world" applied by Anthony Giddens (1999) no longer adequately captures the current situation of near total collapse brought about by a variety of global crises. Such crises include natural disasters—the Asian Tsunami; Hurricane Katrina; the outbreak of SARS; and the spread of contaminated food products. They also include manmade created havocs—the 9/11 terrorist attack; the wars in Afghanistan and Iraq; the Israeli-Palestinian crisis in the Middle East; and the recent global financial meltdown sparked by a subprime mortgage crisis in the United States. No one can deny the unpredictable and risky nature of the world in which we live today. Asia, whose people account for about half of the global population, has a leading, even pivotal, role to play in this global reality. Both the globe as meta-location and globalization as our current reality have been set in crisis mode. Such a situation poses a challenge to the relevance of the discipline of biblical studies for today. I should like to address this question of relevance from the perspective of Asia.

I will pursue my vision of biblical studies in a rising Asia in three stages. I shall begin by discussing various key aspects—economic, political, religious, ethnic, and cultural—of the Asian past, present, and future in relation to Western civilization, the project of modernity, and the current reality of globalization. Then I shall review the brief history of the discipline of biblical studies in Asia, past and present. Lastly, I shall conclude with a series of reflections on "the future of the biblical past" in and for a rising Asia.

ASIA: PAST, PRESENT, AND FUTURE

With the turn of this new century, Asia has become *the* major international focus of attention—be it political, economic, religious, ethnic, environmental, or cultural. Some observers speak of an "irresistible shift of global power to the East" (Mahbubani 2008), while others point to the end of the dominance of the West over the Rest and the beginning of a "post-American world," leading to the "rise of the Rest" (Zakaria 2008). A number of recent publications—such as, for example, *Japan Rising* (Pyle 2007), *China Rises* (Farndon 2007), *India Rising* (Mathur, Richter, and Das 2005), *India's Century* (Nath 2008), and *China Into the Future* (Hoffman and Enright 2008)—signal definitive interest in exploring the ascendancy of Asia as a global and geopolitical power phenomenon of the twenty-first century. Kishore Mahbubani, Dean and Professor in the Practice of Public Policy at the Lee Kuan Yew School of Public Policy of the National University of Singapore, expresses the rise of Asia as a world power as follows:

> For two centuries the Asians—from Tehran to Tokyo, from Mumbai to Shanghai—have been bystanders in world history, reacting defenselessly to the surges of Western commerce, thought, and power. That era is over. Asia is returning to the center stage it occupied for eighteen centuries before the rise of the West ... Asians have absorbed and understood Western best practices in many areas.... And they have become innovative in their own way, creating new patterns of cooperation not seen in the West. Their rise is unstoppable—by 2050, three of the world's largest economies will be Asian: China, India and Japan.... Will the West resist the rise of Asia?.... Asia wants to replicate, not dominate the West.... If the West accepts the rise of Asia and shares power, the new Asian powers will reciprocate by becoming responsible stakeholders in a stable world order. They will lift some global burdens off Western shoulders. But such positive outcomes are not inevitable. History teaches us that the rise of new powers almost always leads to tension and conflict. (2008, front flap)

Given the long history, the varied cultures, and the many peoples of Asia, it would be a formidable task to provide a detailed mapping of the various contexts of Asia and their current developments under the zeitgeist of globalization; any such undertaking lies clearly beyond the scope of the present study. However, as proposed context for interaction with biblical texts, it is necessary to offer an overview of such contemporary realities in Asia. Toward this end, I highlight five specific dimensions here: politics, economics, religion, ethnicity, and culture—a challenging task in its own right. Further, my focus will be on the so-called greater China region (Mainland China, Taiwan, Hong Kong, Macau), giving less attention to its immediate neighbors (India, Pakistan, Japan, Korea, and other Southeast Asia nations).

My hope in this study is to challenge the discipline of biblical studies, long dominated as it has been by Western thought, to rethink its program of engagement with the peoples of Asia. I have in mind two objectives in particular: (1) alerting academics to the inadequacies of established models of research, such as traditional historical-critical scholarship and the scientific-positivist paradigm; and (2) charting new paths for biblical studies as it interacts with Asian cultural realities. Asian critiques that are context sensitive may generate alternative readings of the Bible that are at once original and meaningful.

POLITICS

The rise of the West has transformed the world in unique ways. What will the rise of Asia bring to the world? Will there be peace and prosperity, or will there be conflict and clashes? Mahbubani offer three possible scenarios: (1) Asia's "march to modernity"; (2) a retreat into fortresses; and (3) the triumph of the West. Of the three, he prefers the first choice, arguing that "the greater the number of people who enter the modern world, the safer and more secure our world will become" (2008, 16).

By "march to modernity" Mahbubani means transcending the premodern, a move that involves improvement of the standard of living (beginning with the availability of the "flush toilet" to all Asians), a gradual increase in the buying power of citizen consumers, and enjoyment of the conveniences of modern living. He explains, "as Asians acquire more consumer goods, they are not merely becoming materialistic. More importantly, they are becoming stakeholders in the modern world. When billions of people become stakeholders in peace and prosperity, they steer world history in a positive direction" (17). Mahbubani also argues that, as a society progresses into modernity, poverty is minimized. "Society benefits when people step out of poverty," he writes. "Crime rates decline. Health standards improve. Infant mortality decreases. Life expectancy increases. Education standards rise" (19). Consequently, he adds, the "most important ethical result of the March to Modernity may well be a more stable and peaceful world" (21). By citing examples from the relationship between the United States and Canada and among the European Union, he further argues,

The greatest peak of human civilization is reached not just when nations stop war but when nations achieve zero prospect of war. Some nations have achieved it. The United States and Canada have zero prospect of going to war with each other. So too do the current member states of the European Union.... [W]hat North America and the European Union have achieved today can also be achieved by the rest of the world tomorrow. In short, world peace is not a pipe dream. We have seen how it can be done. (2008, 21)

Mahbubani foresees that many Muslims, taking Pakistan as an example, will want to join the Asian march to modernity, thereby becoming modern religious people. China's project of "modernization" and the concept of a "peaceful rise" also fit well with his perception of peace and conflict in Asia and the world.

For Mahbubani, in the end, the critical element to the success of Asia's march to modernity is the presence of a legal system as the mechanism for making the march work. Such a system, he argues, "almost inevitably leads to a greater adherence to the rule of law" (17). "The presence of laws enhances the sense of certainty and the reality of ownership," he continues. In this way, "the March to Modernity also aids the spread of the rules-based order—domestically, regionally, and globally" (21).

Mahbubani offers many constructive ideas in his analysis of the rising Asian scenario as it relates to the world. What is missing, however, is the factor of political ideology as a crucial element in Asia's peaceful march to modernity. As one of the largest nations in Asia, China embraces communism, a political ideology very different from that of most other Asian countries, although it does find allies in this regard in such countries as North Korea, Myanmar, and Vietnam. India, the other largest Asian nation, is also the world's largest democracy. It has experienced a variation of the economic-political structure laid down by the British Empire, as is the case with a number of other Asian countries—Singapore (constitutional democracy), Malaysia (constitutional monarchy), and Hong Kong (a special administrative region of communist China). Since World War II, there have been both socialist and anti-communist movements in South and Southeast Asian countries, which have torn Asians apart. Indonesia and Vietnam constitute examples of ethnic and ideological conflicts. How well can socialist nations work and live side-by-side with liberal-democratic neighbors? Will political ideology be a critical element for a peaceful Asia and world? How would the biblical text interact with and respond to Asia's political plurality? Such interaction will prove a challenge to biblical scholarship, dominated as it has been by Western conceptions and ideologies.

Asian countries are, with a few exceptions, either constitutional monar-
chies and constitutional democracies or authoritarian regimes and communist
regimes. In the past, conflicting political ideologies have been a major cause
of war in Asia. Since 1949 and into the post-Cold War era, China has been the
largest nation in both Asia and the world to embrace communism as a national
political ideology. Since 1997, Hong Kong and Macau have again become a part
of China; Taiwan awaits its fate in this regard. Tibet continues to pose a major
internal problem. How will the situation fare in these various regions?

Will Hong Kong work as a Special Administrative Region of China, having
once been under the control of the British? More than a decade down the road,
previously treasured values, as well as a sense of the common good, have shown
signs of corrosion. After all, conflicts in political ideology eventually pervade
all everyday socioeconomic activities. Thus it is not surprising if tension exists
between the people of Hong Kong and her communist master motherland over
concepts like democracy and the rule of law. The tenuous situation of Hong Kong
is indeed a creation of historical imperialism-colonialism, set within the modern
"bipolar" political ideologies of communism and Western liberal democracy. The
fate of the people of Hong Kong lies in the hands of the powerful wholly "Other,"
Mainland China, which knows only too well how to play the role of the powerful master. The Taiwan situation is a little more complicated, given its ethnic
and nationalistic dimensions. The issue of Taiwan's identity in relation to China
will remain a key problem, although a focus on the economy by the new KMT
Party, the Kuomintang or Nationalists, may ease political tension over the Taiwan
Strait. The return of Macau to China does not constitute a political issue. However, the Tibetan problem continues to present a complicated challenge, involving
political, economic, religious, and ethnic dimensions. Will a process of democratization help solve this internal Chinese problem, which is tied with the fate of
Asia?

To conclude, Susan Shirk offers a vivid analysis of a rising China in relation
to its neighbors and the rest of the world (2007, front flap):

> We discover a communist regime desperate to survive in a society turned
> upside down by miraculous economic growth and a stunning new openness
> to the greater world. Indeed, ever since the 1989 pro-democracy protests in
> Tiananmen Square and the fall of communism in the Soviet Union, Chinese
> leaders have been haunted by the fear that their days in power are numbered.
> Theirs is a regime afraid of their [sic] own citizens, and this fear motivates
> many of their [sic] decisions when dealing with the United States and other
> foreign nations. In particular, the fervent nationalism of the Chinese people,
> combined with their passionate resentment of Japan and attachment to Tai-
> wan, have made relations with these two regions a minefield.... Rising pow-

ers such as China tend to provoke wars in large part because other countries mishandle them. Unless we understand China's brittle internal politics and the insecurities of its leaders, we face the very real possibility of unavoidable conflict with China.

ECONOMICS

The rise of Asia in the last two decades has had a lot to do with the free market economy and free international trade as the phenomenon of globalization has expanded. However, as pointed out by most economists, the rise of Asia, especially of China and India, has led to the rise of political support for protectionism in both Europe and the United States. The rise of Asia might have caused the West to "retreat" back to its "fortresses," as pointed out by Mahbubani, in the sense of nationalistic protectionism, instead of reaching toward greater free trades. In this regard, Mahbubani argues, the world needs to learn a lesson from history: "The collapse of trade between 1929–1931 had sparked a worldwide cycle of tariff hikes and retaliations beginning in the United States, which had deepened the Depression, closed avenues of escape, and ultimately helped open politics to radical nationalists in Europe and Asia" (2008, 36).

In a speech of 1936, cited by Mahbubani (36), President Franklin Delano Roosevelt captured the situation well: "It is no accident that, because of these suicidal policies and the suffering attending them, many of their people have come to believe with despair that the price of war seems less than the price of peace." Thus in 1945, as President Roosevelt reopened trade and announced the first multilateral trade negotiation, there was hope that nations would have a great stake in one another's security and prosperity and would help create "the economic basis for the secure and peaceful world we all desire" (Gresser 2007, n.p.). However, as Mahbubani further points out, "During the last 20 years, China, India, the former Soviet Union, Eastern Europe and Africa have rejoined the global economy. But the great threat to this is that the U.S. will lose confidence in the free market ideology, and thus the growth of such protectionism in both Europe and the United States will actually cause real danger to the world" (37).

National security and foreign investment are definitely key issues in the peace/conflict equilibrium. Although economics has played a major role since World War II in contributing to the rise of a peaceful Asia, it is becoming an increasing burden for Asia to play its role in the global economy. Similarly, the Western creation of free market capitalism, with its financial market industry (often driven by a greedy elite), is in need of a system overhaul, given the ever-widening gap between the rich and the poor. Perhaps the single most important crisis for the economies of Asia and the world alike lies in the eradication of poverty: raising living standards, improving health, and fostering education—all of which facilitate the restoration of human dignity, without which peaceful living is at risk. Are not all these elements of the global economy concerns of "glocal" humanity? If the Bible has at its core a love for humanity in creation, what do biblical scholars have to say and do about current world economic conditions? Relevance is critically important to the discipline, if glocal humanity is its context and concern.

RELIGION AND ETHNICITY

The rise of the West has been closely linked with the Judeo-Christian tradition. One finds in Asia, however, a multiplicity of religions and spiritualities—Taoism, Buddhism, Hinduism, Islam, folk religions, tribalism, and so on. The three most populated countries in Asia—China, Indonesia, India—have all enjoyed and suffered the realities of multicultural, multi-ethnic, and multireligious societies, where domination has been the name of the game.

As an atheist country, China faces a challenging environment: trying to contain religious activities, while also trying to implement racially impartial economic and political policies for its fifty-five minority ethnic groups. Within the greater China region, religion is seldom the cause of conflict among different religious communities. In Mainland China, however, the State Administration for Religious Affairs regulates all religions, so that only official government-sanctioned religions are legally recognized and allowed to practice. Unfortunately, this discrimination creates tensions. Such state-controlled religious activities prove a challenge to most Western minds, which are used to religious freedom as guaranteed by their constitutions. The lack of such freedom in China does have an impact on Chinese biblical scholarship, slight as it may be.

With the worldwide insurgence of Islamic extremism, Indonesia—alongside such other regions as the southern part of the Philippines, Malaysia, the southern part of Thailand, China's Xinjian—has faced the challenge of disruption to social harmony by religious activists, who often link with extreme religious nationalism and political separatism. In Indonesia, as in India, there seems to be no end in sight to religious and ethnic tensions, causing social disruption, racial strife, and community conflicts—all at the expense of national economic development as well as regional security and stability.

In the case of Sri Lanka's Tamil Tigers (Liberation Tigers of Tamil Eelam), religion and ethnicity merge to create powerful motivation for conflict at a variety of levels—community, national, international. Similarly, in the southern part of Thailand, the close links of the Muslim community with Malaysian Muslims have been the cause of occasional crossborder conflicts with the predominantly

Buddhist community of Thailand. The unique case of Malaysian Muslims has also created tensions within the Malaysian state, because the dominant Muslim majority has, insensitively, put their Islamic religion and Muslim identity ahead of their Malaysian national identity, a postcolonial after-effect of the British Empire. The cases of Islam in Xinjian and Buddhism in Tibet also pose challenges to China in terms of greater openness and tolerance. Pakistan, with its links to Islamic extremists, further represents "a nation at risk" (Nath 2008, 9).

Multicultural, multilinguistic, and multi-ethnic India also has inherited socio-ethnic and religions problems, even though Kamal Nath proudly describes an impartial India:

> In the past 60 years, India has steadfastly refused to accept any single culture or religion as its creed. It has not imposed the language of the largest segment of the population, Hindi, on the rest. In fact, the Constitution recognizes 22 national languages. It also allows the adherences of minority religions complete freedom to practice and profess, indeed to propagate, their faith. They have kept the state and scripture separate. (2008, 9)

Inequalities, social injustice, and poverty in Indian society are threatening its harmonious rise as a world power. Severe oppression has deep roots in religion and ethnicity. As the largest community, Hindus have a caste system that oppresses and ignores the *Dalits* and the *Adivasis*. Religious conflicts will continue to pose a serious threat to the social harmony of a multicultural nation.

CULTURE

The single most important challenge to the West and the world of a rising Asia is perhaps the clash of cultures, though such a "clash" should also be considered a construct of the West. Cultural conflict has a higher probability than most other conflicts. The West has been promoting its secular liberal-democratic culture, while the East has had difficulty embracing such culture in its entirety. Mahbubani has strongly emphasized that the West has brought many good gifts to the East, among them modernity in terms of science and technology. Perhaps it is time for the West also to embrace many of the positive and enlightening cultural values of the East—among them, for example, family filial piety and personal ethical values, which form part of the core social values of Eastern societies, compared to those of individualism and liberal democracy in Western societies.

The recent political situation in Thailand demonstrates ethnocultural concern over how the Western system and Western values are received in an Eastern constitutional monarchy. A government formed through the democratic process via a national general election does not necessarily guarantee a legitimate mandate to govern the nation, unless the monarch and the military give their consent. This is perhaps also a unique Eastern form of appropriating Western democracy.

The Future of a Rising Asia

Despite all the political, religious, and cultural issues and conflicts that have been ever-present in Asia, the fact is that, with the rise of India and China—not to mention Japan, Korea, Taiwan, Hong Kong, and Singapore—contributing significantly to the present global economy, a rising Asia has once again gained its global share in politics and the market economy. As the largest of the seven continents, Asia has long been "the East"—Far East and/or Middle East, depending on one's "center," if there is one—living under the shadow of "the West," in particular under the domination of Western civilization. No longer is this the case, as Zakaria points out:

> [W]e are moving into a post-American world, one defined and directed from many places and by many people.... For the first time ever, we are witnessing genuinely global growth. This is creating an international system in which countries in all parts of the world are no longer objects or observers but players in their own right. It is the birth of a truly global order.... Power is shifting away from nation-states, up, down, and sideways. (2008, 3–5)

A new world system will have to emerge, if Zakaria is right in his estimation. This new system—at least, in terms of increasing interconnectivity—is evidenced by the recent financial crisis, which spread from the United States, the single largest economy in the world, outwards, threatening to collapse the international financial market and forcing the central banks of many countries to act in violation of general rules of operation, thus rewriting the definition and history of capitalism and the free-market economy. These relations will continue to be a challenge not only to humanity historically but also to the relevance of the discipline of biblical studies.

Asia and the Biblical Past

Whatever the experiences of Asia historically and today, the Bible has played a very small role in its development. Most Asians do not have their religious origins in Christianity, and the Bible has largely remained a foreign imperial object. Hence there is little connection between Asia and the biblical past. The rather short history of biblical studies as a discipline in Asia has its origins in modernity, insofar as the discipline was brought by Western civilization and culture. However, the biblical past itself has many similarities with the historical experience of Asia—ethnic tribalism and federalism, international and domestic migration, "river" cultures and empire relations, to name just a few.

In China and its diaspora, according to John Yieh (2007), biblical scholarship reveals four historical stages: (1) Difficult Infancy (1807–1860); (2) Traumatic Childhood (1860–1911); (3) Challenging Adolescence (1911–1949); and (4) Growing Pains (1949–2004). Although one can point, therefore, to two centuries of Chinese interest in the Bible, Chinese biblical scholarship can hardly be measured according to the Western scientific-positivist mode of academic institutional scholarship, mainly due to the use of the Bible for application to everyday life rather than as an object of institutional research. As Yieh rightly observes, Chinese biblical interpretation over the last two centuries is marked by three unique characteristics: (1) the relevance of Scripture to the life of the readers is always treated with urgency; (2) the cultivation of personal character, moral and spiritual, is assumed to be the ultimate concern of biblical interpretation; and (3) the perfection of one's personal character is seen as eventually transforming the whole of society and strengthening the nation (30). Whether these characteristics are rooted in Confucianism is a matter for debate, but the focus on personal ethics and spirituality in relation to national wellbeing has been a traditional concern of the Chinese people, and remains very much so today. The challenge to biblical scholarship will be its ability to relate the biblical text to the common good, the social values, and the national interest of the people of China.

India has a longer history of connection to the Bible than most other modern Asian nations. Devadasan Premnath (2007) offers a well-organized historical description of biblical interpretation in India, tracing its development from the (purported) arrival of Thomas the apostle in South India at around 52 C.E., through the period of the early Catholic and Protestant Missions, to colonial days and postcolonial times. Due to its long history of Christian presence and the colonial cultivation of language and education, India perhaps presents the most advanced experience of biblical scholarship in Asia. In the wake of national independence in 1947, such scholarship has been undertaken with greater indigenous and postcolonial awareness, so there is much to be appreciated and learned from Indian contextual biblical interpretation. Still, biblical studies in India will continue to struggle with issues ranging from parochial dogmatism and religious plurality to ethnic tolerance without compromising the biblical faith, and from social justice and equality to ecological theology. Religious and ethnic conflicts will continue to haunt church and academia alike.

Biblical scholarship in China and India are, for the most part, representative of the Asian experience as a whole: there are those who will continue to struggle with endless interfaith dialogues and other activities involving various religious texts and faiths, while others continue to deal with racial and ethnic conflicts of a religious nature. Biblical studies and methods involving multitextual comparative and interactive analysis will be a real challenge to Asian biblical scholars in multifaith societies, especially in terms of practical effectiveness.

THE FUTURE OF THE BIBLICAL PAST IN A RISING ASIA: A BIBLE IN PUBLIC DEMAND

To make biblical studies relevant to Asians, as is in our best interest as biblical scholars, the text (the Bible) and the context (Asia) need to intersect with each other. How shall this happen in order to make the discipline relevant to Asian people? If there is to be such mutual relevance, making the text relevant to the context and the context to the text, the challenge for the future of the biblical past in Asia seems to be not so much what biblical scholars do inside the academic arena but rather how they present their findings to the people outside academic circles. Thus what are we, as Asian biblical scholars, to do with the Bible in our Asian context? The real question is what has the Bible to do with Asian lives today and tomorrow?

Given my summation of the possible future of the Asian reality in relation to the world at large in terms of politics, economics, religion, ethnicity, and culture, making the biblical text meaningful for and relevant to the public constitutes an unavoidable task and responsibility of Asian biblical scholars. Public accessibility means that the language of scholarship itself must be accessible to the public and must serve as a source and resource for the construction of a better Asia and a better world. Such Bible-aided construction means the construction of personal, social, national, and global ethical principles and values, leading thereby to a new world order and system.

The multidimensional facets involved in constructing a "public Bible" for the future of the biblical past in Asia will require Asian biblical scholars to seriously consider six crucial dimensions: ethics, spirituality, economics, the environment, culture, and politics. Such a focus calls for interdisciplinary integrative studies with a strong sense of orientation to human living conditions, as will be briefly elaborated below. Such a focus is very different from that at work in the scientific-positivist interpretive mode, where historical investigation has priority and where the knowledge gained plays a small role in guiding human beings on how to live and how to contribute to a better world in a glocalized reality.

To begin with, there is a near collapse of ethical principles and values globally. Such has been the case since the advent of modernity and continues to be the case today as modernity marches on globally. Asia is no exception in this regard. Asian leaders have long acknowledged that ethics constitutes the missing critical aspect for a healthy Asia as it rises to world power (Richter and Mar 2004). Old sets of ethical practices are under constant challenge and are often replaced by new sets generated in the social sciences and the humanities. Scientific technological applications also keep transforming modern ethical values and practices. The common good as well as human values have been under serious threat from all fronts. A common platform and/or working standard for the common good in any society is long overdue. The academic communities have been slow to act. There is ethical decline in an age of unparalleled global capitalism and liberal democracy. Furthermore, without addressing this spiritual aspect of humanity, any changes in economic structure and the global financial system will not be enough, for human greed eventually will reverse any economic and political progress. A revitalized awareness of the spiritual aspect of humanity will also aid positively in our attempts to redress environmental degradation. Likewise, an appreciation of the diversity of cultures and cultural experiences can be gleaned from biblical studies, thereby minimizing unwarranted cultural conflicts. Finally, delineating a clear biblical understanding of the common good for humanity and the planet will help in making a positive contribution toward the construction of a political system for governance that could sustain peace and harmony in human societies.

These six dimensions demand, therefore, an accessible, public Bible and a biblical scholarship that addresses these crucial issues. The following ten points elaborate various aspects of these themes.

Peace and Conflict in Asia. The theme of peace and conflict is a major concern for international politics and global economies. Biblical texts that relate to this theme need to be explored in contextual terms and addressed in terms of relevance for the contemporary scene. Thematic and topical studies of biblical words, concepts, or texts that do not in some way address the question of peace and conflict for us today prove inadequate, particularly since this is a major concern in the Bible.

Covenant and Federalism in Union Politics. It is necessary to explore the various biblical concepts that have led to the creation of nations like the United States and confederations such as the European Union, tracing historically their roots to the biblical concept of covenant, which finds its practice in the early Puritan movements in England and America. The rise of the United Nations and the future development of any world system demand contributions from the discipline by way of providing guiding principles for their foundation.

Creation and Environment in Social and Global Governance. Biblical scholarship must address the current conditions of the global natural environment and the responsibility for its governance from a biblical perspective of creation, particularly as our own survival depends on a responsible relation with the planet.

Globalization and the Kingdom in an Age of Empire. Biblical scholarship should explore the various expansions of imperialism (military, political, cultural, socioeconomic, and so forth) and human greed in relation to biblical concepts such as divine grace and providence.

Commandments and the Rule of Law in Liberal Democracy. Biblical scholars should attend to the development of an understanding of a rule-based governing system based on concepts developed from the ancient biblical texts.

Community and Neighborliness in Personal, Social, National, and Global Ethics. A relevant biblical scholarship would explore the biblical basis of various classical and contemporary ethical theories and applied ethics at various levels of human activity, with the aim of contributing biblical ethical concepts and understandings toward the development of contemporary ethical theories and applications. The ethical question is pertinent in terms of Asian and Western differences as it relates to faith. A 2007 survey by the Pew Research Center reveals the following insight, "When asked whether one must believe in God to be moral, a comfortable majority of Americans (57%) said yes, but in Japan and China, 72% said no" (Zakaria 2008, 109). Given the atheistic nature of many Asian societies, there is a need to express this alternative in terms and languages accessible to these societies.

Spirituality and Culture in Social Equality and Justice. This perspective would address the question of a holistic concept of human existence in terms of spiritual and social dimensions. As social beings, we need to explore the biblical understanding of the relationship between personal spirituality and personal/social behavior and whether such a relationship can redress inner as well as social conflict.

Freedom and Responsibility in Civil Society. This area would probe into the biblical understanding of the nature of a civil society under various political systems and governments, especially those of liberal-democratic and socialist persuasions. The question of freedom and its relation to responsibility should also be addressed by biblical scholars.

Knowledge and Power in Science and Technology. As science and technology increasingly envelop our lives and daily activities, to a point of total dependence on them for human life and livelihood, scholars must skillfully negotiate such a phenomenon in terms of biblical ideas and worldviews.

Filial Piety and Education in Modern Social Structures. This branch of biblical scholarship would investigate biblical concepts such as family filial piety and the nature of education with the development of a healthy social model for diverse cultures and societies in mind.

Although some or all of the above issues and topics have long been investigated by various relevant disciplines or interdisciplinary studies, seldom have biblical scholars been interested in cross-disciplinary investigations—often leaving these sorts of questions to their next-door neighbors in the departments of theology. This isolationism is partly due to the comfort and security derived therefrom, for ivory towers are comfortable, after all. Therefore, what is required of biblical scholarship in institutions is serious rethinking and revamping.

CONCLUSION

To speak of a "rising Asia" may be problematic, insofar as such a concept might be a Western construct, perhaps misconstruing cultural change as cultural power. This may be true to a degree, but global power certainly appears to be shifting, as Zakaria cautiously asserts: "The great shift taking place in the world might prove to be less about culture and more about power" (2008, 86). In such a context, global communities find themselves in search of a new world order and system, since the end of the Cold War. With Asia rising, Zakaria looks forward as follows:

> China's awakening is reshaping the economic and political landscape of the world, but it is also being shaped by the world into which it is rising.... Beijing is negotiating the same two forces that are defining the post-American world more broadly—globalization and nationalism.... The stability and peace of the post-American world will depend, in large measure, on the balance that China strikes between these forces (globalization and nationalism) of integration and disintegration. (2008, 88)

In such a shifting environment, it is imperative that biblical researchers make the Bible accessible for Asian communities, showing its relevance and application to the contemporary situation. Such relevance has to do not only with individual ethics and spirituality but also with social and global concerns, including creation itself. Hence, the challenge for biblical scholarship in the "future of the biblical past" in Asia will be to vigorously engage biblical texts with Asian contexts and Asian contexts with biblical texts, making sure that such engagements are culturally relevant and thus hopefully contributing to the transformation of the world. Should this happen in Asia, then at least half the globe will be transformed.

PART 3
EUROPE

7

The Future of a Nonexistent Past:
Biblical Studies in Bulgaria

Milena Kirova

Every narrative addressing the state of biblical studies in Bulgaria should begin with an odd and traumatic situation in the distant past of the country. Christianity was not at all a popular religion until the mid-ninth century. Each of the two tribes comprising the Bulgarian state, the local Slavs and the old Bulgarians (or Protobulgarians), who had migrated from Asia, had their established pantheon and rituals. In contrast to the aristocratic circles in both tribes, various pagan gods coexisted quite peacefully in the lives of the common people. The situation in question took place in the year 865 C.E.

At the time, in an intricate political game aimed at protecting the state from the next-in-a-row military campaign of the Byzantine Empire, and for the sake of his own power, the ruling monarch Boris was secretly baptized in the camp of the Byzantine Emperor. Upon his return to the Bulgarian capital, he ordered a mass christianization of all *bollyars* (the aristocracy), most of whom were Bulgarians. Their refusal brought on a bloody massacre in which almost all the *bollyars*, along with their extended families, were slaughtered. This was followed by deft political maneuvering in Rome, where Boris managed to provoke a violent clash between the envoys of the Roman Church and the Byzantine Church. As a result, Bulgaria became an Eastern Orthodox country with its own patriarch. However, the enforced conversion to a scarcely familiar religion, as well as the horror of the blood-spattered events, left an invisible wound in the spiritual flesh of the new-born Christians. In the centuries to follow, Bulgarians never grew acutely fond of this religion (or of any other). In fact, medieval Bulgaria turned into a flourishing place for heresies. Some of them reached the country from the Near East while others, like the doctrine of the notorious priest Bogomil, originated within Bulgaria itself and entered the social lives of large groups of people, expanding to western and central Europe.

From the late-fourteenth century, Bulgaria was forcefully brought into the boundaries of the Ottoman Empire. This situation lasted for five centuries and doubtlessly influenced the unpopularity of Christianity. The consequent lack of a Bulgarian government, Bulgarian institutions, and a Bulgarian church for five hundred years resulted in the preservation of many pagan traditions in the life of the common population, about 95 percent of whom were peasants. Yet the most savage wound on the religious conscience of Bulgarians was caused by communist ideology, even though it lasted for only forty-five years.

At present, 27 percent of Bulgarians consider themselves Christians, 8 percent see themselves as Muslims, less than 1 percent belong to some other religion, and the rest identify themselves as atheists. In addition, the majority of Christians are so only in a vague social sense: for the most part, they are not acquainted with Christian philosophy, nor do they practice its mandatory traditions. Moreover, after 1989, which marked the fall of communist rule throughout Eastern Europe, including Bulgaria, being Christian became a "democratic" fashion. Belonging to this belief somehow validated a status of "proper" morality, particularly in the public sphere. After 1989, we witnessed intriguing scenes along these lines. For example, former activists of the Communist Party, currently political leaders, began to attend church frequently and would make the sign of the cross with enviable fervency. Similarly, Mafiosi bosses and businessmen of the grey economy consecrated their offices with earsplitting religious parties, while proceeding later on, in a most nonChristian manner, to set off a bomb in the very same offices.

I am telling this story in an attempt to explain why biblical studies in Bulgaria has never distinguished itself in any special way. Perhaps I should have begun by explaining that, as recently as ten years ago, such studies did not exist as a secular science. Sporadic comments on biblical texts appeared, in fragmentary fashion, in other fields of the humanities, above all in literary studies. Even in such cases, however, biblical books were interpreted by means of some type of "exogamic" methodology, and in most instances the aim was to illustrate a point of nonbiblical import.

The few academic researchers who could be considered somewhat competent in biblical studies were in the field of Old Bulgarian studies. This is a group of sciences which study the language and culture of Bulgarian society until the end of the fourteenth century, that is, until the country came under the rule of the Ottoman Empire. Old Bulgarian has been preserved and can be studied mainly in liturgical documents. It may also be found in religious literature, not designed for use in church services, yet always written by priests of higher or lower rank. The language itself is quite different, and far more complicated, than contemporary Bulgarian. As a result, the study of this literature constitutes a hermetic discipline. Only a limited circle of experts are competent in religious literature written in old Bulgarian; further, their comments on such literature have always been in the nature of comparing various Bulgarian biblical translations, rather than for the sake of studying the Bible as such. In light of this situation, the only space in Bulgaria where the roots of biblical studies could take hold was in the field of theology.

THEOLOGICAL BIBLICAL STUDIES IN BULGARIA

The systematic progress of theological biblical studies in Bulgaria began in the year 1923, when the subject was institutionalized. The first faculty of theology opened then: it was the sixth faculty of the University of Sofia, which had been founded in 1888—a decade after the resurrection of the Bulgarian state. As a result of the atheistic politics of the communist regime in the years 1951–1991, religious studies were ghettoized within a Theological Academy founded especially for this purpose. Other university lecturers did not dare to jeopardize their careers by visiting it; religious researches were in general marginalized and designated as nonscientific. Only after the democratic changes of 1989 did theology return to the university. In those early years, the very sight of young bearded priests in black cassocks strolling through the busy passageways of the university buildings was a bizarre, quite exotic, spectacle. Elderly visitors would do the sign of the cross upon encounter with these students, as if they were at church.

Today there are four theological faculties in different universities in Bulgaria. They have a common curriculum, which is the same as the one established in 1923. Biblical studies is one of the four basic units of theology, alongside historical theology (mainly church history), systematic theology, and practical theology. All together, about fifty subjects are taught. Women have been able to enroll in theological studies since 1992, yet the first three female doctoral students were accepted only in 1999. At present, there are about ten women who teach theology in Bulgarian universities, but none of them has received a *Habilitation*.

Biblical research represents a growing area of Bulgarian theology, although so far its achievements have been modest. Ivan Markovsky is considered to have initiated this field in the 1920s and 30s. Since then, there have been other important names: Boyan Piperov, Nikolay Shivarov, and Slavcho Vulchanov in the areas of biblical archaeology and the hermeneutics of the Old Testament; Nikolay Glubokovsky and Christo Ghiaurov in the interpretation of the New Testament. Research has focused on the preparation of students for religious ministry. A great part of such research has involved commentaries on a variety of biblical books: Genesis, Exodus, Proverbs, Daniel, Ezekiel, Jeremiah, Ecclesiastes, and Isaiah. Most of these studies were published in the Yearbook of the Theological

Faculty at the University of Sofia. Remarkably, there are no monographs. There are also very few publications in foreign languages. Again, the explanation lies with the half century of disruption brought about by the communist regime on these newborn traditions, which had just begun to develop in the 1930s and 40s. Actually, during the years of communism, there was a publishing house of the Holy Synod (the Bulgarian church headquarters); however, having a book published by them was a long and troublesome process, entirely under the control and censure of the government. To speak of biblical studies was permitted only under the mask of Old Bulgarian studies. For example, Ivan Panchovsky wrote a study in *Methodology of Christian Ethics* in 1962. In order to get the book published, he was forced to insert a separate chapter on the Bulgarian national saint Ivan Rilsky, who is considered a factual person, in the midst of his discussion of ethical problems.

Periodicals in which biblical research can be published are not very well developed. The main venue for publication, as already mentioned, is the Yearbook of the Faculty of Theology at the University of Sofia. The Faculty also publishes its own journal, *Theological Reflection*, as does the Holy Synod, a journal titled *Spiritual Culture*. The first religious periodical in Bulgaria was the *Church Herald*, with a history that goes back over a century. A secular journal, *Christianity and Culture*, started at the beginning of the twenty-first century. Works in Christian ethics and philosophy, as well as in the political history of the Christian church, can be found in the pages of a new magazine, *Altera Academica*. One of the latest journals in Bulgaria, *Money and Culture*, has quite recently published an article called "The Bible and Money."

Secular Biblical Studies in Bulgaria

Secular scholarly research on the Bible is thus a novelty in Bulgaria. It appeared about ten years ago and was very well received, especially by researchers from other disciplines of the humanities. Today, critical attention to the Bible is no different from the critical attention at work in all modern disciplines and methodologies, which were little known in Bulgaria before 1989 but which have flourished during the last fifteen years. Since the moment of their (Bulgarian) birth, secular biblical studies proved a provocative interdisciplinary science. These big leaps and breathtaking changes are characteristic for Bulgaria, as every long period of stagnation brings about zealous compensation.

The first author to publish in Old Testament studies is Moni Almalech, a professor of linguistics whose main field of interest is the semiotics of colors. He studied biblical Hebrew in Jerusalem. His exploration of the hermeneutics of the

Hebrew Bible combines profound scientific knowledge with interesting topics and a nontraditional approach. His most substantial work so far is *The Colours in the Pentateuch: A Linguistic Picture of the World* (2006). Almalech is a prolific writer who has published a great number of biblical articles in periodicals and on the internet.

My own book, *Biblical Femininity: Mechanisms of Construction, Politics of Representation* (2005), appeared exotic against the background of a rigid theological tradition. Its methodological approach is pointedly interdisciplinary: it brings together gender studies, psychoanalysis, literary studies, and the history of religion. A colleague from the faculty of theology told me about the symptomatic effects generated by the volume: it intensely encouraged the work of the few women who teach there and, even more, their ambitions to overcome the stiff norms of the Eastern Orthodox tradition. Yet again, even more symptomatic is perhaps the fact that none of these women made any attempt to contact me for a conversation on biblical or nonbiblical subjects.

At this point, I should like to share another intriguing observation on the meeting point between tradition and new methods in Bulgarian biblical studies. What I have in mind is the manner in which theological biblical researchers perceive this newborn secular research. Perhaps better put, I have in mind the total lack of any public reaction on their part, as if nothing has happened or could ever happen in a field in which the parameters for comprehending the Bible have been drawn once and forever. This deliberate blindness definitely does not help theology itself. It actually makes theological studies even more hermetic and unable to adapt to the changes that are taking place.

Regarding such reaction, I should also mention that it is still easier to work on the Hebrew Bible. A nontraditional approach to the New Testament interferes directly with the Christian upbringing of the writer's audience, although in Bulgaria this upbringing is less emphasized than in countries such as Greece, Russia, Poland, or even Serbia. The resistance in our case is of a moral rather than religious nature; it concerns the personal identification of the individual, thus begetting an irrational negativism accompanied by a hyperbolized emotional reaction.

Still, life goes on, even in the humanities in Bulgaria. I myself keep working with the methods of gender studies, although lately in the field of masculinity. My new research bears the temporary title of *History and Masculinity in the Hebrew Bible*. Almalech is writing on the Creation story. New authors, from the youngest generation of scholars, are eager to pursue new paths, as in the case of Nikolay Atanassov. After graduating from the University of Sofia in the Department of Bulgarian Studies, he emigrated to the United States. There, while working in nonacademic fields, he researched homosexuality in the Bible and published last year a provocative study in the journal *Altera*, the first of its kind ever published in Bulgaria.

The Bible in Bulgarian Literature

To gain a complete view of interest in the Bible in Bulgaria, mention should be made of its increasing presence in fiction literature after 1989. Bulgarian literature has apparently followed a similar and widespread tendency in world literature in this respect: it has produced in the last quarter of the twentieth century a stream of bestsellers. The aesthetic quality of these books is debatable, yet the fact cannot be denied that the provocative attitude taken toward biblical events in these books has begotten a renewed interest in the Bible itself. This interest has much to do with the fact that these novels focus to a great extent on the documents that were "expelled" from the Bible as well as on those aspects of interpretation that traditionally have been suppressed. The very tendency of bringing back to life alternative facts in the history of Christianity and incorporating them into a narrative has a strong background—both documentary and legendary—in Bulgaria itself. Let us recall that the country was a blossoming center of heresies until the end of the fourteenth century. Several interesting novels along this line appeared on the market.

Vladimir Zarev's *Four Lives of Saints for Father Bogomil and for the Perfection of Fear* (1998) is a narrative about the life and doctrine of the infamous heretic who possessed a charismatic personality, ironically (according to the church) named Bogomil ("dear to God"). The book, sprinkled with references to the New Testament, offers philosophical and psychological insights into the eroticism present in the relationship between the religious leader and his followers. Unlike the traditional image of an ascetic wise man, the notorious priest is depicted as a handsome, ardent seducer, who mesmerizes folks with his religious passion.

Anton Donchev's *The Peculiar Knight of the Holy Book* (1998) has an intriguing and symptomatic history. According to the author, the story was created in the 1970s as a scenario for a Hollywood adventure movie. The movie project did not bear fruit, although the text was actually very suitable for Hollywood, with its medieval settings, legendary characters, and the personality of the Superman-Knight. At that time, such a story would have matched a wave of novels and movies with plots built around the quest for a vanished sacred book. (In fact, if Donchev is to be believed, his book would have preceded Umberto Eco's *The Name of the Rose*.) The story is situated in mid fourteenth century Bulgaria, and again "Bogomilism"—the doctrine of Father Bogomil, with its practical realization in the form of large social groups—is central to the plot.

In 2005 Emil Andreev's *The Glass River* was the winner of a national novel competition. The plot proceeds as follows. Somewhere in present day Bulgaria, an international team of young archaeologists digs out the remains of an ancient village whose inhabitants had practiced strange mystical religious rituals and produced heretical Christian artifacts. The mystic past interferes with the lives of the young people. Thus history, legend, and reality mix together in this story. The title, *The Glass River*, is a metaphor for the ethical message of the book. It comes from a "Bogomilian" redaction of *The Book of Enoch* found by the archeologists amidst the remains of the ancient village. According to this apocryphal fourteenth-century text from Bulgaria, the giants born of the marriage between the sons of God and the human daughters used to go and sit by a river of melted glass and boiling amber. There they wept and mourned the loss of their God. Their tears dropped into the river and hardened it. There was no water in it any more, neither were there fish; iced in the glass were only human dreams and passions.

A common feature of these three novels, as well as of this literary tendency in general, is the random combination of documentary facts, biblical allusions, and fictional narrative, as well as the freely invented additions to history and a tendency to psychologize from a contemporary perspective. Attention, in Bulgaria as everywhere else, is drawn to the hidden, repressed sides of the Christian history, especially to the alternative religious phenomena and practices of the past. As noted earlier, it was precisely Bogomilism that inspired modern Bulgarian writers, for it is the most distinctive national contribution to the rise of Christian heresies in medieval Europe.

In line with this interest in heretical Christianity, we must place also the appearance, within less than fifteen years, of two different translations of the book of Enoch. The first appeared in 1994 and the second in 2008. Both present the Ethiopian and the Slavic redactions of Enoch. Moreover, the Slavic redaction is actually written in Old Bulgarian. Both books are by Boriana Hristova, an academic researcher in Old Bulgarian who is also director of the Bulgarian National Library.

Biblical symbols and messages also appear in the newborn Bulgarian *écriture féminine*. They are particularly characteristic of the works of the major author of this wave, Emilia Dvoryanova. Her university degree is in philosophy, and she is a devoted Christian. Her doctoral thesis is titled *The Aesthetic Nature of Christianity* (1992), and her latest novel is *The Earthy Gardens of the Holy Mother* (2006). The novel is built upon the biblical personality of the Virgin Mary, entwined with the ancient legend of her journey with St. John to the island of Athos after the death of Jesus. This journey resulted in the appearance of the first friaries on the island, which later formed the "monastic republic" known as the Holy Mountain. There, from the very beginning to our days, any female creature, be it a woman or a cat, is denied access. Dvoryanova's novel has a strong political message of rebellion against the unjust segregation created by the Eastern Orthodox Church, as well as passionate protest against the dogmas that impose sexual limits on human love for God.

I should also mention the latest "feminine" novel with biblical motifs, namely, the story *Adriana* by Theodora Dimova (2007). A rich and spoiled woman in the 1930s, Adriana is purged and spiritually reincarnated after seeing Jesus himself on a lonely beach. The story demonstrates a not-too-successful attempt to unite social themes, which traditionally are very strong in Bulgarian literature, with biblical personalities and Christian implications in order to find new solutions to old ethical problems.

Unlike prose, Bulgarian poetry tunes itself less willingly to Christian thematics. We could find episodic decorative mentions of biblical images and motifs in the light of their allegorical or philosophical or daily moralistic usage. In general, Bulgarian poetry was not brought up in the necessity to express religious feelings on the part of its authors. Such was the case not merely during those forty-five years when political circumstances downplayed religious feelings. Exulted with the new possibilities that came with "the dawn of democracy," the literary historian Michail Nedelchev compiled in 1999 an anthology of the most prominent Bulgarian religious poetry from the late nineteenth to the late twentieth century. The outcome was a meager book of sixty pages, including preface and afterword, which contains the works of about twenty poets. No more than half of them regard Christianity as something more than a collection of moral directives.

An atypical figure in present day Bulgarian literature is the young poet and university lecturer in West European literature, Kalin Michaylov, who also is a devoted Catholic. In 2007 he published a book of poetry that had a consistently religious character, *Shed In Your Name*. Everything in it appears to be "genuine" and "as it should be": the passionate moralistic confession of the texts, the lyrical hero's identification with the solitude and torments of Jesus Christ, and the numerous associations with biblical symbols and personalities.

THE FUTURE OF BIBLICAL STUDIES IN BULGARIA

At this point, having noted the significant characteristics concerning the role of the Bible in the past and present of science and literature in Bulgaria, I shall endeavor to summarize those tendencies which guarantee, to a certain extent, its future.

I would put in first place the existence of an appropriate receptive environment. There is still in Bulgaria, mainly as a result of the encyclopedic traditions in the educational system, a relatively large and well-prepared audience. This audience is emphatically interested in modern research in the fields of literary studies, philosophy, the history of religion, and the social sciences. Under these circumstances, secular biblical studies has an excellent chance of being at the center of attention, provided that it develops two basic features: a modern methodological orientation and a definite interdisciplinary character. That would enable biblical studies to preserve as large an audience as possible, an audience as versatile as possible in their professional backgrounds. Should biblical research follow instead the way of narrow specialization, the result would be the creation of yet another marginal space in academic science, which has fallen abruptly, in the course of the last decade, into marginality. Even if we suppose that somehow—let us say, by education abroad or by diligent self-education—individuals appeared on the scene who could write in an innovative and competent way in an exclusive area of biblical studies, such scholars would suffer from the lack of a suitable professional environment in the country.

In such a situation the most reasonable action to take is to look at the options that are available through translations of works in biblical studies from foreign languages. In the 1990s, for instance, it was precisely such literature in translation that greatly compensated for the big gaps in and the slow progress of the humanities within Bulgaria between 1944 and 1989. Even if such works were to be translated, a surprise would await us. Up until now, almost all translations of works in biblical studies have been sponsored by one or another religious institution, usually a church or a Jewish foundation. This, of course, predetermines the choice of the works translated. The main issue becomes the ideological meaning of the religious message which serves, more or less directly, the interests of the sponsoring institution. A good example is the translation of a twenty-two volume commentary on the New Testament under the common title The Bible Speaks Today (1999–2005). The editor-in-chief of the English edition, and author of many of the volumes in the collection, is John R. W. Stott. The initiative belongs to the Bulgarian publishing house New Person, which is entirely religion-oriented and connected with the Anglican Church. The advertising poster for these volumes offers a curious observation: "Books are read easily—they carry the reader away (unlike most commentaries)." The publishers presume that potential readers are, to begin with, intimidated by technical theological terminology and the particularly boring style of Eastern Orthodox (not only Bulgarian) theologians.

Very few of the newly published translations are free of religious motivations. Further, they are faulty in other ways, insofar as they have been selected at random rather than as a result of a systematic plan of publication. By "faulty" I mean that the translations are either of books that lack particular scientific value or are of books that might have had merit in the past. For example, in late 2008 the publishing house Cybea triumphantly presented its very expensive (especially for the Bulgarian market) edition of Abraham Cohen's *Everyman's Talmud*—a book that may have been up to date in the early 1930s, but is no longer so. In fact, the most substantial work of translation in biblical studies today is the *New Bible Dictionary*, published by New Person (1996). It was originally published in English by the conservative InterVarsity Press. In order to adjust the translation to the Bulgarian reader, the dictionary includes newly written columns concerning Bulgarian history, written by a large team of lecturers from the faculty of theology at the University of Sofia.

Thus we return to the deeply theological nature of biblical studies. We have also arrived at the point where we need to consider the future of this tradition of biblical criticism, along with the future of secular biblical criticism. The two seem to run parallel to one another. As we can gather from the advertisement of New Person, theological biblical studies is notorious for its constraints and its unwillingness to divorce itself from its archaic lexicon, its cliched means, and the inevitably prudish tone of its reflections. Until now, it has never attempted to adapt to the modern needs of secular society and continues to live in some oneiric certainty that society shall strive to adapt to it.

Secular biblical studies, in turn, does not need to be lectured in the traditions of Bulgarian theology. It finds—although with much difficulty, because of the total lack of such literature in Bulgarian libraries—information and models in literature published in other languages, mostly in English. It is clear that there is little likelihood of a possible rapprochement between these two traditions in biblical studies, at least in the foreseeable future. Each will continue to undermine the efforts and achievements of the other, yet without being too aggressive in its disapproval. In the communist era such a stance was labeled "peaceful coexistence": it expressed the new approach to the differences between communist society and capitalist society, an approach that developed after the Cold War. It seems that some things never change, especially in social praxis.

It seems to me that theological biblical studies in Bulgaria will make its first steps towards epistemological modernization and linguistic democracy very slowly and very painfully. Why?

The last two generations, to which all associate professors and professors in the theological faculties belong today, were brought up in a context of inflexible theological orthodoxy. It is not as if these individuals cannot change; it is rather that they *do not want* to change. Moreover, these scholars reproduce themselves by educating future university teachers in similar fashion. Some university lecturers (usually assistant professors) do sense the limitations of this approach; they may feel, perhaps, some inner resistance. However, they dare not initiate anything that might involve them in a conflict. One can hardly expect that they will produce any "heretical" observations in monographs. University teachers in Bulgaria write monographs mainly for the purpose of working their way up the academic hierarchy. The existing system inherited the complications of the one in place before 1989; as such, it continues to require four monographs for completion of the cycle. This means that, if a university teacher wishes to become a full professor, he/she has to have written four monographs. Two of these are doctoral theses: a "small" one grants the title of PhD; a "big" one, more difficult, bestows a higher degree known as a Doctor of Science, given in a number of specific areas, such as Doctor of History, Doctor of Philology, and so forth. The other two monographs are for the process of habilitation: the first, toward the rank of associate professor; the second, which must follow the acquisition of the "big" doctoral degree, toward the rank of full professor. Under such conditions, every young university lecturer becomes dependent, for a long period of time, on his/her good relationship with colleagues, especially those who have received habilitation and represent his/her potential referees.

Yet even in the face of such a clumsy and convoluted system, various demands for change have emerged among young theologians. I have already mentioned the excitement that my own anti-traditional book about biblical femininity stirred among women teachers. Another example is the volume *The Biblical Jonas* authored by Ivaylo Naydenov, an Assistant Professor in biblical studies (Old Testament) at the University of Sofia. The book begins with a short foreword to the reader, which clarifies the ambivalent position of a young theologian (he was born in 1969). In effect, *The Biblical Jonah* was the author's doctoral dissertation, which was originally titled *The Book of St. Prophet Jonah: Exegetic and Isagogic Aspects*. The author frankly states that he tried to rework the original text by eliminating some of the reasons why it proved difficult to read. One of these deserves special attention. Dr. Naydenov formulates it as the "distorted link between the reader and the theological literature." "This is why," he says, "I tried to replace scientific dryness with an intriguing narrative in order to make peace between the reader and the Bible." Honestly, an "intriguing narrative" is far too ambitious a claim to make regarding the text that follows. However, the more interesting question is: who is the reader who has to make peace with the Bible and its story? Bearing in mind that few people in Bulgaria read the Bible, and that the majority of this small audience is made up of atheists who do not encounter special ideological problems with the text because they accept it as mythology and literature, the conclusion can only be that it is the religious reader who must come to peace with his/her sacred text.

In spite of everything, secular biblical studies does have, I believe, a future in Bulgaria, considering the interest of a broad reading audience and the willingness of students, especially at the Master's level, to attend lectures in this subject at university. Such popularity runs into a number of problems, such as the continuing lack of a systematically formed academic preparation outside the theological departments, the difficulties in absorbing a vast amount of information in the absence of critical secondary literature in biblical studies, and the lack of knowledge of Hebrew. (Biblical Hebrew is taught only in the theological faculties; there is not one single textbook in Bulgarian, and the majority of Bulgarian Jews do not speak Hebrew, let alone the biblical language). In such a situation, the training of nontheological researchers depends to a great extent on their willingness for self-study and on the possibility of completing their qualifications in foreign academic institutions with advanced biblical studies. Access to foreign libraries (since even Amazon declines delivery of books to Bulgaria) and communication with foreign specialists would be of crucial importance for the future of secular biblical studies in a country in which the discipline has no past.

8

UNITY AND DIVERSITY IN NORDIC
BIBLICAL SCHOLARSHIP

Hanna Stenström

The topic before me is Scandinavian biblical scholarship: Old[1] and New Testament studies during the twentieth century and up to the present, with a brief reflection on their future(s).[2] I understand "Scandinavian" in its wider sense, that is, as Denmark (with Greenland and the Faeroe Islands), Finland (with Åland),[3] Iceland, Norway, and Sweden—in other words, the five nations called "the Nordic countries" by us who live here. That is why I use this terminology, except in established expressions and phrases such as "The Scandinavian School."

The overall aim of this essay is to show that "Nordic biblical scholarship" is not a specific kind of scholarship with a common identity but a phenomenon characterized by both unity and diversity that has grown out of a shared history and a shared idea of Nordic community, as well as out of pragmatically motivated collaborations.

Although the Nordic countries may seem homogenous to an outsider, this region is, in fact, characterized both by a considerable number of affinities in social and cultural life, which have grown out of a long common history, and by undeniable sociocultural diversity (Ryman et al. 2000, 16). Descriptions of Nordic biblical scholarship by outsiders tend to obscure the academic and confessional

---

1. "The Old Testament" is a problematic designation that presupposes a Christian perspective. I use it only as an established, conventional terminology as, e.g., in "Old Testament Exegesis" or if a Christian perspective is intended.

2. I hereby express my gratitude to Inger Ljung and Roland Boer, who read and made valuable comments on earlier versions of the essay.

3. Greenland and the Faeroe Islands and Åland have a certain degree of autonomy within Denmark and Finland, respectively.

diversity of the region. The best example of this is the designation "the Scandinavian School of the Old Testament," which was not originally a self-designation but
was coined by outsiders (Ringgren and Hartman 1992, 1001).[4] This designation is
problematic, since it presupposes a unity among scholars who were actually connected through a network of influences and relations, not as devoted disciples
of the same professor or as subscribers to a program (Anderson 1990, 609). The
designation also renders invisible any Nordic research that does not have the
characteristics of the "School," including practically all Finnish and Icelandic Old
Testament research (613).

However, although I want to problematize the very idea of "Nordic biblical
scholarship," I am at the same time convinced, on empirical grounds, that it exists.
I have experienced it in real life, and I have read texts by many others who have
had similar experiences. So the question is: What can be said about the Nordic
biblical scholarship that actually exists, even though it is not homogenous and
cannot be described in a simple formula?

Biblical Scholarship in the Nordic Countries: The Context

The Nordic countries today are five independent nations with a total population of about twenty-five million. Each nation has its own distinct identity, but
the countries also share a common, at times difficult, history that includes both
peaceful cooperation and bloody wars (Syren 1995, 225–26). Two of the five
nations, Sweden and Denmark, have been independent since the Middle Ages,
while the others are young nations that gained full independence during the
twentieth century. Nordic interaction dates back in time, but after World War II
forms for developing collaboration among the Nordic countries in all spheres and
at all levels of society have been an important political project, including collaboration in research and funding of research.[5] "Norden" (to use our own term) may

---

4. I want to express my gratitude to Mikael Winninge, who drew my attention to this fact and
to the importance of discussing insider and outsider perspectives on Nordic biblical scholarship,
when a draft for this essay was discussed at a seminar in Uppsala in May 2008.

5. For facts about the Nordic region, see www.norden.org, especially the shortcut "Facts
about the Nordic region." A short survey of Nordic history with focus on inter-Nordic relations
and Nordic collaboration is also available, under the subheading "The History of Nordic Cooperation."

be regarded today as a kind of imagined community, characterized by both unity and diversity. Three aspects of Nordic unity and diversity that are relevant in this context are language, culture, and church life.

To begin with language, Danish, Norwegian, Icelandic, and Swedish are closely related Germanic languages. Those who speak Danish, Norwegian, and Swedish can communicate in their native tongues, though not always without difficulty, and read all three languages. For historic reasons, Finland is bilingual, one language being Finnish, a Finno-Ugrian language totally different from the other Nordic languages, and the other Swedish, the native language of about 6 percent of the population.

Regarding culture, a common history has created a number of cultural affinities, although cultural differences should not be disregarded. There is also an indigenous minority with a distinct culture and language of their own, the Sami people, in the north of Norway, Sweden, and Finland (see, for example, Ryman et al. 2000, 15). In the context of biblical scholarship, it may be mentioned that the Jews form a small minority, both now and earlier in the twentieth century. There are few Jewish voices in academic and public discourse, if by "a Jewish voice" we mean someone who identifies him or herself as Jewish and speaks as Jewish, and not a person of Jewish origin who is totally assimilated into the dominant culture.

Today the Nordic countries are in a process of change from rather homogenous societies into multicultural societies. Due to this development, a number of different religious traditions are becoming visible in society. At the same time, the secularization of the native population (and of public and political life) has been central in the development of the twentieth century. It is, for example, difficult to imagine the use of religious rhetoric to support the foreign policy of any of the five countries. Even in this respect, however, there are differences. Sweden is often regarded as the most secularized society. Similarly, the development into a multicultural society is not identical in all the countries; it is more rapid in some (Norway and Sweden) than in others (Finland and Iceland). The situation in Denmark is unique. Here, xenophobic movements have gained acceptance even in official policies and have generated political efforts to support and safeguard "Danishness" in various ways, including the formulation of a "canon," a list of works that should (shall) be known by those who can claim to be true Danes (see, e.g., Fatum 2006, 242).

Concerning church life, all five countries have Lutheran national churches (normally called "folk churches" in the Nordic countries) that have dominated religious life since the Reformation and that have had, through their close relations with the state, a considerable influence on society (Ryman et al. 2000). Today, 75–90 percent of the respective populations are members of these churches. Finland is different, with its two national churches, the Lutheran and the Orthodox (the latter with about 1–2 percent of the population as members). At the end of the twentieth century, the ties between church and state were loosened in all the countries, though not to the same degree. The Lutheran Church in Denmark is still a state church, while the Lutheran Church in Sweden has the greatest degree of independence. Today the international churches, Protestant as well as the Roman Catholic Church, are also represented in all Nordic countries.

The Lutheran national churches have certain similarities but also considerable differences. For example, a High Church movement was important in the Church of Sweden during the twentieth century, and for a period of time New Testament scholars played an important part in its development, in a manner alien to the other Nordic Lutheran churches (as evidenced by Ryman et. al. 2000). Revivalist movements in the national churches at the end of the nineteenth century and the beginning of the twentieth century appeared within the churches everywhere except in Sweden, where most grew into independent communities and churches (Baasland 1995, 147; Ryman et al. 2000, 12–13). That is why the Lutheran national churches in Norway and Finland include larger groups of conservatives than the Church of Sweden and also have, as a result, more tension between conservatives and liberals (see, e.g., Bentzen 1949, 295).

With a few exceptions, biblical scholarship in the Nordic countries during the twentieth century was located at theological faculties in nonconfessional state universities. However, especially at the beginning of the century, this did not exclude close relations between biblical scholarship and the Lutheran national churches, since these churches were a dominant force in society. The history of biblical scholarship is connected with changes in the relations between churches and society (see further Lodberg and Ryman 2000). During the twentieth century, the theological faculties became more and more independent of the national churches. The relationship between academic theology and the churches differs among the different countries. Sweden is the country where the separation has been the most definite, at least at the official level (Ringgren 1976, 48–49; Hartman 1992, 1003; Baasland 1995, 147; Heine 2000, 130–34). Even if a church-affiliated, privately funded, theological faculty, Det teologiske Menighetsfakultet, has been in existence in Norway since 1908, it is only during the last few decades that church-affiliated academic institutions (with an academic education officially recognized by the state as equivalent to those given at the state universities) have had a visible presence in Norway and Sweden (for Denmark, see Heine 2000, 133). Today, at least in Norway or Sweden, there are also biblical scholars working at state universities that lack theological faculties and where theology and/or religion are located in, for example, the Faculty of Arts.

NORDIC BIBLICAL SCHOLARSHIP:
A CATEGORY TOO NARROW AND TOO BROAD

One way of describing the diversity of Nordic biblical scholarship is to argue that the very term "Nordic biblical scholarship" is problematic: it is too broad. Having said that, however, it is also important to remember that it is also too narrow. (For a similar discussion on the cultural conditioning of the "Scandinavian School," see Syren 1995, 225–28, 235–37).

A CATEGORY TOO BROAD

The first reason for considering such a category too broad is that the large number of exegetical works during the last hundred years makes it impossible to write the history of Nordic biblical scholarship without making too many simplifications and exclusions.[6] Furthermore, the differences between the countries make it impossible to do justice to the issues concerning relations between biblical scholars/scholarship and their contexts in anything shorter than a series of publications by a Nordic group of scholars.

However, some examples can be given. One issue concerns the possible roles of biblical scholarship in societies developing from cultural homogeneity towards multiculturalism. The really interesting aspects of this issue become visible when looking at specific national contexts: for example, how Danish biblical scholars today are discussing issues of canon (see, for example, Engberg-Pedersen et al 2006, esp. Fatum, 242–55), or participating, at the University of Aarhus, in interdisciplinary networks concerned with the interpretation of normative texts in various religious traditions.[7] This work is not conditioned by something generally "Nordic" but by the very specific Danish context, where it is impossible to mention "canon" without associating it with political dimensions and the possible oppressive uses of a "canon," and where cultural diversity is a hot topic on the public agenda (see "Denmark" in Encyclopedia Britannica Online; Fatum 2006, 242–44, 253–54).

Another possible issue for discussion is the relationship between biblical scholarship and the churches; here, too, it is necessary to be more specific. In Sweden, the position of all the disciplines at theological faculties changed in

---

6. See, for example, the *selected* bibliography covering works on the New Testament (the absolute majority exegetical) from the period 1939–1949 in Lindeskog (1950a): it covers fourteen pages in small print, Iceland not included.

7. www.relnorm.au.dk.

the 1950s when a professor of philosophy at the University of Uppsala, Ingemar Hedenius, called the existence of theological faculties at modern universities in question because of the theologians' (open or hidden) religious agendas. The response of university theologians, including biblical scholars, was to keep the term "theology" in the name of the faculties but to define it as *religionsvetenskap* ("science of religions" or "religious studies") and emphasize its nonconfessional, academic character (Ringgren 1968, 176; 1976, 48–49; Riesenfeld 1968, 179; Ringgren 1976, 48–49; Hartman 1976, 58–59; Hartman 1992, 1003; Baasland 1995, 147; Olsson 1999, 121–24; Ryman 2000, 54–55). The stories of the theological faculties in the other countries are different (Heine 2000, 130–34), even when they are located in nonconfessional state universities and have a strong concern for academic freedom.[8]

Another reason for claiming that "the Nordic countries" is too broad a category is that the national academic environments are very small. Although the situation is different today, for most of the twentieth century, one or two universities in each country provided education and research in biblical scholarship, and some of them had for long periods just two to four exegetical professors, not counting doctoral students who did some teaching (Baasland 1995, 147; Olsson 1999, 73; see also Moxnes et al. 2000, 33). In such a situation, one or a few individuals (read: strong professors) can determine the development of their discipline in the whole country (Moxnes et al. 2000, 33). When the personal characteristics and convictions of one individual become so important, the histories of biblical scholarship become very different, even when the social and cultural contexts are rather similar. This is a real challenge if the aim is not to produce writings of history in which the history of biblical scholarship is the history of its professors, but rather to understand scholarship in the framework of social structures and processes.

To be specific, the fact that New Testament scholars, with some notable exceptions, played an important role in the resistance to ordination of women in the Swedish Lutheran national church—due to the convictions of some men who at that time were important in a small world—is something specifically Swedish, not some general truth about "Nordic New Testament scholarship" (Reumann 1966, iii–vii; Riesenfeld 1953, 96–127; Stendahl 1966; Olsson 1999, 119). In the 1950s, New Testament scholars in Sweden could be regarded by the media and in public discourse as guardians of the patriarchal order in the church (see, e.g., Lutteman 1959, 90–91, 116; Rydstedt 1953). The story of how in Norway a New

---

8. See, for example, the website for the Faculty of Theology at the University of Helsinki, which stresses the nondenominational, academic character of the faculty: www.helsinki.fi/teol.

Testament professor, Jacob Jervell, in the 1960s and 1970s came to be the one who played the role of "the modern Christian theologian" in the media and in public discourse is a different story, quite dependent on one man's personal characteristics (Moxnes et al. 2000, 44–45).

To take an additional example, the history of the slow and gradual breaking of male dominance involves not one single and unified Nordic history but rather a number of different local histories that are strongly dependent on both contexts and individuals.

A Category Too Narrow

However, when all is said and done, "the Nordic countries" is also too narrow a category to be used in a description of biblical scholarship, since current biblical scholarship in these countries is fully integrated into international scholarship—in its Western form(s)—and reflects its diversity.

Actually, modern Nordic exegetes have had strong relations with international biblical scholarship since the beginning. When historical-critical exegesis was established at Nordic universities in the late nineteenth and early twentieth centuries, relations with northwest European—especially German—biblical scholarship were very strong, as will be shown below. After World War II, relations with the United States and the English-speaking world in general became more important. For this reason, attempts to find traits that make Nordic biblical scholarship unique will most probably not succeed. Even in those cases where it gets a distinct identity—as in the "Scandinavian School of the Old Testament" and when some feminist scholars criticize and formulate alternatives to Elisabeth Schüssler Fiorenza's form of feminist exegesis (Fatum 1991 and, to a certain degree, Økland 2004, and then Schüssler Fiorenza 2007, 16–19)—this identity is created in relation to the non-Nordic research it criticizes.

Today, relations with international scholars are often more important for individual scholars, and more usable in characterizations of scholarship, than relations with local contexts such as the national churches or public debates (so Byrskog 2005, 16–17). This raises a question: Under what circumstances is it possible for biblical scholars to create a world of their own? Most probably, it is at least easier in welfare societies like the Nordic ones, societies that are not haunted by serious inner conflicts or in a state of war, and where secularization makes issues concerning biblical interpretation rather irrelevant to public debate. Thus, the fact that biblical scholarship is highly independent of its local social contexts is most probably a very context-dependent and context-specific phenomenon.

The History of Nordic Biblical Scholarship

Thus Nordic biblical scholarship since the beginning of the twentieth century is too wide a topic and too diverse a phenomenon for a short overview. A number of articles can be recommended for parts of this history. Concerning Nordic New Testament scholarship, Ernst Baasland covers its development up to the mid1990s, giving a number of references to works and scholars (1995). Concerning Hebrew Bible/Old Testament scholarship, I have not managed to find a corresponding article, although some important traditions are presented by Helmer Ringgren in *Anchor Bible Dictionary* (1992: 1001–1002) and G. W. Anderson (1990). Ringgren also gives a short bibliography (1002). The accompanying *Anchor Bible Dictionary* article by Lars Hartman (1002, also with a useful bibliography) can be read as a complement to Baasland's article (Hartman 1992).

However, it is possible to present a very simple sketch of developments. There are other ways to approach the subject. For example, one could study the role of biblical scholars and scholarship in translations of the Bible in Nordic countries during the twentieth century, or the series of commentaries written, or the histories of societies concerned with biblical scholarship; but I have to leave these possibilities aside for the sake of space.

A first phase, which saw the establishment of modern biblical scholarship at Nordic universities, began at the end of the nineteenth century and the beginning of the twentieth and ended (roughly) in the 1920s. The scholars who were active in this process had studied at various European, often German, universities and brought the biblical scholarship they had learned back home. They were not so much internationally active scholars with a profile of their own as intermediaries of international research for their own contexts: universities, churches, and the general public. In most cases, it was a moderate kind of scholarship that could be introduced without severe conflicts with the church, at least if the scholar managed to maneuver slowly and carefully (Gyllenberg 1944, 5–16, 23–25, 31; Bentzen 1949, 295; Lindeskog 1950a, 232; Ringgren 1976, 41–42; Hartman 1976, 51–53; Baasland 1995, 149–50; Olsson 1999, 74–75, 77–84; Moxnes et al. 2000, 33–37; Thelle 2000, 17–20; Ásgeirsson 2008. For Nordic New Testament scholarship, excluding Iceland, before 1945, with references, see Baasland 1995, 147–50).

Developments in Norway were the most dramatic: here, an alternative theological faculty, Menighetsfakultet, with a conservative theological profile, was founded in 1907–1908, as a result of conflicts concerning not only biblical scholarship but liberal theology in general (Lindeskog 1950b, 301–303; for tensions between conservatives and liberals in the other countries in the early period see: on Denmark, Lindeskog 1950a, 232–33; on Finland, Bentzen 1949, 295; on Sweden, Hartman 1976, 52–53).

The strong relations between German and Nordic biblical scholarship, especially before World War II (Baasland 1995, 147; Syren 1995, 226–27; Olsson 1999, 74–75; Moxnes et al 2000, 34; Thelle 2000, 19), were not only the result of the dominance of German biblical scholarship at that time. They were also due to the general German influence on Nordic Lutheran theology and national churches since the Reformation (so Baasland 1995, 147) and to a decisive German influence on cultural life in the Nordic countries up to World War II (Syren 1995, 226).

In the 1920s, roughly speaking, some scholars brought more radical impulses from the History of Religions School in New Testament studies to some Nordic universities (Gyllenberg 1944, 26–27; Hartman 1976, 53; Olsson 1999, 85–90). Nordic scholars in History of Religions/Comparative Religions also started to exercise an important influence on biblical scholarship, especially on Old Testament studies but also on certain New Testament scholars (so, e.g., Gyllenberg 1944, 10; Bentzen 1949, 274–75; Ringgren 1976, 42; Anderson 1990, 612–13; Ringgren 1992; Baasland 1995, 148–49; Olsson 1999, 102–5; Stendahl 2002, 208–9. For examples from later periods, up to the 1990s, see Olsson 1999, 90–92, 102–5). Academic biblical scholarship slowly began to develop independence from the Lutheran national churches, and scholars appeared who were primarily academic, not churchmen and teachers of future clergymen (Hartman 1976, 52–54; Olsson 1999, 78. For Nordic New Testament scholarship, excluding Iceland, before 1945, with references, see also Baasland 1995, 147–50. For the situation in Finland in the 1920s, see Gyllenberg 1944, 10, 17–22, 26–27, 31).

At this time, some Nordic scholars moved away from being disciples of great Germans and claimed the right to speak and act as professors in their own right in the international scholarly community. They started to develop independent biblical scholarship in the Nordic countries in ongoing interaction with international exegesis (Syren 1995, 236; Stendahl 2002, 207–9). Internationally, the best known of these scholars was the Norwegian Old Testament scholar Sigmund Mowinckel (See e.g., Mowinckel 1921–1924; Mowinckel 1951; see also Bentzen 1949, 274, 279, 209–306; Barstad and Ottoson 1988; Anderson 1990, 609–11; Ringgren 1992; Thelle 2000, 17, 20–23; Hjelde 2006). Another Norwegian, Anton Fridrichsen, Professor of New Testament in Uppsala between 1928 and 1953, is a further example (Fridrichsen et al. 1953; Fridrichsen 1972; Fridrichsen 1994; Lindeskog 1950a, 306–9; Hartman 1976, 53–57; Hartman 1992, 1001–2; Gerhardsson 1994, 8–83; Olsson 1999, 108–19). An important part of the latter's project was to create an internationally recognized biblical scholarship that could still be relevant for the church (Fridrichsen et al. 1953; Reumann 1966, x–xi; Hartman 1976, 53–54; Olsson 1999, 108–14, 116–19). He also fostered a number of scholars who gained academic positions around the world (see further Fridrichsen et al. 1953; Fridrichsen 1972, 1994; Lindeskog 1950a, 306–9; Reumann 1966, x–xi; Hartman 1976, 53–54, 56; 1992, 1001–03; Gerhardsson 1994, 8–83; Olsson 1999, 108–19).

This is the context for the so called "Scandinavian School of the Old Testament," where works by the Professor of History of Religions in Copenhagen, Vilhelm Grønbech (Bentzen 1949, 274–75; Lindeskog 1950b, 288–89), and the Danish Semitist, Johannes Pedersen (Bentzen 1949, 277–79, 294), influenced biblical scholars, beginning with Sigmund Mowinckel (Bentzen 1949, 275–77; Anderson 1990, 609–10; Ringgren 1992, 1001). This "School" is best understood as relations and streams of influences among Danish, Norwegian, and Swedish scholars who shared a good many ideas but also differed in important respects (see further Bentzen 1949, 274–92, 294, 303; Anderson 1990, 609–10; Lindeskog 1950b, 288–89; Ringgren 1992, 1001; Syren 1995).

In addition to Mowinckel, mention may be made of the Swedish scholar Ivan Engnell, who appeared on the scene in the late 1940s, with his "traditional-historical approach," which also influenced New Testament studies, and the "Uppsala School of the Old Testament," which emerged through his work (Engnell 1943, 1969). This "Uppsala School" can be regarded as part of the wide network of Danish, Norwegian, and Swedish scholars that was called the "Scandinavian School" (Bentzen 1949, 316–27; Ringgren 1976, 43–48, 1992; Anderson 1990, 611–13; Syren 1995; Olsson 1999, 105–8; Gerhardsson 2005, 392–93).

The years around and during World War II, from the 1930s to the late 1940s, can be regarded as a new phase of consolidation and intense scholarly activity interrupted by the war (Gyllenberg 1944, 22–23, 27–29, 31–34; Bentzen 1949; Lindeskog 1950a, 1950b; Olsson 1999, 75, 116–19; Stendahl 2002. For Nordic New Testament scholarship before 1945, excluding Iceland, with references, see Baasland 1995, 147–50). In national histories of research, we can find fragments of what the war meant to biblical scholars and scholarship (Bentzen 1949, 273–74, 294, 309, 327; Hartman 1986; Gerhardsson 1994, 43, 47, 53–55, 59–60, 96–97; Sollamo 1996, 159; Moxnes et al. 2000, 37. For the Swedish situation, see the article by the historian Oredsson 1997, 170–71, 174–75, 177).

Following the war, from the late 1940s to the mid 1970s, Nordic biblical scholarship flourished (Prenter 1964; Riesenfeld 1968; Ringgren 1968; Baasland 1995, 150–59; Sollamo 1996, 159–65; Olsson 1999, 75–76, 114–24). The first international articles I have managed to find on Nordic biblical scholarship were published during this period, around 1950, covering the 1930s and 1940s (Bentzen 1949; Lindeskog 1950a, 1950b). If a more thorough investigation confirms that these articles are the oldest international presentations, the late 1940s and early 1950s may be said to constitute a decisive period in the construction of "Nordic biblical scholarship." From the outside, such scholarship was now seen as an independent phenomenon worthy of description, while from the inside its identity was beginning to be constructed through the telling of its history.

After World War II, the direction of its international relations shifted from Germany, although relations were never abandoned, to the United States and the English-speaking world at large (Baasland 1995, 150). During the 1950s and 1960s, some Nordic biblical scholars, such as Krister Stendahl from Uppsala in 1954 and N. A. Dahl from Oslo in 1964, were called to the United States to participate in developing U.S. biblical scholarship (Baasland 1995, 150). Nordic biblical scholarship was at that time certainly no longer a community of disciples of great German professors but a community (perhaps rather communities) of internationally active scholars with distinct identities who contributed to international development (Baasland 1995, 150–59; Moxnes et al. 2000, 37–45). In this period, Scandinavian biblical scholarship was perhaps most often associated with tradition-historical work in both testaments and, therefore, with scholars like Ivan Engnell and Birger Gerhardsson, as well as with the collective designation "the Scandinavian School" (in either Old or New Testament, or both). However, there were other forms of research during this period, such as Septuagint studies in Helsinki, while New Testament scholarship was more than just tradition history (Hartman 1976, 58–64; Anderson 1990, 611–13; Riesenfeld 1968; Ringgren 1968; Hartman and Ringgren 1992; Baasland 1995, 150–55; Sollamo 1996, 159–65; Olsson 1999, 122–24).

Marking 1975 as the beginning of a new phase, still ongoing, is, of course, a simplification. It is a way of saying that the Nordic countries form part of the same development as international biblical scholarship: from the classical historical-critical paradigm to a diversity of methods and theories. The mid 1970s are (roughly) the time when this development began (Olsson 1999, 131–33; Moxnes et al. 2000, 45–46; Thelle 2000, 17–18; Byrskog 2005, 16–20).

In this period of growing diversity, various groups of scholars appeared on the national scenes to give biblical scholarship in their own countries or at their specific universities its own profile. In Helsinki, for example, we find those doing Septuagint studies (Baasland 1995, 164; Sollamo 1996, 165–68), those led by Heikki Räisänen, engaged in redaction criticism in the 1980s (Baasland 1995, 161, 165), and those still working with Nag Hammadi texts, e.g., Antti Marjanen. Other examples are: in Sweden, the shift to textual linguistics and other forms of text-oriented work during the 1980s (Hartman 1976, 64–65; Kieffer and Olsson 1993; Baasland 1995, 162; Olsson 1999, 125–30); and in

Denmark, the "Copenhagen School" with its minimalistic understanding of the history of Israel (Carroll 1998b, 52–57).

There was also a shift in New Testament studies during this period, from the Jewish to the Hellenistic context of Early Christianity, as manifested in research projects in Denmark and Norway (Baasland 1995, 159, 161) and associated with scholars such as Troels Engberg-Pedersen in Copenhagen. Social-science approaches entered into New Testament studies through, for example, Bengt Holmberg (Lund) and Halvor Moxnes (Oslo); feminist/gender studies did so through Lone Fatum (Copenhagen), Turid Karlsen Seim (Oslo), and Lilian Portefaix (Uppsala). Although in many places Old Testament/Hebrew Bible studies kept its traditional focus on historical work, some scholars turned to literary approaches, such as Kirsten Nielsen in Aarhus, and to new historical approaches, as evidenced by the issue of the *Scandinavian Journal for Old Testament Studies* on the topic of "History and Ideology in the Old Testament" (Barstad and Tångberg 1994).

As for the biblical theological approach, it is now done very differently. In the 1930s and 1940s, it was at that time regarded as an approach to the New Testament in Uppsala that actively tried to maintain relations with the church. Nowadays, it is seen as a descriptive task independent of the church, especially by Heikki Räisänen (2000a), who follows along the lines sketched by Krister Stendahl in that famous article on biblical theology that began as a way of handling the hermeneutical issues connected with the debate on ordination of women.

The history of biblical scholarship in Iceland, the smallest of the Nordic countries with about 300,000 inhabitants and one university, differs from that of the other countries and is often excluded in works on Nordic biblical scholarship (for an effort to include Iceland, see Bentzen 1949, 281, 299). One reason may be limited resources. There has been a chair in Old Testament Studies since the University of Iceland was founded in 1911, but all professors of the faculty shared the teaching of the New Testament until a New Testament chair was established in 1974. Another reason is that Icelandic scholars, who more often than not have studied outside their country (especially in other Nordic countries and in the United States), have only recently started to publish in international languages and to be active members of international scholarly work, although those who do so are still few in number (Ásgeirsson 2008). While often absent in presentations of Nordic biblical exegesis, Icelandic scholars are present in current Nordic work, as will be shown below.

Through this history it can be seen that streams of influence, formal and informal, and personal relations and collaborations come together to form something that may be characterized as "Nordic biblical scholarship."

Contemporary Biblical Scholarship in the Nordic Countries

In what follows I will give examples of how Nordic biblical scholarship today can be described as going beyond a unique and common content.

Growing Diversity

Contemporary Nordic biblical scholarship is as diverse as international biblical scholarship. Such diversity covers the whole spectrum of criticism—from those who continue to do traditional historical-critical research to those who persistently try to create a new paradigm out of a critique of earlier scholarship from explicit perspectives of power. Therefore, those more specific traits that once existed have faded during the last few decades (Hartman 1992, 1003; Olsson 1999, 76–77; Byrskog 2005, 16). Thus, for example, since Nordic exegetes today relate more and more to the international community of scholars, they seldom publish in their native languages for the general public (Olsson 1999, 76). Even in this respect, however, the picture is not homogenous. There is still a tradition of publishing both academic and popular works in Danish in Denmark.

Another reason for growing diversity is, I believe, the fact that the era of great and strong professors is over, at least partly due to democratic changes at the universities and in society at large. Teamwork involving a group of teachers has in most places replaced the rule of the great professor. Biblical scholarship is also taught at more institutions now than even twenty-five years ago (Moxnes et al. 2000, 45). Although the number of teachers at these institutions is often small, the total number of active biblical scholars may be higher than in the 1950s.

The international scholarly community to which Nordic biblical scholars relate is mainly in northwest Europe, the United States, and the English-speaking world at large. However, liberation theology and other Third World theologies are known in the churches and in academic theology (Moxnes et al. 2000, 49). There are examples of formal relations between universities in the Nordic countries and in the South—for instance, between the University of Umeå, Sweden, and Stellenbosch University, South Africa[9]—in which biblical scholars are also involved, although such relations are not a dominant element in biblical scholarship in the Nordic countries.

---

9. Confirmed in an email dated 2 September 2008 by Mikael Winninge, who taught biblical studies at the University of Umeå for a number of years.

There is also a growing diversity of subjects, a breaking of the dominance of white, male members of the Lutheran national churches. If I focus not on the personal characteristics of individual scholars but on new groups that are becoming visible, I first notice that the number of women is slowly growing. Secondly, I have the impression that the majority of biblical scholars in the Nordic countries are still Christians, but there is today a diversity of confessional affiliations. Even those who identify themselves as agnostics or atheists, or as religious but without identifying themselves with an organized religious tradition, most often come from a Christian background. Immigrants working as biblical scholars at Nordic universities are still normally white Europeans or North Americans (with the exception of some PhD candidates and visiting scholars). There is no audible "Jewish voice" in Nordic biblical scholarship.

So far, the picture of diversity that I have portrayed in biblical scholarship in the Nordic countries today and in the recent past has been rather harmonious. Yet living in a period of change and coping with diversity are never easy. The problem is how to describe the difficulties since, as far as I know, they have not yet been subjected to scholarly analysis. For that reason, my presentation merely shows what is visible on the surface, leaving aside problematic issues connected with diversity and change.

However, what can be said, based on my personal experience and perspective, is that this growing diversity in biblical scholarship in the Nordic countries, both methodological/theoretical diversity and a diversity of subjects, makes it more and more difficult to keep biblical scholars in the Nordic countries together as a group. In scholarly work, methodological and theoretical positions always interact with extra-scholarly factors (such as gender, ethnicity, religious and/ or political beliefs if any, personal experiences, and so on). The more different possible combinations there are of such factors with theoretical/methodological assumptions, the more diverse the category of "biblical scholars" becomes, until a point is reached when it becomes difficult to gather them together on the grounds that we are all biblical scholars living and working in the Nordic countries. The fact that approaches which make the political dimensions of scholarship explicit—feminist/gender perspectives, postcolonial perspectives, and the like—are attracting more and more Nordic scholars contributes to this diversity and to the difficulty of assuming that biblical scholars have enough in common to get together on a regional basis.[10]

---

10. The integration of gender and postcolonial perspectives in contemporary New Testament Scholarship is well illustrated by the conference volume for the Nordic New Testament Conference in 2007; see Holmberg and Winninge (2008).

When talking about diversity, relations between biblical scholars and Jewish communities may be mentioned. Since there is no visible presence of Jewish scholars in the exegetical communities, it was possible for those biblical scholars who wrote biblical theology before and during World War II to read the Hebrew Bible unreflectively as the Christian Old Testament and to reproduce problematic stereotypical images of Jews without having to face criticism from real Jews. At the same time, the Jewish context for early Christianity had been for a long time an important topic in Nordic New Testament scholarship (Hartman 1976, 56–57, 61–62; Hartman 1992, 1003; Baasland 1995, 149, 157–59, with many references), and the first Nordic department for Jewish studies started as part of biblical studies at Åbo Akademi in Turku.

Today, scholars in the Nordic countries share the awareness present in international research regarding anti-Jewish biases in biblical scholarship. Two examples may be mentioned. Swedish New Testament scholars have shown anti-Jewish, not to say anti-Semitic, traits in earlier Swedish New Testament exegesis (Bengtsson 2006; Stendahl 2002, 211–12). Further, in the Danish reception of the "new perspective on Paul" that we find in *Den Nye Paulus og hans betydning,* it is made clear to the reader that one important aspect of this "new perspective" is its contribution to a critique of anti-Jewish biases in biblical scholarship and Christian theology (Engberg-Pedersen 2003s, 11–19). However, for these Danish scholars—I suppose because Jews are a small minority in Denmark—other aspects of the perspective are more important, such as the development of Pauline studies with a strong academic character, not characterized by Lutheran biases, and the development of new theories and methods for the study of the Pauline letters, such as social-science approaches (Fatum 2003, 120–25; Tronier 2003, 158, 179).

Another important aspect of growing diversity has to do with institutions. As mentioned above, biblical scholarship in the Nordic countries during the twentieth century was normally located in theological faculties within nonconfessional state universities, with Menighetsfakultet in Oslo—today an academic institution on a par with the universities—as the notable exception. The nonconfessional character of theological faculties is sometimes seen as a characteristic of the Nordic countries. Relations between theological faculties and national churches have varied over time and among countries, but it may be said generally that these relations have weakened during the last hundred years. However, today there are also in Norway and Sweden academic institutions with an explicit relation to a particular church that provide education recognized by the state as equivalent to the universities. It is important to remember that these institutions may be conservative alternatives to the universities, but they are not always so.

The intention may also be to give ministerial candidates the possibility of integrating academic training and personal faith, theory and praxis.

This development has aroused a number of discussions and questions, still at a beginning stage. From what I have heard and thought, and here I take the risk of being subjective, such issues include the following:

1. Are such church-affiliated institutions places where academic freedom and integrity are constantly under threat, or can they maintain high academic standards while adding other values such as an integration of academic reflection and Christian faith? Can academic freedom and the integrity of scholarship be guaranteed by the internalized professional ethos of biblical scholars who participate in national and international scholarly communities? Is an exegetical education in which Christian perspectives are integrated an equally legitimate consequence of the death of a positivistic ideal of science as is, say, the integration of postcolonial perspectives, or is there something about explicitly Christian perspectives that makes them illegitimate in the academic community? Or are both Christian and political perspectives illegitimate in academic circles?

2. Is it really possible to claim that the state universities are free from biblical scholars with conservative theological agendas? Since the answer is no, the question follows: Is it fair to criticize only those institutions where Christian agendas are explicit, and thus possible to discuss openly? The basic presupposition behind the whole discussion is often, as I have understood it, that the theology behind church-affiliated academic institutions is conservative, not to say reactionary. Is that necessarily the case? Why not imagine such institutions as agents for change in churches and society, motivated by, for example, feminist theology—and as a counterforce to fundamentalist movements in the churches? On the other hand: this may be possible, but is it what is really happening?[11]

CONTEMPORARY NORDIC BIBLICAL SCHOLARSHIP: EXAMPLES

Diversity, however, does not represent the whole story. I will now turn to concrete examples of how the designation "Nordic biblical scholarship" can still be

---

11. I want to express my gratitude to Lars Olov Eriksson and Thomas Kazen for questioning my opinions about church-affiliated academic institutions when a draft of the essay was discussed.

used with reference to cooperation within the framework of a historically given community, and not to a specific and common kind of research. Such cooperative ventures may be analyzed as examples of how "Nordic biblical scholarship" is both presupposed and actually produced through common projects.

My first example is the *Scandinavian Journal for Old Testament Studies* (*SJOT*), which has Danish editors and an editorial board of scholars from all five countries. This journal grew out of a critical discussion in the 1980s about the heritage from "the Scandinavian School in the Old Testament" (Jeppesen and Otzen 1984). In the first issue, its founders programmatically declared that *SJOT* was to be a pragmatically motivated project. It was intended as a platform from which biblical scholars in the Nordic countries who do not have an international language as their native tongue would have an opportunity to speak in international languages in international debates and make the results of their scholarly work, with all their differences, better known internationally.

The programmatic statement makes it clear that the aim of *SJOT* is not to defend "the Scandinavian School" or to replace an old Scandinavian School with a new one. Rather, the scholars working with the journal are united in a common attitude. This "attitude" is not described but, as is also evident from the issues of *SJOT* throughout the years, has to do with research as something dynamic, as a process in which scholars do not defend their results and hypotheses at all costs until their last breath, but rather present their current results and are willing to change their opinions if strong arguments for another option are presented. This "attitude" includes an affirmation of diversity. The *SJOT* is thus an example of how "Scandinavian/Nordic OT studies" is something pragmatic and historically given, not something with a common identity.

Another example, more local in character, from New Testament studies is a collection of articles titled *The Nordic Paul* (although *The Finnish Pauls* seems a better title) and edited by Lars Aejmelaeus and Antti Mustakalio (2008). Its pragmatic and historically given point of departure is the existence of a number of Finnish scholars, Heikki Räisänen as the most influential one from an international perspective, working with Paul's letters. The volume consists of responses by other Finnish scholars to Räisänen's works. The contributors share an academic context, and their work with Paul may also be motivated by the importance of Paul in the Lutheran national church. The aim of the collection is not to reach consensus but to provide a meeting place for scholars who share a context but have different understandings of the biblical texts they study. This work, together with the aforementioned *Den nye Paulus og hans betydning* (Engberg-Pedersen 2003b), which represents a Danish reception of "the New Perspective on Paul," may well be seen as examples of the local receptions of international developments.

Other examples could be taken from various recent and current research projects at different Nordic universities. It would be possible to write a chapter in the national histories of research that focuses on how the conditions for biblical scholarship have changed—for better or for worse, or both—through political decisions concerning the funding of research. The story of the formation of a "Centre of Excellence" in Finland from 1999 to 2005 constitutes a clear example of such developments. It began with work by individual scholars in Septuagint and Nag Hammadi studies, who then proceeded to form research projects in the late 1970s and 1980s, since this was the way to secure financing. In the 1990s such projects were brought together in a Centre of Excellence as a result of political decisions. Here scholars from both Helsinki and Åbo/Turkku worked together on "The Formation of Early Jewish and Christian Ideology" (www.helsinki.fi/teol/hyel/CoE).

Even more interesting in the context of this essay are the networks funded by *NordForsk*, a "Nordic Research Board operating under the Nordic Council of Ministers" and "responsible for Nordic collaboration in research and research training." *NordForsk* is another reason for keeping Nordic scholars together in research networks, conferences, and the like, for which there is an established funding structure. Such *NordForsk* networks formalize, coordinate, and develop contacts among universities and individual scholars that may have grown out of informal relations.

One reason for Nordic collaboration among biblical scholars is that the national groups of scholars are often small. Even those working on internationally important fields, like the Dead Sea Scrolls or feminist exegesis, are often alone at their universities, and maybe even in their countries. However, on a Nordic level it is possible to gather a group of scholars working on the same material or with similar theoretical assumptions, without having everything in common. Such networks may also involve PhD candidates, thus providing them with a broader network beyond their own institutions. *NordForsk*-funded networks and Nordic research groups are also of a manageable size and represent good points of departure for making connections with international scholarship. Among the networks that have been funded recently or are currently being funded, mention may be made of the following: the "Nordic Network on Early Christianity in Its Graeco-Roman Context"[12] with participants from all five Nordic countries and Estonia; the "The Nordic Nag Hammadi and Gnosticism Network"[13] also with

---

12. www.tf.uio.no/ec/index.php. Participants include Halvor Moxnes (University of Oslo), Troels Engberg-Pedersen (University of Copenhagen), and Jon Ma Ásgeirsson (University of Iceland).

13. www.hf.uib.no/ikrr/proak/NNGN.html. The network is interdisciplinary and includes

participants from all five Nordic countries; and the "Nordic Network in Qumran Studies," with scholars from Denmark, Finland, Norway, and Sweden.[14]

Another kind of *NordForsk* network is "Old Testament Studies: Epistemologies and Methods," in which several academic institutions with doctoral program in Denmark, Finland, Norway, and Sweden collaborate with the University of Göttingen to create a wider context for doctoral students and senior scholars.[15] As a consequence of the growing diversity in biblical scholarship, scholars are more specialized now than they were fifty years ago. At the same time, the number of scholars working at each institution may be small. It is therefore difficult to guarantee the necessary breadth of competencies and interdisciplinary connections for a satisfactory doctoral program or internationally valid research in all exegetical fields at every university. The aim of this network is to create a satisfactory academic environment by uniting the forces of a number of universities and scholars.

Finally, different forms of studies on the reception, uses, and effects of the Bible and its interpretations in various contexts today form part of the exegetical agenda in the Nordic countries as well, as seen in publications like *Litteraturen og det hellige* (*Literature and the Holy*) (Davidsen 2005). For example, interdisciplinary work on the Bible and religion in literature at the University of Uppsala has resulted in a number of exegetical dissertations (Olsson 2008). The current professor of Old Testament in Reykjavik has worked on the reception of the Old Testament in movies and in Icelandic poetry (Àsgeirsson 2008). In some places there are institutionalized forms for this kind of work, such as the interdisciplinary Nordic Network for Religion and Literature (including scholars from Denmark, Finland, Norway, and Sweden) based at the University of Aarhus and the "Centre for the Study of the Use of the Bible" at the University of Copenhagen (www.teol.ku.dk/afd/csbb).

Is There a Nordic Biblical Scholarship?

At the beginning of this essay, I questioned the whole idea of a "Nordic biblical scholarship." I hope that I have been able to show that there is something that can be given that name, but that it is not to be defined or described with reference to a common set of theoretical or methodological assumptions, and that it is cer-

---

Antti Marjanen (University of Helsinki) and Einar Thomassen (Institute of Classics, Russian and History of Religions, University of Bergen, Norway).

14. www.nnqs.org. The network was interdisciplinary and coordinated by Torleif Elgvin, Høgskolen i Staffeldsgade, Oslo.

15. www.tf.uio.no/otsem.

tainly not identical with "the Scandinavian School," or any other school. "Nordic biblical scholarship" is a historically given and pragmatically motivated phenomenon that is characterized by both unity and diversity. It is today in some cases also supported by structures for funding research created by political means. It often takes advantage of cultural affinities and in some cases also of the possibility to communicate in one's own language across national borders, although cooperation involving scholars from all five countries on equal terms has to use English as the common language.

In addition to what has already been mentioned, some common characteristics may be noted. It is reasonable to assume that the importance of the Lutheran churches, with their strong emphasis on the preaching of the word of God, in all five countries has contributed to giving biblical scholarship a central position at theological faculties and in theological education. It is clear that the Lutheran context has directed the interest of scholars to parts of the Bible that are important in Protestant theologies, such as the prophets, the Psalms (Thelle 2000, 18), and the letters of Paul (Engberg-Pedersen 2003b). However, the same can most probably be said about biblical scholarship in all places where Protestant churches have a decisive influence. Thus, the Lutheran contexts give Nordic biblical scholarship some of its traits, but these are not always unique. To find something more unique, mention must be made of the streams of influences that led to Sigmund Mowinckel's works on the Psalms. In addition to mentioning the relevance of Pauline studies in Lutheran contexts, mention must also be made of the lines of development that led to the contributions of Krister Stendahl and Heikki Räisänen to the formation of the New Perspective on Paul.

Another characteristic of Nordic biblical scholarship that is sometimes mentioned is a consequence of its history. In both the past and the present, there have been close relations with European, especially German, biblical research and intellectual traditions in general, as well as with the new trends in biblical scholarship in the United States. Therefore, Nordic scholars can act as intermediaries between different scholarly traditions, thereby contributing to international work. This is, for example, explicitly stated as one of the rationales for the formation of the "Nordic Network on Early Christianity in Its Graeco-Roman Context" (see also Baasland 1995, 159).

The Future of Biblical Scholarship in the Nordic Countries

In addition to what has been said about national and Nordic research policies, an important factor already at work has to do with political decisions about academic education and research in the European Union. Developments on the European scene will be decisive for Nordic biblical scholarship in the future.

There will in all probability be a great deal of research in the future on historical problems, text-oriented analyses, linguistic problems, and the like—all that we today include in the wide field of biblical scholarship—in close contact with international developments and from various theoretical perspectives. The possible developments I mention below are not something that I believe will happen instead of such research, but in addition to it.

One set of issues that will be important in the future is the location of biblical scholarship: whether in state universities (in nonconfessional theological faculties or departments for religious studies) or in church-affiliated institutions, or both. Perhaps Nordic biblical scholarship will become even more diverse, or divided, than today. To begin with, between countries where education and research in biblical studies recognized by the state as academically valid will only be possible in nonconfessional state universities and countries where we find academically valid biblical scholarship in different kinds of institutions, including those run by a church. Second, between biblical scholars who openly do their research in relation to the needs and concerns of a certain church and those for whom it is of the utmost importance that their work remain independent of the churches. Lastly, between those church-related scholars who have conservative theological agendas (open or hidden) and those for whom the very point of pursuing biblical scholarship in relation to a church is to be a bulwark against such theologies.

We can also imagine different developments for biblical scholarship in universities. In some places today, biblical studies are located in small departments for religious studies and/or theology in a Faculty of Arts. It will be interesting to see if these new institutional locations have any consequences for the development of education and research. At least opportunities are opened up thereby for more interdisciplinary work in the fields of reception of the Bible and cultural studies.

The development of Nordic societies into multicultural societies also makes it urgent that biblical scholars work in interdisciplinary projects concerning the interpretation of authoritative texts in the past and the present, within the framework of larger projects concerning religion as a social and political factor at various times and in various contexts as well as the problem and possibilities of diversity. The project on "Religion and Normativity" at the University of Aarhus provides a good example of this type of endeavor (www.relnorm.au.dk).

Due to growing religious and cultural diversity, religion is again becoming visible in public spaces and discourses. Religious issues—not formulated by the national churches but by people who do not conform to the cultural norm—claim a place on the political agenda. At the same time, knowledge of religion—not only of non-Nordic churches and nonChristian religions but also of the Christian tradition in its traditional Nordic forms—is diminishing in secularized native populations. Even rather elementary knowledge about the Bible, for example, is becoming something for specialists. There will, therefore, most probably be a strong need in the future for scholars of religion and theology, not only in academic education and research but also in adult education of all kinds and in the public debate.

All those needs and opportunities for interdisciplinary research present biblical scholars with challenges and possibilities. However, we do not know if these challenges will be met and these possibilities turned into realities. I am somewhat pessimistic, and that is not due to any distrust of the goodwill and capacities of biblical scholars. My pessimism is due to the fact that the development of new interdisciplinary networks and projects is only possible if there are a number of scholars with tenure who have time for reflection, time for building relations with scholars from rather different academic traditions and cultures, time for formulating projects and applications, and time for engaging in university politics where they can promote this kind of work. The future lies not only in the hands of scholars but also in the hands of politicians, those who make decisions on funding and those with power at universities who decide if a vacancy shall be filled or not and the nature of the division of time between teaching and other kinds of work for university staff. On the other hand, perhaps power holders at all levels will be enthusiastic about interdisciplinary networks and projects that have an immediate relevance for burning issues in society. Will they be, however, as enthusiastic about research into historical issues or text-oriented studies, textual criticism or Coptic?

The future of Nordic biblical scholarship is connected not only with the future of the universities but also with developments in the churches. Will the national churches still be interested in having clergy with a good knowledge of biblical exegesis, or will more immediately usable disciplines, mainly concerned with contemporary issues, be seen as more important? Without having any studies to rely on, I assume that the churches may even choose different paths. We still do not know what role churches with a more fundamentalist theological stance will play in the future and what the consequences of such a development will be for biblical scholars and scholarship. Will biblical scholars who belong to churches become counter voices to growing fundamentalism? Will they play an important role in churches that are proud of their "liberal" character? Or will they become marginalized in both churches and societies, since biblical scholars of a more evangelical kind in more conservative churches are the only ones who still have a voice outside small, specialized, academic circles?

Perhaps it will be necessary, therefore, for the survival of biblical scholarship, at least in some contexts, that the interdisciplinary connections and cooperations I have suggested above are developed and that biblical scholars show that they have contributions to make to wider fields of study of culture and society in the past and the present. Such biblical scholarship may also be better equipped than so far to work with the issues that I have merely touched upon in this essay: issues concerning the relations between biblical scholarship and its contexts. They may thus deal with issues concerning what happens when biblical scholarship becomes a discipline for persons who are not male members of Lutheran national churches, issues concerning the reception and uses of biblical scholarship in churches and society, issues concerning biblical scholarship in countries where the universities are central in the process of becoming independent and building the nation, and issues concerning biblical scholarship in times of war and times of peace and in societies undergoing rapid change.

PART 4
LATIN AMERICA AND THE CARIBBEAN

9

LIBERATION IN LATIN AMERICAN
BIBLICAL HERMENEUTICS

Pablo R. Andiñach

A combination of social changes, the political climate, and various incipient new winds in the life of the Christian churches supplied the fertile ground in which a new mode of reading the Scriptures began to germinate. Around 1970, the need for other tools with which to understand the Christian mission became evident in Latin America, and what would later come to be called the Theology of Liberation was born, a different way of approaching theological reflection. Alongside this theology, as faithful companion, an alternative way of interpreting the Bible came to be, as well. This is what Juan Luis Segundo (1975, 11–46) developed in his volume *Liberación de la Teología* and what finds its best exponent in the biblical field: the birth of a new hermeneutic out of social and political praxis.

NOVELTY OF LATIN AMERICAN HERMENEUTICS

It is imperative to underscore this sense of novelty, for it distinguishes the new hermeneutic from almost all that had preceded. Latin American biblical hermeneutics does not emerge in centers of theological studies, nor is it the product of an individual author who creates a school of thought and whose work is then continued by disciples. It is, rather, the result of bringing intellectual order on what Christians were already doing in their congregations and parishes. At the same time, it is also a search for deepening reflection on the Bible in order to construct, on the basis of such a praxis of liberation—that is the hermeneutical *circle*—a new way of reading the sacred texts that sustains the work of believers in their quest for liberation and justice.

J. SEVERINO CROATTO

A fundamental work in this movement is a small volume authored by Severino Croatto, *Liberación y Libertad* (1981). This is a hermeneutical exercise that takes the paradigm of the exodus and reads the different parts of the Old Testament and the New Testament in the light of it. The volume follows the narrative sequence of the Bible, yet this order is inverted at various times by starting with the exodus and then moving on to the narratives of Genesis. The latter are thus read in the light of the exodus, and not in canonical order, as had been the case up to that time. The volume presents the prophets as those who assist human beings in becoming conscientized with regard to their condition of oppression, and who call them to rebellion in accordance with the word of God. With regard to the New Testament, the volume explores the liberating attitudes of Jesus and how such attitudes are reread by Paul, who proposes a way out of the threefold alienation affecting human beings: sin, death, and the law. It is the paschal understanding—and the link with the exodus from Egypt should be noted—that sheds light on the message of the Gospels.

The impact of this volume could not have been more revealing for the new generations of biblical scholars in Latin America. The book explains how biblical theology finds its structural frame in the concept of liberation and in the historical experience of recalling that the God who guides the people during their pilgrimage in the wilderness and throughout the whole of their subsequent history is the same God who triumphed over pharaoh and who delivered their ancestors from slavery. As a result, the memory of liberation from oppression and death became a constitutive criterion for reflection and for the development of theological thought—the spiritual and religious support—first on the part of the people of Israel and then, later, on the part of the nascent Christian church. The volume covers the various parts of the Bible and analyzes how the paradigm of liberation lies at the basis of a good number of its postulates and expressions. These general readings Croatto would later expand into works of great magnitude, such as the commentary on Genesis 1–11 and the great commentary on Isaiah, which now, regrettably, are largely forgotten.

CARLOS MESTERS

At about the same time, Carlos Mesters was beginning to develop his search for a popular hermeneutic. In the process, he produced an immense range of materials for the propagation of the Bible on a key of liberation, which materials served to encourage the expansion of the base ecclesial communities. These communities saw their numbers multiply on a daily basis among the poor sectors of Brazil and, in time, of other countries of Latin America. Given their social and political commitments, they posed a challenge to traditional ecclesial structures. More importantly, they took part in popular movements and contributed to struggles for justice throughout the continent. These communities became one of the sources of raw materials mined by the biblical hermeneutic of liberation in its more sophisticated reflections.

The main value of Mesters' work lay in translating the often complex interpretation of the biblical text into the language of the poor. This was especially true insofar as such translation sought not a simple rephrasing of the biblical narratives but rather a foregrounding of their political and social consequences as well as of their incentives toward a praxis of social transformation (1983, 154–68). This he did in dozens of books and articles, which reached those sectors of society most removed from knowledge of the Bible and invited them to engage in mature and committed reflection. At the same time, Mesters, like few others, proved successful in incorporating the language of the poor and of the communities into their own reflections. Thus he not only rendered the Scriptures in popular language, but he also took popular language—its concepts, cosmovision, desires, and so forth—and played with it in the reading of the texts. The impact of his work has been immense and its enduring value is beyond measure.

Jorge Pixley and Gustavo Gutiérrez

At approximately the same time, other authors, such as Jorge Pixley and Gustavo Gutiérrez, were exploring the possibilities of the biblical text in terms of concrete situations. Pixley began by publishing a commentary on the book of Job (1982), in which he dabbled in the critique of theological language and its consequences for the process of liberation. Later he moved on to a commentary on Exodus (1983), a work that was written from within the very context of the struggles for liberation in Nicaragua. This work represents an attempt to take the contextual nature of reading to its ultimate consequences, bestowing on biblical narrative the character of a structural framework for revolutionary action. Pixley succeeds in making the context of the reader the key to reading, as well as the criterion for choosing among the various options for interpretation. In so doing, he also succeeds in making the text into a hermeneutic for the times in which the reader lives. This is its greatest virtue as well as its limitation. Read at a distance, Pixley's Exodus reveals itself as a boundary that closes off the horizon for other possible readings, leaving the reader little space for successive applications of the text to new situations. For Gutiérrez, it is the incomprehensible character of human suffering and the lack of sensibility in reacting to it that lead to his commentary on Job (1986).

It is curious to see two authors choose to work, at the dawn of Latin American biblical production, on a book from the Wisdom corpus. This section of the Hebrew Bible is considered to be a production emerging from the context of the palace and hence attached to the tranquillity of its halls. It is a corpus quite removed from the prophets, with their urgent and explosive literature, which is more in keeping with the times actually lived in Latin America at that point and, at the same time, closer to the needs for ideological sustenance on the part of engaged Christians. Clearly, however, such analysis of Job made it possible to see Latin American biblical hermeneutics as more than a simple selection of texts that could be easily transferred onto the social situation and the struggles for liberation of the continent. In effect, the Bible was not being used as a tool at the service of ideology—no matter how sympathetic such ideology should prove to the interpreter to be; rather, all corners and all possibilities of the Bible were being explored.

What is surprising is that precisely in the Wisdom corpus, which the manuals state is focused not on issues of urgent social concern but on a discurse that looks like metaphysical meditation. Pixley's reading finds that the book of Job constitutes a "fundamental critique of theological method" (1982, 16) and points out that the friends of Job and Elihu represent the traditional thinking of the Israelite sages who construct their thought on unquestionable premises, which they then use to approach a changing reality. Such is also the way, Pixley continues, of contemporary idealist philosophy, which remains unaware of the real historical processes at work and leaves aside the suffering of the masses. A "theology that rests on a violation of human dignity," Pixley concludes, has neither future nor entity. Pixley declares, "Traditional religion and theology have been cruelly unmasked. The worst part is not that they have been unable to explain correctly the suffering of Job, but rather that they have contributed to the suffering of a just man" (1982, 15).

In his volume on Job, Gutiérrez points out that the book exposes the human drama at play in the suffering of the innocent, who are not understood by those around them. He finds that millions of people lived in his continent, at that point in time, the same ancient drama: society—and the church—contemplates unjust suffering and death, attributing to the victims the responsibility for their fate. They assume that it is the sins of those who suffer that stain and darken their souls, or that it is their laziness and lack of economic initiative that condemn them to poverty and marginalization. Gutiérrez seeks in Job answers to the anguish of witnessing millions of human beings consigned to social and cultural death, a death that, without falling into concordism, resembles the experience of this biblical character, upon whom fall all sorts of calamities without his knowing or being able to imagine the reason why. At times, Gutiérrez's interpretation moves toward a spirituality that attempts to account for the only thing that remains for Job: his life, his feelings, his intimate conviction of his innocence. Gutiérrez, however, is not deceived. He observes the evidence of the injustices and their prolongation in time, leading him to question the responsibility of the Creator in the history of oppression and human suffering. "Justice by itself," Gutiérrez concludes, "does not have the last word in speaking about God" (1986, 160). There is more to be said, and that is the subject matter of Job's drama.

Various Contemporary Hermeneutics

As a natural consequence of the criteria that served as the foundation for Latin American hermeneutics, a variety of new hermeneutics began to emerge in response to challenges previously unforeseen. The last decade of the twentieth century witnessed the rise of new actors on the social and political scene who modified the terrain of social struggles and who had remained, up to that time, at the margins of political reflection and, hence, of theological reflection as well. Once more, we can observe how social practices generate their own word, their own language, and give expression in thought to the aspirations that lie behind them, the utopias that call them together, and the life that gives them support. In our continent, this word that is forged in the secular arena is not foreign to the theological task. Indeed, not long upon its appearance, theological reflection follows, pointing to the commitment of Christians in various spheres of social reality.

In Latin America, the work of biblical scholars is intimately tied to the work of those theologians to whom we customarily refer as systematic, even if they may not be so in the strict sense of the term. In many cases, the two disciplines go together in the same individual (e.g., the works of Gustavo Gutiérrez, Juan Luis Segundo, José Míguez Bonino). In others, the relation is also close, so that, even when the two fields are distinguished, it proves difficult to set them clearly apart. What cannot be denied is that in Latin America theological thought always goes hand in hand with a specific way of understanding the Bible, thereby encouraging and supporting a particular hemeneutic. In what follows I shall mention four such approaches represented by four different authors, who in turn represent different movements, groupings, and tendencies—all of which intersect with one another in good measure. Three of these have an enormous body of works, so that I take one from each in order to simplify my exposition.

Humberto Ramos Salazar

Ramos Salazar passed away before his time but left behind his Aymara Theology (1997). In this work, a product of his life experience as both an Aymara and a Christian, he sought to approach Christian theology from the context of the Aymara people.[1] Such a task, however, he was unable to carry out without first setting forth their cosmovision, their understanding of God, their clash with Western culture, their despoliation, historical and ongoing, at the hands of the white world. How to be both Aymara and Christian, when such a religion arrived as a companion to the injustices perpetrated on and the condemnation passed on the culture of his ancestors? How to accept the Bible, given its use, historical and ongoing, to justify the destruction of their social network and the conquest of their lands? Such questions as these constitute the structural framework for the work of Ramos Salazar, which it pursues in depth, seeking to find that point at which the message of Jesus of Nazareth casts off the clothes of the invaders and the vestments of the oppressors and begins to shine like a word that liberates and calls for the restoration of life.

In this search Ramos Salazar came to the conclusion that Aymara theology must find nourishment "in the God of Israel, who reveals himself to his ancestors, who is the liberator that guides the people during the exodus, the God who comforts the people in exile and accompanies them in reconstructing their history. This is the God whom the people call by a variety of names" (1997, 132). Let us pause for reflection on this statement. In it a biblical hermeneutic comes to expression that includes a number of elements that strike a chord in the experience of the Aymara people and other native peoples. The key terms in question are: "ancestors"; "liberator" God; "guides the people"; "exodus"; "the God who comforts in exile"; "reconstructing their history." It is difficult not to see such words as an invitation to find in the God of the Bible the God who stands beside the Aymara people, helping them to overcome their situation of postponement. From the appeal to the ancestors to the reconstruction of a mutilated history, the reading proposed by Ramos Salazar is profoundly rooted in his cultural experience, as well as in his search for a biblical faith that may serve as an efficient tool for the rescue of all that Western expression and culture relegated to oblivion and misery. Today there is an exile that reclaims a new exodus; there is a history repressed that must be reconstructed; there is a pain that calls for consolation, not in order to find resignation but rather to discern the hope of a liberated future.

On the very same page, after this statement, Ramos Salazar concludes by stating that Aymara theology should be constructed on the basis of the God of the New Testament. This aspect of his position is not in contradiction to the above; rather, it provides for him the theological framework with which to read

---

1. See also the issue of *Revista de Interpretación Bíblica Latinoamericana* dedicated to him (27 [1997]). The Aymara constitute one of the major native peoples of present-day Bolivia. Ramos Salazar was a pastor in and later president of the Lutheran Church in Bolivia.

the Old Testament. The Aymara people seek orientation from the biblical narratives about struggles and longings, and they see in the Christ who died and rose the love of God that they did not find in the mouths of the Christian conquerors. It is there, in Christ, that they find the criterion for reading the Old Testament.

Ivone Gebara

Gebara has explored the link between ecology and the condition of woman in numerous works (2002; 2004). While her work does not belong to the field of biblical studies as such, it has had such an impact on them that one would be hard pressed to find any biblical scholar who makes no reference to her thought in the grounding of a feminist approach to the biblical texts. From a theological point of view, her thinking is also eccentric. Its point of departure lies neither in reason nor in faith as such. It explores, rather, the roots of religious experience as part of an interior quest in which she finds nourishment toward a profound spirituality. She discovers that the oppression of men over women has a parallel in the destruction of nature, and she argues that only in overcoming both can we cease from destroying one another as human beings.

Her approach to the Bible proves more problematic. Gebara does not seek in the Bible a reading of liberation from male oppression. She looks upon the Bible, rather, as a product of patriarchal ideology, for which the texts serve both as expression and as religious legitimation. From her perspective, the Bible is a book that can be helpful in our thinking, taking the old stories about the fathers and mothers of antiquity as point of departure. It does not constitute, however, a special revelation—a word that bears greater authority than others and that must serve as orientation for our theological thought. Despite such a position, her influence on the theological and feminist movement has been significant and has led to a rereading of the Scriptures on the issue of gender. In fact, the latest works from Latin America on gender criticism have begun to include theological reflection in their repertoire. As a result, it is no longer possible to think of a hermeneutic that does not take into account, at least as one of its semiotic actors, the question of gender.

Leonardo Boff

Boff has been one of the most prolific authors of Latin American theology. Although his emphasis has not been on biblical studies, the influence of his work on those who engage in hermeneutics in pastoral circles has been notable. In his most recent works, Boff, like Gebara, has placed the topic of ecology at the center of his reflection. The expression, "the earth cries out and the poor cry out," which is taken from the title of one of his books (1996), reveals his awareness that the act of oppressing the poor bears the same face as the act of destroying the house in which we dwell. One need not agree with all that Boff argues in his book—many Latin American theologians have distanced themselves from its central theses—to realize that the relationship of human beings with the earth finds itself at a critical point, and that it is imperative to bring about changes in the mode of production and exploitation if life is to be preserved.

The original aspect of Boff's thought in this regard lies in his construction of a theology based on the following twofold observation: the world that has emerged from modernity has ruptured the alliance between human beings and the cosmos, and the Christian tradition bears a good deal of responsibility for such a rupture. Moreover—and this is particularly of note for this study—Boff holds that a number of biblical texts support the attitude of human domination and oppression over nature. Texts that promote such "domination of the earth" (Gen 1:8, 9:7; Ps 8:6–8) are viewed as the theoretical support for that thirst of bringing all under the control of human beings, without limits of any kind. As a result, domination has led to the exploitation of nature beyond measure, and such exploitation has led in turn to devastation (1996, 104–105). From this point Boff proceeds as follows: first he develops a critique of monotheism, anthropocentrism, exclusivist tribal ideology, and other elements characteristic of the classic Christian theological tradition; then he offers to reconstruct theology from a model to which he gives the name of eco-spirituality. This consists in a "relinking" (a term he coined to mean "to join together again") with the cosmos, discovering a new form of spirituality that goes beyond human beings to include the resurrection of nature, of the inanimate world, and even of celestial bodies (237–38).

Boff does not develop in his work a particular approach to biblical interpretation as such. However, his thought does open up new ways, which are already being traversed by other authors, although they have not yet come to expression in major works. As the ecological crisis continues to move toward center stage in the discourse of our societies, a theological and biblical word will come to expression. In this regard, the reflection of Boff on this topic has been trailblazing.

Néstor Míguez

What has come to be characterized as the intercultural reading of the Bible constitutes a bridge among different discourses. Míguez has elaborated both a biblical and theological reflection and a practice regarding this space of encounter among cultures. In so doing, he has joined a process of reflection that has been taking place around the world (2004, 334–47; 2006, 120–29). This hermeneutical path reveals the following features: (1) reading is shared with readers from different cultural contexts; (2) the different modes of approaching the text are compared; (3) how different aspects fo the text are highlighted by different cultural context; and (4) the influence of the cultural context of readers upon their readings is foregrounded. The contrast with classic "culturalist" interpretations is clear. The latter, upon pointing out the influence of the cultural context upon the reading, proceed to relativize its conclusions by assigning to it—and precisely on such grounds—inferior value, as if the presence of the cultural element weakened the interpretation in question. Intercultural interpretations move in the opposite direction: they assign value to the cultural ingredients and look upon them as a key with which to open dimensions of the message absent in other cultures. This is a hermeneutic that builds on convergence rather than exclusion.

Intercultural criticism proves quite rich not only when European and Latin American readings are juxtaposed, but, above all when readings from the world of the West are juxtaposed in Latin America with readings produced by believers from the world of indigenous peoples. Major communities from among the native peoples of America are reading the Scriptures and producing a renewal of interpretation by situating the Scriptures at the heart of their own traditions. Nevertheless, Míguez does warn that readings coming from the Third World have a tendency—still perhaps in a majority of cases—to reproduce the theology of the missions. He states, "The basic orientation of the missionaries and of the denominational origins persists, more than people realize, beyond their presence and through various experiences" (2004, 340). At the same time, intercultural reading helps to put in perspective our own interpretations, which we tend to regard as normative and unquestionable. Such a confrontation with the reading of the "other" signifies, to a certain degree, a first step in self-critique of our own understanding of the text, leading toward the realization that another view of the text is possible and that other parameters exist for assigning value to the Scriptures.

A constitutive element of intercultural reading is a new understanding of the "ordinary reader." To place the text at the heart of a community and to engage in shared reading calls into question academic reading, even the reading offered in commentaries for lay people, which have recourse to simple language but reproduce the "technical" interpretation and thus rescues the reading undertaken in the base communities. This type of reading is not new in Latin America, as reference to the work of Mesters and others has already shown. It does, however, pose a dilemma that remains unresolved: how to prevent "spontaneous" and popular readings from reproducing the dominant ideologics or from being insufficiently critical of their own point of view. Intercultural reading does represent a way of overcoming regional and limited reading. At the same time, however, the question remains to what extent such reading remains a product of academic contexts that seek to access the world in its global and transcultural dimension. This challenge is still open for reflection in this interesting new perspective on approaching the Scriptures.

Synthesis: Encounters and Mis-Encounters

Various other hermeneutical approaches at work in Latin America could be described. It might be worth pointing out that the examples referred to above are usually traversed by a variety of critical methods. One should at least mention two tendencies that do not exclude but rather feed one another. These define, more or less, the particular points of emphasis of any given author. One can say, therefore, that tension exists in Latin American hermeneutics between a reading that privileges the sociological dimension and a reading that privileges the literary dimension.

The sociological reading has been characterized as a reading "from the four sides." This is based on the visual image of a frame of which each side represents a concept—political, ideological, social, and economic. Texts are analyzed from these four angles of reading not in mechanical fashion but certainly by making use of analytic tools adopted from sociology and politics, as well as critical tools taken from the so-called "materialist reading" of texts. This way of reading has yielded quite interesting and fruitful results, even if it probably reveals, in its most direct application, a hermeneutical limit.

Sociological reading has two commitments as its foundation": (1) that the conditions of production of the text and the social and political actors that took part in its constitution can be identified; and that their interests—in terms of class, gender, economics, and so forth—can be exposed, to a degree. Once the actors have been identified, it is then possible to read the text by unmasking its hidden ideological intentions and seeking to reconstruct its message by overcoming contradictions. This approach clearly entails confidence in the tools of historical and social reconstruction, as well as a disposition to look for the message in the deep semiotic relations of the text rather than in the form of the text as it stands.

To my mind, a twofold critique of this approach is in order. First, such a reading privileges a hypothetical reconstruction of the text. Second, such a move may lead, in turn, to a hermeneutic built on a weak foundation. At the same time, the ability of this reading to expose the factors of power and ideology that lie hidden between the lines of narratives is notable. This is true in both respects: on the one hand, there are texts that reveal themselves as justifying the usurpation of lands (such as the book of Joshua); on the other hand, liberative elements are discovered in other texts that had remained previously undetected (as in the case of certain psalms or in the creation texts of Genesis).

The literary reading, with its privileging of the literary features of texts, derives from the work of Croatto, especially his *Biblical Hermeneutics* (1994). Here Croatto examines the possibilities of exploring the text as text, seeking to analyze its internal relations, its literary aspects, and its deep structures. Far from confining himself to a so-called structuralist reading, he proposes to go beyond any such technical application by placing hermeneutics, strictly speaking, as the final aim of textual analysis. One can readily understand thereby the convergence of different methods in the final leap, whose purpose it is to bring to light the *reserve of meaning*—what is in the text but goes beyond the intention of its first author, and thus what is forged in the contact between the reality of the text under investigation and reflection and the reality of the reader. This reality of the reader is personal and intimate, as well as social and political. Consequently, hermeneutics represents the last step, following the analysis of the text in its three dimensions: the "archeology" of the text, disclosed by historical-critical methods; the text "in itself," analyzed by means of the structuralist method, with its focus on surface and deep relations; and "the forward of the text," which has to do with its *kerygma*, its relevance for the reality of the reader. Once all such roads have been explored, the reader comes to the final moment: reading the text from within life itself. At this point, the context of the reader—social, cultural, personal, and so forth—is illumined by the text, and the text, in turn, reveals its secrets when read from such a context.

As is the case with every method, this one too has its limits. In effect, should the critical tools not be used properly in the analysis of the text, the result may be a reading that is personal or naive or that is ideologically biased, regardless of direction. At the same time, when used to promote the popular reading of the Bible, the literary approach has proved most fruitful for biblical interpretation. Even though the academic version of this approach demands a great deal of knowledge and sophistication, results of the communitarian and popular reading carried out in study and reflection groups have been especially noteworthy.

In no way do the social and political reading of the texts and the literary approach exclude one another. To the contrary, critics make use of both, depending on the critical direction in question. One should note, however, that these readings have recourse to different fields of study: the sociological appeals to the social sciences and, in biblical studies, to classical archaeology and history; the literary appeals to linguistics and hermeneutical theory (for example, Gadamer and Ricoeur). To my mind, the best work in Latin American biblical studies happens where these approaches convergence and enrich each other.

Conclusion

Over and beyond all that has been said above, it is still the case that in Latin America, biblical interpretation continues to be a reflection in search of collaboration with the concrete quest for liberation. That quest is not the same today as it was in decades past. The reality of marginalization and poverty has in many cases grown worse. This is a situation that inevitably generates its own social praxis and, with it, its own word. This word, insofar as it is theological, proceeds to feed again the hermeneutical circle, setting biblical reflection on its course. Once again, new social actors and new challenges to believers will enrich such work and bring encouragement to new generations.

10

Paper Is Patient, History Is Not: Readings and Unreadings of the Bible in Latin America (1985–2005)

Nancy Cardoso Pereira

The Bible in Latin America is many things at once.[1] As a "book" of a historically imposed religion, the Bible participates in the religious and cultural polyphony of Latin America in a way that is conflictive and marked by ambiguities. As a religion imposed, Christianity has no positive contribution to make. There is no way to change such an assessment without compromising facts as well as historical interpretations well known to all.

Milton Schwantes and Pablo Richard address this imposition from the point of view of the indigenous peoples (1992, 3): "After 500 years of conquest and colonization, the indigenous peoples of Latin America are still alive! It has been the indigenous religions that have fundamentally allowed the indigenous peoples to resist and survive, many times in spite of and in the face of 'Christian evangelization.' The Bible was, oftentimes, used as an instrument of spiritual conquest." Such imposition should also be considered historically and culturally from the perspective of the enslaved black peoples of Latin America, as does Heitor Frissoti (1994, 48): "The Bible is *a wound* because it was not neutral. During the colonial period, it was called upon as witness that God was on the side of the King [*sic*], the slave master, the rich man, the bishop, the white man, man. A wound, and a mortal wound, that managed to kill the liberty, the dignity, the faith, and the identity of black people," to which he subsequently adds, "It was used then to legitimate the condition of suffering of the black man and to 'curse' his race. The text most often used was Gen 9:18–27, with which Africans were identified as the cursed children of Ham."

---

1. This essay has been translated from the Portuguese by Fernando F. Segovia.

Christianity ceases to be an imposed religion when it finally looks into the eyes of the continent, into the many faces of many peoples, when it accepts to be one religion among others, one possibility for salvation among others. The process of inculturation of Christianity in Latin America demands the collapse of the hegemonic models of Christianity brought from the outside, Catholic as well as Protestant, and launches a complex and uninterrupted process of ecclesial formatting. In this way Christianity can stop being an imposed religion and become instead a welcomed religion. This is an exuberant process, which finds its most developed explanation in the efforts of liberation theology, but it cannot be limited to this expression.[2] The same may be said with respect to the Bible, as Milton Schwantes puts it:

> In Latin America the Bible is being rediscovered. This rediscovery reveals a new way of understanding Scripture. A new approach to the texts is being tested. The new reading is, in the first place, profoundly liturgical. It is rooted in the coexistence of the community, in its songs, in its prayer, in its Eucharist. It was not conceived in academicism or in the rational world. Its cradle is the communitarian liturgy. It comes from and addresses community practice. It is the struggles for land and a roof that, among us, push and inspire the rediscovery of biblical history. It is the oppression of poor women and the spoliation of the working class that drive the optic of reading. They demand an interpretation that departs from what is concrete and what is social, from the pains and the utopias of the Latin American people. (Schwantes 1989, 87)

Thus it is that the Bible is everywhere! In places important and unimportant: always present! In its simplest commonsense use—as in fenders of trucks, on the doors of homes, as names of stores, and even in the churches. In its systematic and plagiarized study in theological seminaries and churches. In its distrustful and reticent treatment on the part of academic research.

The paths of this liberating reception of the biblical text in Latin America, its achievements and trends of the last twenty-five years, may be approached in various ways (see Gebara 2005). My own presentation here is but one possibility among others. I would like it to be an exercise in polyphony, an exercise in interpretation in which—in the words of the Zapatista rebels of Chiapas, Mexico—many worlds can fit. My odds in so doing, in offering such a comprehensive vision, are small. Here Wolfgang Fritz Haug is to the point: "Interpretation is historically situated. It is rooted in its own point of view and its perspectivism is unavoidable. Thus, the interpreter should know that he is also not protected from blunders and mistakes, the admission of which gives sense to his critique. Paper

---

2. For the fundamentalist reading of the Bible, see Zabatiero 1998.

is patient, but history in flux is not" (2000, 146). For that reason I hope to be able to present how I construct my assessment of biblical reading in Latin America during the period 1985–2005, taking as point of departure the so-called popular reading, its variations, objections, and crises.

The volume put together by Raúl Vidales in 1982, *Volveré … y seré millones*,[3] presents a reflection on "The Historical Subject of Liberation Theology" ("El sujeto histórico de la Teología de la Liberación"), leading to a debate with Enrique Dussel, Hugo Assmann, Jürgen Moltmann, Luis Rivera Pagán, and others. (This was a time when we female theologians did not yet exist, they would say!) The questions and debates are extremely honest, almost severe, difficult. Nothing remains untouched; everything can be critiqued. Dussel sallies forth, "If theology departs from theology, then I take up Kittel's Wörterbuch. If theology departs from the Christian community, then I depart from the history of the church. But if theology should like to depart from the concrete reality of action on the part of those oppressed minorities, the problem is far more complex and demands a greater precision in categories as well" (1985, 6). In this dialogue one can sense the concerns of liberation theology and the methodological implications for biblical research: the Bible is not even the point of departure, nor the motivation. The assumption, then, should be that the "peasant/popular subject" is Christian and reads the Bible. One would then need to establish that the Bible is central to the religiosity of this "peasant/popular subject."

I formulate this exercise of mine with this recollection in mind: We learn with Marx and Engels that ideas have no history. Naturally, that there is a history of ideas is not a point for discussion. What is meant, rather, is that the driving force behind such history is not ideas, but the material history that constitutes the subtext of ideal history.

The popular reading of the Bible in Latin America does not have a history of its own. It moves, rather, within history as part of a larger theoretical field that one might refer to as Latin American critical thinking.[4] It does so as praxis for the production of knowledge starting with popular education (Schinelo and Pereira 2007) and the plural experience of participation on the part of Christian communities in popular struggles and movements (Mesters and Rodrigues Orofino

---

3. The title recovers the phrase attributed to Tupac Katari, a native leader in the struggle against colonial violence: "I shall come back … and will be millions."

4. See *Cadernos de Pensamento Crítico Latino Americano*, Clacso/Expressão Popular. This publication venture is described by the joint publishers as follows: "Why Latin American critical thinking? Because it has vindicated our historical trajectory in the face of eurocentric paradigms and has tried systematically to strengthen our identity, calling into question the conservative thinking fostered by the main powers of capitalism."

2007). Even if one acknowledges that the popular reading does not have hermeneutical hegemony, its effects and shifts during the past twenty years can sustain a critical assessment and the contradictions thereof.

I select various examples of the Latin American reading of the Bible of the past twenty-five years, all of which are characterized by the mystique of groups of study and reflection and a common effort of socialization and publication. I should like to refer in a special way to the Projeto do Comentário Bíblico Latino Americano and the Revista de Interpretación Bíblica Latino Americana (*RIBLA*).[5]

THE POPULAR READING OF THE BIBLE (1985–2005): WHO IS THE PEOPLE?

The following brief story offered by José Comblin forms part of his *Introdução geral ao Comentário Bíblico* (Comblin 1985). The text begins by stating, "This is a Latin American commentary of the Bible." By means of a parable, Comblin addresses the character and motivations of the Latin American Commentary.

A peasant found it odd that the priest would read a passage from the Bible every Sunday and that every Sunday the Bible would prove him right. The peasant would say: "It cannot be that the Bible always proves the priest right but never us, the peasants. I think that the priest does not read it all but chooses only what suits him." And so it was: the readings proposed by the liturgy were chosen and the preachers would comment only on what suited them. Now, what interested the peasants was precisely what was left out, what the clergymen would not read, much less comment upon.

On the one side, one finds the "peasant" and his distrust. On the other side, there is the "parish priest" and his control over the biblical text. This encounter between the distrust of the peasant and the power of the priest takes place "every Sunday" within the space provided by the liturgy. The power of choosing and commenting on the biblical texts belongs to the priest, who undertakes his reading with the authority to "choose only what suits him." The peasant has the power of suspicion, of listening to the reading and identifying the lacunae of meaning, identifying the text as accommodated to the "reasons of the priest" and de-authorizing the Bible for its lack of interest in "peasant reason." The distrust of the peasant comes to expression in the formula, "It cannot be!"—an intuition that the Bible is not being communicated in its entirety—"the priest is not reading all

5. For information about *RIBLA*, see: http://www.RIBLA.org/. There one can access all contents of all volumes in Spanish. For information about the Comentário Bíblico, see: www.loyola.com.br/livraria/detalhes.aspx?COD=12193.

of it"—and a demand that the Bible be read in terms of what "interests the peasants."

This text translates well the situation of Latin American biblical reading in 1985, within the framework of the struggles for liberation that spanned the continent, the movements of resistance against the violence of the military dictatorships, and the evangelical radicalism of liberation theology. The conflicts of the class struggle come to expression as well in the ecclesial space, on "Sundays" and its "liturgies," in the unequal power between priest and peasant, in the biblical reading marked by opposing interests, in the struggle for the process of producing, managing, and socializing the meanings of belief.

The reading of the Bible controlled by a priestly-intellectual bureaucratic corps prevents lay people from having access to the hermeneutical process and participating in the production of theological meanings. More than the clergy-layperson opposition, Comblin's commentary assumes the class contradiction in the framework of biblical reading, in the opposition between a segment that controls knowledge and the knowledge of the "peasant."

In the last twenty-five years, this perception of the field of reading, studying, and interpreting the Bible as a field of power and conflict was vital for the development of critical and creative work in methodologies, procedures, and strategies that might constitute the "distrust of the peasant" as an epistemic site and a site of spirituality that characterize Latin American biblical reading.

The *Comentário Bíblico* project thus assumed hermeneutical partiality as a value, rendering impossible any attempt at or presumption of universality and objectivity on the part of any other commentary. All knowledge produced, within the field of biblical sciences as well, is historically and politically engendered, linking concepts and theoretical and interpretive formulations to lived and experienced social relations of power. The *Comentário* puts it this way:

> This commentary seeks to gather an interpretation of the Bible as lived by the practice of the Christian people in Latin America at the end of the 20th century. It is conscious of the partiality of meaning thus gathered. However, even though it is partial, it has the advantage of being lived. It has nothing to do with a meaning that is purely abstract; it has to do, rather, with something experienced.

It may be said that all commentaries do the same thing. There is, however, one difference. Academic commentaries do not always explicitly state the practice from which they emerge and do not formulate the practice that they wish to establish. This commentary makes it a point to explicitly state both the practice from which it emerges and the practice to which it aspires. It does not hide its origins or its trajectory.

In this sense the Latin American biblical reading expressed in the project of the *Comentário Bíblico Latino Americano* reflected the political and pastoral practices in solidarity with the social movements and liberation struggles of the continent during the period following the military dictatorships (1960–1985). The *Comentário* gathered—and continues to do so still—biblical scholars from universities, churches, and pastoral organizations to create a common space for reflection, study, and production.

The desire to gather the interpretation lived by the practice of the people is presented as a project that is admittedly "partial," "lived," and "experienced," a project inserted within a real practice, within a trajectory. This explicit disclosure of the conflictive character of the production of knowledge and meaning is vital in methodological formulations and implies an acknowledgement of a Latin American religious field marked by class struggle and class interests.

The Social Locations of the Popular Reading of the Bible

This emplacement of 1985 is not limited to the space and figures of the *Comentário Bíblico Latino Americano*. It finds vigorous expression as well in a number of other venues: the *RIBLA* project; the processes of articulating the movement of popular biblical reading, its courses and publications, organized today by REBILAC (Rede Bíblica Latino-Americana e Caribenha); the project of the Bibliografía Bíblica Latino-Americana;[6] and in countless initiatives of biblical popular reading that have taken place throughout the continent since 1985.

These initiatives were collectively generated by a group of biblical theologians who identified with liberation theology and who had a very clear strategic and political vision: ideas do not make history. It is new practices that alter the ways of reading reality and the world. Such questions were duly addressed at various points during the course of the Latin American journey. The very first issue of *RIBLA* proposed a title for such practices: *The Popular Reading of the Bible in Latin America* (*A leitura popular da Bíblia na América Latina*). Its third issue proceeded to clarify it: *The Option for the Poor as Criterion of Interpretation* (*A opção pelos pobres como critério de interpretação*).

The demand to take the concrete reality of the masses as point of departure demands greater precision in the categories of analysis, but this does not substitute for the "action of the oppressed masses" that was assumed as the locus of experience. The Latin American biblical reading assumes the lived experience of

---

6. See: http://www.metodista.br/biblica/.

the oppressed masses as epistemic and hermeneutical location. Here a distinction between point of departure and motivation may be important.

To take the experience of the oppressed masses as point of departure may reduce the experience of reality to exemplary cases, without real intervention in the construction of knowledge itself. This can, in fact, be seen in texts and readings of this period that assume the reality of the oppressed masses as prologue to exegetical and hermeneutical studies but without effective interference in the procedures of criticism and analysis of texts, confining themselves many times to a delimitation of the topic. The result was evident: popular topics, introduced by narratives taken from the life of the people, followed by traditional exegetical procedures.

If we understand the reality of the oppressed masses as motivation, then we should identify the materiality of this experience, interfering in and modifying the method, subordinating exegetical procedures to the materialities of the oppressed masses. From this point of view, the scientific procedures do not remain intact, and the biblical scholar is no longer interested in keeping the location of the Bible in culture and the church. If it is the oppressed masses who do the reading and the interpretation, the location of the scientific categories needs to let itself be swayed by elements from the action itself of these masses, leading to modification of the comfortable and preformatted framework of the study of the Bible and of its authority in culture.

A reflection that seeks to engage popular religiosities should accept the challenge of revising the form of the discourse. The affirmation of the reflection constructed on the basis of the expressions and narratives of religious practices on the part of the popular classes—especially poor women—contradicts the competent discourse governing reality on the part of the dominant—especially men—and its instruments of control through science, history, documentation, and meaning. The plurality of expressions should not be seen as an obstacle to the objectivity of the reflection but rather as fundamental raw material for the production of a knowledge of the real that acknowledges the social fabric as a complex web of relations.

The emergence of new social actors previously neglected and the acknowledgment of the multiplicity of constitutive processes and agents at work in the popular social practices show the need for both a critique of disengaged methodologies and the construction of tools that take account of the presence of such actors—women, children, minorities, races, workers in the informal economy—and their cultural and religious expressions. This process of concretization with respect to the reason of the peasant/the oppressed masses undergoes ever greater diversification through the difficult articulation involving class, gender, and ethnicity. This comes very much to the fore in the issues of *RIBLA* published during this period of time.

The Intensive Bible Courses also served to strengthen the biblical movements throughout Latin America.[7] These courses brought together between forty and fifty people for six months for the purpose of studying the Bible, always taking concrete reality as point of departure. They were ecumenical in character and fostered the participation of lay people and agents of the popular movements. These courses have taken place in ten countries, bringing together researchers, male and female, with local leaders involved in biblical reading to address the challenges presented by the reality of the oppressed masses (natives, blacks, peasants, women, workers, and children) as well as ecology and art, taking always as starting point the cultures of the continent. These courses have had a significant impact in the socialization of biblical knowledge and the appropriation of exegetical procedures (including knowledge of Hebrew and Greek).

The articulation of the biblical movements is carried out by REBILAC,[8] which develops short-term courses, encourages pointed readings ("supportive economy," "urban tribalism," "masculinity"[9]), and organizes continental conferences. In El Salvador, the work of BIPO (popular biblical scholars) and similar movements of the Central American web stands out.[10] In Brazil, CEBI has functioned as the space for diverse processes of popular reading, yielding a significant production of popular materials and spaces for formation.[11] Other initiatives seek to offer biblical formation and materials from a popular perspective, creating links with academic formation and the production of audio-visual resources, as in the Centro Bíblico Verbo Divino in Brazil[12] and in other countries.

By understanding the Latin American Biblical Movement as part of the empowerment process of the oppressed masses, as part of class-based social movements that find voice today in the political profile of elected governments with center-left political agendas, we would be able to acknowledge the significant contribution that these processes of biblical reading have made to the political life of the continent. This is not a mechanical relation, nor is it one without contradictions. In fact, a good many of the new political leaders within the new community and labor movements received a basic foundation in the base

---

7. On these courses, see: http://www.uca.edu.sv/bipo/cursos.htm#CIB.

8. See http://ar.geocities.com/rebilac_coordcont/cronica.

9. See www.dimensioneducativa.org.co/aa/img_upload/e9c8f3ef742c89f634e8bbc63b2d ac77/Escu.

10. See http://www.uca.edu.sv/bipo/redbca.htm.

11. See http://www.cebi.org.br/noticia.php?secaoId=12&noticiaId=132.

12. See http://www.cbiblicoverbo.com.br/.

communities and were trained in the hermeneutics of liberation. In this process, the reading of the Bible begins with a reading of reality and finds expression in a reading of the objective and subjective conditions of the community.

When a peasant was put off by the reading offered by the priest at the liturgy on Sundays, such a reaction was forged within the communitarian and militant reading of the Bible. This was a reading that entailed training in the tools of analysis and interpretation and that formed, and continues to form, countless communities, which proceed to read the Bible with reality as point of departure. Method yields to material life, everyday life, and turns biblical hermeneutics into a communitarian exercise in the construction of existential and social meaning. The Bible is a religious book. The Word of God is not in the book but, rather, in the encounter of life in the text with life in reality. I am, as many others are, an heir of and an apprentice in this process at work in the last few decades in Latin America. Conscience is material.

In a conversation between Jürgen Moltmann and Hugo Assman recorded in the volume edited by Raúl Vidales (1982, 134), an interesting exchange having to do with method takes place. Moltmann asks, "Why did I have to become a Christian? If I start with this method, I see no reason for becoming a Christian." A young Assman responds,

> Here I do turn into a materialist. It involves the last material moment of real life. Neither Marx nor I have ever said anything else: life, the production of real life, the reproduction of real life, the reproduction of the conditions of real life.... Conscience is material. The working of all that implies the ability to be happy, the ability to think, the real ability to enjoy beauty, all this is material, because it is inscribed in the material being of humanity. That last material moment of life for me ... cannot be answered without the intromission of transcendentality in the midst of real life ... in the encounter between historical materialism and the most original demands of the Judeo-Christian tradition.

We were not alone, however. The Bible is many things at once in Latin America: let us talk about the "not-read" reading of the Bible.

THE BIBLICAL ABSENCE OF WRITING AND POPULAR CULTURE

How can one say that these efforts, studies, and practices of the biblical movement express/materialize the reason of the peasant or the reason of the oppressed masses? How does the popular reading of the Bible participate in the emancipatory effort regarding the construction of the reason of the oppressed in Latin America and their revolutionary projects?

Christianity is a religion of the book, of reading, of literate people. This is as true of the fundamentalist model of literal repetition as it is of the historical-critical model of interpretation. However, in Latin America, the oppressed masses, especially the peasantry, benefit only in limited fashion from educational opportunities. The oppressed masses are sub-literate. More importantly, they belong to a world without the written world, that is, a world of cultural representation and where writing/reading is not hegemonic.

If it were true that there was/is a systematic and creative process of "literacy" in the experience of the base communities and the social pastoral groups, in the expression of the processes of popular education, the interpretation of reality, the interpretation of the biblical text, and in the experience of the communities as agents of intervention and spirituality, such a model cannot be idealized, nor can it silence other cultural forms of the oppressed masses. If, on the one hand, one finds an effort to translate the Bible into indigenous languages and to produce more accessible translations using contemporary parlance, the great challenge continues to be, on the other hand, not to allow the centrality/authority of biblical reading/writing to serve to destroy cultural forms dependent on reading/writing. Bruna Franchetto (2004, 11), for instance, points to some of the main issues of concern for linguists with respect to the situation of "linguistic endangerment or languages in danger of extinction": "In the 500 years that followed the arrival of the Europeans, approximately 85% of the native languages of Brazil were lost"; and "Brazil continues to be a country with the highest linguistic density (many different languages in the same territory) and one of the lowest demographic concentrations per language (many languages and few speakers)."

The popular reading of the Bible should also be identified on the reverse side of the base groups organized in the form of social movements, that is, in the complex world of pentecostal practices in Latin America. These practices have in common a relationship of autonomy vis-à-vis the formations of historical Christianity (Roman Catholic or Protestant). The Bible functions as an object of power, with no call for historical-critical treatment, yielding to a use that is simple, narratival, allegorical, and full of images. The Bible is carried around. The Bible is sung. The Bible is repeated, with no need for study, no need for specialists or translators. The real danger of fundamentalist and low readings is relativized by the extreme fluidity of the text and the excesses of interpretations. Such fluidity reveals an accelerated process of de-normativizing the text and a constant movement of displacement of biblical authority. Without the instruments of power and authority, ecclesiastical and scientific, the book can be readily accessed and used, preventing interpretive hegemonies.

Another most diverse and quite old variation has to do with the presence of the biblical text in popular feasts of the country, where it is very difficult to tell where the religious movement begins and ends. In this regard, A. C. Mello Magalhães states, "The greatest contributions of the Bible to national culture were: construction of a corpus of material for the different narratives of Brazilian literature; biblical narratives and plots began to serve as themes for many artistic expressions; religious practices began to use it as a particular devotion; narratives and characters became part of the national imagery" (n.d.).

The presence of biblical narratives and imagery in the popular feasts of Brazil also presents a challenge to the discursive and controlling logic of the traditional churches. In appropriation by the laity, not as dogma but as performance, popular feasts dialogue with biblical traditions in hybrid spaces of the sacred and the profane and in the ambiguity of the religious calendar of Latin America.

For example, in the June festivities associated with Saint John the Baptist and in the *cururu* chants of central-west Brazil, the life and death of the Baptist are reinterpreted by mixing biblical material with elements of the local religious culture (Souza 2004). Similarly, in the feast of the *Sairé*, the story of the flood is recalled, as one can see from the following description,

> Promoted almost 300 years ago by the community of Alter do Chão, in Santarém no Pará, the Sairé is a semicircle made out of wood that contains the biblical account of the flood: a big ark represents Noah's ark; mirrors, the light of day; sweets and fruits, the abundance of food available in the ark; cotton and a small drum, the foam and the noise of the waves during the 40 days of the flood. The three semicircles symbolize the Sacred Trinity.[13]

Further, in the festivities of the *Folia de Reis*, celebrated between Christmas Day and January 6, groups of singers and musicians wearing colorful costumes roam the streets of small Brazilian cities, singing biblical chants that commemorate the journey of the three kings to Bethlehem to welcome the child Jesus. Outside, clowns wearing masks and representing the soldiers of King Herod of Jerusalem, dance to the accompaniment of guitar, tambourine, and *cavaquinho* (small four-stringed instrument of the guitar family), reciting verses as they do so.

These popular festivities are lived simultaneously with church practices normalized by the Bible, thus escaping theological as well as exegetical stares; they are thus best studied within the field of cultural anthropology (Pessoa and Félix

---

13. See http://www.horadobrasil.net/index.php?option=com_events&task=view_detail&agid=90.

2007). Such ambiguity is well captured by the following report appearing in the weekly paper *Jornal Tribuna do Planalto* (Santos 2007):

> For some it is superstition, but for the revelers it is but faithfulness to the biblical narrative. It is thus that they are rigorous with respect to norms and rituals, always remembered and studied, before continuing the course. Reinaldo Pessoa, a young man of twenty-four years of age, is among the most enthusiastic and engaged. No wonder. His role, as an ambassador, requires improvisation, agility, verbal facility, and, above all, knowledge of the tradition. "In the midst of revelry, I narrate the story by singing.... Nothing is learned by heart. Everything is improvised. What one needs to know is the story of the Three Kings."

Therefore, the reference to the reason of the peasant or the reason of the oppressed masses cannot be reduced to ecclesial forms of organization. Rather, such reason should be an inclusive and complex expression of the religious forms of the popular classes of Latin America. Reductionism to the established forms of the base ecclesial communities or to other ecclesial processes in the practice of biblical reading limits and atrophies the vital dimension of the presence of the Bible in many forms of Latin American popular culture, such as resistance, autonomous appropriation, and challenging the power imaginaries of the imposed religion (See Norget 1997). Here the words of Humberto Cholango, in his response to Benedict XVI as President of the Confederation of Peoples of the Kichwa Nationality in Ecuador, are very much to the point: "Life has taught us that 'a tree is known by its fruit,' as the Christ said, and we know how to distinguish between the one who serves the poor and the one who is served by them. The Pope should know that our religions NEVER DIED, [*sic*] we learned to syncretize our beliefs and symbols with those of the invaders and oppressors" (2007).[14]

Beyond systematic theology, beyond dogmatics and metaphysics, beyond the text framed by methodologies, the popular reading of the Bible escapes efforts to control it and realizes itself as language, unraveling the intentionality of an oppressive project of evangelization/colonization and blending with other figures, other myths, other possibilities, and diverse rituals.

More than a theology of the hermeneutics of symbol, as Dussel has argued (1985, 283), that exhausts itself in identifying popular culture as a form of resistance, the challenge facing a theology of liberation continues to be the dissolution of ecclesiological and christological borders, refusing any sort of Latin American

---

14. See http://www.katari.org/archives/respuesta-indigena-al-papa-benedicto-xvi.

Christian triumphalism and relocating the Bible accordingly. This has nothing to do with the clean-cut and subtly violent syncretism at work in inculturation that perpetuates the conversion and insertion of the sacred realm of others within the tolerant disposition of Christianity. It means, rather, understanding the religion of the Bible as one among others—in plural, de-centered, fragmented, and conflictive fashion (Canevacci 1996, 14).

These challenges have been and continue to be faced in the space for study and production provided by *RIBLA*, especially in volume twenty-six, *La palabra se hizo India (The Word Became Indian)* (Jiménez 1997). This volume seeks to investigate the relations between biblical relations and native cultures in their contemporary situation in Latin America, not as a record of the past but as an actual cultural and theological dialogue. This effort comes across in a very special way in the essays by Severino Croato, "Simbólica cultural y hermenéutica bíblica" (Croatto 1997b) and Victoria Carrasco, "Antropología andina y bíblica—'Chaquiñan' andino y Biblia" (Carrasco 1997).

The attempt to adopt the realities and the readings of the oppressed masses had a significant impact on the forms of interpretation and study of the Bible in Latin America. New hermeneutical mediations imposed themselves, based on the reading practices and the lived experiences of the poor with regard to the Bible. Such possibilities were pursued in volume twenty-eight of *RIBLA, Hermenéutica y exégesis a propósito de la Carta de Filemón* (Reyes Archila 1997a). The editorial introduction of Reyes Archila is worth quoting at length (Reyes Archila 1997b, 27):

> The body (word, gestures, dances, the senses, sexuality, pleasure, and so forth), feelings, culture (land, religious symbols and myths, cultural and religious traditions, the festive and the ludic, solidarity, and so forth), community, the meaning of time and space, and so forth. One finds a displacement of the merely objective to the subjective, of the exclusively rational to the bodily and the affective, of the purely political to the cultural, of written language to symbols and myths. This displacement implies enrichment rather than a negation of previous mediations.
>
> There are new criteria or tools for going into the Bible and rummaging around for the meaning of life for us today: suspicion, imagination, dreams, intuitions, specific questions, playfulness, dance, songs, poetry, and so forth. The displacement of the objective to the subjective is evident, of the scientific to the artistic. This experience of direct contact with the text and with life has become the new pedagogical criterion of authority that grounds biblical exegesis and hermeneutics. In this sense the displacement has been highly significant. It is no longer the authority offered by the major exegetical methods (and the major exegetes) of the "first" world that justifies the validity, the seriousness, the relevance, and the depth of the exegesis that we do.

In a very concrete way the feminist reading of the Bible in Latin America has achieved a positive, critical, and creative dialogue with women and feminist movements in the continent. In this way, it has made the female majority of the oppressed the hermeneutical and epistemic point, as one can see in various volumes of *RIBLA*. In the course of the past decades, both women and feminist reading have ceased to be a minority in the meetings and volumes of *RIBLA*. They have gone from serving as a strategy for specific thematic volumes, such as *RIBLA* 15 and 25—*From manos de mujer* (Cavalcanti 1993) and *¡Pero nosotras decimos!* (Cardoso Pereira), respectively—to being a presence in all volumes. In volumes fifteen and twenty-five, the women collective of RIBLA presented the results of specific meetings that sought to concretize the journey in common.

The Popular Reading of the Bible Enters the University

All through the course of these years, many problems and challenges came to the fore that called for critique, self-critique, radical action, and the reevaluation of strategies and methodologies. It was clear that there was no desire to copy the processes of research in Europe or in the United States, even though many of the biblical scholars had pursued their studies outside Brazil. More concretely, from the end of the 1980s, it became possible to do specialized studies as well as master's and doctoral work in Bible in Latin America without having to emigrate physically, emotionally, or epistemically.

Institutions such as the Instituto Superior Evangélico de Estudios Teológicos (ISEDET; Buenos Aires, Argentina), the Universidad Metodista de São Paulo (UMESP; São Paulo, Brazil), the Universidad Bíblica Latinoamericana (UBL; San José, Costa Rica), the Pontificia Universidade Católica de Rio de Janeiro (PUC; Rio de Janeiro, Brazil), and the Escola Superior de Teología de São Leopoldo (EST; São Leopoldo, Brazil), among others, developed the first formal possibilities for the scientific study of the Bible in the continent, producing a growing number of students and researches—both men and women! Finally, the Bible had entered the university.

The end of the 1990s in Latin America brought significant transformations through the consolidation of processes of re-democratization. These were characterized by intense negotiations/violent encounters on the part of the bourgeois élite with the new forms of social resistance and popular struggle. This moment coincides with the process of the dismantling of so-called "real socialism" and the victory of the capitalist model of the West. Latin America occupies a peripheral place in the globalization of capitalism, coexisting with a growing process of accumulation of wealth and the expansion and consolidation of the exclusion of the masses.

This new scenario, which gained strength in the 1990s and through the beginning of the 2000s, had a significant impact on social/labor movements as well as on social pastoral groups. The new arrangements of bourgeois democracy announced the end of utopia and the end of history, stressing the impossibility of economic and political ruptures. The institutional arrangements of capital attempted to destroy popular and direct forms of participation in political life through processes of co-optation, corruption, criminalization, and bureaucratization vis-à-vis the demands of the oppressed masses. The meaning of such mechanisms for academic and university life was twofold: a demobilization of the concept of "praxis" (practice, theory, intervention) and a loss in the importance of reflection on "work" and "politics." The call to the university was to pragmatism, to the functional realism of a possible society, namely, that of Western capitalism with global pretensions.

Faculties of theology and centers of biblical studies were not spared such pressure. If by the end of the 1990s a difficult but creative dialogue still existed between the universities and the movement of popular reading of the Bible, the new millennium demanded that academic theologians resist the naiveté and spontaneity of popular reading. With great ease—which only goes to show the fragility and inorganic character of relations between the university and social movements/pastoral groups—specialists and researchers of the Bible became realists, spirits for change, democrats of moderation, artists in negotiation, and sober critics. They took command of the process of neutralizing the tools of social critique and any type of research with social transformation as aim.

The questions and suspicions of the peasant did indeed call for the end of history and utopias. However, contrary to what the theologians of academic bureaucracy understood and undertook in this regard, such a call was for the end of Western history and its reason, its model and its rationality, its system of production of values and goods, and its utopia of progress. The readings of reality-Bible-community carried out by the oppressed majorities demanded an alternative relation of power and knowledge, new plural subjects, the de-centering of economic reason by ecological reason. In effect, they demanded the possibility of an alternative world. This scenario forms part of the class struggle and its new meanings in Latin America, which update the challenges of liberation theology and its spirituality. Such spirituality insists on denouncing the forms of domination and exploitation as well as on announcing popular alternatives for another possible world. Whoever continues "to do" Bible and theology in this way is neither a pragmatist nor a realist; consequently, such a person has no place in theological institutions.

At this point, the assessments diverge. Of this I am well aware! Other interpretive paths could be advanced, such as, for example, the contribution of Professor Erhard S. Gerstenberger, a friend of mine, to *The Blackwell Companion to the Bible and Culture* (2006). Starting from an ornamental understanding of the class struggle at the international level, a bourgeois liberal view, and a hasty accommodation regarding the Latin American processes, he responds to the question regarding the Bible in Latin America in orderly fashion by way of four phases: (1) the discovery of the Bible; (2) twenty years of opposition (1965–1985); (3) the Bible in the traditional churches; and (4)twenty years of accommodation (1985–2005). What Professor Gertenberger calls "accommodation" should be understood as an expression of the class struggle within the religious realm of Latin America—its processes of censure, interdiction, and interruption on the part of ecclesiastical hierarchies and theo-exegetical bureaucracies. It should also be understood as an expression of the vitality of the Bible (both read and non-read!) in spaces for the construction of conscience, imagination, and the struggle of the oppressed classes. Here I too declare myself a materialist!

Yes, the "priest" of the parable recounted above—who could also be a pastor—continues with Sunday readings that express fidelity to the liturgical and ecclesiastical order as well as to the theological formation received in seminary. It is true that the efforts and practices, the spirituality and mystique of the popular reading of the Bible, did have an influence on theological formation and did have an impact on the curriculum and programs of theological faculties and post-graduate studies. Nevertheless, such efforts were duly demobilized and displaced by two mechanisms of control wielded by Christian patriarchal hierarchies: the impulse given to the world of gospel culture and the process of professionalization of theologians.

The emergence and strengthening of the mistrust of the peasant and his lived experience of faith and of Bible reading in organized and organic fashion, a fashion that served his own interests, unleashed, on the part of churches and institutes for theological formation and publishing houses, strategies for containment that combined the repression of theologians, the demobilization of communities, a shift in the profile of the episcopacy, and the marginalization of theological voices and segments. Fearing the hegemony of the poor in theology and the church, church hierarchies found it preferable to sell and yield its spaces to the marketplace of symbolic goods, handing its followers over to manipulation by the media and exploitation by the mass processes of consumerist faith.

Biblical circles; Bible groups in the jungle, in the tracts of newly cleared land, in the slums, in the city; contextualized readings done by lay men and women formed by many courses on the Bible and the methodology of reading; processes of popular education that nourished the whole dynamic of the popular church; the church of the poor and its theology; liberation theology—all this was deliberately demobilized by the church hierarchies. In their place, singing priests, bands for JESUS, psalms and verses in ballad form, and mass events were substituted.

This process, which affected Catholics as much as Protestants, should be understood within the framework of the class struggle during the years of the so-called democratization of Latin America.

The other process involved the professionalization of theology. Here the forms of participation were broadened by way of access to the formal study of theology, especially for sectors that had been excluded until then (blacks, women, lay men and women), but without socializing the formal spaces of production, which were still in the control of the church hierarchies and their intellectuals. Marked by academic and scientific logic, processes and individuals from social pastoral groups and movements under the influence of liberation theology had to submit to the norms of the university, letting go of their motivations and practices. The call was for scientific treatment of the Bible—objective, correct, well-grounded—a replication of the processes of biblical research in Europe and the United States. In effect, affective and epistemic migration was imposed without having to leave Latin America. The evaluation of Milton Schwantes in this regard is quite pointed (2008, 13–14):

> There is little that is new in the theological academy when it comes to the Bible. I hear many common phrases in the halls, coming out of the classrooms. However, when dealing with the Bible, the tendency is still to render it extremely complicated. It does not seem to me that the study of theology has achieved such innovation in the use of the Bible that such study is actually at the service of the struggles of the Latin American people. The Bible as studied remains foreign to the local soil. It comes wrapped with the ropes and chains of the conquering invasion, without touching sufficiently the local ground and dust.
>
> There are exceptions, it is true. However, in general, according to the books that are translated, what is studied here is what is of Europe. Worse still, what is studied here has already been superseded in Europe. It is useful in this sense: We are at the bottom of the landscape, where garbage is dumped. We turn over the garbage of the "masters." We study the leftovers. However, our biblical bibliography is, almost in its entirety, completely outdated. It is out of step by many years with what is studied in Europe, but we want Europe to continue to serve as our standard.

The distrust and the question of the "peasant" were not limited to the matter of comments on the Bible on Sundays. They had to do as well with a certain role of the Christian religion in the Latin American continent. They called into question the social relations of power and gave expression to new forms of being church, as much with regard to the format of the base ecclesial communities as with respect to the plural forms of social pastoral groups and specific pastoral groups (minors, marginalized women, the land, the incarcerated, the slums, blacks, natives, and so on). It is not so much a matter of the Bible-in-itself but of the Bible-for-itself!

All this is due to the fact that the Latin American popular reading wants to keep the text alive, fertile, speaking—beyond issues of methodology. In the relation between the gravity of methodological interventions and grace mixed with alienation-resistance, the Latin American reading insists on a liberating spirituality—one that does not ask for the sacrifice of the text in the reduction of its complexity, that does not bless the fetish of consumer religion, but that accepts to live this mystique of disorder that gives order to research without killing the text. This is the miracle! The text becomes flesh in reality.

This reality, a cauldron involving class and ethnic struggles, forces the text to reveal its conflicts: the peripheral peasantry, imperialism and its abuses of power, the daily character of poverty (hunger, insanity, and illness), the marginality and abandonment of women and children, the reinvention of ways of living together and sharing.

The Latin American reading chooses, selects, and prefers, without fear of being happy. It does so starting from questions about reality. It accepts the sweat of method, whichever one, and the sweat of the scholar who balances history, sociology, archeology, anthropology, and geography. Far from being a simple approximation to nearby scenarios or a juxtaposition of similarities, the Latin American exegetical and hermeneutical piracy reinvents the scenario and the context of the cultural contact between text and reality, accepting and openly showing the social relevance of research and the researcher. God with us.

11

LIBERATING THE BIBLE: POPULAR BIBLE STUDY AND ITS ACADEMIA ALLIES

Jorge Pixley

By popular reading of the Bible we mean in Latin America the use of the Bible in small groups of believers, usually led by a pastoral agent, either a woman religious (a member of a religious order) or, in most cases, a priest. In Protestant circles, where parishes are not so large, a local congregation is usually the place for this type of Bible study. In introducing Catholic and Protestant—including Pentecostal—groups, a brief reflection is necessary.

For Catholic groups, the use of the Bible is more or less a novelty. Pastoral practice has not usually focused on the Bible. The groups themselves are usually natural communities of a certain place, usually a rural area or an urban slum. These communities share some needs—a school, a clinic, dealing with a common land holder, water scarcity, and so forth. When they discover the Bible, they look for guidelines in dealing with these everyday problems. Protestant groups, on the other hand, are drawn together by their acceptance of a plan of salvation. Of course, they also share similar community problems, but these are not matters to which they look for solutions in the Bible. The Bible is viewed as dealing with "spiritual" or "heavenly" matters.

As such, Protestant groups need the leadership of a creative and courageous pastor to show them that the Bible also has something to say about their daily community needs. The question of leadership is also critical for Catholic groups, but for different reasons. Catholic believers tend on a first reading of the Bible to find too few links to their church practice and too much historical material of no relevance for their daily lives. Here some use of what the academy has gained in the last two centuries can overcome roadblocks. Protestant groups are prone to a reading which views the miraculous as actual historical events, being unaware of the dynamics involved in the production of myth as well as the production of religious Scriptures. In both cases, among Catholics and Protestants alike, a basic knowledge of academic Bible study is a pastoral necessity. This calls for a connection between the academy and the popular community. Since it proves unworkable even for leaders to take the time off required for regular degrees, we have resorted, with excellent results, to intensive courses of one month or, in some cases, several months.

Such contacts are not only of benefit to the groups of believers; the connection is not a oneway passage from academy to group. Scholars also learn in the process, as they discover the questions that their research must address in order to keep their feet on the ground and be able to channel the Bible to the liberation of their people. Because the popular communities want to solve concrete problems, they want their study to be relevant to the political and social development of their societies. From the scholars' point of view, this means keeping abreast of political developments and sociological theories that help them understand the communities within their contexts. This also is a matter that requires attention at the regular meetings mentioned earlier.

When all of this works, it can be a very effective tool in the lives of the communities of popular believers. Needless to say, these are communities of poor people, and thus the specific sources of this poverty as well as effective strategies for overcoming it are part of what must be considered.

The Last Fifty Years

The late 1950s and especially the 1960s saw a tremendous influx of missionaries into Latin America. These came from both Europe (especially Spain, Ireland, and Holland) and the United States. For Catholics, such a development had something to do with the call of Pope John XXIII for tithing the resources of the wealthy churches to evangelize the baptized Christians of Latin America. For Protestants, the surge followed the closing of China to Western religious leaders in 1949. Within the Catholic context, the newly arrived church workers were mostly sent into areas where local priests did not wish to go, precisely remote rural areas and urban slums made up largely of recent immigrants from those rural areas. Here the foreigners were shocked by the levels of poverty among Christian believers. Within the Protestant context, missionaries felt the same shock to some extent, lessened in their case by the need of families to keep in touch with good schools for their children, which meant that missionaries often lived in middle class areas while working with the poor. This wave of missionaries into poor areas of Latin America, alongside the emergence of radical groups of Christian students, provided the spark for the emergence of liberation theology.

Liberation theology is the first Latin American theology in our five hundred year history. Universities had been established already in the sixteenth century in Mexico and Lima, with prominent theological faculties made up of Spaniards trained in Spain and a student body of *criollos*, men born in the New World to Spanish parents. Even though it had been determined in the first years of Spanish knowledge of the New World (later America) that the natives were not naturally slaves (as were Africans), it was still presumed that they were incapable of being priests and, hence, unable to study in the universities. Until the seventeenth century, natives were excluded totally from theological schools, which meant that theology in the Latin American universities was a reproduction of European theology and did not take into account the special circumstances of Christianity in this new world. The early Christian missionaries were mostly Franciscans, Mercedaries, and Dominicans. Very few of them were interested in learning about the culture and religion of the natives, which meant that the schools of theology regarded these religions as irrelevant for true religion. Even in the seventeenth and eighteenth centuries, native priests were a very small minority, and most of them were of mixed blood (mestizos).

It was not until the second half of the twentieth century that liberation theologians and church historians recognized that the church in Latin America was not simply an extension of the Spanish and Portuguese churches. The presence within it of majorities of natives or mestizos made this church and its religion quite different. With its option for the poor, liberation theology treated the native elements no longer as suspicious infiltrations and possibly distortions, but rather lifted them up as genuine aspects of Latin American Christianity.

I mentioned earlier that it was the influx of missionaries in the 1960s that drew attention to the Christian faith of the poor in this continent, especially the concern of that faith for creation, as well as for the defense of life, both human and other. Of course, not all missionaries embraced the cultures of the poor or liberation theology when it appeared. Many continued the Eurocentric emphasis of previous missionaries, condemning themselves to theological irrelevance. Those who embraced mestizo peoples and their culture received with gratitude the sudden emergence of a full-blown liberation theology in the early 1970s, with the publication of books by Rubem Alves, Gustavo Gutiérrez, Hugo Assman, and José Porfirio Miranda—all published in 1971, and all were original Latin American editions, with the exception of the volume by Alves, which was a translation from an English original.

Among Catholics, Gutiérrez, a parish priest in Rimac, a poor sector of Lima, and a protégé of Archbishop, later Cardinal, Juan Landázuri Ricketts, OFM, had an immense impact. Among Protestants, Alves and Miranda had the greatest impact—the former was a Presbyterian minister in the southern cone and the latter a Jesuit priest in Mexico whose publication was profoundly biblical in character. A year later, in 1972, Miranda resigned from the society, along with three other leading Jesuits of the province of Mexico, accusing it of betraying its commitment to the poor. From then on, his worship of God on Sundays was his work with labor unions in and around Mexico City, where he made his living as a professor of philosophy at the Metropolitan Autonomous University. Assman came across as politically more radical; his following was among Christians on the left, both Catholic and Protestant. At this time, during the writing and publication of his volume, he was a political exile from his native Brazil and lived with the Jesuit Juan Luis Segundo in Montevideo, Uruguay.

A note on Segundo is in order. Assman tells of Segundo's grave misgivings, a matter which he came to appreciate later with the failures of so many revolutions. Segundo himself was a magnificent scholar whose base community was a group of professional people, and hence, in his opinion, he was not qualified to be a liberation theologian. In the opinion of most, this was a serious mistake. His volume *Liberation of Theology*, based on a course given at Harvard, qualifies him as such regardless of his pastoral base. It should be noted in this regard that Miranda also denied that he was a liberation theologian. He had trained as an economist in Germany and rejected Marx's theory of value and placing of the origin of classes in the process of production, locating it instead in the circulation of goods. It was this background, he felt, that disqualified him as a liberation theologian.

Liberation theology was a fact at the pastoral level, where the use of the Bible was most important. Pastoral agents lived out the option for the poor and learned to read the Bible as a book of the poor and for the poor. A growing number of biblical scholars found their place with these groups.

ACADEMIC BIBLICAL SCHOLARSHIP

We have made a deliberate attempt in Latin America to keep the popular study of the Bible and its academic study in contact with each other. This did not just happen that way. Several developments were influential in this regard.

CEBIs IN BRAZIL

A major influence was the experience of the Brazilian CEBIs, the communities of biblical study. Their importance was due in part to their number: probably over one hundred thousand groups of approximate fifteen people who met regularly to debate their community problems and to study the Bible with the assumption that biblical study would guide them in resolving such problems.

It was a very sensitive Carmelite priest with an excellent biblical education, Carlos Mesters, who played the key role of midwife in the birthing of this massive movement.

Annual meetings were held in different states across the vast country of Brazil to share experiences with each other and with Mesters. At these gatherings, he would sit with legs crossed, feet clothed only in sandals, a notebook and a pencil in hand. As the various groups, state by state, described their experiences and their challenges, he would take notes in his diminutive handwriting. After gathering their experiences, the next session would focus on the study of the assigned biblical book, which had been determined the previous year at their meeting. Again Mesters would take notes on what the groups had discovered in the word of God. Within a few months, there would be a commentary on the book in a cheap edition and in simple language available to ordinary people. Mesters would bring his academic training from Europe to clarify difficult matters when necessary. This was the model for the interchange between popular Bible reading and academic reading.

The hermeneutics of this process was worked out in Mesters' volume *Flor sem defesa* (1983). The volume advanced a triangular scheme: pre-text, text, and con-text. The pre-text was the physical and social reality of the reading group. The questions and problems posed arose from this reality; indeed, without making that reality a shared vision in the community the reading would not work. Next came the text. This included not just the reading of the translation in Portuguese but also some coaching on the origins of the text and the difficulties concealed behind the translation. It was at this point that the academician proved helpful. Finally, the con-text involved finding the importance of this text for the community engaged in the study of the Bible. Needless to say, the situation was more complicated than this, especially given the vast diversity that is Latin America. Yet Mesters' simple hermeneutic outlined in this book proved a guiding light for many biblical students, both professors and pastoral agents.

In terms of biblical themes, the one that caught the attention of both the popular groups and the scholars was the God who liberated the people trapped in forced labor in Egypt and who led them out under God's prophet Moses. The God thus revealed in the Scriptures was viewed as one who hears the cry of the oppressed and this, of course, gave much hope in a continent that felt oppressed both by the United States and by local tyrants supported by that empire. For a time, the Creator God that had been so important to the native peoples of the New World was put in the shadow of the liberating God. The consolidation of the Cuban revolution, in spite of the constant threats of the nearby empire, gave grounds for hoping that the same liberation could be achieved in countries farther away from the United States. As the Soviet Union became the guarantee of food and energy for the Cubans, it promised to serve as a crutch for other revolutions. Human rights, so important in the United States as a moral distinction from the USSR, were not respected by the tyrants supported by the United States and seemed much less important at the time than the freedom to make a country's own path in independence from the United States.

Academic Studies

In addition to the phenomenon of the CEBIs in Brazil, a number of academic studies had a profound impact in those days of hope in revolution.

José Porfirio Miranda

Miranda's volume of 1971, *Marx and the Bible*, published with his own personal financing, was based on European-style scholarship. Miranda took the theme of justice and traced it through the Prophets, the Psalms, and the Gospels to show how God was known by doing justice. Jeremiah 22:15–16 emerged as a basic text for understanding the liberating God revealed in the exodus: "Are you a king because you compete in cedar? Did not your father eat and drink and do justice and righteousness? Then it was well with him. *He judged the cause of the poor and needy: Is not this to know me? Says YHWH.*" It is by doing justice, argued Miranda, that we know God. There can be no true theology without doing justice. This was powerful stuff.

It was also the basis for his acceptance of Marxists as companions in the struggle for the Kingdom of God. Whether they thought they were atheists made little difference, if they showed with their deeds of justice that they knew God. Miranda's volume was dense and offered a lot of food for thought. To biblical scholars it gave a sense of direction from God's Word. The fact that Miranda gave up on the church and did his evangelical work with labor unions dampened the effect of his work. He did not found a school of interpretation as such, even though he did write a few more biblical works. Even so, his demonstration of the effective results of a close reading of biblical texts in the original languages did have an impact.

Clodovis Boff and Jorge Pixley

Boff and Pixley collaborated on an early volume within the important series Teologia E Libertaçâo, entitled *Opçâo pelos Pobres* (1986); it was dedicated to the important theological topic of liberation theology, the option for the poor. At the time, we were dealing with biblical reading by groups of poor people, and soon it became clear that important parts of the Bible had been written by the poor and thus "belonged" to the poor. Here the stories in Genesis and in the Gospels were prime examples, although there was no concealing that these popular stories had been co-opted by royal and/or priestly elites in Israel. The biblical part of this volume advanced the following argument: The people who had been rescued from bondage in Egypt had been poor peasants, who, like all Egyptian peasants, were slaves of the kings and worked royal lands and performed construction tasks when called to do so. Because of their relative freedom in their villages under the rule of their elders, some were able to respond to Moses's call. In the desert they bonded into a people, Israel. This volume was translated into Spanish, Italian, and, later, other languages as well.

Pixley followed up this lead by working on the history of Israel as seen from the perspective of the poor. Eventually, this work was drawn together in a book, *Historia sagrada, historia popular* (1990), that had an immense effect on the study groups of the poor throughout Latin America, given its translation into Portuguese. The Portuguese title, *Historia de Israel a partir dos pobres*, is descriptive of its content as a history of Israel from the perspective of poor peasants. It provided a framework that a great many popular study groups used to understand the Bible. In terms of current studies of the history of Israel in Europe and the United States, the book is unaware of important questions regarding the validity of some biblical traditions. It begins the history of Israel with the exodus and views the Davidic monarchy as a betrayal of the popular laws drawn up to make it difficult for the tribes of Israel to "return to Egypt." These are difficult issues not settled even in First World scholarship.

José Severino Croatto (1930–2004)

Croatto was the finest linguist of ancient semitic languages yet in Latin America, but he was also a member of a popular Bible study group and a supporter of that movement. After teaching at several institutions, notably the University of Buenos Aires (1964–1974), he joined the ecumenical theological school in Buenos Aires, ISEDET, where he taught from 1974 until his death in 2004. Hermeneutics was a key interest of his. After writing a number of technical books on the subject, he wrote a popular work entitled *Hermenéutica práctica* (2002). His basic thesis was that classical books are always read from the situation of the reading community and that they are continually reread as new circumstances present themselves. This is a process which he documents with abundant examples of rereading from within the Bible. This was a scholarly way of legitimizing the popular reading of the Bible. He by no means meant to cheapen academic study; in fact, his was a very careful reading of the Hebrew text, exemplified in three tomes of commentary on Genesis 1–11 and three on the book of Isaiah. His students constitute a distinct school of close reading of the Bible that remains sensitive to popular Bible reading without feeling bound by it.

The year 1988 marked a significant advance in the popular reading of the Bible with the appearance of the first volume of the journal *RIBLA, Revista de Interpretación Bíblica Latinoamericana* (*Journal of Latin American Interpretation of the Bible*). Its presentation, as conveyed in the first issue, stated, in part:

> This journal is situated. It situates itself in the midst of the experiences of faith and the struggles of communities and churches. The Bible is being rescued by the people. The pains, utopias, and poetry of the poor took for themselves, through the communities, hermeneutical mediations that are decisive for Biblical reading in Latin America and the Caribbean. This journal has as its cradle the long-suffering life of our peoples and their stubborn resistance toward a dignified and just existence. The communities of poor people there inserted are a ferment for biblical hermeneutics.
>
> Similar publications already exist, scattered through all of Latin America. *RIBLA* fraternizes with them. It does not replace them. It has no intention of taking the place of local, national and regional initiatives. It takes them for granted. It considers them indispensable. The route of Latin American reading is situated. It is concrete. It is specific. It is incarnate in the local context in a historical context. *RIBLA* intends to be a link which interrelates local, national, and regional experiences (vol. 1, 1988, 1).

From its beginning, *RIBLA* appeared simultaneously in Spanish and Portuguese, the two main languages of Latin America. At first, it was funded by subsidies from the World Council of Churches, but soon it became self-sustaining and has remained so to this day. Usually, issues of approximately 180 pages in length appeared three times a year.

Because it was conceived by academics who intended to make it a vehicle of biblical support for communities of poor believers, the journal had a duality from the beginning that was to be a defining characteristic and one with which the writers had constantly to struggle. We intended to be as up-to-date as possible, considering the limited bibliographic resources of our academic institutions. Yet we intended to listen to and address the questions that came from the communities. The journal was to be monographic, that is, each issue was to center on one biblical book or theme or on a theme that grew out of the life of the communities.

Two vehicles were established to make our dreams reality: the scheduling of regular meetings among journal contributors for the sake of planning the issues, and the development of so-called Intensive Bible Courses. On the one hand, we held such regular meetings in different countries. The local hosts would always devote part of the time to look at the situation of the host country and its particular problems. In this way we also recruited new and young scholars from the various countries to join our circle, with its popular and ecumenical bent. On the other hand, we committed to six-month courses in basic Bible knowledge in order to introduce pastoral agents to critical biblical study. Our hope was that such intensive courses would be ecumenical in nature, but usually out of some forty participants, all but three to five were Catholic. This was a result of our lack of funds to offer scholarships, whereas the religious orders would give sabbaticals to their members. Each host country established the theme of the six-month course and selected the teachers, privileging insofar as possible the authors of *RIBLA*. After fifteen years of these courses, we had trained an important core of pastoral agents with a more than average knowledge of the Bible.

At the same time, *RIBLA* authors had a chance to test our understanding of the problems the communities were asking of the Bible. Important new themes emerged. In Brazil, the dimension of feminism in biblical study was explored with the assistance of important feminist scholars. In the Dominican Republic, we dealt with "negritude," the set of issues particular to the African peoples of our lands. In Mexico and especially in Bolivia, the lives and anthropological reality of the native peoples and their impact were explored. In Colombia, a peasant reading of the Bible was explored, which is relevant for most of our countries. The list of examples could go on and on.

RIBLA was published in Brazil by Editora Vozes, the Franciscan press based in the city of Petrópolis, within the State of Río de Janeiro. Vozes has its own chain of bookstores in the main cities of the country and was thus able to put the journal on a sustainable basis very quickly. The Spanish edition was a greater problem: while its potential readership was larger, it was divided by many national borders and entailed great postal costs. We went through a publisher in Chile and another in Costa Rica before settling in Quito, Ecuador, with Verbo Divino, which has proved very successful at coping with the challenge and is now commercially successful. In recent years, internet subscriptions have been used to overcome prohibitive postal costs. The task of translation into Portuguese and Spanish has proved a continual problem, and for this we have partially relied on volunteer translators. Each issue will have some articles written in Spanish and others in Portuguese, and all must be ready for publication in both languages reasonably near the projected publication schedule. We have kept going twenty years now. The future is not secure, but whose future is? We have all learned a lot that we were not taught in graduate schools, which for most of us meant Europe and the United States.

The result of such endeavors has been that we now have a new generation of young scholars who received their doctorates in Latin America under the direction of some of our own *RIBLA* colleagues at Sâo Paulo or Buenos Aires. Soon, we expect the Latin American Biblical University of San José, Costa Rica, to offer doctorates in Bible. Many of the younger scholars are women, and they are already having a major impact on our journal and our work.

Issues facing Latin American Biblical Studies in the Future

To begin with, we need to consider the existence of other Scriptures besides the Christian Bible. Most of the native sacred texts were destroyed by the invading Christians, but the Mayan *Popol Vuh* certainly merits careful examination from biblical scholars, something which, surprisingly, it has not received. In addition, there is the Qur'an. Most of our countries have communities of Arab exiles in our midst as a result of various political developments over the years: the problems caused by the Ottoman Empire; the conflicts due to the establishment of the State of Israel in Palestine; and, more recently, the efforts on the part of the United States to reorder the state of affairs in Iraq and its environs. It is a matter of duty to examine the texts of the Qur'an carefully, especially where poor Christian believers live in close contact with Arabs, who are relative newcomers to our cities (there are really no rural Arab immigrants). Finally, there are the Scriptures of the Jewish community, which look like our Old Testament but are organized differently and do not include the Deuterocanonical books, which at least some Christians have in their Bibles. The Torah-dominated Jewish Scriptures have a different global meaning than the Old Testament. The different order of the Book of the Twelve, which Christians often call the Minor Prophets, gives it a different meaning than it has in our Bibles. Jewish communities are well established in countries like Argentina, Mexico, and Panama, though often in areas where poor Christians have less contact with them than they do with Muslims. The study of the Jewish Scriptures casts a new light on the Christian Old Testament, which is very important for our people.

Second, we need to carry out a careful study of the real down-to-earth lives of rural and urban poor people, including the effects of the continuing massive migrations of peasants to urban slums. We claim in our biblical studies to be a support for communities of poor believers, but for the most part our knowledge of the sociological forces buffeting their lives is superficial. Here we need to build alliances with our colleagues in sociology. In the well-established method of see-judge-act, we have relied until now on the insights of poor people themselves when it comes to seeing their reality. The way in which believers see their reality will always be a privileged entry to that reality, and it would be a grave error to despise it. However, sociological scholarship can uncover causes and consequences of phenomena such as wars and rebellions in rural areas, which the poor peasants suffer but do not fully understand. This is, therefore, an important task ahead for biblical scholars, following in our tradition of support for popular Bible study.

Third, we need to explore the option for the poor in the writings of the church fathers, to whom we must add Origen, that great biblical scholar and teacher of the third century C.E., whose teachings were maliciously declared heretical in the sixth century in a context quite removed from his own. The option for the poor is a fundamental pillar of liberation theology, and liberation theology undergirds the popular Bible reading that we practice. The church fathers up to and including Augustine and John Chrysostom believed that the gospel required a privileged attention to the poor, but we have not really pursued the theological importance of this point for their overall religious theory and practice. We need scholarly research to explore this matter in order to put our Bible reading on a solid basis in the faith of the early Christians.

Fourth, we need to examine the issue of historicity regarding the emergence of Israel. For most of us, a belief in the freedom established by the Sinaitic laws for the people who emerged from slavery in Egypt has been a basic pillar of our understanding of the Bible. Yahweh was the God "who brought out from the land of Egypt, from the house of bondage" and in so doing proved that the gods of the pharaoh and his people were impotent when faced with a liberating God who made the heavens and the earth. The historicity of the early period of a tribal Israel has been put in doubt by recent scholarship in the First World, and many scholars would begin Israel with the monarchy or even later. The fact that the biblical books were all written during or after the Babylonian exile has led some to doubt even the account of kingship in our biblical books of Former Prophets. After years of training poor people to read the Bible as a book about liberation, we cannot possibly give up on the liberation motif, which is anyway not limited to tribal Israel. Jesus and Paul announce liberation, each in his own way. However, for us the cornerstone of it all has been the formation of tribal Israel in a context of social formations built on a tributary mode of production. It will be painful, but we must reexamine this. We must not necessarily give it up, but we need to have an open discussion of the matter and pose the question, What would it mean to affirm a biblical liberation without a historical tribal Israel built on Sinaitic laws to bolster it? Our faith cannot and does not rest on the results of historical research, so we must be open to exploring the alternative we have so far been afraid to face.

Lastly, keeping the tie between biblical scholarship and pastoral practice is a permanent problem that will never be resolved decisively. Each generation must explore it anew. For this generation, coming to terms with Pentecostalism is fundamental. Pentecostal churches have grown exponentially in our countries, and they understand themselves in the light of the Bible. Even though there are unworldly elements in their Bible reading, they do find connections with the daily lives of poor people. This is not done in the manner of *RIBLA* and still seems alien to our movement. Bridges must be found. These churches are joining ecumenical organizations; why not organizations devoted to Bible study?

12

BIBLICAL STUDIES IN THE ANGLO-CARIBBEAN: PAST, PRESENT, AND FUTURE CHALLENGES, OPPORTUNITIES, AND POSSIBILITIES

Gosnell Yorke

Christianity came to the Caribbean as part and parcel of Spanish, French, British, Dutch, and finally, North American colonialism. The church went on to assist these powers in building colonial societies: it endorsed slavery, and helped to entrench racial and class divisions after emancipation (Sunshine 1985, 16).

The Caribbean (historically shaped in its identity formation by Africa, Asia, Latin America, and Europe) is home to four major linguistic groups, a plurality of Afro-religious and some Indo-religious traditions, including some indigenous ones (Nettleford in Hall 2006, 6–7; Murrell 2009), and a kaleidoscope of cultures (Sunshine 1985, 7). For that reason, it is an extremely complex region (Davis 1990, 5–7). This makes writing about the rainbow-like region of the Caribbean an exceptionally difficult task.

Current statistics suggest that 70 percent of Caribbean peoples of some sixteen million are of African descent, although we should not overlook the well-organized way of life of our Amerindian ancestors in the region as well. The indigenous peoples such as the Arawaks, Caribs, and Tainos antedate Christopher Columbus, the Italian who got himself lost at sea while traveling under the Spanish flag and who was dubbed the so-called discoverer of the "New World," when he arrived in the Caribbean initially in 1492. Nor should we be oblivious to "the studied assault on the Amerindians and their life style [*sic*] which Columbus' arrival triggered, amounting virtually to genocide" (Thompson 1994).

In this study, emphasis will be placed on the *Anglo-Caribbean*. This is important to point out at the outset, given the fact that a number of Anglo-Caribbean biblical scholars and others write about the "Caribbean" when what they really have in mind is the Anglo-Caribbean—seemingly unmindful of the rich multi-lingual tapestry of the region as a whole (see, e.g., Reid-Salmon 2008 and Titus 2010). For still others, a discussion, ostensibly of the Caribbean, is sometimes restricted to an exclusive treatment of the Hispanophone Caribbean such as Cuba (see Ulloa 2010, 480). In addition, the region tends to get overlooked in a number of publications supposedly meant to target the "Third World," or, more accurately, the "Two-Thirds World." One such omission is exemplified by the editors of the journal *Third World Libraries* (Spring 1995, vol. 5, no. 2), in which mention is made of Africa (Kenya, Nigeria, and Ethiopia), Bangladesh, and Latin America. No mention is ever made of the Caribbean. The giving of short shrift to the Caribbean also manifests itself in a volume Ursula King edited in 1994, *Feminist Theology from the Third World: A Reader*. Again, there is no mention of Carib-bean women, such as Hyacinthe Boothe, the biblical and feminist scholar who once served, among other things, as Director of Graduate Studies at the United Theological College of the West Indies (UTCWI)—UTCWI being the Theol-ogy Department of the University of the West Indies (UWI–Mona [Kingston] campus). Instead, mention is made of Asian and Black South African women.

THE HISTORICAL ROLE OF THE BIBLE IN THE ANGLO-CARIBBEAN

Unlike in the Euro-American tradition generally, biblical studies, as a distinct dis-cipline with its various subfields, such as Hebrew Bible (HB) and New Testament (NT), does not enjoy a long and strong tradition in the Caribbean. Integral to the complex history of the region, however, especially since its contact with Europe as empire as of the late fifteenth century, is the role the Bible itself has played—a rather ambivalent one at best, in that it has been used both to oppress the early slaves on the sugar plantations in the Anglo-Caribbean and as an instrument of liberation, especially by the Baptists (Williams 1994, 6; Gregory, ed. 1995; Ers-kine 2000, 209; Yorke 2000, 2004, 153–66; Jennings 2007, 49–62; Brett 2008; Dick 2010; and Yorke et al. 2010, 39–44).

Historically, the Bible has also contributed substantially to literacy develop-ment among many Anglo-Caribbean peoples (Peebles 1993, 8; Cvornyek 1999, 203). Scholars who write about the historic disequilibrium in the relationship between Europe and the "New World," which spawned the colonial subservience of the latter to the former, lose no time in reminding us that the *ménage à trois* involving the three Cs of Commerce, Civilization, and Christianity must be con-sidered inseparable in any meaningful and defensible discussion of how Europe succeeded in extending its cultural influence throughout the Caribbean. One can also account for Europe's cultural diffusion throughout the world by aligning one-self with Ali Mazrui's rather provocative thesis regarding the three Gs. He writes:

God, gold and glory! Captured in a slogan, these are in fact the three basic imperatives in the history of cultural diffusion. Why do men [*sic*] burst forth from their boundaries in search of new horizons? They are inspired either by a search for religious fulfillment (the God standard) or by a yearning for economic real- ization (the gold standard) or by that passion for renown (the quest for glory). (Mazrui 1990, 29)

Whether we see the colonial legacy of the Caribbean as a whole through the prism of the three Cs or that of the three Gs, the fact remains that the Bible was integral to the total process of empire construction. The Bible was foundational to the christianization of the Caribbean, and it authenticated the restless search for religious fulfillment and meaning that might well have driven not a few of the early missionaries to the region—be it the Roman Catholic Bartolomé de las Casas among the indigenous peoples, such as the Arawaks, or later, a Moravian such as Count von Zinzendorf to the African slaves themselves.

Sugirtharajah identifies the Authorized Version of the Bible(though never formally authorized by anyone [Gilmore 2000, 25]), more commonly known as the King James Version or the King James Bible, as England's greatest cultural product (1998b, 14). One should not forget that the original version of 1611 came with a four-page preface prepared by Myles Smith, one of the translators and later Bishop of Gloucester. The preface was a dedication not to God as such but, "To the most high and mightee [*sic*] Prince, James ..." (Rhodes et al. 1997, 1). It was this version which was exported to and transported throughout the Anglo-Carib- bean. Similar observations can be made regarding the *Louis Segond* version in relation to the Francophone Caribbean, the *Reina Valera* version in the Hispano- phone Caribbean, and the Portuguese (of Portugal) *Almeida* and the Dutch *State Bijbel* versions wherever the Portuguese and Dutch influences were sufficiently strong such, as in the Netherlands Antilles.

Also, it must be said that the Caribbean region as a whole has been character- ized historically more by a relatively robust record of *distribution* of the Bible than actual *translation*, per se, since it was assumed, perhaps rightly, that the region did not yet boast sufficiently developed "Caribbean" languages or creoles, in terms of both prestige and number of speakers, to warrant the translation of the Bible (or a portion of it) into those languages/creoles. However, times have changed and continue to do so in this regard. Before I expand on that, however, perhaps it would be useful to share some relatively recent figures regarding the distribution of Bibles translated in English, French, Spanish, and Dutch. The figures involve complete Bibles—not New Testaments, which would have increased the numbers substantially—as presented in table 1 (United Bible Societies 2002).

In spite of the understandable economic and even political uncertainties facing the Caribbean as a whole, induced, for the most part, by the unrelenting

Table 1.

Caribbean Countries/Islands	Bibles Distributed in 2000–2001
Cuba	45, 857
Dominican Republic	102,998
East Caribbean	13,394
French Antilles	24,212
Haiti	113,237
Netherlands Antilles	8,177
Puerto Rico	106,227
Suriname	15,661
"West Indies" (Bahamas, Belize, Cayman Islands, Jamaica, Turks and Caicos Islands)	78,321
TOTAL	508,084

forces of globalization, it is still true to say that one of the historical and even contemporary phenomena characterizing this linguistically and religio-culturally complex region is a stubborn postcolonial commitment to assert itself on the world stage. In contemporary parlance, Caribbean biblical scholars of whatever stripe are seeking to keep a "glocal" perspective on things.

In the Caribbean, it should also be pointed out, the imposed European powerful High (or H) languages—be it English, French, Spanish, or Dutch—have undergone the not-yet-fully-understood processes of pidginization and creolization. According to some sociolinguists, the Caribbean is one of the best regions in the world in which to study the creolization of European languages (Wardhaugh 1992). According to statistics compiled by Wycliffe Bible Translators Caribbean, for example, out of a total of some eighty creoles spoken worldwide, approximately thirty of them are spoken throughout the Caribbean region as a whole (Yorke 2008). Once considered cultural badges engendering feelings of shame rather than honor, Caribbean creoles are now emerging, more and more, as the mother tongues of many and, therefore, the identity markers and tools with which many now choose to communicate in the region. Among other places, this linguistic phenomenon manifests itself at times in the domains of politics, the church, academia, and the media (Devonish 2007).

One of the more recent domains is that of Bible translation, as well. Today in the region the Bible is not only transported from Europe or North America in Indo-European translations, but it is also being actively translated there. That is, the United Bible Societies (UBS), at times in partnership with organizations like Wycliffe Bible Translators Caribbean, is now promoting in the region—through various bodies like the Bible Society of the West Indies (Jamaica), the Bible Society of Haiti (Port-au-Prince), and the Bible Society of the Netherlands Antilles (based in Curaçao)—the translation of the Bible into the various Caribbean creoles.

In this endoglossic exercise, Caribbean creoles are being valorized, as greater prestige is now being conferred on them. In short, UBS in particular, through its subsidiaries in the region, is not only contributing substantially to the ongoing march towards language retention and revitalization in the Caribbean as a whole but also to the linguistic and postcolonial repositioning of the Bible (including the New Testament) in the Caribbean.

THE ROLE OF THE NEW TESTAMENT IN THE ANGLO-CARIBBEAN

It is perhaps defensible to say that the basic message of the New Testament, in spite of its rich diversity, is really about God's glory made manifest in his all-embracing kingdom-building love made manifest in Christ (Schreiner 2008). This is a message, it seems to me, which ought to be at the very heart of any attempt to engage in meaningful mission to the Caribbean—then and now (Matt 28:16–20; John 3:16–21; Acts 1:1–8, 4:12, 17:16–34; Col 1:15–20; and Rev 14:6–12. See Keown 2008).

I. Howard Marshall is correct, I think, in pointing out that "New Testament theology is essentially missionary theology" and that a "recognition of this missionary character of the documents will help us to see them in true perspective and to interpret them in the light of their intention" (2004, 34–35). In his large two-volume tome (almost 2,000 pages!), Eckhard Schnabel also rightly underscores the centrality of mission in the New Testament as a whole (2004).

Motivated by a sense of Christian supersessionism and armed with texts such as those to which I have just referred, European missionaries, at times risking life and limb, "fanned out" throughout the Caribbean in search of souls for the kingdom, in an effort to be faithful to the missionary mandate as they understood it then (Spickard and Cragg 1994, 298–300). Serving as both sacred text and textbook, the Bible played a pivotal role in the whole kingdom-building enterprise (Dietrich and Luz 2002).

The problem, of course, is that such a kingdom-building missionary thrust was not being carried out in a vacuum but was inextricably linked to that of empire construction as well. For those at the receiving end of this imperial enterprise, especially those falling within the sphere of influence of the various European powers (and later, North America), the "missionary movement" proved to be both a boon and a bane. Spickard and Cragg, are right in pointing out, "The scope of European and North American missionary activity in the nineteenth century was extraordinary. Wherever empire went, there too went missionaries" (1998, 301).

In terms of the Caribbean, we ought to remind ourselves that, during his second voyage to the region (1493), Columbus landed with seventeen ships and fifteen hundred people. Among them were a Rev. Bernardo Boyl and twelve other members of the clergy as missionaries. It is for this reason that scholars like Molefe Kete Asante, in discussing the history of colonialism, juxtapose "missionaries, merchants, and mercenaries" (2007, 209–21). Scholars from the Anglo-Caribbean, lacking some degree of nuance in their use of language, at times affirm that:

The conquest and colonization of the Americas, like Asia, Africa and Australia, were accomplished with the gun and the Bible.... Historically, religion has been used to rationalize and consolidate military conquests, preserve empires through mental enslavement of the conquered, and destroy resistance by debasing and vulgarizing the culture of subject peoples.... The institution entrusted with its propagation was the Christian church—Roman Catholicism and Protestantism. (Hylton 2002, 1)

My basic argument at the outset, then, is this: if those in the Anglo-Caribbean—sometimes made to feel despised and rejected, as is generally the case among Two-Thirds World peoples—are ever to engage in any meaningful postcolonial rehabilitation of the expression "Christian mission" and appropriate it in ways that are entirely wholesome and life-affirming, as God in Christ would wish, then we need to return to the *fons et origo* (source and origin) of the tradition—the New Testament itself—where the justification for that mission is first articulated.

What is quite noticeable, however, among some of the more prominent Anglo-Caribbean Christian theologians, is that they tend not to struggle hermeneutically with the New Testament itself in their attempt to articulate an Anglo-Caribbean Christian theology. For instance, Kortright Davis (1990), who is Anglican and Antiguan, provides us with an excellent articulation of the contents and contours of an Anglo-Caribbean Christian theology, but makes only passing reference to (without discussion of) the *crux interpretum*, 1 Cor 7:21, where Paul addresses himself to issues of slavery and freedom in his Greco-Roman and Corinthian context. In addition, the Corinthian reference does not even appear in the index of the volume, published in the Orbis Series. The late Lewin Williams, from Jamaica, makes passing reference to NT texts like John 12:32 and Rom 11:17–22 in an earlier well-thought-out article but, again, offers no sustained interaction with the passages in question (1991). However, there can be little doubt that the articulation of a relevant and contemporary postcolonial Anglo-Caribbean Christian theology is informed and influenced by a profound commitment to the NT (and the Bible as a whole) as God's liberating word within an Anglo-Caribbean context.

AN EMERGING CADRE OF ANGLO-CARIBBEAN BIBLICAL SCHOLARS

Although Anglo-Caribbean biblical scholars since the early 1970s have earned doctoral degrees from leading universities in America and Europe (e.g., Valentine Chambers, a Jamaican, who earned his degree from Vanderbilt University in Hebrew Bible; and John Holder, a Barbadian, who earned his in Hebrew Bible at the University of London), it cannot be said that there have been well-trained biblical scholars in abundance. However, the times continue to change.

Not to be overlooked in this narrative are those Anglo-Caribbean biblical scholars who were trained in the United States or elsewhere but who have opted, for any number of reasons, either to remain abroad upon completion of their degree program or to return home for a while and then migrate abroad at a later time, thus constituting part of the vibrant Anglo-Caribbean Diaspora. A number of examples come readily to mind, such as the following from Jamaica: Olive Hemmings and Althea Spencer-Miller, in New Testament, both of whom studied at Claremont in California; Pedrito Maynard-Reid, also in New Testament, whose dissertation on James was completed at Andrews University, Michigan, and which was later published by Orbis Books; Bertram Melbourne, again in New Testament, who also studied at Andrews University and whose dissertation was published by the University Press of America; Orlando Moncrieffe, in Hebrew Bible, who studied at Duke University; and Abson Joseph, former Dean of Academic Affairs at the Caribbean Wesleyan College of Theology. Abson completed his studies in New Testament at Brunei University, under the supervision of Joel Green, a fellow member of SNTS. Abson's dissertation on 1 Peter, a narratological reading of the letter, was published by T&T Clark.

Some others hail from other parts of the Anglo-Caribbean as well: one is Melvin Peters, from Antigua who studied Hebrew Bible at the University of Toronto, where he specialized in manuscripts in Bohairic, one of the dialects of Coptic. He is now a full professor of Hebrew Bible at Duke University. Another is Lael Caesar, from Guyana, who studied Hebrew Bible at the University of

Wisconsin at Madison. under Michael Fox, writing his dissertation on Job. As for the present writer, who hails from St. Kitts-Nevis in the Eastern Caribbean, he obtained his Ph.D. in New Testament from McGill University (1987), studying under N. Thomas Wright, with his dissertation subsequently published by the University Press of America (1991). And like a "wandering Aramean" (not unlike other Caribbean migrants, including biblical scholars themselves), the present writer now works and resides in South Africa again after having first spent several years teaching biblical studies in Canada, the United States, Kenya, Nigeria, South Africa, Zimbabwe and Jamaica.

More and more Anglo-Caribbean biblical scholars who are currently working in the Caribbean are also acquiring doctoral degrees from top universities in Britain and elsewhere. Among these are the following: Ian Rock, at the University of Wales-Lampeter, in New Testament, with William Campbell as supervisor (2005); Oral Thomas, at the University of Birmingham, in New Testament, with R. S. Sugirtharajah serving as his supervisor (2007); and Delano Palmer, in New Testament, at the University of South Africa, for whom the present writer served as supervisor (2009). In most cases, one finds not only a competent handling of the New Testament texts—including, as in the case of Rock's work on Romans, the literary and imperial dynamics of the Greco-Roman world—but also a creative attempt to ground discussions within a postcolonial Anglo-Caribbean context. Such is certainly the case with Palmer, a Jamaican, and Thomas, an Antiguan, as their dissertation projects readily reveal: the former's was published by the University Press of America as *Messianic "I" and Rastafari in Dialogue: Bio-Narratives, The Apocalypse, and Paul's Letter to the Romans* (2010); and the latter's was published by Equinox as *Biblical Resistance Hermeneutics in a Caribbean Context* (2010).

Mention should also be made of Anthony Oliver, from Trinidad and Tobago, former Vice-President for Academic Affairs at the Caribbean Graduate School of Theology (CGST, Kingston, Jamaica), an institution within the "evangelical" tradition (a term that is used, according to Trudinger [2004], in too restrictive a fashion nowadays, since all churches are mandated to proclaim the gospel). Oliver completed his PhD in 1996 in Hebrew Bible at Trinity International University in Deerfield, Illinois; his focus was on the book of Amos.

Not to be overlooked are a number of other private, faith-based tertiary institutions which are now offering advanced degrees in biblical studies (Hebrew Bible and New Testament) in the Caribbean as well. One example is the School of Religion and Theology at Northern Caribbean University (NCU) in Mandeville, Jamaica. Established in 1907 by the Seventh-day Adventist church, currently the largest denomination in Jamaica in terms of membership, but acquiring university status in 1999, NCU now offers master's degrees in both Hebrew Bible and

New Testament. In time, it hopes to mount the Ph.D. program for the Anglo-Caribbean in both Hebrew Bible and New Testament as well. Affiliated with the Miami-based Inter-American Theological Seminary which is also owned and operated by the Seventh-day Adventist church, NCU currently serves as one of the sites for the newly-introduced Ph.D. program in biblical studies which is meant to serve, at least initially, the Hispanophone Caribbean and some of the Latin American countries.

Recently, NCU also launched the Biblical Manuscript Research Centre (BMRC), the only such text-critical facility throughout not only the Caribbean but Latin America as a whole. Clinton Baldwin, a Jamaican, who completed his dissertation in textual criticism at Andrews University , Michigan (2007), serves as Director of the Centre; his dissertation was published by Peter Lang.

In speaking with a number of the Anglo-Caribbean biblical scholars themselves, such as Thomas in Jamaica and Ian Rock in Barbados, a felt need was expressed for the creation of better professional structures to facilitate more meaningful interaction. Among other things, this desire to meet together more regularly and to widen the circle of inclusion is consistent with current political trends, as seen, for example, in the initiative of the Caribbean Community (CARICOM) in its call for greater regional integration. The structure being proposed is a Pan-Caribbean Association of Biblical Scholars and Theologians.

The best example of a tertiary institution with regional reach in the Anglo-Caribbean is the most senior such institution, the University of the West Indies (UWI), which goes back to 1948 and was nurtured to academic maturity by the University of London. UWI has three main campuses: Jamaica, Barbados, and Trinidad and Tobago. In each case, a "theology department" is attached to the university. In the case of Jamaica, this involves an ecumenical/interconfessional arrangement, in which ten or so different denominations—including Anglican, Baptist, Church of God, Congregational, Disciples of Christ, Methodist, Moravian, and Presbyterian—have banded themselves together to create the United Theological College of the West Indies (UTCWI). In addition, St. Michael's Seminary, a Roman Catholic institution, is just next door and works in collaboration with UTCWI. In Barbados, it consists of Codrington College, an Anglican College. In the case of Trinidad and Tobago, it is the St. Vianney and Martyrs of Uganda Seminary, a Roman Catholic institution.

CHALLENGES AND OPPORTUNITIES FOR THE FORESEEABLE FUTURE

In spite of the clarion call for greater collaboration, I suspect that it will take some time for any meaningful scholarly camaraderie to develop fully or for a sustained

"coming together" and collaboration to take place among Anglo-Caribbean biblical scholars of all denominational stripes. Given the history, ethos, and mission of
the various denominations in the Anglo-Caribbean (involving those linked to the
three UWI campuses mentioned above, plus the evangelicals and the Seventh-
day Adventists), there is still, it seems to me, an air of suspicion, which might
continue to militate against any meaningful and ongoing collaborative efforts.

On the one hand, those scholars who are linked to UTCWI—and, therefore,
UWI, the regionally established public university—might be viewed as more "liberal" in inclination, insofar as they might be far more willing to take the gospel
to the public square, to experiment with new ideas as they seek to ground the
gospel in the Caribbean soul and soil. On the other hand, those scholars within
the evangelical tradition might see themselves as no less mindful of the need to
opt for the creative contextualization of the gospel but more restrained in doing
so for fear of "mixing religion and politics" too much. What binds them all
together, however, is that most, if not all, of the denominations represented in
both "camps" are members of the Caribbean Council of Churches (CCC) which
was established in 1983 (Titus 2010: 489). In Jamaica, where approximately half of
the entire Anglo-Caribbean population reside, there is also the Christian Council
to which a number of the Protestant denominations belong as well.

For example, the current Governor General of Jamaica, as Head of State,
is a member of the Seventh-day Adventist church, as was the former Governor
General of Antigua and Barbuda. Passing mention can and should also be made
of the fact that the Seventh-day Adventist church has one of the largest single-
denomination relief agencies at work in the Caribbean, the worldwide Adventist
Development and Relief Agency (ADRA). As an active arm of the church, ADRA
responds, at times in collaboration with other agencies like USAID, to natural
disasters like hurricanes and earthquakes. This humanitarian assistance is given
to all and sundry, regardless of denominational affiliation.

In spite of this divide between and among the major sectors of the Christian
community in the Anglo-Caribbean, however, there is one institution that serves
as a point of convergence for all three such sectors: the Bible society. In Jamaica,
for example, the Bible Society of the West Indies benefited in its recent translation of the New Testament into Jamaican (a Caribbean creole) from the input
of biblical scholars in all sectors of the Christian community—UTCWI, CGST,
the Jamaica Theological Seminary (evangelical), and Northern Caribbean University (SDA). This was possible because, for the most part, the Bible serves as the
common denominator among all churches, regardless of orientation and doctrinal persuasion, and because the Bible societies in the Caribbean—as is true of the
Bible societies worldwide—see themselves as servants of all the churches, rather
than as servants of particular churches or denominations themselves.

Such convergence notwithstanding, Anglo-Caribbean biblical scholars have not had much "net practice" working with each other across denominational borders and boundaries. That is a real challenge, which might well remain for the foreseeable future. With such a small but growing cadre of Anglo-Caribbean biblical scholars, however, one cannot afford to ignore any scholars solely on the basis of their denominational affiliation and place of employment. As in North America, Australia, Europe, South Africa, and elsewhere, Anglo-Caribbean biblical scholars should continue to reach out to each other, I believe, in their effort to work together "for the common good," as they confront national and regional challenges in a postcolonial Caribbean setting. They should do so across all denominational lines without having to mask their identities or feel apologetic about their denominational affiliation. Their *modus operandi* should mirror the meetings of learned societies such as the Canadian Society for Biblical Studies, the Society of Biblical Literature, the Society for New Testament Studies (*Studiorum Novi Testamenti Societas*—SNTS), and the New Testament Society of Southern Africa (NTSSA).

By way of illustration, I should like to provide a personal story. When I made an attempt to meet some Anglo-Caribbean biblical scholars, there was an initial excitement and the manifestation of a most accommodating spirit. However, when it was "discovered" that I was from a particular denominational tradition, the initial temperature of warmth and collegiality seemed to have dropped rather suddenly. Making known my denominational affiliation, I thought, was highly irrelevant as a fellow biblical scholar. Of course, not all Anglo-Caribbean biblical scholars operate in that manner. My colleagues at the UTCWI in Jamaica, and no less so at both CGST and JTS, for example, remained most cordial and collegial in spirit throughout.

In spite of this scenario, I am encouraged by some relatively recent developments in the region. In response to their felt need to work more closely and collaboratively, Anglo-Caribbean biblical scholars—and their colleagues in other fields, such as ethics, Christian theology, church history, missiology, pastoral and practical theology—are finding creative ways to come together. Two examples should suffice. First, the Caribbean Evangelical Theological Association (CETA) recently sponsored an event (July, 2010) which was hosted by CGST and to which biblical and other scholars from both UTCWI/UWI and NCU (SDA) were invited for the opening ceremonies. Second, and for the first time ever (January 2011), there was a truly pan-Caribbean theological conference, hosted by UTCWI, to which biblical and other scholars were invited to participate, encompassing not only the three sectors of the Christian community already identified, but also reaching out to the larger multilingual (Dutch, English, French, and Spanish) Caribbean church and community as well. Mention should also be made of SNTS in its ongoing attempt to internationalize itself further in that Latin America and the Caribbean now fall within its purview as well. In time, this should also help to foster greater interaction among Anglo-Caribbean biblical scholars.

In addition, and unlike many biblical scholars in the West, Anglo-Caribbean biblical scholars tend not to operate as "free floating" scholars but instead work and write in the service of the church and its contemporary Anglo-Caribbean postcolonial context. In such a context, the Afro-existential forces at work on Anglo-Caribbean biblical scholars—induced, for the most part, by the unrelenting forces of globalization and its effects of marginalization, vulnerability, and powerlessness—encourage some to transcend disciplinary boundaries and borders (see Kuck 2007). Thus, we find, for example, the biblical scholar who, instead of working exclusively in her/his own silo, interacts with scholars in other fields: ethicists, like Burchell Taylor; Christian theologians, like the late Lewin Williams, former president of UTCWI; practical theologians, like Howard Gregory, former president of UTCWI and now an Anglican Bishop in Jamaica; and church historians, like Lascelles Newman, president of CGST, Jamaica.

Further, the political, economic, educational, cultural, social, and other challenges facing the contemporary Anglo-Caribbean as a whole are also part of the agenda, not only of the Anglo-Caribbean ethicist or theologian but also of the biblical scholar. Granted, in some cases, there is still a need to go beyond a narrow privatist and pietistic fixation on the self, or an escapist and eschatological outlook on life in general, or the undue influence of foreign agendas in particular, to a stance that is much more contextually grounded (see Fanon 1967). However, I am reasonably confident that such "apolitical" and "acontextual" approaches to matters of faith and life will not emerge as the dominant paradigm in the Anglo-Caribbean among biblical scholars and others.

Another challenge facing Caribbean biblical scholars generally is the creative use of indigenous translations of the Bible currently available, as in the following examples: the complete Bible in Haitian Creole; the New Testament and some of the Psalms in Dominican/St.Lucian Patwa; the complete Bible in Papiamentu, spoken throughout the former Netherlands Antilles; and the New Testament in Sranan Tonga, spoken in Suriname. I suspect that, for the foreseeable future, Caribbean biblical scholars will continue to ignore such translations in Caribbean creoles, including, perhaps, the recently published (2012) *Di Jamiekan Nyuu Testiment*, the New Testament in the Jamaican language. This recent translation was spearheaded by the Bible Society of the West Indies (Kingston, Jamaica). Earlier, the Bible Society had already published the Gospel of Luke (2010), with the title "Jiizas: Di Buk We Luuk Rait Bout Im." I suspect that most, if not all, will continue to opt for the Bible (Hebrew Bible and New Testament) exclusively in its

Euro-American linguistic manifestation, whether they fall within Anglophone, Francophone, Hispanophone, or Netherlanderphone areas of the Caribbean.

CONCLUSION

In this by no means exhaustive survey of biblical studies in the Anglo-Caribbean, I have sought—through retrospection (looking back), introspection (looking within), and projection (looking forward)—to give insight into the important role which biblical studies is playing in the region. In spite of the challenges to which I have referred, I am fairly confident that Anglo-Caribbean biblical scholars will continue to "grow and prosper and be in good health." Since, however, like the prophet Amos I am neither a prophet nor the son of one (Amos 3:17, NIV)—or, following the CEV translation of the American Bible Society (1995) based in New York, "I am not a prophet! And I wasn't trained to be a prophet"—only time will truly tell what directions biblical studies will continue to take in a postcolonial Anglo-Caribbean context in the early twenty-first century and, perhaps, beyond.

PART 5
PACIFIC

13

DRIFTING HOMES

Jione Havea

The opportunity to imagine into writing what biblical studies might look like in the future in the islands of the South Pacific (*Pasifika*) is unsettling. There are several reasons for this.

First of all, to write about the future is a foreign practice to the oral cultures of islanders, whose lived world and worldviews are fluid and slippery, drifting and laid-back. Our ancestors, male and female, practiced different forms of writing, like the *tatau* (tattoo),[1] which inscribed their roots and routes on their faces and bodies. The ones who could not bear the cuts of *tatau* chisels, and who were surely more sensible, carved onto tree trunks, some of which became totems, or narrated with strands in mats and patterns in *tapa*. Given that biblical studies have not reached *tatau* stage in Pasifika, this reflection will avoid the illusion of rigidity and finality.

Second, it is unsettling for an offspring of oral cultures to imagine the future as if it will be free of the present. Islanders' sense of time is not linear, as if we move from one point in time to another point in time and eventually arrive at a future point in time which is outside the present point in time. Rather, time has to do with place and relations, which we do not slot up as past, present, and future. Time has to do with connections (*kāinga*), and it is therefore rooted and woven, flexible and routed. We talk and dream about a tomorrow, a next week, and so on, but always in relation to the places we inhabit and the relations that oblige us. The future interweaves with what impacts us in the present. Biblical studies in Pasifika in the future will ebb with the conditions of the islands and the relations between islanders. Both island space (because of climate change) and relations among

---

1. In my native language, Tongan, *tatau* has two other meanings: (1) to "squeeze out" (e.g., water from a soaked cloth/article or milk from scraped coconut) and (2) to attain "equal status."

islanders (migration disperses Pasifika people overseas) are currently drifting. As our island homes and people drift, so does our future and whatever the future of biblical studies might be among us.

Third, it is unsettling to imagine a future since the present of biblical studies in Pasifika is not local (Havea 2008). How may I imagine *our* future when *our* present is not *ours*? Our situation is similar to the situations of aboriginal peoples in Asia, Africa, and Latin America, where biblical studies continue to be a European project. As (some but not all) biblical scholars in the West engage the gifts of womanism, psychoanalysis, postcolonialism, queer and cultural theories, alongside a slew of other interpretive approaches, Pasifika islanders are trapped in the promises of traditional-historical, literary, and theological criticisms. White missionary teachers gifted our fathers and grandfathers with those tools, and "the Western classics" line the dusty shelves of our scanty theological libraries, forcing native students to think and read as if they were Europeans from the nineteenth and twentieth centuries. To imagine biblical studies in the future in Pasifika therefore requires untangling the hold of European modes of thinking from native minds.

Fourth, because I live and work outside of my home island of Tonga, I am suspect in the eyes of the bookkeepers to the politics of representation. Pasifika islanders have not agreed on spokespersons to tell on our behalf the future of biblical studies in our islands. Should that task be a burden only of islanders who live in our drifting island homes? Can the task be free from the snares of nativism, which tends to romanticize natives as exotic subjects? What is the role for islanders who have drifted to overseas lands? Given that there is only a splash of Pasifika biblical critics, it will help to converse and cooperate with other socially and culturally savvy islanders. The mats on which such conversations may occur are still being stranded and woven,[2] and this chapter is a strand for that dream.

These unsettlements point me toward three issues over which I shall spend the rest of this chapter. I will begin to: (1) unpack the gifts that drifting island space offers for imagining biblical studies in the future; (2) decolonize the minds of Pasifika islanders by insisting that we set European modes of thinking adrift; and (3) consider how crosscultural conditionings contribute to forming the future of biblical studies in Pasifika, drawing upon my experience (as drifting islander) of biblical studies in Aotearoa/New Zealand and Australia.

---

2. In response to a special session on "Bible in the Pacific" at the 2008 international meeting of the Society of Biblical Literature (Auckland, Aotearoa-New Zealand), a group of Pasifika islanders, led by Nasili Vaka'uta and Tevita K. Havea, gathered to consider a hope to cooperate in a writing project. Watch for this island space!

I will address these issues in three drifting sections, each exploring different senses of the word "drifting." I am of course assuming that biblical studies can home the Bible in, and complement the future of, Pasifika. The Bible is a drifting home (Havea 2007, 2008), which I will weave in this chapter with Pasifika drifting.

DRIFTING ISLAND SPACE

Pasifika islanders are saltwater people. Our world and worldviews contrast from those of indigenous people from the interior of larger lands with flowing rivers, who are freshwater people. Our saltwater surroundings condition our daily lives and give us the feeling that our sea of islands drift in the currents of the Pacific Ocean. Island space is like bodies that are constantly in motion, drifting toward and away from each other, as reflected in the navigational wisdom of our ancestors:

> Pacific models of ocean navigation differ from western paradigms because they do not flatten and stabilize space through the bird's eye view of nautical charts. Instead, Pacific navigators have developed a complex system of charting a vessel's movement through space where the voyaging canoe is perceived as stable while the islands and cosmos move towards the traveler.[3]
> … Attention to movement offers a paradigm of rooted routes, of a mobile, flexible, and voyaging subject who is not physically or culturally circumscribed by the terrestrial boundaries of island space. (DeLoughrey 2007, 3)

---

3. This navigational wisdom manifests itself in the Tongan practice of *heliaki*, often misunderstood as the Tongan version of metaphors (Kaeppler 1993, 6–9). *Heliaki* is more than metaphorical use of symbols and language. *Heliaki* is intentionally engaging, teasing and troubling, attracting the attention of listeners but at the same time withholding details (through *tupu'a* [riddle], for instance) in order to draw listeners toward the speaker and her/his *talanoa* (story, concern). The speaker uses *heliaki* not in order to conceal meanings, though this happens, but in order to tease listeners to draw toward the speaker. *Heliaki* warms listeners to the speaker. A speaker uses *heliaki* in a similar way that a dancer draws others to dance (*tu'ulāfale*) alongside her/him. Similarly, island navigators imagine that islands move toward them and the voyaging vessel.

Island Space in Motion

We experience the islands as bodies that float, in motion, on the face of the deep. We respond to this sense of drifting in a variety of ways. In light of my task here, I shall discuss two common responses, drawing upon my Tongan roots and native language, and await other islanders to join this performance (see n2).

Both responses can be drawn from the same Tongan proverb, *holo pē tuʻú he kuo ngalu e fasi*—"Keep the position, or relax the stand, for the wave has broken"—which takes me back to the surfs (Havea 2003). This proverb comes from a context in which a group of voyagers or fishers wait for the right wave to carry them onto shore without shattering their vessels, and themselves, on the rocks (compare with the wish of a psalmist upon the little ones of Babylon in Psalm 137). The proverb applies to inhabitants of volcanic islands who drift in the open sea waiting for a wave to carry them up to a platform on the cliff where they can land, as well as to inhabitants of atoll islands who wait for a wave to clear them over the reef. In both cases, the drifters have no control over the part of the saltwater drink where they are. Some members of the group might be eager to get out of the water. Some might be too tired to give attention to the currents and the waves. Some might be too confident that they can ride any wave onto shore. It is for those kinds of restless attitudes that the proverb *holo pē tuʻú he kuo ngalu e fasi* is often uttered, either from one of the members of the group or from someone on shore, and it might be heard as saying one of two things,[4] depending on how one behaves upon the surf, during the wait.

First, the proverb calls the drifters to keep the position, *holo pē tuʻú*, for the wave that could have carried them safely ashore has broken, *he kuo ngalu e fasi*. One opportunity has passed by, and the drifters must wait for the next one. Arrival is on hold, delayed, and the drifters are to be patient and keep their position, for it is better to wait for a safe wave than attempt to ride a wave that will break on the rocks. Patience is a virtue that most islanders are known to have. Sometimes, however, too much patience results in excessive laid-back attitudes and indifference.

In this first sense of the proverb, the drifters are in a deep fluid context, and they float with the illusion that they can keep their position in the sea. This raises questions relating to what it means to keep the position in the ocean. Does one keep the position in relation to the ocean floor? In relation to the waves? In relation to the island? In relation to one's fellow drifters? The illusions of fixedness and of control are not always clear in the minds of the

---

4. The challenge, of course, is how to discern which of the two senses of the proverb would guide one safely ashore, which can only be decided on the surf.

drifters because their concern is not with where they are but how and when to safely arrive where they are going.

These insights can migrate into the spheres of biblical studies, whose practitioners are not always aware of the fluidity of the texts and of their contexts (referring to the contexts both of the text and of the biblical critics) and the illusion of their sense of control. The text is not property to mark and claim, or a container to unpack, but a deep fluid body with many currents, some of which can carry one home and other of which can dash one to pieces. Furthermore, control over the text is an illusion (Aichele 2001).

The second response comes from the same proverb, this time heard as calling the drifters to relax the stand or release the position, *holo pē tuʻú,* for the wave on which they have been waiting is breaking, *he kuo ngalu e fasi.* Oops! In this second sense, the pull of a breaking wave has caught the drifters, and their hope for survival is in letting go of their stand so that they might bob to the backside of the wave instead of rolling in its whirling mouth unto the rocks. Arrival is imminent, with pangs and cuts, hurled from the fluid context unto the sharp teeth of the cliff or the reef. The illusion of control surfaces quickly, and, according to island wisdom, the more relaxed the drifters become the less painful the arrival will be. This could be the difference between wounds and scratches at one end of the spectrum, and between death and life at the other end.

Waves come in all sizes, and every wave may of course take one to shore, near or far. The condition in which one lands will depend on how one rides each wave. It is best to avoid breaking waves, but in the event that a breaking wave rips a drifter, it is better for that person to relax and release her/his stand and hope for the best. Drifters cannot control waves, but they can ride them (Havea 2007). The aim of the drifter is to survive the meeting of the wave and the rocks. Sometimes, this requires relaxing and letting go.

It would benefit biblical studies in the future if this kind of attitude, knowing that there is a time to relax and release one's stand or position, can drift into the minds and attitudes of biblical critics. This call relates to both ideological and methodological positions, and it comes from island spaces from where we see a lot of rigidity and stoniness in Western expressions of biblical studies (see below).

These two responses have to do with how to do biblical studies, with an island twist. They are not about methodology, but about the attitude of doing biblical studies. This is one way of saying that methodology reflects personality, which reflects experience and location, and that some of the Western methodologies we have learned clash with our personalities. Any contribution from our saltwater experiences to biblical studies in the future must therefore include moving the fence of how to do biblical studies from the rigidity of methodologies, which are driven by ideologies and insecurity, in order to give room to the complexity of personalities, which are conditioned by confluent ideologies. Biblical studies came to us, and to indigenous people in mission fields, as a means of controlling how we behave. It is appropriate that we move in the other direction also, to see how our personalities can influence biblical studies.

ISLAND SPACE AND CLIMATE CHANGE

There is a second sense in which island space is drifting, having to do with the many islands that are crumbling and drifting away in the tentacles of the mighty ocean. Climate change is especially devastating against the low-lying atoll islands that spread over Pasifika.[5] The environmental predicament whirls from a pool of ironies: there is too much fresh water in the ocean but not enough fresh water on parched islands. Coral reefs choke from the excess of fresh water in the ocean, impoverishing islanders' sources of food and living. Moreover, it feels as if the floors of the ocean are rising to push waves inland and carry back the shores on their whitewash. The waves of the ocean, energized by climate change, are invading and shifting island borders. Island homes drift in this regard also.

Islanders' concern for the environment is primarily about survival. When one lives on an isolated island with limited resources, the rising of the seawater level means more than the loss of land. Rising seawater level depletes already impoverished lands. Islanders struggle with simple tools to root crops and reap fruits on shallow layers of island soil, and the invasion of seawater makes gardening less productive and our wells saltier.[6] With regard to the drifting islands of Pasifika, therefore, the primary response to the environmental crisis is not about how to save earth but how to survive it. People with privileges and authorities can speak with messianic voices about saving the earth, but drifting islanders hope to survive the often furious and barren earth (Fejo 2000).

Drifting from the struggles of islanders into the practices of biblical studies, what might biblical studies become if the messianic attitudes of biblical critics are exorcised? Biblical studies arrived in Pasifika, as in other mission fields, under the influences of the colonial venture and the missionary drive. The upshot is that

---

5. There are large volcanic islands in Pasifika also, whose inhabitants do not experience the fury of environmental displacement with the same desperation as those from atoll islands. Yet they are conscious of the plights of atoll islanders, who may be their relatives and whose ancestors may have been friends or foes at a previous time.

6. It does not help when the skies do not release its waters on the islands. One of the painful things to see from an island is rain passing at a distance in the open sea, which causes anguish that recalls, though the situation is the reverse, the anguish of the drowning victims who saw the ark of Noah floating away at a distance.

both the Bible, selectively read with christocentric biases, and the natives, whom early Westerners saw as savages, were seen to need rescue. Over time, biblical studies developed into messianic exercises exhibited most fully in the pulpits, from which terrorizing sermons of condemnation (of native/pagan customs) and deliverance (through the Christian/missionary message) ricocheted from week to week. Messianic attitudes created a rift between the two parts of the Bible, in parallel with a crevice between native and Christian cultures. As the New Testament resolved the problematic Old Testament, so did Christian cultures native customs. Messianic attitudes did not help our ancestors, and I cannot see at this point if they will be helpful for our descendants.

We often hear that heroes and winners write histories and construct memories, but we also know that histories and memories look different when survivors tell them. Survivors are not messianic, for they are more concerned with companionship and endurance. What might biblical studies look like if we embrace the patient fortitude of survivors? I imagine that biblical texts will sound different. The garden story (Gen 2–3), for instance, becomes the story of a couple who survived an unproductive situation in what was once (but not at the beginning) a fruitful land space that belonged to a prohibiting landlord (Yahweh), so what used to be lamented as expulsion becomes cause for joy—freedom at last! Eve and the serpent become the parents of survivors (from Noah to Rahab, Ruth, Jonah, Job, Abigail, Stephen, Paul and many others), some of whom led resistance events. One may take similar lines with other expulsion stories, from Cain to Abram to Canaan and Israel, even to the sting of death and so forth. Expulsion and exit, which might come with cuts and wounds, are events to celebrate in the mouths of survivors.

There is a "how to do biblical studies" element here also. The European hermeneutical agenda emphasizes the tasks of "reading" which is linked with "writing" and affirms the structures of literacy and textuality. This system reinforces the interests of the privileged winners who write histories and construct memories. For the sake of survivors and of biblical studies everywhere, I propose that we consider supplementing our dedication to the righteous tasks of *reading* with the enduring leisure of *telling*. The Pasifika word for this is *talanoa*, which refers both to *the act of telling* (as verb) and to *the story* (as noun), so the same word crosses between diachronic (worlds behind and in front of a story) and synchronic (worlds in a story) realms.

One of the dilemmas in narrative and storytelling practices is that narrative readers and storytellers in the end revive, through reading and storytelling, the diachronic traits of stories at the expense of their synchronicity. With *talanoa*, on the other hand, the telling (*talanoa*) is not independent of the story (*talanoa*). Telling (*talanoa*) can imagine a story (*talanoa*) into life, locating it in time and space. On the other hand, a story (*talanoa*) can resist the illusion of time and space that telling (*talanoa*) provides. This affirmation of *talanoa* is for complementation rather than displacement, coming with the assumption that biblical studies will continue to be foreign on the shores of Pasifika as long as it favors the European hermeneutical agenda. For biblical studies to have a future in Pasifika requires engaging the double edges of *talanoa* (Havea 2008).

Drifting European Influences

Natives of Pasifika have multiple local and shared myths of origins. Several groups share a common myth of origin, which claims that our ancestors migrated from a land (which Maoris remember as *Hawaiki*), whose location is now unknown, and occupied islands that Maui (who was 'otua-mo-tangata, god and human, in the Tongan *talanoa*) fished up from the ocean. This particular myth of origin explains why paddling oars (which became war clubs), canoes (*waka*), and fishhooks (*hei matau*) are significant symbols in Pasifika.

Natives nowadays imagine "lost canoes" when we try to explain how we are related to people in other islands. Our *talanoa* claims that all natives of Pasifika came from the same root, but some of the canoes were lost during the journey and ended up in other islands. This raises an obvious question: "lost" in whose perspective, story, or telling?[7]

The joke here is that in the end, depending on the perspective of the *talanoa* (story or telling), all of the natives could have been on the lost canoes. The extent to which natives of Pasifika could claim to be indigenous to the islands is open for debate, but we are of the same mind that our ancestors were seafaring people. Among islanders, we celebrate our roots as the routes of our ancestors. We are descendants of a migrant and migrating people, whose routes are our roots.

When we relate to people whose roots come from outside of the three main groups of Polynesia, Melanesia, and Micronesia, we natives are, in general, xenophobic. People of Chinese roots, for example, have suffered the burning wrath of Tongans and Solomon Islanders, and people with Indian roots have experienced the same among Fijians and Tongans. On the other hand, we are generally accommodating of people from European countries, even though they came

---

7. Usually when scholars echo Spivak's question, "Can the subaltern speak?" they expect the subaltern to speak the master's language. One falls into this trap when one emphasizes the truth or meanings of what one tells. By stressing on the other hand the dynamics of *talanoa*, one encourages the subaltern to speak his/her own language and requires the masters to learn the languages of the subaltern.

as explorers, invaders, colonizers, and missionaries. We accommodate "white people," who came first, but not the "people of color," who arrived later and who still live among us. We uphold "white values and teachings" (which include Christianity and the biblical teachings) even after the "white people" left. I am referring here to the European modes of thinking of early explorers, colonizers, and missionaries, which continue to determine what natives deem as proper for our people today. Is it time to allow such "white values and teachings" to drift away?

I raise these questions not because of an anti-white nativism nor because I want to treat latecomers (from Asia and Europe) equally. Rather, I am concerned that honoring European values and modes of thinking (from the missionary and colonial era) debilitates the minds of native people. To make us think as if we were Europeans (of a particular era) is to make us think as if we were not who we are—native people—in our present struggles. We consequently reject modes of thinking from other cultural settings (e.g., Asia, Latin America, and Africa) as well as recent developments that come from the Western worlds (e.g., feminism and postmodernism). As such, echoing the hope of colonized peoples throughout history, we need to decolonize our minds, requiring us to allow early European influences to drift away.

With regard to biblical studies, I am targeting the historical-critical methodologies and the conservative theological empire-building worldviews. Those were *gifts* of the missionaries that came without a "use by date," but their usefulness has been exhausted. If those influences drift away, there will be room for Pasifika natives to hone the Bible and the tasks of biblical studies.

DRIFTING ISLANDERS

Pasifika migration continues, both into and away from the home islands. Pasifika is more crosscultural now than before due to the arrival of more foreigners and the return of some natives because of remigration or deportation from overseas. Being crosscultural is not a new phenomenon to the seafaring people of Pasifika, for our ancestors borrowed cultures and artifacts along the way to their new homes, but it is more evident now than before. At the home islands and overseas, we are more conscious of crosscultural conditionings.

In Pasifika, we are not always shrewd concerning what aspects of arriving cultures to localize, in part because we too want to be modern and in vogue. As minority groups overseas, for the sake of survival, we do not always have a say in forming our new surroundings. Thinking that we are insignificant, simple islanders in the world of cultured people, we are not always attentive to how we contribute to the conditioning of our settings. We are therefore *drifting islanders* in the sense that we have agile natures and volatile identities. Should we be more resolute in determining who we are and how to define the way we *talanoa* and maneuver? What currents and modes of thinking in our crosscultural surroundings might we accommodate and localize? From my present location, I propose that we accommodate three of the currents that flow in Aotearoa/New Zealand and Australia. I propose these with the hope to encourage *talanoa* along, and in between, the lines of biblical studies.

First, I advocate women-consciousness and sincerity towards sexuality, whose currents generate and chart various waves of feminism. The intersection of the waves of feminism with biblical studies has been encouraged in Aotearoa/ New Zealand and Australia by Judith McKinlay, Elaine Wainwright, and many others. Yet, a forum in which these concerns can engage the *talanoa* of Pasifika is lacking. Thus far, it is the burden of individuals from outside the European maelstroms and whitewash (foams of waves) to relate to and justify our imaginations alongside what dominant people do.

As the tide of biblical studies rises in our saltwater region, it would be helpful if we are tenacious in encouraging women-consciousness and sincerity towards sexuality. Whether these concerns are foreign or local to Pasifika is a question worth exploring. Did Christianity and Western civilizers, upon their arrivals, ostracize women-consciousness and sincerity towards sexuality from native minds? What was lost when missionaries condemned the nakedness and sexual freedom of our ancestors? How one unpacks these questions will vary, and it may not be possible to find out why Pasifika culture is so patriarchal. I believe that advocating women-consciousness and sincerity towards sexuality would help set adrift the deep-rooted patriarchal and homophobic anxieties of christianized Pasifika, which traditional customs and religious values sanction.

Second, I encourage earth-consciousness, which is a strong current in Australia through the works of Norman Habel, who cooperates with scholars from throughout the world to develop earth readings. Attention to earth—which includes land, sky, and ocean—is, of course, a global concern that transcends disciplines (McFague 2008). Several natives of Pasifika have already added island-wise perspectives. Iutisone Salevao (2000) relates land (*ele'ele* and *fanua* in Samoan) to blood and life; Ilaitia Tuwere (2008) attends to the dance of *vanua* (Fijian word for "land"); Winston Halapua (2008) extends the horizon to *moana*, the deep sea, which is necessary in contexts where global warming threatens to drown low-lying islands; and Nasili Vaka'uta (2008) attends to the people of the land. Attending to *moana* and the people of the land obliges us to grapple with the strengths of earth (as sky, land, and sea), through the *talanoa* of people for whom earth has to do with blood, life, womb, dance, celebration, ritual, home, belonging, and more. Given the natural disasters that frequent the shores of Pasifika (such as drought, earthquake, tsunami, cyclone, and so forth), earth-consciousness is a necessary element in the development of Pasifika biblical studies.

The third and most challenging current is the confluence of the various manifestations of critical and cultural theories, such as postmodernism, Marxism, psychoanalysis, queer, public, and postcolonial theories, and more, whose roots creep back under the surface to the Western world. The most energetic surfer of this current in Australia is Roland Boer, whose works embody a broad understanding of critical theory, extending from Jeroboam to Marx to Bob Dylan to Žižek and toward tombstones and beer bottles. Boer's works are radical in that they are rooted (the root of "radical" is *radix* : "root") in the secular contexts of Australia and beyond. More recently, Boer joins the mission to rescue the Bible from right-wing fundamentalists, releasing a manifesto that calls secular revolutionaries to gather at the worldly left (Boer 2007b).

Scientific minds and modernity replaced the passion for faith with the obsession with evidence and reason, so it became unfashionable for biblical scholars to be persons of faith. In the recent past, critical and cultural theories came along promoting rootedness and differences, but these did not revive faith under their umbrellas. Can there be faith in the world of critical and cultural theories (double meaning intended)? What might that faith look like? These are questions that we need to take seriously, as we ponder what the future of biblical studies might look like among the religiously infused people of Pasifika.

In the end, the suggestions I make here beg the obvious question: Am I not herewith promoting the hermeneutical project of the West? Of course I am, with a Pasifika twist: instead of letting the colonial and colonizing interests of the West drive how we engage the three currents I have outlined, I propose that we embrace these concerns not because we want to be chic but because we have a role to play in our crosscultural conditionings. We must tussle with these currents in order to stop being colonized subjects. Herein lurks our dilemma!

In Closing, Drifting into Angatuʻu!

One of the legacies of the Christian mission and colonization, parents to what Rudyard Kipling called "the white man's burden," is the taming of native people's will to resist. With the name and will of God on their tongues, missionaries and colonizers shut natives up and tamed their spirits. The church, which built the halls of biblical studies in Pasifika, inherited these depressing practices; so, if we want to revive the spirit of resistance, we must revive it in those realms first. Resistance can take many forms, from speaking and writing against "the empire" and the abuse of power to marching in demonstrations and taking up arms. Resistance is always for and against something, so there is no room for impartiality.

In closing I turn to one of the Tongan words for resistance, *angatuʻu*, which is the combination of two words, *anga* (will, attitude, custom, way) and *tuʻu* (stand, stop, excrete), and is better translated as a combination of *will to stand, to stop* and *to excrete*. The one who resists must have the will to stand for/against in order to stop and excrete something. In this chapter, the one who resists uses *talanoa* against powers that seek to silence and disadvantage natives. In the past, natives had to listen and obey without talking back to missionaries, civilizers, and colonizers. Encouraging *angatuʻu* is a way of saying that it is now time to talk (*talanoa*) back. Yet, *angatuʻu* is more than just talking; *angatuʻu* is also about custom, way, and actions. If the Western hermeneutical drive favors the will to power and the will to knowledge, the counterpart in Pasifika must insist on the will to stand, to stop, and to excrete. For biblical studies to be *ours*, local in Pasifika, the spirit of *angatuʻu* needs to be kindled.

14

Braiding the Traditions in Aotearoa/ New Zealand

Judith E. McKinlay

... Europe is in our books and in our boxes. We will unpack them slowly. God save this bright air, these untroubled waters. (quoted in Paul Morris et al., 2002, 91)

On Sunday morning, when I was upon deck, I saw the English flag flying, which was a pleasing sight in New Zealand. I considered it as the signal and dawn of civilisation, liberty, and religion, in that dark and benighted land. (quoted in Davidson 2004, 16.)

So writes the Anglican CMS missionary, Samuel Marsden, of Christmas Day 1814, the legendary day of the first Christian service in this land. His text was "Fear not for behold I bring you glad tidings of great joy" (Luke 2:10). Ironically, most of those listening could neither follow nor understand, but Marsden wrote in his journal, "we could not but feel the strongest persuasion that the time was at hand when the Glory of the Lord would be revealed to those poor benighted Heathens ..." (quoted in Davidson 2004, 16).

In Colin McCahon's series of crucifixions, painted in the 1940s, Christ hangs over the New Zealand landscape. Viewing these, the poet James K. Baxter saw McCahon's Christs "reconciled with the fertile hills behind them" (quoted in Simpson 2001, 15). Or are they imposed? Biblical studies in this land poses a similar question: how does the Bible relate to this place? A more personal question might be: how does a descendent of settlers, brought up in a Presbyterian manse, formerly a teacher in a theological college, now teaching in a secular university, provide a balanced assessment of the past, present, and future of biblical studies in this country? What follows is inevitably my view, reflecting who I am, and the traditions to which I belong.

Writing of his Scottish, Gaelic-speaking, community, led here by the charismatic, if autocratic, Rev. Norman McLeod in the latter half of the nineteenth century, my grandfather records:

> [M]any families had a complete set of Matthew Henry's encyclopedic *Exposition on the Old and New Testaments* and many of the older men had a working knowledge of the contents of these ponderous volumes. Thus, their faith was founded on a thorough knowledge not only of the words of the scriptures but of the interpretation of those words as understood at that time. (McKenzie 1942, 200)

Not all were as Bible-centered as this settlement at Waipu.

Tradition meets Tradition in Aotearoa

In a close biblical parallel with the Israelites under Joshua, the settlers had come to a land already populated by a people with their own cultural traditions, their own sacred spaces, and their own gods. My ancestral community may have been relatively small, but from 1831 to 1881 the non-Maori population grew from fewer than a thousand to half a million people (Belich 1996, 278). Christ and the Bible entered with the missionaries. A letter from Jane Buttle around 1853 gives a homely glimpse of this: "I have a Bible class of women each week in our kitchen" (Porter and Macdonald 1996, 91). They came optimistically. Anne Wilson writes in her diary before leaving London in 1832 how her heart "seems drawn" to "the poor heathen" whom "[t]he Lord shall give ... to His son" (Porter and Macdonald 1996, 60–61). For some, Calvinist theology and nineteenth-century views on race qualified such optimism. The Moravian missionary Johann Wohlers writes in 1870: "Should it not be said that God, in His all-wise government, has ordered it so that a Christian race shall arrive, at the time appointed by Him, in the land of the savages, when the latter have outlived themselves, in order to soothe their dying hours by civilized comforts and Christian consolation."[1]

Missionaries apart, the settlers as a whole were not "intensely Christian" (Belich 1996, 439). Yet, as James Belich observes, the fact that "much adherence was not intense does not make it unimportant." The point is that the settlers brought with them their culture, their traditions, and frequently their Bibles. Most significantly, they needed land. If they needed it, biblical warrant could be taken as a given: follow the command of Genesis 1:28 "and emigration follows as a nec-

---

1. *The Evangelist* 2/6 (August 1870), 234. I am indebted to Susan Jones for this quote.

essary consequence" (Stoughton in Gunn 1998, 132). Witi Ihimaera expresses the result biblically in his novel, *The Matriarch*: "In New Zealand, only one horseman of the Apocalypse was needed to bring destruction to the Maori. He was white and he carried a carpet bag into the new South. As he rode the country, he scooped the Maori and his land up with his scythe and, opening his carpetbag, put them both in it" (1986, 239).[2]

However, if the Europeans could turn to scriptural tradition, so could Maori. An editorial in the *Nelson Examiner* of January 26, 1861, expresses the reaction: " … when we find the natives taking up their [i.e. the missionaries'] teachings and describing us as Ahabs, and themselves as Naboths, we fear the effect of the seed they sow" (Gunn 1998, 37).

The other side to this meeting of traditions was that the Bible was welcomed among Maori. Henry Williams wrote in 1832, "We feel the want of books for the natives very greatly—what we at present possess they generally know by heart."[3] The solution came in the form of the CMS missionary printer William Colenso, who by January 1840 had printed 54,000 books (Phillipson 2004, 133), so that by the 1850s, Maori were more literate than the settlers.[4] Bible study had begun in earnest, but in some significant instances Maori biblicism moved on to become markedly different from that taught by the missionaries. Maori prophetic movements multiplied as biblically literate leaders found in the scriptures a framework for ordering their lives both under and against the colonizers.

---

2. Some sales were voluntary, although the payment was usually set well below its true value; some were forced; and some had their land taken, either by force or so-called legal punishment. Sometimes the church and individual missionaries sided with the Maori, but this was by no means always the case. Apirana Ngata writes of Bishop Selwyn's connection with the British forces that it "was one of the things that damned Christianity and its representatives among its Maori converts. It turned all Waikato against the missionaries down to this day" (Sissons 1991, 120, quoting from the *Whakatane Historical Review* XXIII, 1:40).

3. H. Williams to Secretaries, 6 July 1832, Hocken MS 285B, 244, quoted by Phillipson (2004, 129). See Belich (1996, 165), "There is some evidence that Maori initially saw reading and writing, or even books themselves, as magical keys to European knowledge—which in a sense they were.… But … the Christianity-literacy thesis implies that Maori conversion was false, a pretense intended to trick the missionaries into handing out literacy. The Maori interest in Christianity was rather deeper than this." He notes that "[b]y the 1850s, over 60 per cent of Maori counted themselves as Christians."

4. However, the initial enthusiasm had waned by 1844, when Colenso reports that some were destroying these "little silent messengers." Belich (1996, 19) suggests that "[t]his was partly because … saturation point had been reached. Missionaries, like muskets, ceased to be useful for asserting mana when everybody had them. But another factor may have been a growing Maori desire to distinguish themselves from Europe, in religion as in other things."

THE BIBLE AND TE KOOTI: A TRADITION TRANSFORMED

One such leader was Te Kooti Arikirangi Te Turuki. He had been imprisoned on the Chatham Islands in 1867 on dubious, if not illegal, grounds. While lying ill, he heard a voice saying that God had heard his cries and "would teach him the words which he had spoken to 'all your ancestors' (*koutou tipuna*), Abraham, Isaac and Jacob, and their descendants down to David." Then, as he described it in his diary, "His feet appeared like a white cloud, his garments were like the whiteness of snow, his head like a myriad of stars, his crown like the sun, his girdle as the setting and rising of the sun, his fan was like a rainbow, and his staff was such as has never been seen in this world (Binney 1995, 67).

If that was a Revelation/revelation experience for Te Kooti and the prisoners with him, it was the exodus tradition and the promises of Deuteronomy that they (re)made as their own. It was they who now escaped from bondage. It was, as Kendrick Smithyman's poem tells it, the Bible replayed: "When he landed he called the hill ahead Mount Moriah,/reefs in the bay were Tablets of the New Law./He was the Maori Moses" (Binney 1995, 542).

Fleeing inland, they journeyed into the wilderness to (re)claim the land of Canaan, Te Kooti's sermons accompanying them at every stage. On October 24, 1868, it was Joshua 23:5–6 that spurred them on, with its promise of God driving out the land holders (Binney 1995, 115), but if their attack upon the settlers at Matawhero (10 November) was Joshua's battle at Jericho replayed, this biblical zeal was a direct response to injustice and land confiscations. When the reprisals ended, Te Kooti prophesied, "There'll be no more wars … the last will be with me. This is a promise from God to us." Prophetic act followed prophetic word as he buried his sword. Looking to the future he declared, "I've got a Son coming— after me. To finish what I have started" (Binney 1995, 506). The Tuhoe prophet Rua Kenana saw himself as this Son, and, just as Te Kooti had taken the missionaries' Bible study and fused it with Maori experience and Maori tradition, so Rua, in turn, clothed political action in biblical language. As Te Kooti had used the exodus narrative, so now Rua led "the Iharaira (i.e., Israelites) out of Pakeha bondage into the wilderness of the Urewera forest.… As the children of Israel set up camp beneath Mount Sinai, so did the Iharaira make ready their village at the foot of Maungapotahu" (Sissons 1991, 218).[5] In April, 1907 Rua announced in the *Poverty Bay Herald:*

---

5. Other Maori groups, many similarly prophetic, adapted the scriptures in other ways to fit the new colonizing context. Among the converted Christian communities there was the same blending of traditions, seen, for example, in the Maori Madonna carved at Maketu in 1845, which had both Mary and Jesus wearing a facial *moko* (i.e., tatoo) (Belich 1996, 217).

The Israelites gathered together under a booth (Jonah 4:5). A question of land was brought forward by several persons for discussion; and, in consequence, the Leader Hephzibah [i.e., Rua himself] (Isaiah 62:4) has finally determined the said question by having sworn and established before God to be a habitation for God and man the block of land known as Maungapotahu, containing 20,000 acres. (Sissons 1991, 195)

The Ringatu faith had been founded deep in the Urewera country, which may have been remote, but not too remote for the missionary advance. As the Rev. J. G. Laughton, the missionary involved, tells it:

> In spite of Rua's friendship ... the work in Maungapotahu was carried on ... in that tension which was inevitable where a Christian mission was being developed and where, in the Mission school, children were daily being taught the Christian faith within the domain of one who claimed himself to be a divine incarnation. (Laughton 1961, 17)

The various turns of biblical studies had now come to another meeting.

THE CHURCHES FOUND INSTITUTIONS FOR THEIR ACADEMIC TRADITIONS

While Tuhoe children were learning from the Bible in the remote Urewera country, in the centers church authorities were opening seminaries and theological halls, but their academic eyes were firmly fixed on the Europe from which they had come and where they themselves had studied.[6] The Presbyterians soon heard of W. Robertson Smith's dismissal in 1881 from his position in the Presbyterian Free Church College in Aberdeen. His crime? Teaching a critical approach to biblical scholarship judged contrary to the tenets of the Westminster Confession of Faith. A speech at the opening of Dunedin's Knox College in 1909 notes that "[i]n the past the Old Testament has been the battleground, but there are signs that in the near future the conflict is to centre round the New Testament" (Breward 1975, 23).

Disquiet surfaces at various intervals. Dispute followed when the Rev C. H. Garland told the Methodist Conference in 1893, regarding "higher criticism," that, "[t]he theory that most of us have been trained to believe—viz.,

---

6. Bishop Selwyn opened the Anglican St John's College in 1843; Bishop Pompallier established the first Catholic seminary in Auckland in 1850; and the Presbyterians founded a Theological Hall in Dunedin in 1876.

that inspiration is a guarantee of inerrancy, and inerrancy is indispensable to its authority—must give way" (Davidson and Lineham 1995, 206–7).[7] A church member complained in 1934 that a textbook used by the professor of Old Testament is promoting "the principles and methods of modernist and sceptical [sic] scholarship.... It is simply outrageous that such a book on such destructive principles [G. W. Wade's *Old Testament History*] should be endowed by the Presbyterian Church of Otago." The Presbyterian Synod took no action, largely on grounds of a technicality (McKean 1994, 136; Breward, 40)!

"Overseas" scholarship sets the agenda. Allan Davidson observes of the period 1918–1939 that "[w]hile artists, poets and writers were beginning to explore New Zealand identity and take seriously the New Zealand context, theological reflection was largely dependent on external sources for its inspiration" (1991, 114). In 1940 the challenge of Rudolf Bultmann's New Testament theology, including his dictum that "Biblical literature should be treated as secular literature because Jesus was a real man," came directly to Dunedin's Theological Hall, with the arrival on the staff of Helmut Rex (Rehbein), a Confessing Church pastor and refugee from Nazi Germany (Andrew 1999b, 201). For the most part, however, it was a mainline scholarship, as each denomination understood it, reflecting what was being taught in Britain, Germany, or Rome. Although Davidson describes 1960s New Zealand as being in "the last throes of a dependent mentality and reliant on Britain for models of university education, curricula and for teachers who either came from or had undertaken their postgraduate study there" (2000, 205), the situation lasted a little longer in the theological colleges.

A Careful Braiding

Maurice Andrew was one who spent his postgraduate years with Gerhard von Rad in Heidelberg and returned bringing with him von Rad's commitment to Old Testament theology. Yet as early as the 1970s, he found himself "more and more ... expressing Old Testament studies within the framework of New Zealand issues and the relationships of New Zealand peoples" (1999b, 300).[8] As he

---

7. J. J. North, founding Principal of the Baptist Theological College 1926–44, and A.L. Haddon, Principal of the Churches of Christ Bible College 1927–61, both brought an awareness of European biblical and historical scholarship to their students (Davidson 1991, 113). Davidson adds, "T. H. Sprott, Bishop of Wellington 1911–36 and L. G. Whitehead, Warden of Selwyn College Dunedin 1919–50 were among the Anglicans who gave a lead in accepting Biblical and historical criticism" (207).

8. Maurice Andrew was appointed to the chair of Old Testament Studies at the Presbyterian

wrote in 1982, "since the Bible cannot be received without interpretation, theology based on the Bible is also done through interpretation and this is by people in a particular place" (1982, 126).

Interestingly, he made a connection with feminism. He was writing of what he described as the *"furor methodicus"* of the 1980s, in which "[f]ar from Old Testament studies remaining a comfortably familiar realm, new approaches followed each other with bewildering rapidity," and noted that feminism was "the new movement in study that involved the students themselves most." He himself recognized that it "fitted into what I had been doing already" in that "interpretation is influenced by the kind of people doing it" (1999b, 305), and here the kind of people were New Zealanders. Not all were so welcoming to these changes. When I submitted a proposal for a course on biblical women in the early 1990s, after Andrew had retired, there was considerable opposition to its feminist components, including the plan to use Elisabeth Schüssler Fiorenza's *In Memory of Her* as one of the textbooks.

An invitation to write an introductory study for the local Education for Ministry program resulted in Maurice Andrew's *The Old Testament in Aotearoa New Zealand*, a work remarkable for its contextual braiding of traditions. The connections with New Zealand attitudes and circumstances are challenging. For example, Isaiah 5:8–30 is seen as "directed against the kind of people who not only have a house in Dunedin but also a crib at Karitane, a home in Auckland and a *bach* at Muriwai" (1999a, 403). The work is larded with references to biblical passages in New Zealand literature, art, and culture: "The imagery (i.e., of the Garden of Eden) is also alive among quite different people in Aotearoa New Zealand, in quite different places. Judith Binney and Gillian Chaplin write that 'The meeting house Rongopai … bursts with paintings of blossoms and vines, including the Tree of Life.'" (1999a, 32).[9] Te Kooti is here too. If what is conveyed "through these particular Israelite manifestations" can be understood "through New Zealand expressions as well" (1999b, 356), these quite naturally include memories of this Ringatu founder. So it is in the chapter of the biblical mountain experience of Exodus 19–20: One writer has recorded that Te Kooti appeared on top of a hill, and, with the sun shining upon him, he appeared as Moses of old appeared on Sinai (1999a, 110).

Andrew's small publication *Treaty Land Covenant* (1990) had set the biblical covenantal tradition in dialectic conversation with the Treaty of Waitangi. This treaty is New Zealand's foundational document; as our political past, its

---

Theological Hall in Dunedin in 1971.

9. The reference here is to J. Binney and G. Chaplin, *Nga Morehu: The Survivors* (2nd ed. Auckland University Press, 1986) 152.

implications are woven through our present and our future. Signed in 1840 by the Crown and a significant number of Maori chiefs, its interpretation is complicated by the fact that it was written in both Maori and English, with subtle but significant differences leading to different perceptions of what was agreed upon. Biblical language is part of the complication. The missionary translators used the Maori term *rangatiratanga*, which they had used for "kingdom" in the Lord's Prayer. This implied a "sovereign" right, considerably more far-reaching than the Crown intended. Inadvertently, they had bequeathed a legacy of dispute, one that has not yet been fully resolved. Yet a research project in the late 1980s into how the churches were observing the treaty relationship in their theological colleges reported: "[i]n the theology colleges and in New Zealand society as a whole there is a denial of the reality of the Maori world and of Maori identity ... in the theology colleges the theology taught is imported from overseas and fails to address the issues which arise in this country" (Susan Healy quoted in Norris 1999, 127).

James Irwin, the second principal (1964–70) of *Te Wananga a Rangi*, a Presbyterian Maori Theological college, reflecting on the past in 1984, stated that "not enough thought was given to the nature of ministry in a Maori setting," and that "the model of Scottish training for the 'ministry' was too easily taken over without question" (Davidson 1991, 136). Today, Maori are designing the curriculum for Maori at *Te Wananga* and Anglican and Methodist churches are ordering themselves along bicultural (and multicultural) lines. The Auckland School of Theology declared a commitment to bicultural theological education in its foundational mission statement. What does that mean in reality? Elaine Wainwright, Auckland's Head of School, acknowledged at the time of writing that that was still under exploration (2005, 126). This is the context in which we all live and work.

Braiding for Whom?

This context undergirds the other question: whose interest is served by biblical studies? Is it the church, society in general, or the academic guild? Until the late 1990s, biblical studies, for the most part, was taught in church colleges in ministry training programs, by staff appointed and employed by their churches, even if they were also teaching as honorary lecturers within the universities. Much has changed. Theology is now one discipline among many in the secular universities of Auckland and Otago, traditionally the two main university centers for theological studies.[10] In theory one might expect this to make a difference,

---

10. Auckland now has a School of Theology and Otago a Department of Theology and Religious Studies. Church colleges and institutes partly staff the Auckland school, while the full-

that the confessional lens might be significantly lifted. The issue of "confessional" versus "academic" has, of course, been much debated beyond New Zealand. Philip Davies made a strong case in 1995 for two different disciplines: an academic humanist biblical studies and a confessionally based Scripture. Letters flowed in response both to Michael Fox's article "Bible Scholarship and Faith-Based Study: My View," published in an SBL Forum in 2006 and Ronald Hendel's "Biblical Views: Farewell to SBL: Faith and Reason in Biblical Studies," posted in July/August 2010.[11]

Practical realities complicate the issue. Auckland and Otago are very aware that the churches remain significant stakeholders. Both work hard at maintaining an independent academic integrity alongside meeting the churches' confessional expectations. While Elaine Wainwright acknowledges that "theology does not belong to the churches alone," that word "alone" is significant. Her point that, as a university discipline, theology's "vision is multidirectional" and its voice "polyvocal" (2005:139) does not deny the churches' stake. What it does mean is that Auckland students are required to engage with "contemporary approaches, recognizing the multifaceted nature of all biblical interpretation."[12] Otago similarly expects "a spirit of open inquiry" and "a willingness to wrestle with contemporary debates such as the end of 'modernity', the emergence of feminist forms of study, and the renaissance of indigenous cultures." Its students are to "look at what are perceived as the most sacred dimensions of human existence in a critical manner."[13] Certainly there is a contrast in language marking the difference with confessional institutions. Carey Baptist College, for example, expects its students to "articulate a theology of revelation and authority." Where Auckland talks of the "implications for contemporary society," Carey requires an application of the Bible "to life, ministry and mission."[14]

Yet despite Auckland and Otago's care to maintain the academic/confessional balance, the polemic has appeard here also. Chris Marshall has recently charged that "the task of interpreting the Bible has largely been captured by a professional, and often sceptical, scholarly elite" (2007, 8). Although he says "[t]his is not to

---

time staff at Otago have been university appointees since 1997.

11. The case is not necessarily one of opposites. Robert Davidson, both an academic and a church member, writing from Scotland, considers that "it is possible to empathize with a religious tradition without being committed to it and in the context of such empathy to handle it with intellectual insight and integrity" (2002, 169).

12. www.theology.auckland.ac.nz.

13. www.otago.ac.nz/theology

14. Included in the "key learning outcomes" for the course "Understanding and Interpreting the Bible" at www.carey.ac.nz/study_options.

deny the importance of scholarly enquiry unfettered by the controls of ecclesiastical dogma and politics," he goes further, declaring that "the Bible has been exiled from its true homeland in the community of faith and banished to an alien academic society, with its own definite, though often unacknowledged agenda." Marshall's own position is clear: "the wise reading of Scripture" requires "recognition of the *centrality of Jesus to the meaning of the biblical drama* [original italics] … each and every part of Scripture must, finally, be assessed in relation to him" (14). While this is the script of an address delivered to a Bible College of New Zealand audience, Marshall is an academic working and teaching within a secular university, although, somewhat ambiguously, in a position funded by a Presbyterian church parish.[15]

Dealing with the challenges of practical realities, such as government funding policies, is a task the independent colleges also face. Compliances set by a secular state sit uncomfortably with confessional institutions, such as Carey Baptist and Laidlaw Colleger (formerly The Bible College of New Zealand), both of which offer degrees taught by well qualified scholars.[16] They are required to submit data indicating the social relevance of their courses, a utilitarian criterion at some odds with confessional expectations. Similarly, assessment follows the modernist expectation of the rational and objective, where, as Tim Meadowcroft observes, the church has always recognized the "affective and subjective as part of the enterprise of knowing God" (2007, 27).[17]

BRAIDING THE TRADITIONS IN WRITING

Little of this is unique to Aotearoa/New Zealand, just as many biblical quests, such as discovering more of the biblical past, are universal and international. Much of what New Zealanders publish reflects the interests and approaches of scholars

15. Chris Marshall is a New Testament scholar, formerly on the staff of the Bible College but now teaching in the Department of Religious Studies at Victoria University of Wellington. In a dialogue in the same issue, he specifically talks of "Christian interpretation" as being "committed to a canon within a canon on the grounds that the gospel story of Jesus Christ is considered to be the key for unlocking Scripture's true import" (Crawshaw and Marshall 2007, 18).

16. These are now accredited by NZQA (the New Zealand Qualifications Authority) and funded through TEC (the Tertiary Education Commission). There is also a plethora of small faith colleges, most of which consider themselves evangelical and Bible-based, but a Bible interpreted largely through the lens of "the biblical Christianity of North America" (Darragh 2004, 210).

17. The situation for the universities is different as they are dependent on a PBRF funding (Performance Based Research Fund).

with whom they have studied elsewhere. Paul Trebilco's work on early Christianity in Ephesus (2004) and group identity (2012) continues in the tradition of the carefully researched studies of early Christianity associated with J. D. G. Dunn; so too, Elaine Wainwright's *Women Healing/Healing Women: the Genderization of Healing in Early Christianity* (2006) follows the feminist historical tradition of Elisabeth Schüssler Fiorenza. Both break new ground. Publishing is, of course, an international concern. Tim Meadowcroft's study of Haggai in the Sheffield Readings series, for example, was commissioned for an established international series; Tim Bulkeley's hypertext commentary on Amos is international by its very nature as a web-based resource. Studies applying new methodologies, originating "overseas," are mostly read "overseas." Stephen Pattemore's use of relevance theory (2004), Laurel Lanner's use of fantasy theory (2006), and Gillian Townsley's use of Monica Wittig's lesbian theory (forthcoming) are good examples. The recently founded journal *Relegere: Studies in Religion and Reception*, Otago based but with an international editorial board, is another. This is a global world and New Zealanders are a globe-traveling people with wide networks; most biblical writers belong to SBL and other international societies, even though the costs of travel are considerable.

Earlier in the decade, the Australian-based *Earth Bible Project* brought scholars together "across the ditch". For despite New Zealand's much marketed "clean green image," the state of the environment is a concern here too, perhaps influenced by the indigenous spirituality where "everything has life, the stone, the trees, they have a *mauri*" (life principle).[18] Following a significant, if debatable, project principle that "Earth is a subject capable of raising its voice in celebration and against injustice."[19] Alice Sinnott, for example, sought to listen to Earth's voice through Job, who, from his dunghill, "believes that he understands Earth and can speak for her" (2001, 90). Following the books move to a conclusion where Job, who had listened to Earth "with his ears," could now look at Earth and say to God, "My eye sees you," has allowed a fresh exploration of the book's subtleties. Keith Carley, acknowledging that "Earth has no compassionate advo-

---

18. Ruka Broughton, "Incomparability between Maoritanga and Christianity," in *Tu Tangata: Maori News Magazine* 27 (1985–86), 6, quoted by Moore (45).

19. Tim Meadowcroft, in a paper delivered at the Australasian conference of theological schools (ANZATS) in 2000, argued that it is "a thoroughly anthropocentric device," dependent upon reader-response, so that "[a]t the end of the exercise, the voice of the earth continues to look suspiciously like a human creation." In response, the Earth Bible team conceded that the language of earth's voice is metaphorical, but "more than metaphor" and "more than a rhetorical device" in that it provides another hermeneutical tool, allowing humans to "begin relating to earth as kin" and "as partner and co-creator rather than property" (2001, 28).

cate" in the prophetic tradition of Ezekiel, applied the project's eco-justice ethic
and found a basis in Ezekiel's formula of desolation for his own call upon readers to "speak up for Earth," if we are "to live in a more sustainable and generous
way" (2001, 154, 157). Neither of these studies, nor Trebilco's reading of 1 Tim
4:1–5 (2000) related directly to the land of Aotearoa. It was an organic farmer,
albeit with a doctoral thesis on Isaiah, who asked that unsettling question: "Have
the settlers been the snake in this Garden of Eden?" and stated, quite directly,
"Colonisation ripped through *nga tangata whenua* (i.e., the people of the land)
here as elsewhere, wreaking cultural and environmental devastation" (Reinken
2004, 235).

Yet, few studies have taken colonization seriously into account. David Gunn's
1998 essay "Colonialism and the Vagaries of Scripture: Te Kooti in Canaan" and
Mary Huie-Jolly's 2002 article "Maori 'Jews' and a Resistant Reading of John
5:10–47" stand out—the first by a New Zealander working in America and the
second by a former American working in Aotearoa/New Zealand. Contexts are
hard to keep in place. And Te Kooti keeps rising from the past! He, admittedly
with others, lies behind Huie-Jolly's thesis that Maori who defiantly identified
with "the Jews" were shaking the dust of empire from their feet (2002, 110). In
my own 2004 *Reframing Her: Biblical Women in Postcolonial Focus*, I attempted,
in one chapter, to read the female imagery of Revelation with one eye on Israel's
goddess past and another on the strong Ringatu Matriarch of Witi Ihimaera's
novel. In another chapter it was early settlers' letters that brought fresh aspects
of the texts to light, with the focus this time on Sarah and Hagar's narratives.
Yet at the annual ANZABS meetings (The Aotearoa-New Zealand Association of
Biblical Studies), there are few papers making contextual connections with this
country, despite Elaine Wainwright's leadership in providing courses that include
"perspectives that inform interpretation such as ecological, feminist, Māori,
Pacific and other culturally-based approaches" (www.theology.auckland.ac.nz),
and in her own ecologically focused work.

This is not to deny the fact that historical-critical scholars also recognize
the significance of context and place. Paul Trebilco, for example, in asking what
was distinctive about being Christian in Rome or Ephesus or Jerusalem, con-
cluded that "earliest Christianity entered into a dialogue with culture and context,
employing some facets of culture, critiquing others" (2006, 18). In this he was
following Richard Bauckham's suggestion that these small groups were nonetheless conscious of being part of a much more extensive "world-wide" network, and
arguing for a local/global dialectic from Christianity's earliest days. Perhaps that
is an apt description for biblical work here.

But how to engage with the local, which so often seems to arouse suspicion?
The "conscious attempt by specific communities to read the biblical text in light

of explicit ideological commitments, such as radical feminism or postcolonialism or queer theory or whatever" was a concern for Marshall in his address (2007, 9). While he allowed "that advocacy interpreters are simply being honest about the preunderstandings and political biases" and "are usually motivated by a genuine commitment to greater justice" and even that their readings "often cast new light on the text, and expose the power dynamics hidden behind 'received' interpretations," this did not distract from his charge that "sustained ideological criticism" led to a "substantial erosion of confidence in the reliability of biblical meaning" resulting from "sustained ideological criticism." Much hangs on those words, "the reliability of biblical meaning." The counter question is whether in a postcolonial society it is responsible not to apply a deconstructive template to texts that carry ancient ideological agendas with their own power imbalances. Yet such polemical disagreement tends to be muted or avoided at the annual biblical gatherings. When advocacy readings do alternate with historical-critical studies, no one complains or decries the critical mix! The 2011 colloquium on Isaiah and Empire held at Laidlaw College saw a similar range of methodologies and approaches, and yet the very disparate papers were heard with interest and respect. Or perhaps this reflects a New Zealand politeness rather than a respect for the varied hermeneutical choices.

"Local" comes, however, in many guises, for what could be more local than Kathleen Rushton's recent paper, "On the Crossroads between Life and Death: Reading Birth Imagery in John in the Earthquake Changed Regions of Otautahi Christchurch" delivered at the Bible, Borders, Belongings seminar, held in Sydney in 2012? Here the "local" changed in line with the presenters, as it stretched out to cover Oceania, as its "talanoa," explained by Jione Havea as "the confluence of story, telling, and conversation," "drift[ed]" through New Zealand, Australia, Tonga and India (Havea, forthcoming).

THE FUTURE BRAIDING OF BIBLICAL STUDIES IN AOTEAROA NEW ZEALAND

Any crystal gazing sees the hermeneutical mix continuing: traditional methodologies valued for their basic historical-critical tools, but complemented by others. How wide will the range be? What of cross-disciplinary conversations?

There is, on the one hand, a growing interest in the theological interpretation of scripture, with the new Journal of Theological Interpretation, edited both by Joel Green of Fuller Seminary and Murray Rae, the head of Otago's Department of Theology and Religion. A volume of papers from a colloquium, sponsored jointly by Laidlaw College and Otago, is soon to be published by Sheffield Phoenix Press.

This is a very different conversation from those that take place at the annual meetings of the Australasian Bible and Critical Theory Seminar, and which are published in its international ejournal. Once a year, for the last fifteen years, biblical writers and specialists in fields such as literary and political theory, philosophy, cultural studies, anthropology, eco-criticism, Marxism, et al., have been meeting and sharing papers, together with good pub food and wine. New Zealanders "cross the ditch" to join in these critical cross-hatching dialogues. Gillian Townsley's 2007 paper applying Monica Wittig's feminist theory to a study of 1 Cor 11 is a good example. Will there be more of these here on this soil? Biblical papers as diverse as Marxist, utopian, postcolonial and eco-critical are all part of the mix, the link being the concern to apply the theoretical critical eye to reading and texts.

There is need, too, for new voices. While scholars from Asia and the Pacific have long studied here, their voices have largely been muted or forgotten once they leave.[20] For the most part, their studies have followed the traditional approaches with few, if any, contextual connections. This is now changing: Nasili Vaka'uta's paper, "Reading beyond the Reefs: A Sketch of an Oceanic Hermeneutics," presented at the 2005 national biblical conference, was indeed an exploration from beyond the reefs that splashed upon us, and woke us up very appropriately, for Auckland, where he teaches in the University's School of Theology, is the city with the world's largest polynesian population. Papers such as his "Tālanga: Theorizing a Tongan Mode of Interpretation" (2009) and his *Reading Ezra 9–10 Tu'a-Wise: Rethinking Biblical Interpretation in Oceania* (2011), published in the SBL International Voices in Biblical Studies series, are needed here in challenging us to take context into account.

For the question remains, what does it mean to do biblical studies in this postcolonial country of Aotearoa/New Zealand? It has become a truism that readers do not read in a vacuum, that all reading and interpretation is carried out from "somewhere." Those who shy away from "contextual" studies fail to recognize that traditional historical-critical readings are themselves "'context-full' of particular ideological or Eurocentric suppositions" (Lawrence 2007, 532). The ever-widening program of the SBL meetings indicates an awareness in the academic guild of the increasing regional and methodological diversity. While the need to maintain international standards is a given, the question remains: will more scholars in this country wrestle with the question of what it means to inter-

---

20. Paul Trebilco has recently collaborated with Simon Rae, a historian of Christianity in Indonesia, in the writing of a commentary on 1 Timothy for the Asia Bible Commentary Series. While this is a specifically contextual series, and Rae has lived and worked in Indonesia, neither writer is himself Asian.

pret the Bible here, in a society living with the challenge of a treaty not yet fully honored? Can scholars in Aotearoa/New Zealand avoid the critical call of post-colonialism, that understands "imperialism, and colonialism as an omnipresent, inescapable, and overwhelming reality in the world: [both] the world of antiquity … and the world of today" (Segovia 1998b, 56)? What does it mean to do biblical studies in a society that is becoming ever more multicultural, with new generations of New Zealand-born Pacific Islanders, Asians, and an increasingly wide diversity of ethnicities? If the question of what it means to do biblical studies in Aotearoa/New Zealand is not asked, academic biblical studies will be an intellectual discipline isolated from the community in which it works.

Louise Lawrence (re)claims the word "hefted"—originally of sheep with an instinctive and intimate sense of place—for grounded and contextual biblical readings (2007). She is not writing from Aotearoa, but it might be an appropriate term for us, for as the poet Cilla McQueen writes (1982), admittedly a little tongue in cheek, "this place is just one big city with 3 million people with a flock of sheep each." The times are changing: we are now more than three million, and sheep are giving way to cattle and deer. The ways of reading and interpretation are changing, too; but undergirding the complex braiding of traditions, I clearly see a heftedness in my crystal ball.

15

CAUGHT IN BETWEEN: AUSTRALIAN BIBLICAL STUDIES
BETWEEN ASIA, THE PACIFIC, AND THE WEST

Roland Boer

Biblical criticism in Australia has always suffered from an identity crisis: it has hung on to the idea that it is an outpost of Western scholarship at the same time that it exists at the intersection between the Pacific and Asia. For most of that time, it has valued the first while barely taking notice of the other two. So in this survey and proposal for the future of biblical studies in the in-between zone of Australia, I trace the legacy of Western biblical scholarship and ponder the possibilities of a greater meshing with Asia and the Pacific. I have organized my discussion in terms of four types of analysis. If we view biblical criticism in Australia as a room, then these types are windows into that room. We look into the same room, but the window through which we do so affects how we see that room. A small window on one side gives a distinct picture, while a stained-glass window on another side provides a very different insight, a louvered window provides multiple views, and then a large panoramic window on yet another side shows up the whole room in a very different light again. I have called these windows "legacy," "institutions," "caught in between," and "crystal ball."

LEGACY

More than a decade ago I offered a sketch of the background of biblical scholarship in Australia called "Remembering Babylon" (Boer 1998; see also Boer 2008). Looking through this small window, I suggested that the story of biblical studies in Australia might be understood in terms of three phases from the time of European settlement in 1788 onwards: emulation, nationalism, and positive unoriginality. Although these phases mark sequential periods of time, they are not mutually exclusive, for they also represent three overlapping options that have been and continue to be tried out today.

Emulation covers that long stretch of time in which the few biblical scholars who taught in theological colleges were drawn from and continued to imitate the perceived intellectual centers of Europe, especially those that happened to be in the heart of the British Empire. Nothing in the colony was worth much, except perhaps the space and sunshine, so all one could do was try to erase the fact that one was in a very different part of the world, hope to keep up with what was happening in the imperial center, and emulate that great fount of culture and learning in its uncouth outposts. Of course, those who ended up teaching in Australia were driven by many motives, such as less than bright career prospects back home, a scandal or two from which one was fleeing, the solace of the bottle, or the simple reason that one was not born into the right family in the right part of town. These drawbacks did not stop the early holders of teaching posts from wearing the tweed jackets with elbow patches, glasses, and incinerators that passed for pipes—just as the dons did back home. Even today it is not uncommon to find a higher position filled by British or North American scholar—the Australian "cultural cringe" working nicely alongside the attitudes of scholars from the imperial center that a well-paid administrative position "down under" might be a fine way to round out a career, just as members of the British ruling class were granted governorship of this or that antipodean colony or Caribbean plantation as reward for a lifetime's service.

Emulation remains a powerful motivating force for biblical scholars even today. If we consider those who actually published, the names are relatively few, since it was customary only for the odd professor with a writer's itch to produce anything at all. Samuel Angus was perhaps the best known biblical scholar in the first half of the twentieth century. A Scottish don who became professor within the Presbyterian Church, Angus's claim to fame was to introduce critical biblical scholarship to the Presbyterian, Methodist, and Congregational students whom he taught in Sydney. Apart from the waves of unrest and resistance, and even the attempts at a heresy trial, Angus wrote and published. But he already faced a persistent problem, for there were no publishing houses in Australia that would publish anything in biblical studies. So he published with British presses such as Duckworth and T&T Clark. Looking at his work now, one realizes how unoriginal it was, emulating the work done in the United Kingdom, catching the same wave as everyone else "back home" (Angus 1914, 1929, 1933, 1939). Later, others such as Francis Andersen and John O'Neill (Andersen 1959–1960, 1970; Andersen and Freedman 1989; O'Neill 1961, 1972, 1975) would continue the pattern of emulation, moving overseas as a natural extension of that tendency.

In that earlier essay I called the second phase "nationalism," but a better term is in fact "regionalism." Beginning in the 1970s, this is where we find an emphasis on Australian-trained scholars, Australian content, contextual concerns, and the push to bring back to Australia those scholars who had strayed overseas. It has gained pace in the last few years as postgraduate students and established scholars look elsewhere than the United States for study and work. As Norman Habel (one of those who did return after many years in the United States) once put it, at that time we found our own voice for the first time instead of mimicking that of another. For many this is a positive development that continues today, especially as more and more biblical scholars do their postgraduate study in Australia. The down side is that it can become very small-minded and parochial without the crucial interaction with what is happening outside Australia—and by outside I do not mean the faded intellectual powerhouse of the Atlantic but the more interesting developments in the Pacific and Asia. Another problem is that such regionalism often operates on the basis of showing the crumbling powerhouse that something good can in fact come out of Australia, despite contrary expectations. In doing so, regionalism merely re-inscribes the old values of what passes for academic quality.

The third phase I called—a little too cleverly—"positive unoriginality." It was an effort to characterize what biblical studies might be able to do in this part of the world apart from either emulating what goes on elsewhere or asserting regional distinctiveness jingoistically. Positive unoriginality (borrowed from the cultural critic Meaghan Morris [1988, 244; 1990, 10–11]) is meant to be a meeting point of these two options. It is a process of copying which persistently alters the "original" so that it comes out the worse for the imitation.[1] What is appealing about this approach is that it is very good at crap detection. All the posturing and posing by biblical scholars is shown up for what it is: the hierarchies of knowledge become targets, and one learns not to take the international currents of biblical scholarship with complete seriousness. It is also a way of appropriating whatever methodological means are provided on the global theoretical market (this is the "unoriginal" bit) and using such methods in entirely new and unexpected ways (this is the "positive" bit).

I wrote "too cleverly" above since I am not sure whether positive unoriginality is a real phase or option, or whether it is really an exercise in wish fulfillment—something I imagined might be possible in this part of the world. I am no longer happy with the term and what it stands for, so this essay may be seen as an effort to rethink this last category. I will have less to say about the other two phases, since they are still very real in current biblical studies in Australia: a good deal of emulation by unimaginative and overburdened scholars and an equal amount of parochial celebration of regional achievements.

---

1. Homi Bhabha (1994) would call it, in his confused way, mimicry.

Institutions

Second, biblical criticism has been caught between two institutions in its checkered history in Australia: church and university. In order to gain a sense of how it has negotiated these two, I offer the schema shown in tables 1 and 2.

All of these have been and no doubt will be tried again from time to time, depending on economic capabilities, theological direction and struggles, and the ability of individuals to come up with deals. One type that has not yet been tried is one European model (not that of Paris) where theology is a faculty or department wholly within the university and autonomous from any church control. There is a good reason for this. When the structure of the University of Sydney

Table. 1. Types of Independent Theological Colleges

Type	Nature	Biblical Studies	Economics	Quality
Wagons in a circle	Independent theological colleges in order to provide unique brand of ecclesiastical education.	May include languages but more often does not. Emphasis on training for ministry and exegesis for sermons.	Churches relatively wealthy, with enough money for buildings and teaching staff.	Teaching: varies greatly. Research: not encouraged.
Federation	Gathering of independent colleges into a consortium that has powers relating to course approval, granting of degrees and maintenance of standards.	If resources are shared, there may be more language work but focus is still on interpretation and sermon preparation.	Not quite so wealthy. There is a greater need to share resources between colleges.	Teaching: more uniform since the federation oversees quality to some extent. Research: lip service.

Table 2. Types of Relations Between Theological Colleges and Universities

Type	Nature	Biblical Studies	Economics	Quality
Donut	Secular university surrounded by church-based residential and teaching colleges. The best example is the University of Melbourne.	Non-existent in university. Taught by surrounding theological colleges.	Theological colleges remain independently funded but do make use of some university services (internet and library).	As with independent colleges.
One foot in each camp	50/50 deals, such as at Flinders and Murdoch; staff supplied by churches, paid partly by churches and partly by university	Subject to university requirements re course numbers and content. Languages tend to suffer under university requirements for minimum student numbers in courses.	Churches are short of money while universities seek to cut costs on funding.	Teaching: subject to university standards, it is of higher standard. Research: university infrastructure, resources and expectations are more conducive to research.
Old rubber stamp	The university offers the degree and controls course structure but teaching is done almost entirely by part-time staff drawn from churches and theological	Biblical studies a complete part of a theology degree with majors possible in both Hebrew and Greek.	University supplies buildings and pays teaching staff. They are still part-time and still drawn from churches.	Teaching: Better but still varied, since all teaching is part-time. Research: haphazard.

Table. 2, continued.

Type	Nature	Biblical Studies	Economics	Quality
	colleges. Prime example is the old School of Divinity at Sydney University.			
New rubber stamp	Universities like Charles Sturt and Western Sydney offer the degree, but it is taught entirely by one or more theological colleges. The college is the theology department.	Nature of biblical studies taught depends mostly on the college offering the teaching.	Both churches and universities seeking ways of cutting costs and rely on the other to help them do so.	Teaching: university approved but in reality depends on college. Research: no different from independent colleges.

was first being debated in the early nineteenth century, the role of theology inevitably came up for discussion. Some wanted the traditional theological faculty, but others were not so enthused. The reason: which church tradition would be dominant? Would it be Anglican, Roman Catholic, Presbyterian, Methodist, or ... ? The problem was that no tradition could claim to be *the* expression of Christianity, let alone theology, in Australia. So an unholy alliance came into being: some church leaders joined with secular leaders to argue that theology should not be taught at the university, since this would be the best way to ensure the pluralism of religions and religious tolerance. Sydney University and Melbourne following it were established as secular universities in which theology was explicitly excluded.

However, as I write, the University of Newcastle is trying exactly this approach that the early founders of universities in Australia found too risky—theology based "purely" in the university. The arguments put forward are that secular universities have for too long denied theology a rightful and historical place in the university. However, the old problem has raised its head in this situation, for the churches that have put up the money for the new program also feel that they should have a large say in appointments and course content.

Caught in Between

The third window through which I peruse the room of biblical studies in Australia is what I have called "caught in between." If we think of biblical studies as an in-between discipline in Australia, then the following types of in betweenness show up: (1) the drive for "secular" universities that has led to biblical scholars finding room in all manner of strange places; (2) the tension between intellectual subservience to so-called "centers of scholarship" on the one hand and the advantage of being outside such contexts on the other; (3) the history of Aboriginal missions and claiming of the Bible by indigenous peoples in their own way; and (4) the increasing awareness of Australia's context within Asia and the Pacific. I take each in turn.

As with many "new world" colonies, Australian tertiary institutions were established well after the Enlightenment and in the midst of the new drive to secularism. None of them dates from before the nineteenth century and many of them were explicitly established as secular institutions. In response to this situation, biblical critics have had to find their places in both familiar places and strange corners—confessional colleges (the bulk), secular religion departments (Edgar Conrad [2002] at the University of Queensland, Magella Franzmann [2004] for a time at the University of New England), cultural studies (my own experience for a time), ancient history (as at Macquarie University or Anne Gardner at Latrobe), and so on. Many of us have moved between such situations, while a good number have remained outside traditional forms of employment—on unemployment benefits for a while (Michael Carden [2004] and Julie Kelso [2007]), or running finance companies (Noel Bailey), or becoming radio announcers (David Rutledge [1996]). As a result, aspiring graduate students have become very creative in finding ways to study the Bible; often the outcome of their work is just as creative. In fact, unless one is a confessional scholar in a particular denomination's theological college, one has to be highly creative in Australia to do biblical criticism at all. And so, outside the very occasional and safe research that tends to turn up in theological colleges, there is some very innovative work being done in those strange nooks and crannies where biblical critics tend to find themselves in order to pay the rent and find some food to eat (see some of the references listed above). Two examples of that innovative work are the Bible and Critical Theory Seminar and the Earth Bible Project. I will have more to say about them in the last section.

A further feature of in-betweenness lies in our relation with the self-styled intellectual superpowers, both old and new. This is an ambiguous relation, a mixture of disadvantage and advantage, for we are caught between the apparent standards and expectations of such centers and the liberation of being outside those zones. Let me be blunt: Australia never has been a major focus for biblical studies. One day, if it establishes an Australian empire on the basis of coal (especially when oil becomes prohibitively expensive) and uranium, and if it builds a massive fleet of ships for sea and air and space, then it may become such a place. For what would happen then is that Australian tertiary institutions would be able to attract the best (or at least most expensive) biblical scholars from around the world to teach—as happened once with the United Kingdom and the United States when they were empires. I hope that never happens. We have enough pressure to measure up to international standards, so much so that tertiary institutions celebrate a major achievement if they manage a "top 100" placing in official lists (universities such as Sydney, Melbourne, Queensland, Monash, and the Australian National University regularly do, often ousting more fancied institutions overseas). Scholars are expected to travel to international conferences, publish in international presses (not much choice since no press in Australia publishes any biblical studies, apart perhaps from devotional material), and "punch above their weight" whenever possible.

What is far more enjoyable and productive for biblical scholars is to be outside those zones. If I may use a personal example: it is a great relief to go to conferences overseas and find that I don't need to engage in intellectual flexing or posing, that I don't need to join the meat market looking for a job, and that I don't need to rank the places interviewing to make sure they register high enough on my scale of self-worth. Instead, what we find is that creative energies may and can be unleashed in the interstices of the international scene.

A third element of this in-between nature of biblical studies is a legacy of Australia's colonial past and present in relation to Aboriginal people. The brutal arrival to and occupation of Australia by Europeans is a relatively recent overlay of the oldest civilization on earth—that of Australian Aborigines, a civilization that goes back more that 40,000 years. As far as the Bible is concerned, we find a well-documented ambivalence in the midst of that colonial heritage: even though the Bible arrived in the hands of missionaries, it has been appropriated and transformed in the hands of Aborigines. I have written of the processes of Bible translation into Aboriginal languages elsewhere (Boer 2008, 135–59) and of the way the intersection between languages (usually it is from English into a language like Pitjantjatjara) generates new meanings and stories beyond the controls and wishes of the translators. Mark Brett (2008) has brought his experience working with Aboriginal land to his biblical interpretation.

Here I would like to make two points: first, when speaking of Aboriginal religion we must never forget that the main form of such religion is Christianity, transformed and reshaped in distinct ways, and this means that the Bible is a crucial feature of Aboriginal religion; second, we still await the rise of a number of Aboriginal biblical scholars of international standard. Other disciplines now have Aboriginal scholars who can mix it with the best of them. I think of Anne Pattel-Gray in theology (1998) or the Rainbow Spirit Elders collection (1997) or Grahame Paulson (2006). But unfortunately biblical criticism lags behind. Nungalinya College in Darwin is doing a fantastic job training people in biblical studies, but the work is deeply confessional, geared for community needs, and those who study are often community leaders themselves with massive demands on time and energy. So we have a distinct in-betweenness, one that runs between academic biblical scholarship and community-based needs, between traditional forms of accreditation and suspicion of researchers and academics, and between critical scholarship and confessional approaches to the Bible.

A final aspect of being in-between is the way Australia is not quite Asia and not quite the Pacific. I do not want to suggest that Australia is unique, but that it has an identity crisis: a cultural outpost of the West, economically and culturally intimate with Asia and militarily linked (and resented) in the Pacific. As far as the Bible is concerned, there are a number of developments. In the direction of the Pacific, there has been a steady stream of students coming to study in theological colleges in Australia. For example, I recall a class I taught (for my sins) at the United Theological College in Sydney in the 1990s, where more than half the class came from Western Samoa, Fiji, and the Solomon Islands. These were traditional mission grounds for Methodists and the connections remain strong. Those who trained in Australia either ended up staying and working in the church in Australia, sometimes within their own diaspora communities, or went back home to teach. More recently, however, this model has been breaking down. Australia has for too long felt itself to be a resource for the Pacific—in terms of economics, military, religion, and education. But now the teachers have begun to come to Australia. Jione Havea (2003) took up the post in Hebrew Bible at the United Theological College in Sydney and has been there ever since. Although it is stronger in New Zealand, this drawing of Australia into biblical concerns of the Pacific is one direction for the future.

Asia, especially the south-eastern parts, is also drawing Australia into its orbit. I am not revealing anything new by pointing out that this is closely tied up with the economic boom driven by China, but also Thailand, Malaysia, Singapore, and India. It used to be the case, and still is to some extent, that students came to Australia from Asian countries with Christian histories. For example, a steady number of Korean scholars completed their doctoral studies under Edgar Conrad at the University of Queensland before returning home to take up posts in theological colleges. I found that the students who persevered with Hebrew were deeply confessional Korean students keen to know more of the Bible. But there are changes in the air: there is much energy, in terms of publishing, translation, teaching interchange, and conferencing throughout Asia, but especially in China, Taiwan, and India. The Society of Asian Biblical Studies held its inaugural conference in July 2008 in Seoul, and a Bible translation is under way at the behest of the Chinese government. I leave it to the reader to refer to the pieces in this collection by Philip Chia and Monica Melanchthon for more information on developments in greater China and India. Australian scholars are being drawn into this energetic web of biblical scholarship, but much more remains to be done, especially closer to Australia in Indonesia where there are many possibilities for connections with both biblical critics working in the many theological colleges and critical Qur'anic Muslim scholars.

CRYSTAL BALL

I have already begun gazing into my crystal ball, especially with the ways Australian scholars are being drawn into the fascinating and energetic worlds of the Pacific and Asia. But when I look at the ball more intently, I can see five directions for the future. Both overlapping and at odds with each other, they are distinct: the possibilities for greater interaction and collaboration with Asia and the Pacific, the Foundation for Biblical Studies, the Earth Bible, the Biblical Scholars Mutual Self-Help Society, and the Bible and Critical Theory Seminar.

What will be the trigger for greater interaction between Asia, the Pacific, and Australia? It may well come with the arrival of peak oil, the steadily climbing cost of fuel, the increasing restriction of air travel to the wealthy few, and the diminishing ability of Australian scholars to take those cheap long-haul flights to Europe and North America. We will look back on that period of cheap, mass air travel as a strange anomaly once cheap energy has gone. The trip to New Zealand by container ship already costs less than flying, although time slows on the journey and one must recover a more ancient pace of life (as I have done recently on precisely such a journey). The upshot is that the Pacific and Asia will become even more important for Australian scholars. Collaboration, interaction, and conferences in this area will, I suspect, become more common as the longer journeys become less frequent. In fact, in my imaginative moments I begin planning conferences that meet on board a ship, picking up and dropping off scholars on a round trip between—to name but a few places—New Zealand, Fiji, New Caledonia, the Solomons and other Pacific Islands, China, Malaysia, Indonesia, Singapore, and of course Australia.

As for the Fellowship for Biblical Studies, this is a Melbourne-based group with the longest history of such associations in Australia.[2] By far the largest percentage of its members comes from the various theological colleges in and around Melbourne, although there are one or two from other cities and the odd university-based scholar. The fellowship publishes the annual *Australian Biblical Review*,[3] holds four annual seminar dinners, and is the heart of traditional, historical-critical work on the Bible (for example, see Campbell 2005, 2008; Mostert 2002; Painter 1979, 2002). It is deeply confessional, largely male, and upholds what it feels to be the traditions of scholarly excellence.

Compared to the Fellowship of Biblical Studies, the Earth Bible is much more interesting.[4] Brainchild of the untiring organizer and editor, the almost fossilized Norman Habel, the Earth Bible project has its base firmly in Adelaide. Initially involving five volumes of collected essays (Habel 2000–2002), the project has extended to liturgical material for use in churches (with ecological themes introduced at certain points in the ecclesial year and full liturgies developed [Habel 2004]), to sessions at the Society of Biblical Literature meetings, and to further collections of essays (Habel and Trudinger 2008). What the Earth Bible project seeks to do is "listen to the voice of Earth" and exegete biblical texts with this hermeneutical principle at the forefront. It is of course part of a larger "green" push in the humanities, making links with eco-criticism, the new kid on the theoretical block. In the other direction, the project is quite confessional, for it seeks to bring about a green wave of change within the churches. One reason is that churches and their interpretations of the Bible have been part of the dominant technocratic paradigm that tears human beings out of the environment in which we exist. Habel and the Earth Bible project members have a reforming agenda for the churches, although it tends very much to be the "liberal" wings of those churches which are most receptive to the message.

The Earth Bible is one example of a feature of biblical studies in Australia: the need to create your own environment of like-minded people in order to discuss and carry on your research. I recall a discussion with David Halperin (of *Saint Foucault* fame) some years ago when he was about to leave Australia for the United States after a few years here. He found it difficult, he said, to find a group of scholars with whom he could bounce around his ideas. He felt like he was the only person doing what he was doing and longed for that environment back home in the United States. There, he told me, you find such an environment already in place when you land a good job. What Halperin did not realize is that

---

2. See http://www.fbs.org.au/.

3. http://www.fbs.org.au/abr.html.

4. See www.webofcreation.org/Earthbible/earthbible.html.

in Australia you need to create those environments for yourself. It may take some more work, but it is far more creative and rewarding than assuming that such an environment is a given.

Another example of this process of making your own environment is the Bible and Critical Theory Seminar. Meeting, eating, drinking, and sleeping in pubs across the country from Perth to Brisbane and now in New Zealand, the Bible and Critical Theory Seminar has gathered a diverse group of people since 1998. As the name suggests, the group explores the intersections between critical theory and the Bible. The members of the seminar understand "critical theory" in the broad (rather than narrow) sense of a range of approaches that may be brought into touch with the Bible: feminism, psychoanalysis, queer theory, post-colonial theory, new historicism, cultural studies, poststructuralism, Marxism, cultural anthropology, political philosophy, eco-criticism, and so on. Each year the seminar has healthy and lively discussions between historians, philosophers, psychoanalysts, anthropologists, literary and cultural critics, and, of course, biblical critics. The seminar has been the major forum for graduate students to try their hand at presenting papers, experienced scholars to explore new directions, as well as a good number of international visitors. Up until 2008 we met in pubs in Australia, but after the gathering in Auckland in 2008 and the faithful kiwis who keep traveling across "the ditch" to get to Australian meetings, the seminar has begun regular meetings in New Zealand.

By now quite a few publications have come out of the seminar. Many people have tested early versions of essays before sending them to journals, presented various bits of books, and every now and then a volume of collected essays comes out of the seminar. These works have made significant contributions to psycho-analytic and feminist analysis through the work of Luce Irigaray (Kelso 2007), queer interpretation and the history of reception (Carden 2004), semiotics and the question of canon (Aichele 2001; Conrad 2004), eco-criticism (Elvey 2005) along with philosophy (Rose 2005), postcolonial analysis (Brett 2000; McKin-lay 2004; Boer 2008), feminist criticism (McKinlay 2004; Wainwright 2006) in combination with ethology (Cadwallader 2008), ficto-criticism (Boer 2007c), Marxist criticism (Boer 2003, 2007a), and the odd manifesto (Boer 2007b). A couple of volumes of collected essays drawn from the seminar have also appeared (Boer and Conrad 2003; Boer 2006). The Bible and Critical Theory journal first emerged from the seminar, although it has moved well beyond its beginnings, having become a significant international journal in biblical studies.

The seminar provides a forum for those who work in secular institutions, for those who work as secular biblical critics without any confessional standpoint, and for those who do work in theological colleges but are interested in newer directions of research. In short, it is one of the main powerhouses for innovative research in biblical studies in Australia and New Zealand. Again and again, someone hears about the seminar and says, "I didn't know this existed! I thought I was all alone." And so each year a few new people come out of their holes and corners and connect with a wider and energetic discussion.

However, I finish on a different note: the Biblical Scholars Mutual Benefit Society. Half joke, half serious, the idea for "Bibmut" arose when we were discussing how many capable and innovative biblical scholars were unemployed or underemployed in this country. Very soon there were almost twenty on the list. They are all people with PhDs, well-published, regular attendees and presenters at conferences, people who must do odd jobs here and there to make ends meet. We joked about getting a land grant and setting up a commune. We plotted lobbying the education department of the federal government and the universities about overpay and over-employment of existing staff. We pondered suggesting that pay levels and work levels drop to reasonable levels so that more could find work and live reasonable lives. As I write, plans are afoot for a web-lobbying campaign to pepper politicians and university leaders and granting bodies for some insight and wisdom, which seem to be in short supply. If not, we may find that the really interesting work comes from a few caravans, mud huts, and trailers in a biblical commune or two.

PART 6
NORTH AMERICA: CANADA AND THE UNITED STATES

16

READING THE BIBLE IN "OUR HOME AND NATIVE LAND":
EXPLORING SOME MARGINS AND MIGRATIONS IN
CANADIAN BIBLICAL STUDIES
(THROUGH THE LENS OF PSALM 137)

Fiona C. Black

In Canada, it appears that biblical scholars do not often avail themselves of the opportunity to reflect on how their political, historical, and social contexts impact their work on the Bible.[1] This does not mean that Canadian biblical scholarship is not "engaged"; rather, I suspect that it has more to do with a perception that there is not much about biblical studies in this country that marks it as distinct—as any different, say, from American biblical studies in general.[2] In fact, the reluctance to think about what makes biblical studies in this country *Canadian* could look a little like a crisis of identity, which actually is something that could be said to affect our entire national consciousness and not just our academic discipline.[3]

---

1. There are only a few exceptions that appear to contextualize biblical-critical work from a Canadian context: Erin Runions (2000), John Kessler (2007), Christine Mitchell (2008), and Harry O. Maier (2002, 2005, 2007). See below for discussion.

2. Or even European biblical studies? This is an impression that I admit I had when I was first approached to write a chapter for the present volume. I am grateful for the input of Christine Mitchell, Harold Remus, and Francis Landy on these matters at a recent CSBS meeting, and for their encouragement to keep thinking about these matters. I also appreciate the feedback of Francis Landy and Erin Runions on a draft of this paper.

3. Some fifty years ago, Northrop Frye famously quipped that a Canadian is an American who rejects the revolution (1971, 14). In his essay, he was trying to differentiate Canadian political ideology from American via discussion of Canadian poetry, but his comment seems to be repeated in such a way that it is used to sum up our essential *sameness* with American identity, the original civil disputes notwithstanding. More promising—if we were to continue the

What, I wonder, would it look like to engage in biblical studies that incorporates a desire to understand the discipline's history in this country, as well as its unique dynamics in Canadian culture, politics, and history? A voluminous project, to be sure. How might one make a start? And why might it be important to do so?[4]

If we are to survey biblical study[5] here in this country, part of that picture must be to consider what it means to be Canadian, that is, whether and how national identity (or identities) impacts the way we read the Bible. Indeed, how do Canadians negotiate their *Canadian-ness*, sandwiched as we are historically, culturally and geographically, between two empires? What particular aspects of our history, our complicated context as colonized and colonizer, impact biblical studies in Canada? We might, thus, also ask some difficult questions about "home" and "native," as my title, borrowed from the national anthem, indicates. Whose home? What is native? And what might *Natives*—our First Nations peoples—have to say to the discipline as it continues to grow and change in a changing Canada?

Since an essay of this type threatens to become encyclopedic, I focus my exploration of biblical studies in Canada in conjunction with two significant issues for Canadian identity: cultural diversity and Canada's relation to two colonialisms. After some discussion there, I suggest some matters we might begin to think about, if, as scholars here, we see the value of thinking about our context in a critical way. By way of a conclusion, I turn toward a specific biblical text (Ps 137) and a particular hermeneutical community with which I am connected, that of Caribbean Canadians.[6] The psalm is apt here not only for its importance in Caribbean hermeneutics, but because it might be both symptom

---

discussion with Frye—are his comments about our ideas of cultural difference from America, prompted by the geographical landscape in Canada (10). See Scott's comments about Canadian identity (or the lack thereof) in literature.

4. The conversation needs to be more protracted than what I am able to offer in this initial foray; I hope that my comments might spark further interest in the Canadian context as it impacts the use and interpretation of the Bible.

5. I use a general term here, not "biblical studies," because I want to leave room for the many aspects of study of the Bible that are not official or disciplinary ones.

6. Some other work that I am currently undertaking pursues the Bible as it intersects with the African-derived tradition of Obeah and as it comes to be negotiated in Caribbean hermeneutics, notably with respect to the Bahamas. This work already had me thinking about culture and identity, about the displacement of peoples and the effort to remember what has been lost in the process of transplantation. I have also been thinking about what can be reasonably repurposed in the context of that new culture, and how those factors may be crossfertilizing. My comments can only be brief, but I make them because I am hopeful that what makes the surveying of biblical studies in any context useful is to focus it eventually toward reading biblical material.

and therapy for the Canadian context: it expresses longing for what is lost and hope for new beginnings.[7]

Biblical Studies in Canada

To begin, it is important to relate the myth of origins of the discipline of biblical studies in Canada as it became manifest in both theological and "secular" university departments and in the creation of the Canadian Society of Biblical Studies (CSBS). Conveniently, the history of both is partially reproduced by John S. Moir in his book, *A History of Biblical Studies in Canada* (1982), which, as far as I am able to determine, is the only such work of its kind. There, Moir describes the discipline's origins as being quite similar to those of the United States, where it developed in connection with theological (seminary) studies, eventually to break with them and morph into the more secular or liberal arts contexts that were developing in national universities during the 1960s and 70s. This century-long process naturally connected with the expected ideological shifts taking place in university education. In Canada in the early years, it also involved the question of the usefulness and availability of biblical languages to students. Part of that picture as Moir develops it is that secular departments, such as that in the University of Toronto,[8] became established at the end of the nineteenth century because they were able to offer what seminaries could not or were uninterested in offering. Moir suggests that these trends were directly related to developments in German biblical scholarship and to the eventual pursuit of graduate degrees in Germany by Canadian students. Of particular interest is Moir's tracing of the somewhat alternative movement at the University of Toronto during this time towards the "higher criticism." Deeply controversial, the wrangling over the intent and effects of such new methods were to plague the department for some years.[9]

---

7. To offer up a reading of a biblical text is not only pertinent for biblical scholars. Canada is a nation that, despite popular belief to the contrary, is still noticeably Christian. Though immigration may of course be slowly altering this profile, our history, laws, culture, and social practices are built, as Western culture typically is, on Jewish and Christian ideas and texts. It is not a stretch to ponder the influence that a psalm such as Ps 137 may have on the picture that I paint here. It is also not unreasonable to assume some degree of biblical literacy amongst Canadians, though such an assumption is, naturally, difficult to prove.

8. Formerly "Orientals," now the "Department of Ancient and Near Eastern Languages and Literatures."

9. At the University of Toronto, a new charter cleared the way for a program to be pursued in "Orientals" that allowed the teaching of biblical languages and literatures, quite separate from theology. The movement was not without its critics. To twenty-first century eyes, the comments

The CSBS's roots were "central" too, geographically speaking. Moir's telling of the society's history shows that it was, for many years, a small collection of like-minded scholars from central Canadian provinces who met intermittently to discuss their work. The depression and the intervening war further complicated the growth and regular assembly of the society. Nevertheless, it persisted, and today—at a respectable seventy-six years of age—has a membership of some four hundred strong. This is small potatoes, of course, compared to SBL or AAR, but it does reflect quite accurately the small size of the group working in Canada. It also reveals consistency in numbers over the last couple of decades, as well as in research interests and approaches (more on this below).

As Mark Noll points out in his review essay on the Bible in America (1987), however, histories such as Moir's suffer from problems of conceptualization, among them, that they are intensely political, paying little attention to demographics, origin (of scholars), and the like.[10] Noll observes that Moir's book is mostly a "study of scholarship at the University of Toronto and its affiliated colleges" (507). I would also point out that it has a peculiar interest in documenting (without further commentary) the number of Jews and women who are occasionally members of the society, once it is formed. The mention of the former group is particularly interesting, given our Delitzschian roots (see below). It would be useful for the field to have the same history of what were actually similar nego-

---

of dissenters such as Samuel Blake (a prominent Toronto lawyer, a governor of the University of Toronto, a cofounder of Wycliffe College—a theological college associated with the Anglican Church of Canada—and a "strident champion of a rigid and aggressive evangelicalism" [Moir 1982, 29]) that students were being encouraged to think of the Bible as a collection of "old wives' fables," seem an amusing objection, given the degree to which the discipline has developed in the intervening years. According to Moir, Blake seemed to uphold the secular intentions of the university, but his objections were over the discussion of biblical literature in such a way that it actively promoted skepticism or disbelief. He was assured by the university chancellor that the Bible was being studied with "no dogmatic teaching and no work of interpretation being carried on" (30), yet that students did need "some cognizance of [biblical] literature" as part of a well-rounded education. To this he responded: "There is a very wide difference between taking 'some cognizance of the literature' and using this liberty as an opportunity to assail the authenticity of the Bible, to introduce and advocate the views of the higher critics, to instill a disbelief in the Messianic character of the Old Testament prophecy, and to introduce the idea among Students that large portions of the Bible, accepted by many as God's Word, are mere myths or allegories and to be rejected as 'old wives' fables'" (31).

10. This narrowness of sampling in Moir's research is actually emblematic of similar histories in America that Noll examines. The focus of his review essay is predominantly the SBL Centennial Series, with publications on topics ranging from general histories (e.g., of the SBL), to particular approaches (e.g., feminist approaches to scripture), to specific scholars (e.g., Amos N. Wilder).

tiations and developments in such universities as McGill or McMaster—and perplexingly not in others, such as the University of British Columbia or the University of Alberta. Comparative analysis of all programs and histories might have shed some light on how most came to renegotiate the relationship between theology/confessional biblical studies and their secular or academic cousin as time moved along—a relationship that still profoundly affects our universities (and our academic society). Whereas in the United States, certain (private) schools have been able to maintain their distinctive and confessional approach, in Canada this possibility exists only in the Bible college.[11]

Moir's emphasis on Toronto and on the historical developments of schools and programs also means that he is less interested in the work of particular persons or fields; less, indeed, with exploring what biblical scholars actually worked on in Canada and what interests or ideologies governed their work. This becomes an issue especially given his final comments in the book regarding the dominance of the Toronto department and its chosen area (Hebrew Bible/Old Testament studies), the lack of New Testament personnel in the country, and the relatively small output of biblical scholars here (in terms of publications). This means that as a Canadian discipline, both in our places of work and in our academic society, we have no collective memory, no established history of what we as biblical scholars actually *did*. Quite apart from our failure to be good conservators of our own traditions, then, we have a paucity of information on what might characterize us in our work and in any contextually-mediated approaches to the Bible. Here might be at least one reason for the perceived crisis of identity that I suggested that we are suffering.[12]

---

11. Some colleges have, over the years, transformed themselves into independent Christian universities, privately funded, and with no affiliation to public universities. There are, to date, a handful of these around the country, such as Crandall University (formerly Atlantic Baptist University), Trinity Western University, Concordia University College of Alberta, etc.

12. The fault, I hasten to add, is not Moir's (who is not even a biblical scholar), but ours. Surely, even if resources are limited, part of the writing of the story of biblical studies in Canada must be to establish the legacy of those who worked in this national and academic context. Those such as James Frederick McCurdy (the "founder of the CSBS," according to Moir's dedication), R. B. Y. Scott, George B. Caird, Stanley Frost, George Johnston, among many, merit closer examination: were they merely transplants from German biblical scholarship or the highly influential University of Chicago (Moir), or did their particular contexts affect how they interpreted, wrote about, and preached the Bible? In other words, what effects did Canadian history, politics, and culture have on their work? A recent attempt has been made with Manson's tribute to the life and work of R.B.Y. Scott. The article is a little thin on Scott's voluminous contribution to biblical scholarship (though some work on the prophets is discussed), however, and he is lauded more for his Church-related work and his "vision of a just, fair and free society" (2005, 32).

One final issue with regards to Moir's history requires comment, and that is the closing observation in his study:

> In Canada no "schools" of biblical interpretation, whether centred on one person or on one institution, developed. Overall, individual Canadian scholars made their greatest contribution to biblical studies through their teaching. Canadian biblical scholars have produced many articles in their field—some have been literally prodigious in this area—but less frequently have they authored monographs. In international scholarly journals and organizations they have contributed as much if not more than could fairly and proportionately be expected from such a restricted group.... The most distinctive and lasting traditions of biblical studies in Canada, however, are still the strong emphasis on language as the basis of further studies and that essentially conservative position assumed by most Canadian scholars in matters of interpretation, a position that J. F. McCurdy described as "a sense of proportion." (1982, 108–09)

Would biblical scholars in Canada agree with Moir's evaluation, I wonder? To be sure, some twenty-five years have passed, so we must account for the developments in the Canadian scene. We might speak, for instance, of some important contributions made in such areas as Dead Sea Scrolls;[13] of the trailblazing of now retired scholars such as Robert Culley in the shift from historical to literary approaches;[14] and of the extremely influential work of some current historians and literary critics.[15] And one cannot, of course, describe the publication of monographs by Canadian scholars as "less frequent"! Moreover, no longer could we assert that Toronto's influence remains as pervasive in national biblical scholarship as Moir indicates that it was in those early years.

These sorts of successes and shifts can be expected in twenty-five years of academic development. In part, they reflect the movements taking place in the

---

13. Consider, for instance, work by Martin Abegg, James Flint, and Eileen Schuller. One should also mention the Dead Sea Scrolls Institute of Trinity Western University.

14. Culley is well known for his interest and work on oral traditions at a time when they were not at all *en vogue*. More latterly, he was a founder and an active proponent of alternative approaches in the journal *Semeia*, and edited two volumes there on textual indeterminacy. Most interestingly, he seems to have assisted in the spawning of some biblical scholars with decidedly "alternative" interests.

15. The contributions of some of the more well-established scholars (some actively working still and some recently retired) in the country to the field have been voluminous, not only in our own national context, but in the field at large, to name only a few: Donna Runnalls, Peter Richardson, Art van Seters, Adele Reinhartz, Eileen Schuller, David Jobling, Ehud benZvi, Francis Landy, Wili Braun.

discipline away from historical studies to incorporate other interests.[16] They also have to do, it seems, with increased numbers in the discipline in Canada (from 1982) and with the internationalization or globalization of the field. The shifts and developments also are connected with the reorganization, amalgamation, or erosion of many religion departments, wherein schools can no longer afford to serve the broad range available in biblical studies in its entirety. Student interest has a profound impact on what is offered, if my own context in a small, Atlantic Canadian undergraduate university is any measure of the national situation. As one might expect, part of the (mostly publicly funded) Canadian university scene is that economics drives biblical (religious) studies in many ways: (1) funding to particular university humanities departments; (2) research money available, both in specific university contexts and in the broader national competitions;[17] (3) in the demands made by ecclesiastical or denominational interests, where applicable.

A survey of academic departments in universities, though, is but one part of the picture. One cannot legitimately develop a history of biblical studies in Canada without investigating the strong and longstanding tradition of small independent institutions—Bible colleges and schools—which began to develop in the latter part of the nineteenth century.[18] Many of these institutions exist in their original formats, functioning as places where laypeople, with or without a

---

16. A qualification is necessary here: though the discipline at large might be moving in a certain direction, it is not entirely clear that Canadian biblical studies is eagerly going along with it. Meek's observation in 1958, before Moir even assembled his history, still gives me pause: "Near Eastern studies have occupied no mean place in the Canadian scene, but one could wish there might be more research, spread over a wider area" (260). Nevertheless, there is some definite movement from the picture that Moir describes in 1982. See below for more discussion.

17. This is often under threat in an age of reduced government funding for education and in renewed efforts to make what "counts" in the university context as that which has a clear and present translation to industry. Recent funding cuts to SSHRCC (Social Sciences and Humanities Research Council of Canada) by the present conservative government are a case in point. SSHRCC's policy to align fundable research in the humanities and social sciences with business and finance are perhaps one piece of evidence of the council attempting to cope with funding slashes.

18. That history is far too complicated to elaborate fully here. Denominational differences and the huge number of schools that developed, many of them in small-town/rural Canada, make it a long story. A brief history of a variety of colleges is excellently presented in McKinney's article (1998). Bowlby and Faulkner's survey of religious studies in Atlantic Canada is also useful for understanding the history of the Maritime context. As McKinney points out, though, the Maritime context was not the part of the country that "birthed the majority of Canadian Bible schools" (35); it was, instead, the prairie provinces.

high school degree,[19] might further their knowledge of the Bible and strengthen their faith. They might also prepare for missions or the ordained ministry here, depending on the requirements of specific denominations. In some cases, it has become expedient for these schools to merge with local university campuses (as, for example, with some colleges affiliated with the University of Alberta), and in other cases, to recast themselves as liberal arts colleges with a Christian focus.[20] There is some communication between these colleges and secular or theological university programs but, if it occurs, it appears to be achieved through denominational connections or at the professional level, where, for instance, faculty are members of the CSBS or other societies and make connections there.[21]

All of the above describes institutionalized biblical study, even if the various arms do not have much to do with each other at all. Is it possible to determine who *else* reads the Bible, however, and can this be accounted for in any concrete way in an essay such as this? One thinks, for example, of various collaborative projects between First Nations communities and the Canadian Bible Society to translate the biblical text into traditional languages.[22] Though I have yet to locate

---

19. Originally, the schools did not require high school diplomas for entrance; this was one factor which made them so accessible and attendance well subscribed (McKinney, 46).

20. For example, Concordia University College of Alberta has transitioned from a Lutheran (Missouri Synod) seminary (1921), to offering first and second-year courses for the University of Alberta (1967, 1975), to becoming a degree-granting institution in its own right (1987), to ending ties with the University of Alberta (1991) and changing its name to Concordia University College (1995) in order to best reflect its independent status and liberal arts profile. Other conversions from colleges to universities include Trinity Western University (which despite its original aims did not receive government permission to grant degrees until some seventeen years after its inception in 1962, then accreditation by the AUCC five years after that), and Crandall University.

21. What I mean by collaboration is that it is not very often that Bible colleges and university departments have had or presently have a sense of shared vision or goals in their elaboration of the biblical text. On both sides, the perception is of a certain exclusivism and/or elitism. University programs might be suspected of perceiving themselves as "academic" and rigorous over against the others; the colleges appear to harbor suspicion of their counterparts as sacrificing faith and embracing secularism. Denominational differences further divide colleges from collaborating with each other, in many cases, though regional proximity will sometimes bridge those gaps. These differences are not just about historic developments of institutions (their charters and statements of faith, for example), but in the past have been linked to the different educational backgrounds of faculty. In other words, the formation of these scholars and teachers was, historically, different, as elaborated in Moir; so were the perceived aims of the study of the Bible. What would be encouraging is to see connections being established between the two in the future, where there is common ground.

22. One such example is the *First Nations Bible*, which is a project to translate the NT and approximately 30 percent of the HB/OT into Mohawk. See www.firstnationsbible.com and www.

direct evidence of strictly interpretive work, such as commentaries and the like, of course translation provides its own kind of context-motivated interpretation. These collaborations revive centuries-old endeavors to provide translated texts for various communities, but they are also doing something that is essential for the twenty-first century. In working with elders, linguists and translators, the committee is seeking to find a way to record and preserve native languages that are rapidly being lost due to various encroachments on traditional life and culture. In this way, the Bible exceeds its importance to communities as religious text and somewhat ironically becomes a tool for the preservation of First Nations culture.

What's Canadian about Canadian Biblical Studies?

Though I found the idea troubling when I first read it, I wonder if Moir's observation (quoting McCurdy) of the "sense of proportion" that affects Canadian Bible scholars, the "sane and tactful course" that occupied their work in the early part of the twentieth century, might be interrogated (1982, 109, 23).[23] To be sure, contemporary Canadian biblicists are rigorous, dedicated, excellent scholars, but many if not most *are* proportionate in their choice of research subjects or their methods. Why should this be? Is it a reflection of early attitudes toward the historical background of their discipline as it developed here, or of the context (the theological schools and universities) in which many work?[24] Is it a case of sheer numbers—that a small demographic (compared to the United States) suggests one is less likely to find nontraditional scholars in such a small pool? Is it an indication of religious adherence or interest?[25] Or, is it something to do with the

---

biblesociety.ca.

23. The latter refers to a response to the methods and advances of the "Chicago school," which, Moir explains, was acceptable to churches around the turn of the century as long as scholars pursued proven facts over imaginative theories (23). The conservatism that marked Canadian scholarship at this time, in response to Chicago (which had risen, meteor-like in North American esteem) is evident in the comments of H. P. Whidden, a graduate of the same and eventual chancellor of McMaster, a Baptist school: "It is not exactly a hot bed of Heresy, and yet pretty tall heretics have grown there and will continue to grow there for some time. For a man who has thought through … things a little, it is not a very dangerous place; but I am quite satisfied that I did not take my regular Theological Course there" (71–72).

24. I refer to contexts, as I indicated earlier, which may be working out that delicate balance between confessional (theological) and secular biblical studies.

25. Or is it a reflection of my own perspective, that what makes radical (or "disproportionate") biblical studies is that which is iconoclastic, or which attempts to move against the main-

national context in which we work? In other words, is *Canadian-ness* a synonym for proportionate? And if so, why should that be?

Of course, one might immediately take issue with this idea of a sense of proportion: what exactly does it mean? McCurdy seemed to indicate (as I read via Moir) that it has something to do with engagement with higher criticism. Canadians appeared to be willing to learn the skills and to engage with the academic debates of historical criticism, but in essence they were conservators of tradition (academic and religious). They were sensible, not radical; they were not about to substitute any bathwater for babies. These inclinations are, according to Moir, thanks to our Delitzschian roots, where the Leipzig school fostered "rigorous and scientific" methodology, a moderate tone and "verifiable results, as opposed to radical and speculative interpretations that would shock and challenge both scholarly and popular orthodoxy" (1982, 107). Is there, then, a correlating strategy—conscious or not—among today's Canadian scholars? It would be hard to make such a generalization without examining the work of each person in the field. There is, however, still the strong grounding in matters philological and historical in most programs across the country. Informal polling of colleagues suggests that this is still the most sensible way to teach biblical studies and to prepare students for graduate work in the field. Moreover, a brief exploration of the papers presented and the seminars hosted at the CSBS over its seventy-five years or so shows a predominance of historical approaches and interests, even up to the present. The so-called literary or cultural-critical readings of the Bible and interest in what one might refer to as the newer methods of biblical scholarship seem consistently underrepresented in the society.[26]

There is every reason to value solid background in linguistic and historical studies of the biblical world. The only problem, of course, is that our "roots" have been used as tools to "conquer and subjugate other peoples' texts and stories and cultures" (Sugirtharajah 2000, 49). They appeared to liberate European readers from ecclesial and theological constraints, but as Sugirtharajah points out, the liberated were Western, male, white and middle-class; others were shackled by historical criticism's totalizing (colonial) impulses. Franz Delitzsch, moreover, provides a rather interesting example of these matters in his own life and work. Known for his rigorous scholarship, particularly his thorough commentaries on the Psalms, Song of Songs, and Job, he is also known for his somewhat

---

stream?

26. Naturally, these methods or interests are no more value-neutral than is historical criticism. The point is merely that, if following Moir, our historical critical roots point to our conservative interests, and if those roots have not shifted much in their own right, or towards other methods, then it follows that conservatism must still mark our discipline, in broad terms.

"ambivalent" opinions about Judaism. On the one hand, he was a radical and vocal supporter of Judaism before World War I, and, on the other, he could not reconcile his ideas about the truth of Christianity with the existence of the first covenant. He was, in other words, supersessionist in his thinking (Levenson 2002, 383). This accounts for his formation of a missionary society for the conversion of Jews and his translation of the NT into Hebrew (*ha-Brit ha-Chadashah*). Levenson evaluates this conflicting stance in Delitzsch as allosemitism, which is a troubling skeleton indeed to have in our collective closet.[27]

At this juncture, I cannot make too much of the connection with Delitzsch: it cannot be suggested that Canadian biblical scholarship is by its nature antisemitic, philosemitic, *or* allosemitic. (One might certainly look back at its history, however, to see if and how clearly Delitzsch left his mark.) What I would ask, though, is what we might do with such knowledge about our collective formation. It is not enough to ignore it or simply to be different. Should such history not be foremost in our minds as we engage the Bible? Further, might not the "ambivalence" of Delitzsch be rather useful heuristically, as well? It is reminiscent of our apparent difficulty as Canadians to negotiate the matter of our own "schizophrenia," as it relates to our history as colonial subjects of the British Empire and to our role as perpetrators of the colonization of First Nations people (and, one might argue, new immigrants to the country).[28] Both colonized and colonizer, our schizophrenia brings to light even more troubling histories of the Bible in Canada than our connections with Delitzsch.

To address these dynamics briefly, one need only point out that postcolonial studies concerning Canada have, broadly speaking, had to deal with the complex nature of Canada's relation to colonialism in the manner described above, but also as it bears on matters of distinct societies (French Canada) and on official thinking on cultural diversity/multiculturalism. What these issues mean for biblical studies per se has yet to be investigated, but each issue brings with it a host of events or practices that implicate Christianity and/or the Bible in complex and often troubling ways. For instance, Canada's troubled relationships with its First

---

27. It would seem that the younger Delitzsch, also at Leipzig and equally influential for Canadians according to Moir (9, 10, 15, 31, 39), took his father's ambivalence a little further. Gossai quotes him as being of the opinion that the Hebrew Bible is "full of fraud and immorality that had damaged the moral fibre of Christendom and should be no longer read as sacred literature by Christians" (152).

28. That may seem a radical statement, but many have written about the creation of a third class of immigrants, many of them professionals, who are being forced into poverty, menial labor, or servitude in this and other Western countries. Canada, with its nice talk about multiculturalism and diversity, is not exempt from such practices.

Nations peoples involve a plethora of ills, such as forced conversions, co-opting land, stolen generations,[29] continued displacement/fights over land claims, and numerous social and medical problems caused by locating communities in "reservations." Scholars of Quebecois culture and history write voluminously and often about the formative and, at the same time, difficult participation of the Catholic Church in the lives of French Canadians. Current thinking on immigration and cultural diversity is hampered by decidedly fuzzy policies that have little or no interest in religion as a major category for understanding or facilitating immigrant arrivals.[30] This means that there is little effort made to educate the receiving communities about religious customs and difference, creating strained relations between "Christian Canada" and others.

Lists of this sort are endless. The point is to ask whether and how this speckled history, part of the complicated picture that is Canada, might inform biblical scholars as they go about their interpretive business. The issues appear to have little to do with a reconstruction of Persian Yehud, of the impact of a particular temple scroll, of the literary contours of Isaiah, of the language of the lament psalms, and yet, one must ask (must one still ask?) whether it is possible to engage with a text or series of texts that has its own political demands and implications without considering an interpreter's own. Given the ethical imperative in reading biblical texts that has been identified by Elisabeth Schüssler Fiorenza, Fernando Segovia, and R.S. Sugirtharajah, among others,[31] to engage with mat-

---

29. In particular, one might mention the residential schools policies of the late 1800s and early 1900s, where native Canadian children were removed from their homes and "educated" in church-sponsored schools across the country. There they suffered physical and sexual abuse, the denigration of their culture, and numerous other injustices. The Canadian government is currently (but slowly) assessing claims and attempting to make reparation for these injustices.

30. See Bramadat (2005) and Bowlby (2003) particularly; the latter argues that governments ignore religion at their peril. Indeed, religions establish "authentic precedents on which we can build the future of a multicultural society" (46).

31. I mention these three names in the field because of their initiatory and extremely influential work. For an early exploration of contextual reading (really, the impact of cultural studies as it might be realized on biblical scholarship), see Segovia and Tolbert (1995a; 1995b), both volumes. Biblical studies now comfortably boasts a number of learned contributors to this field, however, many of them the contributors to this present volume. See, in general, the work of Kwok Pui-Lan, Musa Dube, Tat-Siong Benny Liew, Erin Runions, Roland Boer, Gerald West, Stephen Moore, Laura Donaldson, Archie C.C. Lee, and so on. The work of these scholars engages, implicitly at least, with Elisabeth Schüssler Fiorenza's much quoted SBL presidential address in 1987, wherein she calls for the decentering of the discipline. Observing a shift in the field towards a rhetorical-ethical or rhetorical emancipatory paradigm (what Segovia labels as critical cultural studies), she insisted (and continues to; 2000) that the "theoretical frameworks, methods, and strategies of biblical interpretation," along with its "institutional locus and its scholarly

ters of politics of place, culture and identity as we interact with the Bible, it is especially incumbent upon us who are working in this field in Canada to write from *our* context. Moreover, the responsibility seems to extend further back than that. Perhaps greater attention paid to Canadian life and culture (in the academy and outside it) by us as scholars and citizens—an interest in the question, "What is Canada?"—needs to be addressed before we can even begin to open "the Book" and read.

It would seem that if we are to conduct the sort of rigorous self-analysis that I perceive these scholars to be advocating, we might come upon some serious matters. The first and most obvious would be the apparent crisis of our own identity, the apparent reluctance to explore ourselves as a nation and as biblical scholars in that national context. The second is to understand that our implication as biblical scholars in our own colonial history cannot be neutral when it is conflicted itself and when the central thread of the biblical story is about land and conquest. The third is more positively connoted: far from being an antiquated or solely historical document(s), the Bible surely has something to offer the diversity and complexity of our time and context. Matters like these affect many culturally various and dynamic nations, to be sure. Can the Bible help us to explore Canadian identity? Does it pose challenges to it? Do not our history and our chosen text for analysis (from whatever hermeneutical circle we operate) prompt more from us in terms of ethical and socially critical responses to what we see in the world around us and what we read?

MIGRATIONS AND MEANDERINGS IN CANADA

For the edification of the nation, HISTOR!CA[32] provides a series of advertisements of historical moments in Canada's creation. One is about the importance of Laura Secord in the War of 1812. Another is about the nontraditional teaching methods of a woman (!) who teaches her pupils to read using the Bible (the Bible!); and so on. A third shows a young man who dares to correct a priest—struggling to converse with First Nations peoples on behalf of explorer Jacques

---

and educational formations" (30) be rigorously scrutinized. She continues to insist on this, as indeed others do, because it seems that the discipline still questions the validity of other voices in its midst, especially when those voices challenge the positivistic, scientific center. See the discussion between Schüssler Fiorenza and Heikki Räisänen as a case in point (2000b).

32. HISTOR!CA is a nonprofit organization dedicated to teaching Canadians about their history. The commercial I refer to can be found at http://www.histori.ca/minutes/minute.do?id=10123.

Cartier—that "Canada" means not "country" or "land," as he infers, but "village": "that village over there." The priest, because of his status, persists in his interpretation. So it is that we learn that our nation's name actually means "village" and, more importantly, that our perceptions of ourselves are based on mistranslation (and a certain dose of ecclesial arrogance). This commercial is instructive, at least, but perhaps not only in the ways that *HISTOR!CA* might have hoped. I find it thought provoking for its insistence that we remember to focus away from the general and on to the particular.

"That village over there" is naturally another way of talking about diversity. It engages directly with the current debate in Canadian society and politics over exactly what multiculturalism or cultural diversity is.[33] Critics argue it is not so much a matter of having a policy that does not resemble America's notorious "melting pot," but one that actively seeks to preserve and value difference. Will Kymlicka and Norman Brown sum up the contention as this: "[H]ow to show respect for diversity in a pluralistic society without at the same time damaging or eroding the bonds and virtues of citizenship" (Scott 2002, 117). For my purposes, "that village over there" is a useful way of signaling the diversity in background and interpretive context (academic or personal) of particular interpreters; yet, the television commercial, as facile as it may be perceived to be, visually marks "that village" as another's space. In that case, it is a First Nations space, where contact and negotiation take place on their terms.[34] "That village" is also vital for pointing out that it is important to resist the tendency of biblical studies (especially biblical studies in Canada) to be monologic. Monologism here applies to methodological approach, subject choices and desired outcomes of biblical study. Diversity of voices and villages might well prompt us to ask ourselves, How diverse are we?

I mentioned above several "exceptions" to my general statement that Canadian biblical scholars seem disinterested in addressing their Canadian context. These are examples of some who have taken up "that village over there," to ask what it is about their historical and geographical contexts that inform how they look at texts. These three, Maier, Mitchell, and Runions, have set the stage for the kind of thinking that I am advocating. Their work is not necessarily thematically or methodologically connected, but, as Mitchell writes, these kind of steps set us well on our way to "develop a distinctively Canadian body of work" (2007, 274).

---

33. Canada's multicultural agendum has by no means been uncontested. One of the major detractors, Neil Bisoondath, argues that Canada's policies rely on "stereotype, ensuring that ethnic groups will preserve their distinctiveness in a gentle and insidious form of cultural apartheid" (1994, 191; quoted in Scott, 115).

34. Sadly, history went badly and bloodily for the Mic'maq people after Cartier's contact. I wonder if there will be a commercial made about that.

Taking up John Kessler's model of a charter group for Yehud, Mitchell reads the story of Saskatoon, a temperance colony, intertextually with Haggai. She argues that her understanding of one influences the other, and vice versa, so that in effect, by her presence in Saskatoon and her interest in its history, the two are inextricably linked in a kind of hermeneutical circle. What she wonders eventually is if this kind of reading might be a typological framework for doing biblical studies in Canada. Though she does not explicate here how this might work, she leaves us with a tentative but tantalizing beginning: "I suggest that it is the Canadian's liminal space and context (in between colonizer and colonized; in between historical empires—British and American; both inside the Anglo-American scholarly sphere and also outside it) that leads so many down this road ["working in Persian period texts and contexts"]" (2007, 273). Absolutely, there are connections between the nature of the materials we (choose to) read and our context. As I have indicated, what we need are sustained interrogations of those connections, not only to understand ourselves (and our texts) better, but also to answer to the ethical imperatives that our history and our texts make—to recognize, analyze, and respond.

Sophisticated movement in this direction is made in an article on Numbers 16 by Erin Runions, a transplanted Canadian, who is now directing her analytical energies toward American politics—alas for Canada. The article pits the rebellion at Korah against two other "rebellions:" that of the siege at Gustafson Lake, British Columbia, in 1995; and that of a blockade of the OECD conference in Montreal in 1998 by activists who were protesting the MAI (Multilateral Agreement on Investment). The point of her analysis, as she says, is not to imply a causal connection between Bible and contemporary responses to colonial ideology, but to show how ideological underpinnings of violent repression of objections to colonialism are remarkably similar (2000, 184).[35] This is a provocative reading, and it is the kind that biblical text and interpretive context demand of readers. Of course, some readers may be less than comfortable with connections that are not apparently direct (or causal) but are merely intertextual. What Runions' work acknowledges and makes use of in a powerful way, though, is that intertextuality is always part of the interpretive exercise.

Similar movement is made by Harry Maier, and in disparate ways. His involved study of the book of Revelation led him first tentatively to explore the connections between his own upbringing as a German immigrant in Canada in a book-length study of the text (2002). These are later focused sharply in a

---

35. She adds: "This observation is at the very least interesting, and perhaps also significant, given that the Bible has been used as a tool of colonization, and that the narrative of the promised land has authorized more than one conquest" (185).

provocative reading of Revelation among immigrants (2005), which is fully contextualized in contemporary North American politics, in his own family memory as German refugees after World War II, and in Canadian postwar sociopolitics, all of which form him as a reader of Revelation. They also constitute the backdrop of an ethical approach to the text: "To read Revelation in the contemporary first-world comfort of the middle class—that group for whom religious apocalyptic entertainment is marketed—is to risk coming away with a sinking sense that one is a Laodicean" (78).[36]

These three readers so far take us into a realm where we have yet to tread fully as Canadian biblical scholars. Each piece is fully contextual, autobiographical, and particular to a given historical or contemporary set of events. Also, Runions and Maier, by virtue of this and later work, have been thinking about the ethics of biblical reading in a sustained way, Maier especially for Canada. The perceived difficulty with this kind of work may be that such intertexts—even if sensibly and legitimately filtered through the autobiographical stance of the reader/writer—might not be perceived as legitimate avenues for biblical scholarship, especially by Canadian audiences. Or such an approach may simply not be in the *interests* of every person writing here in Canada. Conservatively, one might respond to such objections that as long as this type of work is represented here in some capacity (through more frequent publication of it and the encouragement of forums for dialogue and exploration, in the academy and beyond), then we are on the right track. Surely, though, there is the possibility of contextually engaged reading in every reading. Does not the text demand it of us, in its own difficult contours? And in the current disciplinary climate, where at last we might assent to the personal in the textual, do not our *selves* bring about an engagement with the Bible that demands that we listen to what constitutes us as readers—our interests, our chosen methods, our intentions for the text? Finally, we must ask: what is our country to us that it remains a silent partner in our midst?

---

36. That is, it "offers prophetic admonition for the rich and self-satisfied who are tempted by idolatry" (70). In a completely different context, Maier also writes about the paradoxes of doing biblical/theological study in the culturally diverse context of Vancouver. His prescription here is this: "I urge commitment to the familiar made strange by learning to become 'strangers to ourselves'—to grow into awareness of the often poorly understood desires, commitments and embodied traditions that constitute us as historical subjects and predispose us to act and interpret in often hidden ways" (2007, 86).

A Prescription?

Here might be some indications of directions for biblical studies in the country along these contextually-mediated lines that I have been discussing. (I hasten to assert that it is as much a prescription for my future thinking—a raising of my own consciousness—as it is directed to others in the field who want to think about these matters.)

First, biblical studies in Canada might look critically at its own origins (or myth of origins). It might consider the preponderance of historical and philological work in this country, not because there is something wrong with those approaches and interests per se, but because, like all aspects of the discipline, they are rooted in particular ideologies, make particular assumptions, and exclude other voices in asserting their own privilege.

Second, Canadian biblical studies might interrogate those historical-critical beginnings as they are framed in the context of colonialism in a way that jumps off from the important beginnings already made in the field. It might ask whether its European roots (German and British) have left a lingering Eurocentrism as their legacy here in Canada. It might ponder the use to which biblical texts were put in the process of colonization (in its complex duality); conversely, it might also explore the liberating history of those texts as they were used by the colonized to resist violence and enforced assimilation. Those who choose to write and research in other directions have the responsibility to understand the context of these other methodologies. Asking the reasons behind the shift (from, say, historical to literary or literary to cultural studies) is one part of the picture; asking about the ideological structures inherent in certain post-structuralist or postmodern approaches is another.

Third, Canadian biblical studies must consider itself in relation to otherness of two kinds. One is the otherness that it encounters in its midst, in the form of society's (and the academy's) marginal voices and those disenfranchised by cultural hegemonies, notably Christian. Similarly, the other "other" is that which has always been here in the form of the country's original peoples. Can one promote biblical study in this country without addressing the impact that the Bible and its related religious traditions have had on these others? And, as a means of redress, could biblical scholars in Canada seek to engage with precisely these grassroots hermeneutical communities in their own work? What a potentially rich and enervating connection this might make.

Fourth, biblical studies must consider itself in light of the traditions with which it is implicitly (if not explicitly) connected. The current divide in our academic world between secular and sacred, or liberal arts and theological, is as false as that which Canadians seem to assume marks our society: a separation between church and state. Even if we, as I do, refrain from explicitly theological study in bible classes and research, the influence and legacy of the tradition(s) impacts how these texts have been read and taught and used. Teaching students, for example, to "bracket out" theological questions as they ask others of the Bible may seem commonsensical, but it may be naïve and, worse, unethical.

Then, as Noll argues and Schüssler Fiorenza has also indicated, a complete account of the state of the Bible in the federation needs not only to hear the voices of the Bible as mediated through academia, but through Canadian culture as well, and in those (perceived) in-between spaces of Bible colleges and Bible belts around the country. Northrop Frye has fallen out of fashion in biblical studies lately, but he wrote extensively about the intersections between literature, Christianity (Bible), and Canadian culture. Is it time to go back to Frye? Are there ways to bring other contexts into conversation with academic biblical studies that could be mutually comfortable and beneficial? And what of our cultural heritage? Canadian culture is a tricky field to negotiate, since so much of what we adhere to is common to American culture as well (media, literature), but these are not totally contiguous expressions in all cases.[37]

By the Rivers of Babylon

I turn in a different direction now to look at "that village over there," or one small part of the dynamic puzzle that encompasses Canada. My attention is directed toward a hermeneutical community with which I am connected, that of Caribbean immigrants to this country. Through this community, I want to think about memory and the hope that memory brings, and obfuscates, in the midst of migration. I think about them in the context of Canada as a nation of people largely from elsewhere, a collection of those who have been collected. In general, these matters pertain to admittedly broader questions: how immigrant identity is configured in the context of the new land, how diasporas are created, and what impact these have on Canadian identity.

As I indicated, these questions are also autobiographical: I am an immigrant to Canada from the Bahamas. I am, however, largely invisible as such, because in ethnic appearance, in accent, in education and acculturation, I "read" as born and bred Canadian. I am also deeply aware of the potential problems of inserting myself as someone *also* of European descent into the discourse of Caribbean

---

37. The use and impact of the Bible on Canadian literature is one possible resource. See Kyser's PhD thesis on the Bible and Canadian literature (2004). Also, see the special issue of *Literature & Theology* (16.2), devoted to Canadian literature.

hermeneutics and liberationist readings. I struggle with this, because my time in my land of birth was formative; my heritage is "mixed." My immigrant identity is part of who I am, not as whimsy or nostalgia, but profoundly: this land calls to me; it calls me to come home. These impressions have intensified in the last decade as I have made myself aware of issues of poverty and the geographical and cultural erosion of the Bahamas. I feel pain and powerlessness. I feel anger at the subsuming of a proud nation by its domineering colonizers (past and present) and at the apparent lack of good leadership to stop the damage. I have begun to think of myself, if not as part of a diaspora, then at least as uncomfortably spread across two worlds—part of two homes.

Into this mix, I am also proposing to throw the Bible, of course. As I have been arguing in the first part of the paper, Canadian biblical studies must consider matters of readerly context, especially when that context is as multiple and complex as is this country's. So, for this reader, looking at that village over there— the Caribbean immigrant community—means addressing a Canadian context or identity as well as a Bahamian one. Naturally, it is important to resist essentializing *or* eliding these two[38] natures/nations of readership and instead allow the conflicts as well as the conflations that arise from such readings to coexist. Does the Bible have anything to say to such reading communities and their challenges? I think in particular of Ps 137, one of the paradigmatic texts of exilic mourning, and one with particular resonance for Caribbean peoples in diaspora. In both Canada and the Bahamas, along with other nations, the psalm is well-known enough culturally that we can assume familiarity with it, both through the faith communities of both Jewish and Christian traditions and in non-religious communities with some degree of (biblical) literacy. In addition, due to its exposure in reggae and other popular music, it is also a text with which one should assume that North American and Caribbean cultures generally are familiar, though those cultures may have long lost the referent for it.[39]

To the displaced (by enslavement, political exigency, war), the psalm is a bitter expression of the disconsolation of the exiled, of their failure to sing in cel-

---

38. Or, perhaps "multiple" is a better description, since my membership in either country is compromised by either naturalization (Canada) or European descent (Bahamas). It would seem that a failure to "fit"—in the politics of belonging—actually multiplies possibilities for identity, rather than limits them.

39. See Runions (2009) on the use of the psalm in Boney-M's musical version as a tool to abuse prisoners at Abu-Ghraib. Runions explores links between American ideology and warfare and (often inconsistent in culture) metaphorical language related to Babylon. Her question, "what does it mean when a country that likes to proclaim itself as beyond slavery plays a song about freedom to people it is torturing?" is most pressing, and provocative.

ebration of their home in triumph. It is also a testament to the misunderstanding and mockery that they suffer at the hands of others. But then again it is a troubling text, for in the context of a vow, it offers imprecations on the speaker's own person—a reversal of the usual complaint genre that sees these effects imposed upon the speaker by God or enemies (e.g., Pss 13:1–2; 22:7–8; 35:11–12, 15–16; 69:5; 88:7–9). It is also terribly violent in ways that perhaps affect us more viscerally than any other kind of violence waged against the innocent: the slaughter of babies by dashing them against rocks.

In terms of its applicability as a text for discussions of diversity and immigration, Ps 137 certainly laments the calamity of the exile and the desolation of displacement; it stages grief over the loss of land and generation; it emboldens the bitter desire for retribution. One might object that it is about *enforced* absences, though, and not about those undertaken by the directions of one's own will. And yet, perhaps such differences are unimportant, for the psalm profoundly articulates loss, no matter its cause—the loss of land, the desire to remember what is gone, the recognition that return is not possible. Even if it were possible to go back, the psalm intimates that the homeland would not resemble that land of memory or history. In fact, in Ps 137, *that place* vacillates between identities—Jerusalem and Zion, between Babylon and not-Babylon—showing itself to be out there, away from here, but not entirely locatable. Correspondingly, diaspora too becomes a place of the imagination (Berns-McGown 2008), where "here" is always in reference to there, to what once was, to what it is hoped might be recreated.

And yet, as if boldly asserting a paradox, the psalm also speaks to the real or the particular, to certain aspects of Canadian society, to [a] specific diaspora[s]. Once, the text provided solace for Huguenots exiled to Canada and America. The text was also used to give voice to the mourning of slaves as they considered their transplantation into a life of slavery and disconnection from their land and culture. It had particular poignancy for those who travelled (to Canada) on the underground railroad. It was also eventually recast into the service of Jamaican political interests in the context of Rastafari and through the music of the Melodians, Bob Marley, Burning Spear, and others. There, like the Bible does everywhere, it experienced the mutations and augmentations as cultural need shaped it to meet its ends.[40] These experiences and the augmentations

---

40. In the song version, for instance, Ps 19:14 is added in as part of the text. This gives a startlingly different flavor to the psalm, not least of which because it intersects with the rest of Ps 19, which is in large part a wisdom psalm that underscores the laws of Yahweh and a social system whereby the rewarded are seen as righteous and the oppressed as sinful. The two psalms read together, in fact, are jarring.

that accompany them find their way, through migration and generation, to our own country, where they form part of the collective memory of people from the Caribbean, of descendants of slaves, and of others enslaved in other lands and other times.

For Caribbean hermeneutics, the psalm provides a rich resource. Nathaniel Samuel Murrell writes of the double-edged influence of the Bible in slavery and settlement of the Caribbean. On the one hand, Columbus landed there "with the Bible in one hand and a sword in the other" (2000, 11), and subsequent settlers used Christianity and its Scripture as means of "production, control and domination" (14). On the other hand, Murrell acknowledges the uncontainable nature of the text, of its use in underground traditions that still afforded captives a voice and a private spirituality. Murrell frequently writes of a more modern-day example of such subversiveness in the use of the Bible in Rastafarai worship and politics. Their particular interpretive strategies of "citing up" (the use of word sounds and language instead of context and acknowledged meaning to support a particular view) allows the Bible to be used as a resource for the present, for an "I an' I" spirituality that contravenes any colonial interests that the establishment (Babylon) is perceived to represent. Ps 137 is of particular interest and use in this context (Murrell 2001).

These conflicted dynamics of biblical "ownership" and use are visible in many texts, of course, but are intriguingly evident in Ps 137. Perhaps somewhat understatedly, Patrick Miller argues that the psalm puts readers into a state of conflict. On the one hand, they are lulled into the familiar strains of the lament, exacerbated perhaps by their familiarity of it in tradition, liturgy, and even popular culture. On the other hand, they are snapped out of their reverie as they respond to the violence of the retribution that the speaker advocates (1986, 55). I think Miller is correct, though I wager that these contradictions run deeper than he identifies. Initial readers/hearers also knew that the familiarity of the psalm relies on memory, on the exiles reliving the traumatic event of their captivity and estrangement. It relies on them being able to insert themselves into the minds of the "we" described in v. 1. The language is affective, surely. It generates the same remorse, the same visceral hatred and desire for revenge, that the speaker himself expresses. This pertains as much to original audiences as it might to later ones throughout the interpretive tradition.

Moreover, the psalm is a plethora, a compendium of inversions and oppositions. There is the tension expressed between remembering and forgetting. The speaker remembers Zion, vowing retribution on himself if he forgets it. Yet within this there is also a desire both to remember Zion and to forget the trauma that got him here. The psalm also pits familiarity against violence, the comfortableness of memory (no matter how disturbing its events) and the sudden, harsh, and final plan for the captors. There are the voices of the captors who taunt the captives, and there is the lone voice of the captive, who desires a hearing. We see here also the tracings of rescue, the familiar refrain of lament psalms, and speakers who wish for better times; these are poignantly and startlingly contrasted with imprecations against the enemy (again familiar). There should be rescue for the speaker but its opposite for those who have oppressed him. Finally, there is generation and loss of generation. It is through memory (passed down from generation to generation, one infers) that the people of Israel continue, despite the odds. This same hope is cut off from the captors, in figurative and literal ways.

Do not these inversions/tensions/contraversions speak powerfully to the conflicted nature of Canadian society, in its many parameters described above? To be sure, the obvious bottom line is that the psalm resonates with communities in diaspora, the Caribbean community in particular, on a number of levels. The first is obvious, in that it contains the memory of another oppressed, another enslaved people. Moreover, the psalm carries memory with it in its interpretive cache; it works as a vocabulary for grief and memory in part because it has worked so well before. Like many similar biblical texts, it provides a means of articulating grief and loss, of providing a means to hope for reparation. In so doing, it also allows grief to be generative, along the lines of what Rose Lucas has argued in her study of the poetics of mourning as impacting the subjectivity of those on the move.[41] Second, and further, these contradictions or inversions of the psalm mirror the hybrid identities of immigrants, pushing them not to identify wholly with the land that is lost or the land that is new, but to negotiate their existence somewhere between them.

Indeed, the in-between spaces of immigrant identities are integral in a country that seems to be negotiating its own self-understanding not only by virtue of its increasing immigrant membership, but also between the spaces of two colonies, *and* between the fictional space of an *ideal Canada* and the material place that wrestles with the historical realities of its own origins and the practical permutations (including the problematic, violent ones) of accomplishing its goals of cultural diversity. Does such a text, therefore, speak to a country that needs to settle issues over the nature and goals of cultural diversity? Can an acknowledgement of the pain and loss described herein address new pain and loss? Can the psalm in its complexity create and preserve community through its articulation of trauma and at the same time guard against the dangers of cultural apartheid (Bisoondath 1994)? More than simply a soothing balm, a place to sing what

---

41. Specifically, Lucas writes about how mourning effects in the mourner a process whereby he or she comes to acknowledge the loss (38:4), but also, coterminously with the creation of art (poetry), establishes a speaking position (38:3).

cannot be sung, it is a clarion call for us to think more closely about the politics of what it means to displace and to be displaced. It means, in short, that dispossession is not a simple matter: that life in all its complexity is not erased when one leaves a land and enters another, no matter through what circumstances one arrives.[42] It seems to mean that this is a text not just for the displaced, but maybe also for the displacer. Ps 137 looks, thus, to be a national text not for a few, but for many.

Further, I suggest that the contours of the psalm engage the listener to think hard about violence, both as it operates excessively in our midst and as it frames the backdrop of the experience of the displaced in our midst. In other words, as I have just been intimating, violence forms the immediate memory of the speaker, but it also speaks to his past (colonial power) and future (revenge to be exacted). So visible is this violence, in fact, that the speaker makes it excessive: it is inflicted upon children; it is aimed at destroying generation; it is the vile taste in the mouth at the end of the song of the displaced. By casting light into the shadows of this psalm, it is of course important not to obscure real suffering, or deplete the aptness of the text for its own and countless generations who use it. But the violence herein does indicate that the rivers of Babylon (the multicultural bliss of Canada? the tropical paradise of the Bahamas?) offer no mere comfortingly tranquil setting for the singing of songs, but they are in places turgid and muddied, pulling singers into their midst. The psalm, in other words, crosses from here to there, from lament to violence, from desolation to contempt, in ways that ought to leave many readers uneasy.

And what of the Bahamas? Its own complexities, expressed as it struggles to identify itself as a postcolonial nation, proudly independent of Great Britain since 1973, are compromised by its physical and economic proximity to the United States. Most visitors to the Bahamas are American, and an increasing majority of land ownership is foreign, often American. Tourist expansion now threatens the so-called family islands of the Bahamas and at great cost to the nation's natural resources. Bahamians eschew their own culture in favor of American visual culture, consumer goods, and food. So the neocolonization of the Bahamas repeats the old, but this time with a greater complicity on the part of Bahamians, who see it as welcome progress. Moreover, the country fails adequately to deal with its

---

42. I mean here that the psalm speaks of loss and violent displacement, to be sure; it also suggests, however, that there might be other situations behind migration that complicate the victim/perpetrator dynamic. Though it may be reading on the margins, the speaker's imprecations against himself if he forgets Yahweh and Yahweh's deeds brings to mind the fact that the people of Israel were colonizers, too—that they violently displaced or exterminated those in their midst when they were strangers in their land.

own neo-slavery in the form of its complex treatment of Haitian immigrants.[43] The questions that I just asked of Canada, in other words, are surprisingly true for the Bahamas as well.

Perhaps, though, it is possible to learn from contradictory texts and the painful realities of migration that might be represented there. Psalm 137 signals that to belong means we must not attempt to fix identity and claim those factors that come with it (voice, power, privilege), but be comfortable in their failure to contain us. Rather than choosing to remain unsettled by such crossings (actual and textual), M. Jacqui Alexander (2005) allows herself to be prompted to explore them for their pedagogical value. They mirror the crossing of the Middle Passage, to be sure, and as such, aid memory, as well as implicate other migrations.[44] Specifically, they ask us to think about what Alexander describes as spiritual labor,[45] which means a keen observance of the relations between sacred and secular and, most promisingly, about "living intersubjectivity that is premised in relational solidarity" (8). In other words, and to simplify Alexander here, contradictory texts and migrations teach us how better to understand ourselves, and potentially to create diasporas and communities that embrace diaspora in better ways. It might be that such labor is what is needed for Canada—and the Bahamas— as it looks to its past and attempts to articulate its present. And what might a Canadian biblical studies that is rooted in living intersubjectivity be like? It would espouse an entirely different "sense of proportion" (so Moir) indeed.

---

43. Currently, and in order to stem the perceived enormous tide of illegal migration to the Bahamas, the arrivals of Haitians are strictly monitored (there is even a separate holding and interviewing area for Haitian nationals in the airport). Haitians, like many foreign nationals, may not be granted citizenship of the Bahamas (ever) without a Bahamian parent, nor may their children, even if born in the nation (the Bahamas' citizenship laws operate, for individuals born after 1973, on the principle of *jus sanguinis*; Treco). And yet, the Bahamas relies heavily on Haiti to provide cheap labor and domestic service, especially in the tourist industry. By contrast, anyone may purchase and own indefinitely Bahamian land. See, fairly recently (2002), Treco for the history of Haitian migration to the Bahamas and some discussion of these complexities.

44. In sites of crisis and instability, as evident in the Middle Passage and other migrations— but which I think may legitimately be read in pertinent texts as well—Alexander finds a space opening up between sacred and secular, between dispossession and possession, between materialism and materiality, and the like. It is these that she wishes to open and explore "ways of being and knowing and to plot the different metaphysics that are needed to move away from living alterity premised in difference to living intersubjectivity premised in relationality and solidarity" (2005, 8).

45. I am leaving the matter of gender aside in this paper. For Alexander, such spiritual labor is usually undertaken by women. I cannot interrogate this fully here, but surely, as one explores the dynamics of immigration with respect to religion, one would discover that gender would have an integral role to play here.

17

THE VIRTUAL BIBLE

George Aichele

Within every book there lies concealed a book of nothing. Don't you sense it when you read a page brimming with words? The vast gulf of emptiness lying beneath the frail net of letters. The ghostliness of the letters themselves. (Wharton 2001, 75–76).

The Bible has always been virtual and so, therefore, has the "biblical past." Not only are the various and inconsistent pasts and futures narrated or implied within the Bible's texts virtual, but the past and future of "the Bible" as a Christian[1] entity is virtual, as well. This does not mean that the Bible is somehow unreal or incomplete, nor does it describe another Bible—a Bible that is somehow "other" than the one that people read. Indeed, the virtual Bible is the only one that we know. The virtuality of the Bible is perhaps its most important feature.

According to Katherine Hayles, "Virtuality is the cultural perception that material objects are interpenetrated by information patterns" (1999, 13–14). Hayles comments that "we participate in the cultural perception that information and materiality are conceptually distinct and that information is in some sense more essential, more important, and more fundamental than materiality" (1999, 18; see further her discussion on 248–51). In other words, virtuality entails what Jacques Derrida calls logocentrism (1976, 12–15). Gilles Deleuze argues that the virtual object corresponds to a desire for reality which "governs and compensates for the progresses and failures of ... real activity" (1994, 99. His discussion of virtuality runs throughout *Difference and Repetition*, especially 103–5 and 205–14[2]). Thus, the virtual is by no means unreal, or even optional; on the contrary, "The

---

1. I restrict my comments here to the Christian Bible. There is a virtual Bible in Judaism also, and much (but not all) of what I say below applies to it as well.

2. See also Deleuze/Parnet (2007, 148–52) and Williams (2003, 7–11, 164, 198–200).

virtual ... is the characteristic state of Ideas: it is on the basis of its reality that existence is produced, in accordance with a time and a space immanent in the Idea" (Deleuze 1994, 211; emphasis added).[3] According to Deleuze, the real is reciprocally determined by the virtual and the actual. As Roland Barthes says, reality itself is an effect, "an unformulated signified" (1986, 139; see also 141–48). The virtual is "real without being actual, ideal without being abstract" (Deleuze 1988, 96). Thus, virtuality is the means and the meaning through which we encounter the real, and without which there is no "real." It belongs to the realm of ideology.[4]

Apart from the virtual Bible, there could be no concept of "the Bible," and consequently no real Bibles. The virtuality of the Bible is not at all unique, and yet the relation of the Bible's virtuality to anything actual is rich with ideological overtones. The virtual Bible does not tell the truth, but rather it produces truth.

Digital and perhaps especially online versions of the Bible make us especially aware of its virtuality, but the virtuality of the Bible is not limited to such texts. Instead, the Bible's virtuality is closely bound to the fact that the Bible has always been a writing. As Edmund Husserl says, "The important function of written, documenting linguistic expression is that it makes communications possible without immediate or mediate personal address; it is, so to speak, communication become *virtual*" (1978, 164; emphasis added). Writing makes possible the formation of ideal objects that remain the same across time and space; but, as Derrida notes, commenting on Husserl's words, "That *virtuality* ... is an ambiguous value: it simultaneously makes passivity, forgetfulness, and all the phenomena of *crisis* possible" (1978, 87; Derrida's emphases). No text can speak for itself, but written text inevitably escapes its author's control and falls into the hands of a reader, who may be anyone, as Socrates recognized long ago in the *Phaedrus* (see Derrida 1981, 61–171). A text is a machine that makes meaning; or, rather, it is part of an intertextual machine through which readers make many and various meanings. Unlike oral communication, writing/reading inevitably produces virtualities, which in turn produce the crisis of repetition and difference.

In writing, the meaningful connection between signifier and signified is neither tight nor exclusive, and it is always artificial. As a result, this connection must itself be explained. The message is not simply received; it must be interpreted— that is, it must become virtual—and this inevitably requires yet other signs which themselves must also be explained, and so on. The realm of meaning is divided

---

3. See also Deleuze (1994, 279), Deleuze and Guattari (1994, 140, 157) and Eco (1979, 23, 29).

4. See Eagleton (1991) for a detailed review and critique of some of the more important understandings of ideology. For an examination of ideology theory in relation to biblical studies, see Boer (2003).

into signifiers and signifieds, but this division is constantly collapsing, for every signifier may also be signified, and every signified may be itself the signifier of yet another signified. The seemingly clear semiotic channel is deconstructed, and instead of a well-controlled flow of meaning, there is a flood. Umberto Eco notes that "signification ... by means of continual shiftings which refer a sign back to another sign or string of signs, circumscribes cultural units in an asymptotic fashion, without ever allowing one to touch them directly, though making them accessible through other units" (1976, 71). Semiosis flows without limit, in both the direction of the signifier and that of the signified, and both the First Signifier and the Last Signified of any utterance disappear into referential abysses. As a result, meaning is elusive and fluid, and connotation runs wild (de Man 1979, 208). There is no absolute anchor to which a proper meaning could be attached.

This unlimited semiosis characterizes every text, but it is particularly problematic in relation to written texts and becomes a serious challenge to any text that is desired to have a definite and authoritative meaning—that is, any Scripture, any text that is believed to transmit the "word of God." This challenge has been recognized by a growing number of scholars, ranging from Werner Kelber (1983) to Stephen Moore (1992, 1994) to Daniel Boyarin (1994) to Harry Gamble (1995), among others. See also the groundbreaking work of Walter Ong (1967), as well as the early writings of Derrida (1973, 1976, 1981).

The Bible is not simply a collection of such sacred texts, but it is an intertextual mechanism—a canon—that directs and limits the flows of semiosis (Aichele 2001). The canon of scriptures forms an authoritative structure that defines for its Christian readers a single, coherent message. As Yvonne Sherwood says, "A deeply ingrained cultural sense of the Bible as the 'Word of God,' or at the very least a homogeneous canon, means that we expect that separate textual voices will be gathered into a single consciousness.... This book, of all books, is expected to process life into a gigantic metanarrative, to frame the world in a Great, all-encompassing Code" (2000, 217). For Christian readers, all of the biblical books "speak" clearly together, expressing "a single consciousness."

According to Julia Kristeva, "The term *inter-textuality* denotes this transposition of one (or several) sign system(s) into another ... its 'place' of enunciation and its denoted 'object' are never single, complete, and identical to themselves, but always plural, shattered, capable of being tabulated" (1984, 59–60; Kristeva's emphasis). Meaning is never neatly packaged in a text, to be unwrapped and displayed by careful *exe*gesis. Rather, meaning is stretched between texts, as they are brought together in the various understandings of actual readers—that is, through *eise*gesis. Intertextuality contains and directs semiosis, breaking its flows and bringing it decisively to an end. This concept of intertextuality is thus quite distinct from the notion of historical sources or influences that still dominates biblical studies, even though that notion has also confusingly been called "inter-textuality."

The intertextuality (in the Kristevan sense) of the biblical canon naturalizes the component texts, making them appear familiar and normal. They seem to belong together. In this way the canon is profoundly ideological (Barthes 1974, 206). Ideology creates an illusion of reality; it makes the meaning of the text seem obvious by providing a set of conventional codes that allow the reader to recognize the text as a meaningful work, to identify its structures, and to make sense out of its message. Virtuality is the arena of meaning, and ideology shapes the virtual Bible through the intertextuality of the canon.

Like unlimited semiosis, and unlike historical criticism, intertextuality locates the meaning of a text firmly in the reader. Intertextuality lies in spaces between texts that are formed by tensions between signifiers and occupied by readers. Each reader is a living repository of texts, a network of potential connections, and thus each reader is herself both the product and the event of intertextuality, the point at which an intertextual network comes to bear upon a text. She is the means through which the actual text (physical signifiers) becomes virtual and thus meaningful. The biblical canon limits the reader's network of texts, bringing together precisely *these* texts in precisely *this* sequence in order to control the way that she reads these texts—that is, to shape her thoughts and her life, her understanding of herself and the world.

Thus, the canonical control of meaning does not appear in the individual texts themselves but rather in the ways in which texts are juxtaposed with one another in the interpretive practice of faithful readers. The Bible's story, Sherwood's "gigantic metanarrative," grounds reality for such a reader, describing her world (cf. Barthes 1974, 76). The canon responds to the "crisis" inherent in the "chaotic literalness" (Derrida 1978, 88) of the written texts by obscuring their diversities and assimilating them into the theological unity of the "Word of God." It forms a virtuality, a producer of reality.

The single codex of the Christian Bible connotes to many people that the Bible is one single book, and it assembles the canonical, intertextual network in a format that can be easily used as such. "The codex is an existential code unto itself, a unifying factor of a culture" (Debray 1996, 141). The singularity of the biblical codex plays an important role in signifying its single, coherent message for a united, universal Church—that is, in its virtuality. The canon was formed by Constantinian Christianity to deter the pursuit of heretical connotations of the "Scriptures" and to justify its own claim to be the "new Israel," the chosen people of God. According to Jon Berquist, "The canonical text is not a unified whole; it is not a body of literature at all. Instead, it is an assemblage held together only by the imperialist power that first created it" (1996, 28). This "imperialist power" is not merely confined to the initiatory moments of the canon (like the dynamite charges that compress fissionable material in a nuclear bomb), but instead it is a dynamic intrinsic to the canon itself and closely related to the long imperial history of Christianity.

This is the virtuality of the Bible. However, the canon is not the same thing as the virtual Bible, nor is the codex; indeed, the distinctions between them are very important. We recognize that the Christian Bible appears in various different canons and different physical forms (not to mention languages, translations, and manuscript variations), yet despite these differences, we usually talk as though there is just one Bible. The virtual Bible is the dream that the canon seeks to realize. The Bible as an actual book would never have come into existence if it had not already existed as a virtuality in the thoughts and desires of Christians. The Bible as a canon of texts cannot exist apart from its virtuality, and the actual Bible cannot be read apart from the virtual Bible. Nevertheless, the canon is precisely that which makes the Bible the Bible; for without the canon there is no Bible, but merely an assortment of more or less unrelated texts, which may or may not be "Scriptures." If there were no canon, but merely a collection of texts or even of "Scriptures," a different virtuality or virtualities would appear. This is elementary semiotics: without both the actual signifier and the virtual signified, there is no sign, no reality effect. This point must be qualified twice.

First, the intertextual context of any text, even the most ancient or authoritative ones, is always finally the *here* and *now* of the living reader. In other words, the act of reading is always anachronistic and local. Readers today may have some sense of historical conditions under which the canon was produced or how other readers understood or understand biblical texts, but our awareness of such circumstances and other readings is itself always conditioned by our own contexts, interests, and commitments. Ancient or foreign readings always stand at an inherent disadvantage to the *contemporary, local* readings through which they are inevitably filtered, thanks to the virtual Bible. The ideology "in" the canon is always refracted through the reader's own ideology, even when it challenges that ideology.

Second, just as no single text can explain itself, so no collection of texts can explain itself. Although the canon is a powerful intertextual mechanism, it is never entirely successful. It deeply influences the deciphering of its component texts, but its control over those texts is inevitably loose and incomplete. Lively and significant disagreement over the meaning of the Bible, or the extent of the canon (or the best translations or manuscripts), will always occur. Thus the virtual Bible is a somewhat fuzzy concept. Even binding the canon into a single physical codex cannot guarantee that the reader will assemble the various texts in the "proper" way, and so additional assistance, in the form of extracanonical commentaries, introductions, sermons, catechisms, and other guides on "how to read the Bible," is continually required.

The dangers of unlimited semiosis are exacerbated when formerly hand-written texts are mass (re)produced by means of the printing press. The transformations that occur between manuscript and printed text are just as important as the changes that occur between oral and written text, but we are only beginning to become aware of them (see Benjamin 1968, 217–51 and, especially, Eisenstein 1979). Walter Benjamin compares printed texts to photo-graphed paintings, and he argues that once it has been mechanically reproduced, the painting or writing loses its "authenticity" (1968, 220[5]). The painter respects the integrity of the artwork, but the cameraman impersonally invades and dis-members it. The picture produced by "the painter is a total one, [but] that of the cameraman consists of multiple fragments which are assembled under a new law" (1968, 234). Benjamin argues that "within the phenomenon which we are here examining, from the perspective of world history, print is … [a] particu-larly important case" (1968, 219). Like the photographed painting—perhaps even more so—the relation of printed text to a handmade "original" is highly problem-atic. As a result, the reader's relation to the text changes.

The biblical canon was formed in part to stabilize the hand copying of its component texts[6] and to produce a standard collection of Scriptures for use throughout the newly-imperial Christian church. With the appearance of print technology, control over reproduction of the Bible passed into the hands of com-mercial publishing houses, freeing the dissemination of texts from control by the churches. Since the print revolution, the Bible has functioned less and less as the communal property of Christian churches, and more and more as the private property of individual readers—that is, as a commodity to be bought and sold. As a mass-produced text, the printed Bible makes the reader more aware of the Bible's virtuality, even as the printing process replaces ecclesiastical, canonical assurances of the Bible's authority. Ever since the Protestant Reformation—which occurred at the same time as the print revolution—we have become more and more aware of the multiplicity of the Bible: multiple canons and multiple trans-lations, as well as the multiplicity of texts that has always been there within the Bible. The virtual Bible has become even fuzzier.

Today, the Bible appears on numerous Internet pages and in other electroni-cally mediated versions, and the effects of the mechanical reproduction of text are amplified greatly. The dissemination of digital texts via the Internet spreads now

---

5. This point is developed further in Benjamin (1968, 83–109). For a similar judgment in regard to geometry and science, see Husserl (1978, 168–170).

6. On the instability of text in manuscript culture, see Gamble (1995) and Ehrman (1993).

out of anyone's control. The Bible on a computer screen is not a printed Bible, just as printed Bibles are not the same as manuscript Bibles (see further Nunberg 1996). The digitized Bible is not a discrete object like a codex or scroll that you can hold in your hand and read with your eyes. Its countless bits and bytes are invisible, recorded in arcane storage media and accessible only through complex networks of sophisticated electronic technology. The canon has no significant impact on digital access to biblical texts, and "canon," once separated from the materiality of the codex, becomes once more an abstract idea. Stored in databases, which make the texts easier to retrieve but which also decontextualize them and make them available for uncontrolled recontextualizations, the texts are fragmented to the level of the lexia[7] and beyond—but a database is not a canon.

With the advent of electronic culture, the reader becomes even more aware of the physical stuff of text and of the tenuous connections between text and meaning. The number of technological stages between the sender and the receiver of a digital message adds to the reader's consciousness of the frailty of the connecting media, reminding her that reading and writing are themselves artificial technologies. Readers become more conscious both of their own need for meaning and of the constructed character of meaning. At the same time, digitization gives the reader greater control both over the individual text, which can easily be rewritten, and over the extent and structure of the textual collection, for whole texts can easily be added or deleted. Just as writing has made us aware of semiosis in a way that pure orality could not, so the various mass media of electronic culture now make us aware of virtuality in ways that we were not previously. The digitized Bible makes it more evident than before that the Bible is and has always been virtual.

We are only now in a position to appreciate the virtuality of the Bible, and to begin to understand some of its consequences. As a virtuality, the Bible is the clear, ideal object of a community of understanding. The meaning of the Bible may not be clear, but the idea and value of "the Bible" is. The virtual Bible is always the same in every translation and edition. It is a global Bible, transcending history and culture. Of course, actual Bibles are multiple, local, ephemeral, and polysemic, and their many truths and values are disputed; but this ideal of universality, changelessness, homogeneity, and singularity defines the ideological concept of "the canon of Christian scriptures."

Electronic culture is a global phenomenon. The old colonial empires are increasingly replaced by multinational corporate "empires" such as Microsoft,

---

7. "The [Bible] verse is an excellent working unit of meaning; since it is a question of *creaming* (or skimming) the text.... For us, a verse is a lexia" (Barthes 1988, 229; his emphasis).

Disney, Shell, McDonald's, or Mitsubishi. The divisions between rich and poor, strong and weak, will be realigned but not eliminated. Those who have access to digital technologies are already privileged in the new imperial order, just as those who have access to books and print technology have long been privileged (and still are), even as the world of print culture fades. Hayles reminds us that "70 percent of the world's population has never made a telephone call" (1999, 20). As she says, the "experience of virtuality" is "exotic." Much of the world's population remains in effect isolated in circumstances typical of print or even oral culture, and in many of these communities the canonical authority of the Bible is still strong. Yet today's global, electronic culture shapes the lives of people in the most remote villages just as much as it does the inhabitants of New York or Tokyo, even though that shaping may be far less obvious. Thus, both the relative isolation of these communities and the apparent vigor of the Bible within them are also products of electronic culture.

Additional millions of people in less isolated circumstances continue to believe that the Bible is the authoritative word of God, but for these people, the Bible no longer signifies *as a canon*. The loudness of believing communities' protests on behalf of the canon is itself a symptom of the withering of the canon's control. The Bible remains active today within the discourse of both believers and nonbelievers, but increasingly only as a talisman, a sign in its own right: a marker of Christian identity, a self-explanatory symbol of cultural superiority, moral righteousness, and personal salvation. Some remarkable examples are surveyed by R. S. Sugirtharajah (2003a). In effect, the Bible has become a husk, an unopened codex, the illusion of a book. The Bible is no longer valued for what its various texts actually say, but for what "we all know" that it says. Thus preachers and politicians, as well as bumper stickers and billboards, can dogmatically assert that "the Bible says ... , " without ever having to justify their claims—and get away with it. The Bible does not convey a universal, apostolic message, but it has itself become the message.

Like all cultural products, the Bible has become a commodity to be sold in competition with a wide array of other products in a global market. As Robert Carroll says, "When the market drives, there are no limits to human folly or to the production of what will sell, and ... bibles will continue to be produced in whatever forms are dictated by the consumerism of a commodity culture" (1998a, 60). Carroll's groundbreaking work has been furthered by Sherwood (2000) and Hugh Pyper (2005). The Bible is now available in reader-friendly "dynamic" translations in comic book or magazine formats (see further Beal 2008). In its many consumer-oriented forms, the Bible stands on market shelves beside comic books and hot rod magazines, as well as Beanie Babies, mp3 players, video games, and countless other "entertainment" items, competing for the buyer's attention. The Bible's status as popular commodity transforms its authority.

In today's globalized, digitized world, when the Bible signifies, it does so in increasingly noncanonical ways. As the canon increasingly fails to control the meaning of the biblical texts, different sorts of cultural play with or upon those texts take its place. Many forms of such intertextual play with the Bible are readily to be found among competing cultural products, including novels, movies, music and video recordings, comic books, and electronic games. In many cases, this interplay simply reflects prevailing ideological positions and thus reinforces dominant canonical understandings of the Bible—for example, Mel Gibson's movie, *The Passion of the Christ* (2004). Now this movie, for many of its functionally illiterate viewers, has effectively entered the canon and replaced the gospels, or perhaps the entire Bible. Other instances offer radically different translations or contextualizations of biblical texts, provocative rewritings that in effect remove the text from the canon of the scriptures. In such cases, the biblical texts take on remarkably different meanings apart from the canon, as noncanonical intertexts channel the semiosis. A striking recent example is the transformation of both the Eden and Christ stories in Philip Pullman's controversial novel trilogy, *His Dark Materials* (1995, 1997, 2000).

A growing number of scholars have begun to explore these myriad transformations of biblical texts in popular culture (Aichele 2000; Aichele and Walsh 2002; Beal 2002; Kreitzer 2002; Pyper 2005; Sherwood 2000; and Walsh 2003, 2005, among many others). The biblical texts are recycled and recontextualized, and their semiotic potential is played out in a wide variety of ways. The multiplicity of the Bible is highlighted yet again as it is broken up, reassembled, and often decanonized. The old imperial forms of power and desire reflected in the canon become less and less viable.

The authority of the canon as a whole, the ideological illusion of a powerful and coherent Bible, slips away further with each passing year, as the various texts that once were thought to "speak" with one "voice" the word of God are seen to transmit different messages, in different ways, to different people. The idea of the Bible as a canonical entity is fading away. Will we continue to think the virtuality of the Bible in a world where the canon increasingly appears only as a list of titles, as in the writings of early Christians? If the canonical totality of the Bible is no longer a factor in the way that the Bible's texts are read, then its exclusive juxtaposition of writings that guarantees that these texts (and only these) all speak together the authoritative and universal, coherent Word of God—that is, the virtual Bible—disappears. And if that happens, can the actual Bible continue to exist? The individual texts will continue to exist as long as people continue to read them, but if those texts are no longer seen as part of a larger, authoritative whole—a virtuality—then will people continue to read them? What sort of future will the biblical past have then, and what sort of future will "biblical studies" have?

18

What Has Been Done? What Can We Learn? Racial/ Ethnic Minority Readings of the Bible in the United States

Tat-Siong Benny Liew

For most people—at least those in the academy of biblical studies—racial/ethnic minority readings of the Bible in the United States started in the 1970s. Michael Joseph Brown's account of African American biblical scholarship, for instance, dates the rise of what he calls "blackening the Bible" to this same decade (2004, 19). What is also helpful in Brown's account is that he accounted for the rise of this scholarship, at least partly, on the basis of the pioneering work of black theology in the 1960s (2004, 16–19). The sixties was, of course, a decade of popular or grassroots movement against the racism and imperialism of the larger U.S. society, or what Daryl J. Maeda calls "the twin 'Chains of Babylon'" in his book about how people of Asian heritage in the United States came to become a collective or community known as Asian America (2009, ix). Even in this brief narrative account, or recount, we can learn that racial/ethnic minority readings of the Bible cannot be limited to the discipline of biblical studies.

Biblical readings became more colorful as a result of James Cone's black theology (1969, 1970), Gustavo Gutiérrez's theology of liberation (1973), Choan-Seng Song's story theology (1979, 1984), and Ahn Byung Mu's minjung theology (1981). All of these pioneering Christian theologians referred to the Bible to construct what they hoped to be a sociopolitically relevant and thus contextually specific theology. This crossing between theology and biblical studies—often taboo among traditional biblical scholars, who also believe in a clean separation between focusing on what a text meant in the past (exegesis) and what that same text might mean today (application)—is but a small clue to how racial/ethnic minority readings of the Bible will blow things wide open, not only between theology and biblical studies but also between biblical studies and disciplines outside of theological or religious studies (see Schüssler Fiorenza 2010, 381–82).

Kwok Pui-Lan, with what she calls "parallel processing" (1998a, 80), suggests that one must transgress disciplinary boundaries to break new ground in biblical studies. Without other disciplines, theological and otherwise, one would be stuck and restricted within the disciplinary norms or regimes of truth already established within biblical studies, the history of which is not devoid of race and racializing dynamics (Segovia 2000a, 157–77; Kelley 2002). Or, in the words of Susan Buck-Morss, "Discipline boundaries allow counterevidence to belong to someone else's story" (2000, 822). It is the anthropological principle that going overseas and encountering another culture might open one's horizon to see that one's own cultural way of doing something is not necessarily the only way or best way. Talking about going beyond disciplinary boundaries, David Palumbo-Liu (1995), a secular Asian American studies scholar, has suggested that rigid disciplinary boundaries are actually built upon assumptions of origin and purity that are similar to those in national debates over immigration. Such assumptions idealize an "originator," who owns a certain intellectual space that will only be sullied by trespasses or transplants. With the resulting "inside/outside" or "pure/impure" binary oppositions, a power differential is created to downplay and arrest "guerrilla action within more 'traditional' (i.e., institutionally sanctioned) fields" (Palumbo-Liu 1995, 57).

The connection between interdisciplinary study and racial/ethnic minority readings of the Bible should be evident by the "border-crossing" language I intentionally employ. Racial/ethnic minorities in this country, despite their nativity, are often racialized as perennial border-crossers who do not really belong. One can see in the recent controversy surrounding President Barack Obama's birth certificate that, as this world becomes more and more global, African Americans are also not exempt from such racializing dynamics. The assumptions and arguments that Palumbo-Liu identifies are used to patrol not only racial/ethnic borders within a nation but also disciplinary borders within the academy. In both the nation and the academy, despite the rhetoric of freedom, movements and pursuits are often circumscribed by invisible, but equally inhibiting, barbed wire (Dutta-Ahmed 1996, 340–44). The first important lesson we can learn from racial/ethnic minority readings is that interdisciplinary study of the Bible is indispensable to resisting a tyranny of purity in both academic and racial/ethnic terms.

By Whom? For What?

Before I actually talk about what has been done in racial/ethnic minority readings of the Bible since the 1970s, I would like to clarify that racial/ethnic minorities—scholars and otherwise—did not actually begin racial/ethnic readings of the Bible.

In other words, it would be inaccurate—in fact, wrong—to blame racial/ethnic minorities for racializing the Bible, or for making everything (including the Bible) about race/ethnicity. Space will not allow me to give more than a few examples.

When the United States became a world power through its expansion into Asia in the late nineteenth century, and Chinese, in (re)turn, started to seek entry into the nation from various shores, Greenberry G. Rupert helped popularize the threat of a "Yellow Peril" with his book of the same title. Most telling, however, is the book's subtitle: *Or, The Orient Vs. the Occident as Viewed by Modern Statesmen and Ancient Prophets*. Rupert's phrase, "ancient prophets," was actually a reference to the Christian Bible. Understanding people from "China, India, Japan, and Korea" through the phrase "the kings of the east" in Revelations 16:12 (King James Version), Rupert himself made a religious, racial, *and* political prophecy that Jesus Christ would stop these "kings" and their menace against the western world (1911, 9–22). Rupert's "introduction" provides three main questions that he thought "the world" would need to settle, because they would determine the ultimate question of "who shall rule the world" (1911, 6). Rupert's three questions are: (1) "the race question ... between the colored races of the world and the white race"; (2) "the religious question ... between the eastern nations, who are not professed Christians, and the western nations, who profess to be Christians"; and (3) "the financial question involv[ing] the wealth of the world" (1911, 6). In one short page and three succinct questions, Rupert demonstrated the intricate intersections between religion, race, and imperialism/capitalism against Asians, just as post-9/11 Islamophobia has once again shown.

Even Elizabeth Cady Stanton's book of protest at the end of the nineteenth century, *The Woman's Bible*, is racially implicated, given her commentary on Numbers 36 that women who marry outside their own tribes must be lacking in "nob[ility]," "virtue of patriotism ... family pride, [and] all the tender sentiments of friendship, kindred, and home" (1898, 1.124).

Of course, the transpacific advancement of the United States was predated by its involvement in the transatlantic trading of black slaves. Given the Bible's role in the history of slavery of this country and the racial nature of U.S. slavery, it should not be a surprise that readings of the Bible by whites—both popular and scholarly—have been key to not only the justification of slavery but also the racialization of persons within the national borders of the United States (see Harrill 2006, 165–92; Johnson 2010). In other words, racial/ethnic minority readings of the Bible must be read within a wider context of readings by whites that can be bluntly called "white supremacist" readings.

Thornton Stringfellow, in an essay published in a 1860 volume, *Cotton is King and Pro-Slavery Arguments*, read 1 Cor 7 and 1 Tim 6 to affirm not only that the Bible and slavery were compatible, but also that slavery was shown in the Bible as a way of salvation for otherwise fallen persons or peoples—which, for Stringfellow, would include his contemporary Africans (see John Byron 2008, 2–4).

Perhaps the best known example is how the so-called "curse of Ham" in Gen 9 has been read as referring to a divinely-ordained subordination of blacks (Felder 1991, 129–32; Johnson 2004). In response, Frederick Douglass writes:

> They have declared that the Bible sanctions slavery. What do we do in such a case? What do you do when you are told by the slaveholders of America that the Bible sanctions slavery? Do you go and throw your Bible into the fire? Do you sing out, "No Union with the Bible!"? Do you declare that a thing is bad because it has been misused, abused, and made bad use of? Do you throw it away on that account? No! You press it to your bosom all the more closely; you read it all the more diligently; and prove from its pages that it is on the side of liberty—and not on the side of slavery. (Speech in Glasgow, Scotland, March 26, 1860; cited in Harrill 2006, 177–78)

For Douglass, reading race or racializing with the Bible did not begin with the enslaved but with the slaveholders. Douglass's words also reveal an insight that might become clear in light of a comment by Tertullian, that late second to early third-century polemist against heresy:

> One man perverts the Scriptures with his hand, another their meaning by his exposition. For although Valentinus seems to use the entire volume, he has none the less laid violent hands on the truth only with a more cunning mind and skill than Marcion. Marcion expressly and openly used the knife, not the pen, since he made such an excision of the Scriptures.... Valentinus, however, abstained from such excision ... and yet he took away more, and added more, by removing the proper meaning of every particular word, and adding fantastic arrangements of things which had no real existence. (*On Prescriptions Against Heresies* 38.4ff.; cited in McDonald 2011, 162)

Those who "excise" the Bible with a knife are easier to deal with, as it is easier to accept different conclusions if one can attribute those differences to the fact that others are looking at different materials altogether. It is kind of like that story about ten blind "Indians" describing what an elephant is like by touching different parts of an elephant's body. Those who "excise" the Bible with a knife are also easier to deal with, as their act can be identified or labeled as a severance of connection. That is to say, those who are looking at different materials and drawing different conclusions are, in a sense, dismissible as outsiders who have nothing to do with "us." It is a similar dynamic when people like myself are told to "go back to where you are from." Not so, however, with those who, like Valentinus in Tertullian's example, draw different conclusions while still sharing with us the same

Bible. Yet another way to illustrate this difference is domestic partnership that breaks up with and without children; it makes a difference if there are shared or common concerns between disagreeing parties.

Racial/ethnic minority readings of the Bible, like the presence of racial/ethnic minority bodies within the United States, end up functioning like a thorn in the flesh that cannot be removed. As Paul tells us in 2 Cor 12, such a thorn, though deemed understandably undesirable, serves a positive function of keeping one grounded—not in the sense that you are not allowed to go out, but in the sense of keeping humble, keeping in touch with reality, including the reality of God's grace. Racial/ethnic minority readings of the Bible not only refuse to let particular readings rule by default by continuing to engage the Bible, but they also have the potential to remind all readers that they are connected to one another through this common book no matter how differently they read.

Besides providing alternatives to dominant readings, there is yet another reason why racial/ethnic minority readings are important. As racial/ethnic climates, even understandings of race/ethnicity, change over time, so also questions of race/ethnicity change, or at least they are not addressable in the same ways. For instance, overt racist readings of the Bible might decrease, perhaps even disappear; yet that decrease or even disappearance does not necessarily mean that issues over race/ethnicity are over and done with. In a society or situation of "racism without racists" (Bonilla-Silva 2003; Ford 2008, 37–92), racial/ethnic minority readings of the Bible, like what literary critic Susan Koshy says about the humanities and arts in general, may become "a generative space" to continue to interrogate and explore what can no longer be addressed in a courtroom, including the expression of grievance (2008, 1543). Regardless of the origins of racial/ethnic readings of the Bible, racial/ethnic *minority* readings have become one significant avenue to pursue and push conversations, education, and recognition about issues regarding race and ethnicity, boundary and community. This is especially so since biblical texts are not only ambiguous and fluid in nature but also deal with feelings, anxieties, desires, dreams, memories, meanings, and values in terms of content or focus.

Mapping Things in Stages

First Stage

When racial/ethnic minority readings of the Bible by scholars began in the 1970s, the main concern was twofold: first, to find minority subjects in the Bible; second, taking a cue from feminist readings of the Bible, to present positive, or at least more complex, pictures or images of minority subjects when they are "found" in the Bible. In sum, the concern was recognition. For instance, Charles Copher, an African American pioneer who received his PhD in 1947 and became the first dean of the historically black Interdenominational Theological Center in Atlanta, made it a mission of his scholarly career to argue that Hebrew Bible narratives presented blacks as both recipients and mediators of God's salvation (1989; 1991). What Copher tries to do with the Hebrew Bible, Cain Hope Felder does with the New Testament. Questioning the "mistaken notion that ... the relation of Black people to the Bible is a postbiblical experience" (1989, xi), Felder goes on to argue not only that Mary and hence Jesus are more like "Yemenite, Trinidadian, or African American today" in appearance (1993, 192–94) but also that ancient writers of the Bible acknowledge and admire ancient Africans for having a great and glorious culture (1991).

In fact, this question about "black presence" in the Bible makes up and takes up one of the four sections of the first anthology on African American biblical interpretation, *Stony the Road We Trod* (Felder 1991). Given the role of the Bible and biblical interpretation in racializing blacks as inferior and bound for servitude, the first two sections of this anthology are appropriately allotted to deal with the authority of the Bible, as well as the method of and resources for biblical interpretation. Slavery is, of course, a central concern for African Americans, so it rightly occupies one section of the anthology. The fact that this section on slavery not only shares the same number of entries with the one on "black presence" in the Bible (three essays in each section) but also shows up after the section on "black presence" speaks volume about the significance of this subject for this first stage of African American biblical interpretation. Brown's account of "blackening ... the Bible" also begins, after an introductory chapter, with Copher and Felder and their "black presence" emphasis (2004, 24–53). African American biblical scholarship starts with this politics of recognition: Blacks are not only qualified interpreters of the Bible, but the Bible itself also contains black presence and appreciation of black culture.

Coming on the scene about a decade after their African American counterparts, the first generation of Asian American scholars of the Bible are also concerned about Asian presence in the Bible, but they go about arguing for it in a different way. Although Felder tends to refer to the ancient Hebrews as "Afro-Asiatics" (1991, 136), Asian American scholars of the Bible are reluctant to claim particular biblical characters as Asians. This reluctance has much to do with the fact that this first generation of Asian American Bible scholars are mainly of East Asian heritage and are thus distant geographically from West Asia and North Africa. Instead, they tend to identify racializing dynamics familiar to Asian

Americans in a biblical text, and then identify with a particular biblical character in that text.

Chan Hie-Kim, for instance, compares the Cornelius story in Acts 10–11 to his own experience as an Asian immigrant to the United States, since both Cornelius and Kim are outsiders interacting with and integrating into a community of another racial/ethnic group (1995). Similarly, Francisco O. García-Treto compares the Joseph story in Gen 39–41 to his own diaspora from Cuba to the United States, since Joseph and García-Treto share a "hyphenating" experience of being a Hebrew-Egyptian and a Cuban-American because of their respective exiles (2000). Chan-Hie Kim does not specify the race/ethnicity of Cornelius beyond the fact that he is a non-Jew; likewise, García-Treto never identifies Joseph as Latino. He only identifies *with* Joseph because of a similar experience of exile and having a hyphenated identity.

As racial/ethnic minority readings of the Bible continue to develop, this attempt to find one's presence in the Bible does not disappear (e.g., Sadler 2007). For example, Uriah (Yong-Hwan) Kim reads the Uriah story in 2 Sam 11 by focusing on Uriah as a readily dispensable "foreigner" who is murdered and forgotten despite, or perhaps because of, his attempt to join and even fight for the people of Israel (2002). Without suggesting that Uriah is an Asian, Uriah Kim simply juxtaposes Uriah the Hittite both with Vincent Chin as scapegoat victims while their respective killers get away with murder and also with himself as "minority" persons involved in identity struggles.

SECOND STAGE

Uriah Kim's reference to identity struggle conveniently clarifies two underlying dynamics in the first stage of racial/ethnic minority biblical interpretation. First, the struggle is mainly understood to be between majority whites and minority persons of color. Second, the minority identity to be recognized is often assumed to be stable and known. It is a collective identity that all members of a particular racial/ethnic minority group should be ready to embrace; it just needs to be recognized by whites and minorities who have yet to come to their racial/ethnic group consciousness. At the same time, Uriah Kim's essay does reveal a stark difference from the work of Copher, Felder, and Chan-Hie Kim. While those in the first group start their reading of the Bible with the Bible and the history surrounding a biblical text, Uriah Kim starts with his context and experience as a twentieth-century Asian American. In addition, one finds, on the basis of footnotes and bibliographical entries in his essay, that Uriah Kim's reflection of his context and experience is informed by scholarship in ethnic studies. In a sense,

García-Treto's essay might serve to illustrate the transition from Copher, Felder, and Chan-Hie Kim on the one hand, to Uriah Kim on the other.

Like Felder's homage to Cone and black theology, for instance, García-Treto begins his essay on Joseph by referring to the theological work of Justo González and Fernando Segovia, but, like Uriah Kim, one finds in García-Treto's essay a reflection of Cuban American diaspora that is informed by nontheological and nonreligious scholarship on Cuban America, though the number of such bibliographical entries is limited to two and this reflection appears in the middle rather than the beginning of the essay. This shift can be understood as moving from "reading Scripture reading race" to "reading race reading Scripture." This simple turn of phrase—for which I am indebted to Kah-Jin Jeffrey Kuan—refers to a change from the earlier emphasis on reading the Bible to find and understand race to a new priority of reading and understanding race and using that as a lens through which to read and make sense of the Bible. The Bible, in other words, is now explicitly *not* the first entry into an exploration. The concern is now less what the Bible has to say about race/ethnicity and more what a particular racial/ethnic group has to say about the Bible. Inverting this process is important because, one again, biblical studies as a discipline is not unaffected by the infection of racial/ethnic discriminations and colonial impulse.

Inverting the process is, in effect, precisely the proposal submitted by Vincent Wimbush when he asks, in the introduction to his encyclopedic project, *African Americans and the Bible*, "How might putting African Americans at the center of the study of the Bible affect the study of the Bible?" (2000, 2; see also Wimbush 2007 and 2010).[1] Of course, the title of the volume itself is telling; it uses the conjunction "and" instead of the proposition "in" between African Americans and the Bible. Racial/ethnic minority scholarship of the Bible at this stage is no longer only about demographics, but includes a shift of framework. As cultural critic Kuan-Hsing Chen rightly suggests, changing one's reference points can lead to "an alternative horizon, perspective, or method for posing a different set of questions" and developing different understandings (2010, xv; see also Gay Byron 2009; Abraham Smith 2010, 91).

Another significant change as racial/ethnic minority readings of the Bible enter what I call its second stage is how the assumptions about struggle and identity we mentioned through Uriah Kim's work also begin to change. In this stage, racial/ethnic readings of the Bible begin to manifest a much greater diversity

---

1. In fact, Wimbush would go further to question if and how finding "black presence" could be "a desperate but ultimately unwise and self-defeating game" (2010, 357). I will have more to say about Wimbush's scholarship in relation to minoritized biblical criticism in general and African American readings in particular.

within each racial/ethnic minority group. To put it another way, identity struggle begins to take on a different meaning with struggle now involving internal differences within a racial/ethnic community and identity becoming multiple and less than stable. Intersections between race/ethnicity and other identity factors, such as gender and sexuality, come increasingly into the picture. After presenting the challenges to Afrocentric readings by female readers like Renita Weems, Clarice Martin, Wilma Ann Bailey, and Cheryl Kirk-Duggan (see also St. Clair 2008), Brown concludes his account of African American biblical scholarship with what he calls a "neo-womanist"—that is, queer—perspective that destabilizes a binary understanding of gender (2004, 175–83). One can also see this turn towards an intersectional emphasis in the works of African American scholars of the Bible like Randall C. Bailey (2009) and Demetrius Williams (2009).

The desire for recognition that we mentioned in the early stage, while still present, becomes perhaps less desirable once racial/ethnic scholars of the Bible recognize that such recognition might come with a price. In effect, racial/ethnic identity can become one dimensional and restrictive, and this pressure to conform can come from one's own racial/ethnic minority community as well as from whites. Frantz Fanon, that early theorist of racialization, laments that whites thought of Africa as a single unit and African advocates of negritude basically replicated that problem (1963).

A good example that demonstrates this more complicated identity struggle within racial/ethnic minority biblical interpretation is an essay by Gale Yee, entitled "Yin/Yang is Not Me" (2006). Yee compares recognition by whites to being an animal in a zoo through what Rey Chow, an Asian American critic in the larger world of literary/cultural studies, "calls ... 'coercive mimeticism,' in which racial/ethnic persons are expected to resemble and replicate certain socially endorsed preconceptions about them" (2006, 154). At the same time, Yee relates experiences of Chinese Americans in China, including her own, when they are forced to become either Chinese or American but not both, as well as research about Asian American women who self-identify as simply "American"—that is, white—to distance themselves from stereotypical images of Asian women living under patriarchal Asian cultures. Her rejection of a single and stable racial/ethnic minority identity then leads Yee to conclude that "an Asian American biblical hermeneutics [is] a hard one to pin down" (2006, 163).

In addition to paying tributes to contextual theologians (like Peter Phan and Jung Young Lee) who help develop Asian American theology and hence inspire Asian American biblical interpretation, Sze-kar Wan himself would help illustrate the methodological divergency, diversity, or fluidity of Asian American biblical interpretation by featuring a "hermeneutics of hyphenation" that can be somewhere or anywhere "betwixt and between" a"historical" or an "ideological" emphasis, for lack of better terms (2006). This struggle to highlight and clarify the heterogeneity among Asian American readers of the Bible can further be seen in Patrick S. Cheng's queer reading of Judg 19 (2002), Mary F. Foskett's reading of adoption in both Exod 1–2 and Rom 8–9 as an Asian adoptee in the United States (2002), and Henry W. Morisada Rietz's attempt to read with a *hapa* identity (2002 and 2006).

Among Latino/a readers, Manuel Villalobos has recently performed a provocative reading of Acts 8:26–40. Beginning with the feminist and queer work of Gloria Anzaldúa, Villalobos reads the borderland as a site of transformation that brings hope to not only the Ethiopian eunuch's body but also Villalobos's own queer body that has often been denied and denounced by fellow Latinos (2011). It is little wonder that Segovia emphasizes "the concept of Latin(o/a)ness" as a "construct" that "is neither self-evident nor determinate ... [but] always subject to interpretation and debate ... always evasive and fragile" (2009, 199–200). In this second stage, racial/ethnic minority scholars of the Bible are branching out beyond a homogenizing identity into "crossroads of ambiguity" (Anna Deavere Smith 2000, 24).

THIRD STAGE

As racial/ethnic minority readings of the Bible move into the twenty-first century, with this emphasis on intersection, internal diversity, or intracommunal negotiation, there are signs that we are inching toward a third stage that also works on intercommunal conversations across minority groups. Aside from an early attempt to establish contact between African American and Asian American Bible scholars in 2002 (Liew and Wimbush 2002), the strongest indication of this inclination is the 2009 volume edited by Bailey, Segovia, and myself, *They Were All Together in One Place? Toward Minority Biblical Criticism*. While individual essays within this volume are not necessarily demonstrating this crossing, the volume as a whole—by putting three racial/ethnic minority groups together in one volume, even if they are not necessarily in one accord—does gesture a desire not only to seek recognition from each other as racial/ethnic minority communities but also to facilitate communication between each other for association, affinity, and perhaps even alliance.

Making Bible scholars of other racial/ethnic minority groups rather than white scholars one's primary conversation partners signals a potential sea change. If racial/ethnic minority readings of the Bible in the second stage show that racial/ethnic identity is not only constructed but also composite—that is, it involves and is made up of different and multiple elements—the crossings we begin to witness in this third stage hint that the underlying framework of our work has changed from a bipolar one about "majority" and "minority" or "whites" and "persons of color" to one that is multipolar or multicentric. I use both terms because what has been happening in the society at large and the guild of biblical scholarship in particular can be the results of either a more complicated, layered, stratified, and triangulated minoritization process on the part of the dominant, or ground being gained by racial/ethnic minorities, or both. Regardless of reason, intercommunal crossings will help all racial/ethnic minority readers of the Bible understand not only the Bible's role in racialization (both for and against racial/ethnic minorities) but also our role in the oppression and liberation of ourselves and others.

This shift to intercommunal conversations across different racial/ethnic minority readers is not only a comparative but also a connective turn. In other words, instead of fortifying boundaries to allow for differences within but continuing to arrest invaders and interlopers from without, racial/ethnic minority readers from separate communities now seem to realize that "differences do not exist independently of each other … [but] converge and conflict and thus participate in each other" (Chuh 2003, 148). Wimbush, after editing *African Americans and the Bible* at the turn of the century (2000), now talks about his desire to do some "comparative work" among "historically dominated peoples" that is not only "transcultural" but also "multidisciplinary" (2010, 359, 363).

Looking Ahead

If this is where racial/ethnic minority readings have been thus far, where might we go from here? Let me make just three suggestions.

First, one of the most frequent feedbacks I hear about this volume on minority biblical criticism is the absence of Native American voices. The low number of Native American biblical scholars aside, I want to point out honestly that unfortunate tensions often exist between Native Americans and racial/ethnic minorities.[2] On the one hand, racial/ethnic minority analysis is guilty of often ignoring the importance of indigenous genocide and colonialism, and thus contributing to the stereotypical trope of the "vanishing Indians." Some, perhaps

---

2. Examples of work that have been done on Native Americans and the Bible include Warrior (1991) and Donaldson (1999). For an interesting example of a racial/ethnic minority scholar of the Bible writing about the Bible and the experiences of the indigenous people, see Abraham Smith (2010, 69–71). Not only does Smith cross the boundary between minoritized and indigenous concerns in doing so, but he also crosses the testamental divide that often exists between biblical scholars. While he himself is a New Testament scholar, the scholarship he discusses is mainly connecting indigenous issues with the Hebrew Bible.

too many, of us are too eager to "claim America" without confronting the United States as a settler state built on indigenous genocide. On the other hand, Native activists *and* academics often argue for their sovereignty and land claims in terms of prior occupancy: "This land is 'ours,' not 'yours,' because we were here first!" One implication of this argument is that it can turn against those who arrive late, including racial/ethnic minorities who came into the United States through immigration and migration. I have, in a contribution to a dialogue between African American and Asian American Bible scholars, questioned if the attempt by Copher and Felder to (re)claim the Bible by proclaiming black presence in the Bible would not only end up reinforcing the ideology of first rights (2002).

Andrea Smith helpfully provides us with a possible alternative to break this impasse (2010). Her suggestion is to (1) replace the temporal with a spatial framework; and (2) emphasize a radical relationality to land rather than a sovereignty that sees space as property to be owned and used (2010). According to Smith, this shift to a spatial and relational framework means that indigeneity can also become expansive and inclusive. Rather than involving the recognition of a particular people, indigeneity becomes a building of relationships with and caring for all peoples and all of creation, especially since the colonial and capitalist world order will eventually oppress everyone and everything. Indigeneity in this sense is less about identity and more about a particular praxis. After half a century of identity politics, we have learned that such politics, despite the progress it has helped make, can create a "beehive" situation (Dabydeen 1991) of "living-apart-together" (Ang 2001,14). I wonder if Smith's work on indigeneity would provide a way for us to—not replace—but rethink racial/ethnic minority readings of the Bible, so these readings can also be more expansive and inclusive. The so-called affective turn in literary/cultural studies in the last decade (Cvetkovich 2003; Ngai 2005; Clough 2007; Staiger, Cvetkovich, and Reynolds 2010), which emphasizes human emotions that know no racial/ethnic boundaries, seems to have a similar goal to move beyond narrow identity politics.

Second, given Andrea Smith's critique of the temporal framework in general and the claim of first arrival in particular, let me go back to the origin story about racial/ethnic minority readings of the Bible. Reading by racial/ethnic minority scholars of the Bible in the 1970s actually did not begin racial/ethnic minority readings of the Bible. As much as scholars might like to take credit for being founders—or worse, "fathers"—of racial/ethnic minority readings, racial/ethnic minorities have been reading the Bible for a long time. Slave narratives in and after the antebellum period, for instance, often include quotation from, comments on, and engagements with the Bible (Callahan 2006). Mindful of what Elisabeth Schüssler Fiorenza calls "the Athena complex," which co-opts women's wisdom and work into a "motherless" lineage made up of only patriarchs, and hence her consistent call to mine the archives of feminist biblical interpretation (1998, 12–15, 51, 73), let me point to a couple of examples.

While the publication of Cady Stanton's *Woman's Bible* at the end of the nineteenth century has become rather well known, if not necessarily read, Virginia W. Broughton—a devout black Baptist missionary and advocate of women's rights—and her 1904 publication, *Women's Work, as Gleaned from the Women of the Bible and the Bible Women of Modern Times* (Carter 2010, 9–21), have remained unknown and unfamiliar to even most racial/ethnic minority scholars of the Bible.[3] Another example would be a contemporary of Broughton: Sui Sin Far, who has the distinction of being called the "First Chinese-American Fictionist" (Solberg 1981), "the founder of the Chinese North American woman writer's tradition" (White-Parks 1995, 6), as well as "the grand maternal figure of *all* Asian American letters" (David Shih 2005, 48). Despite these recent accolades, Sui Sin Far was not a famous writer in her own time and was by no means a scholar. However, her writings are full of allusions to and quotations from the Bible. "[T]he stories in the Bible were more like Chinese than American stories," she writes, "[i]f you had not told me what you have about it, I should say that it was composed by the Chinese" (Ling and White-Parks 1995, 78). One white critic of literature—so not a minoritized Bible scholar—has even suggested provocatively, though only in passing, that the Bible was "the single most important model" of Sui Sin Far's own writings, as it accounts for their "short," almost parable-like format and "didactic bent" (Ferens 2002, 95–96).

Racial/ethnic minorities in the United States started reading and writing about the Bible a long time before racial/ethnic minority scholars of the Bible did so in the 1970s. While I think tradition can change and thus be inventive, I also agree with R. S. Sugirtharajah, a racial/ethnic minority Bible scholar in the United Kingdom, that tracing a historical tradition through archival work can be inspiring, both because it is encouraging and because it equips us to further the work (2003b, 93–94). Simply put, rather than reinventing the wheel, every generation can instead spend its time and energy to invent new elements and emphases to enlarge and enrich the tradition. Just as popular or grassroots antiracist and anti-imperialist movements have facilitated academic developments from new directions in theology, being contextual to new disciplines like ethnic studies, acknowledging, apprehending, and appraising so-called popular readings of the Bible by racial/ethnic minorities past *and* present will only contribute to future developments of such readings.

---

3. There are, of course, exceptions. See, e.g., Williams 2004, 170–72.

Ethnic studies scholar Lisa Lowe has argued that white philosophy on human freedom as a universal right since the Enlightenment came into being only by robbing African slaves and Asian coolies of their freedom as a colonized labor force (2006). As racial/ethnic minority scholars of the Bible, we must not forget what we affirm by dismissing racial/ethnic minority readers outside of the academy. Among racial/ethnic minority scholars of the Bible, Wimbush might have done most on this front, given his work on outlining an interpretive history of African Americans in general (1991) and on Olaudah Equiano (2009a) and Douglass (2009b) in particular. As director of the Institute of Signifying Scripture, Wimbush is also branching out to do ethnographical work on how persons of color today read the Bible in faith communities that are not academic in focus (ed. forthcoming).

Finally, let me return to our earlier reference to Latin America and Asia in linking theology with racial/ethnic minority biblical scholarship. Brown actually does something similar by way of Brazil and Nigeria in his more racial/ethnic specific accounting of black biblical scholarship (2004, 9–15). These references point to another potential crossing that has not really been developed by racial/ethnic minority scholars of the Bible since those incipient intervals of the 1970s. I am referring here to a transnational or transcontinental dimension of racial/ethnic minority scholarship on the Bible.

While most people remember W. E. B. Du Bois's declaration, "the problem of the twentieth century is the problem of the color line," from *The Souls of Black Folk* (1903, xx), many have forgotten that Du Bois actually made that statement first in France as part of the 1900 Pan-African Conference in a speech that he titled "To the Nations of the World" (1995). For Du Bois, arguably the most iconic figure within African American academic circles, the "Negro problem" or the question of race in the United States needed to be dealt with not only in terms of cultural nationalism but also "from the setting and in the name of a transnational gathering of men and women" (Edwards 2003, 2). Du Bois demonstrated, in his typically prophetic manner, that most cultures and societies do not operate in self-enclosed ways. Just as Philip Curtin (1990), Joseph Roach (1996), and Hortense J. Spillers (2003) have highlighted the need to look at black slavery in a larger, transatlantic frame, we need to develop a more frequent and serious crossing between racial/ethnic minority readings of the Bible in the United States and readings in Africa, Asia, and Latin America, so we can—in Curtin's language—go beyond the "plantation complex" and redraw the boundaries to create a different type of transnational exploration and transcontinental comparison. Fanon's other suggestion years ago, when he declared "comparison" as "the first truth" of a colonized black person (1967, 210–22), has been confirmed and shown to be more widely applicable by Yee's trip from Boston to Hong Kong: something dramatic happens when a person of color moves from the metropole to the colony and vice versa (see also Shu-mei Shih 2008, 1349–52). The world might have come to the United States, but we cannot mistake the United States for the world. How do persons of the same race/ethnicity read over here and over there? The Bible is already global; it is read by people around the globe, by people with doctorates and without. The question is whether our readings, including racial/ethnic minority readings, will catch up with that reality.

19

Changing the Paradigms: Toward a Feminist Future of the Biblical Past

Elisabeth Schüssler Fiorenza

I approach the topic of this volume, *The Future of the Biblical Past*, from the vantage point of a critical feminist rhetoric and hermeneutics of liberation rather than from a culturally or geographically defined position.[1] This may place my reflections somewhat at odds with this volume's overall organization, which is structured in area[2] and cultural studies terms around geographical-continental and national-political identity spaces, rather than in terms of theoretical, methodological, or emancipatory[3] struggles. By foregrounding identity in geographical-global terms but not in religious (premodern) or methodological (modern) terms, the volume proposal situates it in the postmodern space of globalization via area studies and

---

1. See my autobiographical reflections, "Changing the Paradigms" (1991a). I use "feminist" as an umbrella term to signify an intellectual and social movement and theory. Such a formal category needs to be contextually specified with, for example, womanist, *mujerista*, Latina, queer, Western, global, critical, liberationist, and so forth, since there are numerous articulations of feminist theory and practice. Such a political use of "feminism" as an umbrella term seeks to avoid the fragmentation and splintering of feminist power that is still marginal in societies and religions around the globe.

2. For a feminist problematization of area-studies conceptualizations, see Ella Shohat (2002).

3. Although emancipation is often used negatively for feminists (in German, *Emanze* is a pejorative attribute) and viewed as tainted by postmodern eyes, I prefer the term over "liberation," since President George Bush used *liberation* for the *occupation* of Iraq. Emancipation is connected with liberation from slavery. The word is defined as both the act of setting free from the power of another (from slavery, subjection, dependence, or controlling influence) *and* as the state of being thus set free, liberation (used of slaves, minors, a person from prejudices, the mind from superstition, a nation from tyranny or subjection). See http://en.wiktionary.org/wiki/emancipation.

asks what the future of the biblical past will be in these discrete globalized spaces.[4] However, we need to explore the future of the biblical past not only in terms of global spaces and cultural identity slots. It is also necessary to explore such a future in terms of religious locations and spiritual identity formations that do not overlook but foreground and problematize the religious-confessional-the*logical[5] spaces where most biblical studies are done.

In order to elucidate why I do not position my critical feminist theoretical approach in terms of national/cultural/geographical identity politics, I will use the metaphor of "resident alien" for characterizing the space of a critical feminist the*logy of liberation. This metaphor is rooted in my experience of living as an actual resident alien in the United States and the attendant experience of dis-location. As a resident alien, I am a senior "resident" in the North American academy and at the same time an "alien," because I am an immigrant woman. My German accent marks me as foreign in the United States, and the American accent ascribed to me by German hearers brands me as foreign in Germany. As a feminist resident alien, I belong neither here nor there! This difficult experience of "belonging nowhere" can be illustrated with the following vignette.

Years ago, I asked an esteemed colleague who was born in Germany but who, as a Jew, had to flee during the Nazi time how he handled the experience of belonging neither here nor there. This question was engendered by my experience of having been accused at a European feminist conference of representing American imperialism in feminist theology, which had deeply depressed me. My colleague was surprised by this question and asked: "What do you mean? I have always had the feeling that I belong everywhere." I was puzzled by his response until a friend explained to me: "Of course he belongs everywhere, at all the scholarly conferences where he is honored as 'one of them,' as the great Jewish-Christian scholar whose path-breaking writings are celebrated and discussed. As a wo/man,[6] you do not belong to the male scholarly the*logical club; as an emi-

---

4. See the discussion in the special issue of *Signs*, Globalization and Gender, *Signs* 26/4 (Summer 2001).

5. In order to mark the inadequacy of our language about G*d, I had adopted the Jewish orthodox way of writing the name of G-d in my books *Discipleship of Equals* and *But She Said*. However, Jewish feminists have pointed out to me that such a spelling is offensive to many of them, because it suggests a very conservative, if not reactionary, theological frame of reference. Hence, I have begun to write the word *G*d* in this fashion in order to visibly destabilize our way of thinking and speaking about the Divine. Since the*logy literally means "speaking about G*d," I also write it with the asterisk rather than alternating between thealogy and theology.

6. To make conscious the power of kyriocentric language and discourse in general and biblical language in particular, I use the expression "wo/men" in an inclusive generic way: to include men, to problematize the essentialist notion of woman, and to signify the differences

grant/immigrant, you do not belong to the club of American or European wo/men; and as a white Euro-American teaching at Harvard, you certainly do not belong either to the Two-Third World male or to the female scholarly contingent."

This resident alien experience of belonging nowhere has marked the theoretical location from where I speak. As a "resident" I am a fully entitled member of the academy, but as an "alien" I seek to articulate scholarship that is different. On the one hand, I have never felt that I am not a legitimate resident of the biblical academy, since I enjoyed an excellent classics German education. On the other hand, as a female scholar who until the beginning of the twentieth century was excluded from academic studies and church leadership, and who is still excluded in many parts of the world and many religious communities, I am a resident alien in biblical studies. Recognizing this "doubled" social-religious locatedness also has its benefits. For instance, as a wo/man excluded from the academy, I do not need to feel defensive whenever German scholarship is attacked, whether from the right or from the left. Growing up after the Shoah, I early on rejected the notion of collective guilt for the past but adopted instead the notion of *collective responsibility*. As a wo/man from a rural lower class background, I knew that neither my ancestors nor I had produced anti-Jewish or colonialist racist biblical scholarship. Nevertheless, I also have always been deeply convinced that I have a responsibility to change biblical and the*logical studies that have done so in the past and still promote prejudice and discrimination today.

Being a resident alien scholar in the Euro-American academy does not excuse me from responsibility but compels me to articulate and teach scholarship that does not continue but change the discourses of the discipline. While most area and postcolonial studies erase the hyphen between Euro (/Asian/African, etc.) and American in order to construct a dominating colonizing and a dominated colonized Other, I have refused to own this hyphenated construct and to define my approach in cultural-regional identity terms. Instead, I have insisted on characterizing my work as "feminist," which I have qualified with "critical" and

among and within wo/men. This writing of wo/men has a double communicative function. It seeks to startle readers into recognition by ironically reversing the use of *man* and *he* as inclusive of *woman* and *she* in kyriocentric languages, instead using *wo/men* as the generic term, which is inclusive of marginalized men. It also seeks to communicate that "wo/men" is a fragmented political name that points to the differences among and within wo/men and asserts that wo/men as a socially constructed group do not have a defining essence in common. I thereby invite readers to engage in a spiritual-intellectual exercise that reverses the usual linguistic practice of using man in a generic sense to include woman. Simply by learning how to speak, men experience themselves as central and important, whereas wo/men learn that we are not directly addressed but are subsumed under male terms. I hope that this use will engender more research on biblical translation and interpretation in non-androcentric language contexts.

with "liberation/emancipation." The space from which I speak is the theoretical space of a critical feminist the*logy of liberation (see Schüssler Fiorenza 2011).

SPEAKING WITH A THE*LOGICAL ACCENT

I have lived in the United States for almost forty years as a resident alien who emigrated from Germany in the 1970s, because wo/men could not teach on the the*logical faculties of German universities. This was the case because of a concordat made between the Roman Catholic hierarchy and the Nazi regime. As the first woman in my university, I had undertaken full the*logical studies and arrived in the States with a thorough scholarly training in both the*logical and biblical studies. Because of this "German Catholic" the*logical hermeneutical accent, I was able to develop biblical studies in a feminist key and to search early Christian writings for a spirituality of survival and well-being.

Whereas biblical studies in Germany were part and parcel of the*logical studies, in the United States they were part and parcel of scientific historical studies. I remember meeting a famous Jesuit scholar who was annoyed when I addressed him as a "the*logian" rather than as a biblical scholar. Although the*logical concepts and arguments crept unacknowledged into the scholarly rhetoric in the United States, the overt self-understanding of biblical scholars was "scientific" and not the*logical. Whereas I operated with an hermeneutic-rhetorical rather than with a dogmatic-doctrinal notion of the*logy, the ethos of biblical studies in the United States advocated value-detached, objective, philological, historical, archeological, exegetical scholarship that sought to articulate biblical research objectively as historical facts.

Such scientist scholarship claimed the task of saying what the text meant in its historical context, but ascribed the task of establishing "the meaning of the text for today" to the*logians and pastors (see Stendhal 1962). For instance, a colleague told me, upon my arrival in the States during the Vietnam War in 1970, that I never should allow students to ask for the relevance and significance of the text, if I did not want to give in to their desire for avoiding critical–historical work. In contrast, my Catholic German training had insisted that the task of the biblical scholar was to research and establish the meaning of the biblical text in the past for today. Biblical interpretation was impossible without also engaging in religious/the*logical meaning-making for today. The intensive hermeneutical discussions had made a positivist scientistic understanding of biblical studies and biblical history passé and out-of-date, or so I thought.

This "the*logical" accent allowed me to understand myself as a feminist scholar and to assert the out-datedness of hegemonic positivist biblical scholarship. Moreover, I came at a fortuitous moment to the United States, when the wo/men's movement in Judaism and Christianity had just gotten underway and feminist studies in religion had begun to emerge in the academy. Although it was considered detrimental to one's career, I became fully involved in the Women's Liberation Movement—as it was called in the late 1960s and early 1970s—in both the academy and the church.

Unlike many of the American wo/men scholars and activists whom I met at the Women Doing Theology conference at Grailville in 1972, my understanding of the*ology was not negative, since I had studied the*logy during the Second Vatican Council and experienced it as exciting and liberating. In the context of this movement, I learned to understand myself as a the*logian who did not just transmit and teach the the*logy of her progressive the*logical "fathers"—such as Karl Rahner, Hans Küng, Johann Baptist Metz, or Jürgen Moltmann—but who articulated the*logy and biblical meaning for the wo/men's liberation movement that sought to change society and religion. This intellectual "conversion" allowed me to delineate theoretically the place from which to speak as that of a "critical feminist the*logy of liberation" (Schüssler Fiorenza 1975), a delineation which articulated my alien status in the academy and my "being at home" in a women's liberation movement for change.

As a feminist the*logian, I argued, the feminist biblical scholar was called to listen to and work with the wo/men's liberation movement in society and religion in order to articulate their research questions and teach biblical-the*logical meanings that foster the well-being of all wo/men.[7] While I participated in many different women's groups, I decided to focus my energy on rigorous academic work, since at the time there were so few wo/men and feminists around who could or would do such work. Over the years, I also sought to develop a pedagogical process inspired by radical democratic feminist liberation movement practices. Such a pedagogy is essential to biblical studies if we want to train future professors, teachers, leaders, and ministers to do the work of a critical interpretation for liberation.

I also sought to articulate my theoretical vantage point and hermeneutical approach in discussion with the emergent liberation theologies of the 1970s. However, my articulation of a critical the*logy of liberation was not derived from

---

7. Whereas most First World feminist scholarship has done its work in terms of the three hegemonic paradigms of academic biblical studies, feminists of the Two-Third World have consistently insisted that feminist reading must be done with grassroots wo/men in the churches. Compare, for example, the essays in the volume edited by Vander Stichele and Penner (2005) and in the volume edited by O'Brien Wicker, Spencer Miller, Dube (2005). I believe it is important that the fourth paradigm heed their call.

liberation the*logy but inspired by the maxim of the Women's Liberation Movement: "Until all wo/men are free, no wo/man is free!" Such a the*logy, I argued, needed to develop a hermeneutic of suspicion to place traditional the*logy and Scripture studies in *krisis*. It needed to rearticulate biblical studies in the interest of the emancipation/liberation/well-being of all wo/men without exception. This required a reconceptualization of the dominant historiography and hermeneutics of biblical studies in feminist terms. I set out to do so first in my books *In Memory of Her* (1983) and *Bread Not Stone* (1985) and have continued to develop this approach in my subsequent work (1992, 1993, 1994, 1998, 1999, 2000a, 2001, 2003, 2007, 2009b).

Speaking with a Feminist Accent

This feminist theoretical articulation has placed me between a rock and a hard place, since the First World postmodern academy is suspicious of "liberation/feminist the*logy," considered to be a child of modernity. Two-Third World feminists, in turn, are rightly suspicious of academic feminist work that is not developed in discussion with grassroots wo/men's movements for change. The theory undergirding my articulation of a critical feminist hermeneutics of liberation, however, is not gender essentialism, nor the "theology of woman," but critical feminist theory.

The wo/men's movements in religion of the 1970s often worked with the essentialist analytic unitary category of " woman," since the nomenclature "feminist" was shunned by the public and the academy as too ideological, too political, or too eccentric, and was often caricatured as man-hating and identified with lesbianism. Hence, many of my colleagues, including those of the Two-Third World, argued that the f-word ("feminist") could not be used in their churches or academic contexts, and hence it would be better to speak of "women's the*logy" rather than of feminist the*logy or feminist biblical criticism.

In my first book, *Der vergessene Partner* (1964), I criticized the "theology of woman" as legitimating the "equal but different" politics of modernity that excluded wo/men as "the Other" from leadership positions in church and society. Biblical wo/men's or gender studies often assume an essentialist understanding of woman and do not recognize that gender is always inflected by race, class, age, sexuality, imperialism, and other identity markers. However, it must not be overlooked that the "cult of true womanhood" does not define the essence of all wo/men but articulates the ideal of "the White Lady."

Hence, I argued that one must refuse to develop a feminist analytic in terms of the essentialist category "woman" and not advocate a "woman in the Bible" or woman's Bible approach. The tradition inaugurated by Elizabeth Cady Stanton's *Woman's Bible*, which focuses on biblical texts about women, needs to be interrupted rather than continued. Such an approach, consciously or not, works with the essentialist notion of "woman" elaborated in the image of the "White Lady" that is propagated by the media not only in Western countries but around the globe. If wo/men are not only determined by gender but also by race, class, heterosexism, and imperialism, it is necessary to develop a critical analytic that is able to deconstruct the global cultural paradigm of the White Lady.

Thus, I find myself not only "in between" different geographical spaces but also "in between" different feminist spaces. Women's or gender studies tend to speak about wo/men and gender, but not about race, class, and imperialism. This assumed gender identity framework engenders the dichotomy between the space marked "white women/ First World women" and the space marked "wo/men of color/Two-Third World wo/men." Identity politics claims that white/First World feminists can only speak for white/First World wo/men and in the name of white/First World wo/men, and thus inevitably must articulate a "white/First World" the*logy and hermeneutics. Over and against such identity politics, I argued as "resident alien" that my identity was not only constituted by my gender but also by my immigrant status, class, education, nationality, race, religion and more, and hence identity must be seen as multiplex and shaped by intersecting dominations.

Because Euro-American wo/men were mostly the first wo/men to gain access to the academic study of the*logy and religion, the beginnings of feminist studies in religion are often judged by Two-Third World wo/men as intrinsically marred by racism and colonialism. This diagnosis overlooks that the first generation of feminist scholars in religion was deeply involved in liberation movements and in the women's liberation movement. It also does not recognize that, exactly at the moment when Two-Third World wo/men entered the academy as speaking subjects insisting on race, class, heteronormativity, colonialism, or imperialism as crucial categories of analysis, the academic discourse switched to gender as a key analytic category. The type of feminism which is conceived in terms of gender essentialism can only reproduce the cultural essentialist identity construction which understands the dichotomy between white upper-class men and wo/men, the Lord and Lady, as the key analytic category of feminism. On the other hand, theories of race, culture, class, colonialism, or imperialism are often formulated without taking feminist studies into account and without making gender a key ingredient of their analytic.

The analytics of feminist, postcolonial, and critical race theories have developed alongside each other but have not been integrated to accomplish an intersectional analysis. The term "intersectionality" was coined by the legal scholar Kimberly Crenshaw and entails "the notion that subjectivity is constituted by mutually multiplicative vectors of race, gender, class, sexuality, and imperialism" (Nash 2008, 3). The theory of intersectionality has been articulated in a threefold way: as a theory of marginalized subjectivity, as a theory of identity, and as a theory of the matrix of oppressions (Garry 2001; Lugones 2007, 2010). In the first iteration, intersectional theory refers only to multiply marginalized subjects; in its second iteration, the theory seeks to illuminate how identity is constructed at the intersections of race, gender, class, sexuality, and imperialism; the third iteration stresses intersectional theory as a theory of structures and sites of oppression. Race, sex, gender, class, and imperialism are seen as vectors of dominating power that create co-constitutive social processes which engender the differential simultaneity of dominations and subordinations (Einspahr 2010).

Intersectional theorists usually conceptualize such social and ideological structures of domination as *hierarchical*, in order to map and make visible the complex interstructuring of the conflicting status positions of different wo/men. I believe that the label "hierarchy" for such a pyramidal system of domination is a misnomer, since it only targets one specific, religiously sanctioned form of domination. Hence, I have proposed to replace the category of "hierarchy" with the neologism *kyriarchy*,[8] which is derived from the Greek words *kyrios* (lord, slave master, father, husband, elite, propertied, educated man) and *archein* (to rule, dominate).[9] In classical antiquity, the rule of the emperor, lord, slave master, husband—the elite freeborn, propertied, educated gentleman to whom disenfranchised men and all wo/men were subordinated—is best characterized by the neologism *kyriarchy*. In antiquity, the social system of kyriarchy was institutionalized either as empire or as a democratic political form of ruling that excluded all freeborn and slave wo/men from full citizenship and decision-making powers.

Kyriarchy is best theorized as a complex pyramidal system of intersecting multiplicative social and religious structures of superordination and subordination, of ruling and oppression. Kyriarchal relations of domination are built on elite male property rights and privileges as well as on the exploitation, dependency, inferiority, and obedience of wo/men who signify all those subordinated. Such kyriarchal relations are still at work today in the multiplicative intersectionality of class, race, gender, ethnicity, empire, and other structures of discrimination.

Rather than identifying kyriarchy in dualistic terms with the binary of male over female, white over black, Western over colonized people, it is best to understand it as an intersectional pyramidal system shaped by race, gender, heterosexist, class, colonial, imperial dominations. Kyriarchy connotes "the multiple

---

8. For a fuller elaboration of kyriarchy/kyriocentrism, see Schüssler Fiorenza 2009a.
9. For the first development of this concept, see Schüssler Fiorenza 1992, 103–32.

relations of ruling that include the way in which gender relations articulate with economies, states, and markets"—and, I would add, religions. A kyriarchal analytic engenders an exploration of relations of domination "as mediating processes of negotiation constituted by complex identities and practices rather than by an assumed universalized unitary, dominating force of male (white, colonial, elite, imperial) domination and female (black, colonialized, underdog) subordination" (Feldman 2001, 1101).

Kyriarchal empires and democracies are stratified by shifting intersections of gender, race, class, religion, heterosexuality, and age. These intersections shape the *structural positions* that are assigned to us more or less by birth. However, how people live these *structural kyriarchal* positions is conditioned not simply by these structural positions themselves, but also by the *subject positions* through which we live them. Whereas an essentialist approach assigns to people an "authentic" identity that is derived from our *structural position*, one's *subject position* becomes coherent and compelling through political discourse, interpretive frameworks, and the development of theoretical horizons regarding domination. Thus wo/men's activism in movements against colonialism, racism, heterosexism, and class exploitation must be recognized as "a kind of subterranean, unrecognized form of feminism and therefore as a legitimate part of feminist historiography" (Shohat 2001, 1270).

In short, a critical intersectional feminist analytic does not understand domination as an essentialist, ahistorical dualistic system. Instead, it articulates kyriarchy as a *heuristic* (derived from the Greek, meaning "to find") concept, or as a diagnostic, analytic instrument that enables investigation into the multiplicative interactivity of gender, race, class, and imperial stratifications, as well as research into their discursive inscriptions and ideological reproductions. Moreover, it highlights that people inhabit several shifting structural positions of race, sex, gender, class, and ethnicity at one and the same time. If one subject position of domination becomes privileged, it constitutes a nodal point. While in any particular historical moment, class or imperialism may be the primary modality through which one experiences class, imperialism, gender, and race, in other circumstances gender may be the privileged position through which one experiences sexuality, imperialism, race, and class.

Insofar as transnational kyriarchal capitalism crosses all borders, exploits all peoples, and colonizes all citizens, it requires a counter-vision and dissident strategy, which Chela Sandoval has called "democratics," a strategy and vision which has affinities with my own attempt to articulate the space of the ekklēsia of wo/men[10]

---

10. For an excellent critical discussion of this concept, see Jobling 2002, 32–60, 142–63.

as a critical radical democratic space of interpretation. Since *ekklēsia* understood as a radical democratic congress of fully entitled, responsible decision-making citizens has never been fully realized either in Christian history or in Western democracy, the expression *ekklēsia gynaikōn* ("the ekklēsia of wo/men") functions as a linguistic means of conscientization. Since the signifier "wo/man" is increasingly used by right-wing religions to draw exclusive boundaries, it is important to mark linguistically the difference between religion as kyriarchal institution and religion as *ekklēsia*, as the decision-making radical democratic congress of the people of G*d.

Sandoval explains *democratics* as one of the methods of the oppressed in the following way:

> With the transnationalization of capitalism when elected officials are no longer leaders of singular nation-states but nexuses for multinational interests, it also becomes possible for citizen-subjects to become activists for a new decolonizing global terrain, a psychic terrain that can unite them with similarly positioned citizen-subjects within and across national borders into new, post-Western–empire alliances.... Love as social movement is enacted by revolutionary, mobile, and global coalitions of citizen-activists who are allied through the apparatus of emancipation. (2000, 183)

However, I am somewhat hesitant to claim "love" as the *sole* revolutionary force or to reduce "oppositional social action only to a mode of 'love' in the postmodern world." Although I am well aware that numerous U.S. Two-Third World feminists have eloquently written about the power of love in struggles for justice,[11] I cannot forget the function of "romantic love" either in the oppression of wo/men nor the anti-Jewish valorization of the "N*w"[12] Testament "*G*d of Love*" over the "Old" Testament "*God of Justice.*" Democratics, in my view, must be equally informed by justice, as Patricia Hill Collins has argued:

> Justice transcends Western notions of equality grounded in sameness and uniformity.... In making their quilts Black women weave together scraps of fabric from all sorts of places. Nothing is wasted, and every piece of fabric has a function and a place in a given quilt.... [T]hose who conceptualize community via notions of uniformity and sameness have difficulty imagin-

---

11. Audre Lorde, bell hooks, Toni Morrison, Cornel West, June Jordan, Gloria Anzaldúa, Maria Lugones, Merle Woo, Alice Walker—to name just a few.

12. Here the asterisk seeks to draw attention to the danger of supersessionism in the label "New Testament."

ing a social quilt that is simultaneously heterogeneous, driven toward excellence, and just. (1998, 248–49)

In this image of quilt and quilting for the making of justice, the decolonizing practices of a global democratics, of the *ekklēsia of wo/men*, and a critical feminist dissident global interpretation converge.

Speaking with an Emancipatory Accent

To conceptualize feminist emancipatory biblical studies as such a critical quilting of meaning in different sociopolitical locations, I suggest, will enable us not only to deconstruct the kyriarchal ideological inscriptions of the biblical past but also to articulate a biblical spirituality and emancipatory vision of justice and well-being for all. To transform the past of biblical studies towards a feminist future, one needs to chart the emancipatory paradigm of biblical studies as a new field of inquiry. If the biblical past should have a future, this paradigm must be emancipatory, since its task is not just postmodern ideological deconstruction but also the production of spiritual emancipatory knowledge of re-vision and re-memory. Such a critical feminist emancipatory paradigm requires a change of the following three areas of biblical studies: (1) the the*logical understanding of scripture; (2) the reading of kyriarchal texts; and (3) the conceptualization of history.

1. An emancipatory paradigm has to relinquish both the apologetic defense of the Bible as well as the critical scholarly disinterest in the*logical interpretation. It has to wrestle the*logically with the understanding of the Bible as the word of God as well as with the estimation of the Bible as a cultural classic which has to be approached with a hermeneutic of appreciation and trust rather than a hermeneutic of suspicion. Hence, it is important to transform this doctrinal-cultural paradigm of authority and to define scripture the*logically not as a dogmatic archetype but as a the*logical prototype open for transformation. Whether scholars are religious believers or not, we have to wrestle with the Bible as Scripture and to articulate emancipatory interpretations of biblical texts, because millions of disenfranchized wo/men still read the Bible searching for visions of hope and transformation.

Because of its ideological inscriptions, the Bible as Scripture and as cultural classic must be approached not only with a hermeneutic of suspicion and evaluation but also with a hermeneutic of imagination, remembrance, and transformation. Reinterpreting a long the*logical tradition that found its way into the writings of Vatican II, I argued for an emancipatory specification of revelation. Rather than to rely on a "canon within the canon" approach, I have argued that a critical feminist emancipatory paradigm also has the the*logical task of exploring what "G*d wanted to put into Sacred Scripture for the sake of our i.e. wo/men's salvation or well-being."

In other words, kyriarchal texts and histories have no truth claims as legitimators of oppression and must be critically analyzed and evaluated in their sociopolitical contexts if G*d's salvific intention should be "revealed" in the process of interpretation. Whether biblical scholars of the fourth paradigm are believers or not, we have to analyze the the*logical rhetoric of Scripture in its different sociocultural and religious contexts.

2. The emancipatory paradigm of biblical studies also has to confront the power of biblical language. In a grammatically androcentric (i.e. male-centered) and kyriocentric (lord/master) centered language system, wo/men always have to think twice and to deliberate whether we are meant or not when we are told, for example, that "all men are created equal" or that we are "sons of G*d." Religious-biblical language tells us that we are made in the image of G*d, who is generally portrayed as male. When reading the Bible as Sacred Scripture or as a Western cultural classic, wo/men internalize not only that the Divine is male and not female but also that wo/men are second-class citizens subordinated to male authority. Simply by learning to speak or to pray, wo/men learn that we are marginal, insignificant "second-class members" of society and religion.

It seems to me, therefore, that only those Two-Third World feminist scholars who have not been socialized into a Western andro-kyriocentric language system, because the languages of their native countries are not gendered, can break this power of biblical male-centered language over us. Scholars who have grown up in a language system that, for instance, is a *status system*, are able to make significant contributions to feminist emancipatory translation, thought, and the*logy. Critical feminist emancipatory research is still very much lacking and promises to become a fecund area of study in the emancipatory fourth paradigm.[13]

3. The civil rights movement and other liberation movements around the globe have argued that it is a sign of oppression not to have a written history. Hence, the rewriting and reconceptualization of "His-story" in a different key was and is an essential task for emancipation and liberation. Historiography in general (and biblical history in particular) has to relinquish its antiquarian moorings and elite orientation. It has to recover history as memory and remembrance.

In writing *In Memory of Her*, I tried to do just that. I was not so much interested in writing woman's history in Early Christianity but to write Early Christian

---

13. See now, however, the very interesting article of Satoko Yamaguchi, "Father Image of G*d and Inclusive Language: A Reflection in Japan" (2003). I hope that this article will engender more research on biblical translation and interpretation in non-androcentric language contexts.

history in a feminist key. I sought to explore whether our sources would still allow us to frame Early Christian history in such a way that not just men but also wo/men would be remembered as central actors in and shapers of early Christian communities and as articulators of religious vision. Since identity is shaped by the story we tell about origins and beginnings, I continue to argue, it is necessary to tell Early Christian history differently. To do so, in *In Memory of Her*, I proposed a model of struggle—struggles between shifting egalitarian relations on the one hand and kyriarchal dominations on the other.

In Memory of Her is often read in terms of the Protestant model of "pure" beginnings and rapid deterioration into patriarchy. However, this is a misreading that does not grasp the historiographical and political model of struggle undergirding the arguments of the book. These struggles did not end in the second century, but they are still ongoing today and have shaped not only Christian but also Western history. In contrast to some postmodern literary theorists who eschew the writing of history as "what must be remembered," I believe that it is important to change historical biblical studies in the interest of liberation/emancipation, if the biblical past is to have a feminist emancipatory future.

Rather than re-inscribing the disciplinary divisions between the*logical and scientific interpretation, between literary and historical methods, between sociopolitical and religious approaches, or between social-sociological and ideological–religious criticism, I continue to argue that critical feminist emancipatory studies must work for a paradigm shift that can overcome these dualisms by conceptualizing biblical studies as a rhetoric and ethics of inquiry and transformation. To conceptualize the emancipatory paradigm of biblical studies as a rhetoric of inquiry and ethics of transformation would engender research in the following areas of interpretation that constitute the fourth emancipatory paradigm:

- global experience and sociopolitical-religious location of the subjects of biblical knowledge.
- systemic structural sociopolitical analysis of the rhetorical and historical situation.
- a hermeneutics of suspicion, which includes ideology and language-critique, a critique of method and epistemology, cultural and literary criticism, and a critique of religion and theology.
- ethical and theological evaluation of texts and interpretations as to how they serve global domination or equality and well-being.
- a cultivation of the interpretive scholarly imagination and ritualization of texts and traditions to create the "other worlds" that we desire and strive for.
- a rewriting of biblical history as emancipatory historical reconstruction, as memory and heritage in the struggle for liberation and well-being.

- a critical praxis of change and transformation in a global world of domination.

These seven areas of feminist emancipatory research require transdisciplinary collaboration and the formulation of new methods of inquiry.

At the same time, these seven areas of research require translation into a practical pedagogical guide for interpretation. I have done so by formulating and developing *the Dance of Interpretation,* which encompasses the following hermeneutical steps: *a hermeneutics of experience, a hermeneutics of domination, a hermeneutics of suspicion, a hermeneutics of evaluation, a hermeneutics of imagination, a hermeneutics of remembrance and a hermeneutics of transformation.* Whereas in *Bread Not Stone* I articulated the four interpretive steps of suspicion, evaluation, reconstruction, and imagination, I have later added the critical feminist steps of experience, domination, and transformation in order to embed the interpretation of biblical texts into a critical feminist context and goal.[14]

This "dance script" can easily be activated through common sense questions to be put to the text. With these steps of the interpretive "dance," a critical feminist interpretation for liberation facilitates conscientization and cultural, social, religious, and disciplinary transformation. It provides intellectual and spiritual resources to individuals—be they scholarly or citizen-readers of the Bible. It provides the means for engaging in the work of emancipatory feminist critical interpretation. Such emancipatory scholarly and citizen reading practices of interpretation provide the rhetorics, methods, and ethics of inquiry for the emancipatory feminist work of changing academic biblical studies.

Engendering a Feminist Future of the Biblical Past: Transforming the Paradigms

In *Bread Not Stone* (23–42), I argued that the discipline of biblical studies consists of three existing hegemonic paradigms: the *doctrinal* paradigm, which understands the Bible as the word of G*d; the *historical* paradigm, which reads the Bible as a book of the past; and the *pastoral-the*logical* paradigm, which sees the Bible as the root-model of the church. I also cited a new emerging paradigm of biblical studies, which I called a feminist paradigm of emancipatory praxis. It is obvious that this paradigm construction of *Bread Not Stone* is firmly situated within liberation the*logical discussions and seeks to gain distance from both the doctrinal and the historical-positivist paradigms.

---

14. For the translation of these research areas into practical strategies of interpretation that can be used by all wo/men engaging in biblical interpretation, see Schüssler Fiorenza 2001.

Fernando Segovia also charts four paradigms of biblical studies, and he does so in terms of *modern* academic biblical criticism rather than in terms of the overall history of biblical interpretation (1995; see also 1998a). Hence he constructs his paradigms in terms of methods of criticism: (1) Historical Criticism, which uses the text as *means*, as the dominant paradigm through the 1970s; (2) Literary Criticism, which dislodged historical criticism in the 1980s, analyzes the text as *medium*; (3) Cultural Criticism, an umbrella term that encompasses lines of inquiry such as socioeconomic and ideological analysis, Neo-Marxist and various forms of sociological analysis, understands the text as *medium and means*; finally, (4) Cultural Studies, which he later replaces with Postcolonial Criticism (1996; 1998b; 2000b; 2000c), which takes account of the influx of marginal voices and locates the meaning of the text in the encounter between the text and the flesh-and-blood reader. Its constitutive method is ideology criticism.

At this point it might be helpful to look again at my own somewhat different paradigm construction, which I have renamed in my latest book, *Democratizing Biblical Studies*, as follows: (1) The Religious-The*logical-Scriptural Paradigm; (2) The Critical-Scientific-Modern Paradigm; (3) The Hermeneutic-Cultural-Postmodern Paradigm; and (4) The Rhetorical-Emancipatory-Radical Democratic Paradigm. Since I still begin with the premodern Scriptural, religious-the*logical paradigm of interpretation, my genealogy of biblical criticism reads somewhat differently from that of Segovia. The four basic paradigms that I have articulated in *Bread not Stone*, and refined and renamed again and again in the past thirty-five years, differ with Segovia's paradigm construction in that they recognize and take into account the the*logical Scriptural paradigm of interpretation.

In line with Latin American liberation the*logy of the 1970s and critical feminist the*logies of liberation in the past three decades, I have argued that the emerging fourth paradigm had to be critical, dialogical, practical, and emancipatory. It has to be oriented not only toward the academy but also toward living communities of faith and/or struggle. Rather than just being beholden to the elite academic study of the biblical past, it has to work for people in and outside organized religions who search for a spiritual vision of justice and love. In contrast to malestream liberation the*logies, I maintained that the emerging emancipatory paradigm of interpretation must be, first of all, critical, approaching the text with a hermeneutic of suspicion. This frame allowed me to develop the emerging fourth feminist paradigm as that of emancipatory praxis. Most importantly, I have sought to articulate this fourth emancipatory paradigm not primarily in reaction to the three hegemonic paradigms of biblical studies but in conversation with feminist, liberation the*logical, and postcolonial theories.

Just as the third paradigm, the fourth emerging paradigm places the Bible into the hands of people, but now makes explicit that biblical interpreters are not only gendered but also raced, classed, and colonialized. Whereas the first two paradigms have excluded wo/men from the authoritative interpretation of the Bible throughout the centuries, the third and fourth paradigms of biblical studies call for a critical feminist reader who is/to be able to evaluate biblical texts and interpretation. Segovia's assumption that only the third cultural paradigm has shifted attention from the text to the reader needs to be corrected. It is the feminist the*logical paradigm that first sought to shift the scholarly focus from the biblical texts to the community of interpretation.[15] It could do so because it connected with the religious-hermeneutical tradition and sharpened it by adding ideology-criticism to its repertoire, a move that called for an ethics of interpretation.

Although I have revised the nomenclature of these four paradigms over the years again and again, I still see paradigm criticism as an important method for creating an alternative ethos/space from which to transform biblical studies toward a feminist future of the biblical past. Paradigm construction has developed a typology of shifting antagonistic practices that shape and determine the discipline of biblical studies and biblical interpretation on the whole. However, I believe for fruitful change to occur, the antagonistic rhetoric of paradigm change needs to be abandoned.

Kuhn, the intellectual father of paradigm construction, was certainly correct in observing that scientific paradigms arise in competition with each other and seek to replace each other. Looking at the history of the discipline of biblical studies, one can easily chart the field of biblical studies in such competitive terms. However, in the context of the fourth emancipatory feminist paradigm, it seems more appropriate to chart paradigms as different scientific domains that correct and supplement each other. In other words, it is important to articulate paradigms not in combative but in collaborative terms. Paradigms can exist alongside each other, or they can be overlapping or remedial to each other. They can utilize each other's methodological approaches, or they can work in corrective interaction with each other.

If one conceptualizes paradigms also in political and not only in disciplinary terms, one can integrate the spheres of the professional and the "ordinary" reader by delineating a paradigm as "a public intellectual sphere" where "citizen interpreters" come together to debate and discuss the Bible in terms of their own theoretical frameworks, methodological approaches, and spiritual interests. Such public spheres—the academy, the church/synagogue, the school and the indi-

---

15. I prefer interpretation over reading since all wo/men can interpret stories and biblical texts but not all wo/men can read.

vidual—in which biblical studies are practiced are overlapping and not exclusive
of each other. In order to communicate with each other, the "citizen interpreters" need to be clear not only about their different theoretical languages, but also
about the different spiritual-ideological emphases and goals of the four paradigms of biblical studies. I contend that by articulating paradigms as different
and overlapping practices in the "public sphere" the dichotomizing tendencies
that still haunt the discipline as well as minority criticism can be overcome.

In such a political vision, the fourth emancipatory paradigm can be seen as
creating a "radical democratic critical public space" from which to interact with
and challenge the the*logical, the historical, and the cultural academic paradigms
to transform their intellectual structures of exclusion and domination. The stress
of the fourth paradigm on ideology-critique and on the analysis of power enables
it to facilitate border exchanges between the four interfacing paradigms of biblical studies.

However, I would insist that the work of the fourth paradigm must not just
be ideological-critique critical but also constructive and visionary. It must articulate biblical visions of liberation and well-being that foster religious identity
formations and spiritual discourses which transform the internalized intersecting
structures of domination. Whereas the task of the first paradigm is the exploration of biblical the*ology, the aim of the second is biblical historiography, and
that of the third is a critical reading of text in culture, the fourth paradigm has the
task not only of tracing biblical traditions of domination and emancipation but
also of asking what *they do to* those who submit to their world of vision.

In order to pursue this task, biblical studies needs to create the conditions
for equal citizenship in its own public spheres. It can do so by articulating a
theoretical platform capable of fostering critical and constructive exchanges and
learning between different approaches and groups that inhabit the diverse and
ever-shifting paradigmatic space of the fourth paradigm. The inhabitants of this
space need to pay careful attention to all the theoretical voices in their midst,
avoid dualistic over-and-against constructions, and create common ground for
the work of producing emancipatory radical democratic biblical knowledges.
Such critical feminist emancipatory work, I venture to say, is able to articulate
and create a feminist future for a biblical past that is inscribed with oppressive as
well as liberatory tendencies.

20

CULTURAL CRITICISM: EXPANDING THE SCOPE
OF BIBLICAL CRITICISM

Fernando F. Segovia

In the mid 1990s, twenty years after the first rumblings of discursive unease and the initial calls for disciplinary redirection, I undertook the task of mapping the given results of such concerns and moves regarding the conceptualization and exercise of biblical criticism by way of paradigms or umbrella models of interpretation. This was an attempt to outline and explain the critical present, to survey the lay of the land, in terms of its past trajectory. Such mapping, in retrospect, followed a twofold impulse of the times. It was a response to a particular development regarding the scope of the field: a growing emphasis, beyond the traditional focus on texts in context, on critics and readings in context. It also formed part of a corresponding general problematic and project: a call for analysis of the relation between critical production and social-cultural location.

Fifteen years later now, as other discursive rumblings and disciplinary calls have surfaced, I take up the task of mapping the envisioned results of such concerns and moves in the understanding and practice of biblical criticism by way of disciplinary parameters, interdisciplinary intersections, and interpretive directions. This is an attempt to imagine and shape a critical future, to conjure up the lay of the land, in terms of its present state of affairs. This mapping also follows a twofold impulse of the times. It is a response to a concrete development regarding the terrain of the field: expanding diversification and globalization alongside heightened emphasis on porousness and dialogue. It also constitutes part of a corresponding general problematic and project: a call for reflection on the "future of the biblical past" on a global scale.

The two mappings are thus very much related. The cartography of the future here proposed, what I characterize as cultural biblical criticism, returns to and expands upon the fourth paradigm, what I designated as "cultural studies," within the vision of the present already advanced. I believe it imperative, therefore, to begin this second mapping by revisiting the first one: outlining its essential structural components; placing it within its own critical context; and recalling its configuration of cultural studies as umbrella model. In so doing, the present exercise can be directly and profitably situated against the background of the earlier one, in light of developments in both discipline and profession since that time.

Mapping the Present of the Biblical Past

Structural Components

My initial mapping of biblical criticism was constructed on a twofold foundation of internal-discursive and external-material elements. From within, I outlined a set of four expansive theoretical-methodological frameworks, which I characterized as in competition but not as mutually exclusive. These I presented in terms of a sequential and progressive plot, whose path was classically threefold (beginning, middle, end) but ultimately ironic (end as open ended). This path was traced as follows: to begin with, a situation of stability, represented by the longstanding dominance of traditional historical criticism, with foundations in historical studies; then, around the mid 1970s, a crisis of instability, occasioned by parallel turns to literary studies and social studies, yielding literary criticism and sociocultural criticism, respectively; lastly, a resolution of the crisis by way of stable instability, signified by ideological criticism, with grounding in cultural studies. From without, I pointed to the pivotal role played in such plotting by a marked shift in the demographic matrix of criticism, given the many new faces and voices joining the ranks of the discipline for the first time ever. In this development, whose beginnings can be traced to the 1970s and which underwent rapid expansion through the 1980s, I identified various group formations. On the one hand, I underscored the influx of women scholars from the West; on the other hand, I highlighted the entry of scholars, women and men, from throughout the non-Western world as well as from among minoritized groups within the West, especially in the United States. The presence and impact of such "Others" in a field that had been totally male and Euro-American I described as central to the crisis and resolution stages of the plot.

This mapping was drawn, in self-conscious and explicit fashion, from the perspective of the fourth grand model of interpretation advanced, ideological criticism. Thus the trajectory of the field was portrayed as leading, through the various impasses and contradictions presented by the earlier paradigms, to the emergence of cultural studies—a discursive framework by then already in full force. Similarly, the ongoing changes in method and theory, even within cultural studies itself, were depicted as hastened and complexified by the changes in critical concerns and objectives brought to bear by the changes in visage and accent among practitioners—a material framework in full evidence by then, as well.

CRITICAL CONTEXT

The critical context for this mapping can be approached in terms of both disciplinary and publishing developments. In 1995, when the proposal was first set forth, biblical criticism was beginning to address, from within the framework of ideological criticism, the role of the critic in the task of interpretation, both in personal (autobiographical-psychological) and in collective (social-cultural) terms. Indeed, the proposal itself was advanced by way of respective introductions to a two-volume project whose objective it was—as its title, *Reading from This Place*, readily indicates— to examine precisely the relation between critical production and social-cultural location. This project was an ambitious one. The first part and volume dealt with this problematic in the United States (Segovia and Tolbert 1995a), bringing together scholars from both the dominant group and minoritized groups, while the second pursued it in global perspective (Segovia and Tolbert 1995b), calling upon scholars from all continents, encompassing thereby both the First World and the Third World.[1] By its venue and placement, the first mapping thus served, in part, as grounding for both project and lens: a grand-scale theoretical and methodological account of how the field had arrived at this particular discursive and material juncture in its history.[2] It was a reading of the past in order to explain the present.

The project was not, however, the first example of this type of critical inquiry. Pride of place in this regard, I would argue, belongs to an earlier volume titled *Voices from the Margin*, a reader published in 1991 and edited by R. S. Sugirthara-

---

1. This project originated as a two-part symposium at Vanderbilt University. Its division was by no means unproblematic or unchallenged, given its isolation of the critical discussion in the United States from that in the world at large. Nonetheless, it was adopted primarily in light of a phenomenon perceived as distinctive of the U.S. scene: the significant number of racial-ethnic minoritized critics at work in the field, which was thought to make such a separate discussion appropriate and even necessary.

2. The introduction to the first volume, "'And They Began to Speak in Other Tongues': Competing Modes of Discourse in Contemporary Biblical Criticism," analyzed the paradigms of historical, literary, and sociocultural criticism and introduced that of ideological criticism (Segovia 1995a). The introduction to the second volume, "Cultural Studies and Contemporary Biblical Criticism: Ideological Criticism as Mode of Discourse," addressed ideological criticism in detail (1995b).

jah. At the same time, while both projects sought to foreground the significance and ramifications of social-cultural location in criticism, they went about doing so in quite different ways.

To begin with, the roster of contributors differed significantly. The *Voices* anthology included only essays from the Third World, all of which had been previously published. This concentration its subtitle, *Biblical Interpretation in the Third World*, clearly specified. In contrast, the *Reading* collection involved studies from all quarters, from dominant and minoritized groups in the first volume, as well as from both the Third World and the First World in the second volume, all commissioned for the occasion. This the subtitles bring out: *Social Location and Biblical Interpretation in the United States* and *in Global Perspective*, respectively.

In addition, the character of the contributions proved markedly different as well. The *Voices* anthology brought together pieces from both inside and outside the academy, deliberately reaching out to popular readings of the Bible. Furthermore, it specifically selected academic readings that were, in some way, in solidarity with the people. The *Reading* collection confined itself solely to the realm of the academy. Moreover, there was no proviso regarding identification with the people on the part of the critics in question.

Further, and most importantly, the tenor of the publications also differed significantly. The *Voices* anthology was put together in geopolitically as well as ecclesially oppositional and revisionist terms. This was a project grounded in the hermeneutics of liberation, focused on issues of marginalization and oppression, and carried out in the face of the established critical practices of Western biblical studies viewed as universalizing and exclusionary. The *Reading* collection, on the other hand, was conceived in theoretically and methodologically oppositional and revisionist terms. This was a project grounded in literary theory, revolving around the topics of multiplicity of meanings and diversity of readings and undertaken in the face of received critical practices regarded as objective and impartial.

As such, the two publications are best approached as variations of the same genre. While both were certainly intent on scrutinizing the relation between location and production, they did so in different modes: *Voices from the Margin*, in terms of a theological First World-Third World divide; *Reading from This Place*, as a problematic inherent in all criticism. To put it differently, while the former represented by and large an exercise in geopolitical and ecclesial liberation—a hermeneutical program arising out of concern for the marginalized and oppressed—the latter constituted primarily an exercise in methodological and theoretical liberation—a hermeneutical program emerging out of interest in contextualization and perspective. Thus, from the point of view of the *Reading* collection, *Voices* might appear as critically much too ambiguous. Are different readings the result of different meanings uncovered in the text or of different applications of textual meaning in different contexts? In other words: Is there a conservative critical position regarding the meaning of Scripture, in which meaning is inherent in the text behind the opposition and revisionism in question? From the point of view of the *Voices* reader, *Reading* might come across as critically much too removed: What do questions of multiplicity and diversity have to do with issues of marginalization and oppression? In other words: Is there a conservative critical position regarding the figure of the critic, in which formalist questions prevail, behind the opposition and revisionism in question?

In the end, however, both publications are very much the progeny of ideological criticism. Further, the differences between the two, considerable as they are, should not be cast in binary terms. Just as there was preoccupation with matters of theory and method in *Voices from the Margin*, so too there was concern for matters of oppression and marginalization in *Reading from This Place*.

Configuring Cultural Studies

At the heart of cultural studies, I argued, lay a focus on readers—real readers—of the biblical texts. Such foregrounding and analysis of flesh-and-blood readers in criticism signified a major deviation from previous approaches to reading constructs. Historical criticism had subscribed to the ideal of the scientific reader: universal, above society and culture; and informed, objective, and disinterested. Literary and sociocultural criticisms had largely followed suit in this regard, preserving the scientific reader construct. At the same time, and hence the presence of the qualifier "largely," both models devoted increasing attention to the question of readers and reading in interpretation, although from quite different quarters. For literary criticism, such focus revealed two different directions: on the one hand, a turn to reader constructs either internal to the text or external as inferred from the text; on the other hand, approaching the problematic of multiplicity in interpretation by granting greater agency to real but abstract readers, either through different activations of multilayered meaning in the text or through different completions of textual omissions. For sociocultural criticism, such interest emerged as the result of ever greater insistence on the gulf between ancient and contemporary societies and cultures and ever greater caution regarding the pitfalls of reading-into, either through presentism or ethnocentrism. Ideological criticism punctured the ideal of the scientific reader, while also going well beyond moves toward other reading constructs in literary criticism and calling into question the sharp divide between past and present demanded by sociocultural criticism. In effect, ideological criticism problematized all real readers, including critics, as irretrievably and inescapably contextualized and perspectival—always situated (location) and engaged (agenda) in society and culture.

The ramifications of such emphasis on flesh-and-blood readers were numerous and profound. Real readers were said to stand behind all theoretical frameworks and reading strategies as well as behind all re-creations of meaning from texts and all reconstructions of contexts in or around texts. Thus, all such constructions and reconstructions, as well as their underlying models and methods, were regarded as constructs on the part of real readers—hence, similarly contextualized and perspectival. Consequently, all representations of the past were viewed as re-presentations—re-creations and re-constructions. Likewise, all approaches to the past were looked upon as concepts and tools of analysis embedded in specific discursive programs and agendas. In cultural studies, therefore, the analysis of readers and their contexts, their ways of reading, and their findings in reading, becomes as important as the analysis of texts and their contexts, insofar as both levels of analysis are seen as interrelated and interdependent, indeed mutually constitutive. Such analysis bears other important ramifications as well: attention to all sorts of readers and reading traditions; consideration of all dimensions of human identity, both in readers and in texts; and a view of interpretation as inherently and necessarily multidirectional and multilingual.

Mapping the Future of the Biblical Past

Given such a representation of the critical present in general and of cultural studies in particular, I should now like to pursue a mapping of the future in terms of cultural biblical criticism. This I shall do by way of a close exchange with a number of other proposals, coming from quite different quarters and perspectives. These have all scrutinized my proposal for a set of four critical paradigms and for cultural studies as one such grand model. The exchange contemplated is thus more along the lines of a continued conversation.

I have three mappings in mind, listed in chronological order of publication: Stephen Moore, from the point of view of postmodernist interpretation; Elisabeth Schüssler Fiorenza, from the angle of a critical feminist interpretation for liberation; and Abraham Smith, from the angle of minority and African American interpretation. Despite their differing contexts and agendas, these critics share a sustained record of reflection on biblical interpretation and, as such, approach the proposal from within their own visions and programs for the discipline—its past, present, and future. Moore points to its lack of discursive interchange, calling for greater input from cultural studies. Schüssler Fiorenza calls attention to its confinement to the realm of academic criticism, arguing for broader analysis of biblical studies as a religious-theological tradition. Smith brings out its limitation to academic criticism as cultural formation, moving toward the integration of other traditions of interpretation. All three engagements I find keenly insightful and decidedly helpful. In fact, I take such critiques as point of departure for this proposal on behalf of cultural biblical criticism.

I shall pursue the proposed mapping and corresponding exchange in three movements. To begin with, I will examine the evaluations and frameworks of these critical engagements. Then I will address the various critiques by way of critical engagement. Finally, I will draw on the major points of contention—no attention to interpretation beyond the scholarly literature; no consideration of interpretation beyond the religious-theological realm in general; and no relation of interpretation to the project of cultural studies—to advance a vision and program for cultural biblical criticism as a way of imagining and shaping a future for the biblical past.

CRITICAL RECEPTION: EXPOSITION

I begin by unpacking the representations and evaluations of the proposal advanced by the various mappings. First, I lay out their respective underlying visions and programs; then, I place the specific judgment rendered on the proposal within this overall background and describe its positive and negative elements, as the case may be. In so doing, I set the stage for the critical engagement to follow. The result is a keen sense of the spectrum regarding the state of the field, its problematic, and its future.

Disciplinary Limitations: Moore

The first engagement, by Stephen Moore, appeared three years after *Voices from the Margin* and *Reading from This Place* in a volume of *Semeia* on approaching the Bible through the lens of cultural studies, for which he served as editor (Moore 1998a). In his own contribution to the project, a programmatic introduction titled "Between Birmingham and Jerusalem: Cultural Studies and Biblical Studies," Moore examines the existing relation between the two areas of study (1998b).[3] This he does in sequential fashion. First, he surveys the established tradition of cultural studies, tracing its path to the present—leading figures, salient developments, characteristic features. Here he finds the near-total lack of attention to biblical matters striking, especially given the ever-expanding range of such studies. Then he turns to the recent phenomenon of cultural biblical criticism,

---

3. This study, it should be noted, was a revised version of an earlier piece that he co-authored with J. Cheryl Exum, "Biblical Studies/Cultural Studies," which served as introduction to an homonymous volume edited by both (Exum and Moore 1998b), in itself the outcome of a colloquium on this interdisciplinary intersection held at the University of Sheffield.

outlining its main variations—leading emphases, major proponents, key developments. Here he finds the almost-complete lack of attention to cultural discourse
noteworthy, especially in light of its forty-year history by then.

Moore's overview is not just descriptive but also trailblazing. His goal is to
surface and address these respective lacunae in order to forge ahead. It is, therefore, a call for a properly informed intersection of the two fields of study. It is a
call formulated from the side of biblical criticism. His emphasis is not so much
on the necessary integration of the Bible and its reading in cultural discourse, for
there is no pointed critique or corresponding call for action along these lines.
Such a need is acknowledged, verbalized in terms of sheer lack of attention, but
remains undeveloped. The emphasis lies, rather, on imperative dialogue with cultural studies on the part of biblical criticism. Here the critique is pointed, and
the call for action explicit. It is a call for "biblical cultural studies" (18)—one that
Moore himself puts into action through his involvement in the two cultural/
biblical volumes of 1998. Such criticism, moreover, Moore views as a "crucial
component" of "postmodern biblical criticism"—indeed, a most promising and
pressing one, insofar as it sheds light on the many uses of the Bible in the contemporary world, many quite "alien and eerie," bringing about thereby a "shock of the
familiar" (23). What the other components of postmodern criticism are and how
cultural criticism relates to them are, however, not addressed.

Within this overview, my proposal is accorded a mixed evaluation. It is
listed as one of three major variations, identified as the first actually to invoke
the designation of "cultural studies" as such, and associated with the ideological dimension of the cultural studies movement. It is, however, like the others,
described as functionally divorced from—"floating free" though "not unaware"
of (21)— the discourse of cultural studies and thus an "outsized" application
thereof, grounded rather in discussions about the problematic of meaning and
reading in criticism. To grasp the import of this critique and its consequences for
the present proposal, a fuller sense of Moore's vision and program is imperative.

In charting the trajectory of cultural studies from the 1950s through the
1990s, Moore constructs a historical narrative involving three stages: (1) gestation, a "myth of origins" (late 1950s through 1968); (2) glory, a "heroic age" or
"Golden Years" (1968–1979); and (3) incorporation, "Cultural Studies Inc." (1980s
and 1990s). Through the formative period, encompassing the first two phases,
the process is exclusively British in nature and has as pivot a research venue at the
University of Birmingham: the Centre for Contemporary Cultural Studies, first
established in 1964 as an annex of the English department and then transformed
in 1987, through union with the sociology department, into the Department of
Cultural Studies. Three characteristics are said to mark the movement as a whole:
a focus on ideology; the study of contemporary culture, popular rather than high;

and an anti-disciplinary impulse, leading to work across fields and the ideal of the engaged intellectual.

A closer look at the various stages proves helpful in dating such features. With the first stage comes a novel approach to the concept and study of culture: attention to the working classes and the popular media (Richard Hoggart) and expansion of the idea of culture as a way of life, with industrial societies in mind (Raymond Williams). During this stage, the Centre is established in 1964 by Hoggart, who becomes its first Director, to pursue cultural studies along these lines. In the second stage an ideological move takes place: a turn to marxist analysis of culture, first along the lines of Louis Althusser (institutional systems) and later in dialogue with a variety of other marxist thinkers. At this time, the figure of Stuart Hall becomes crucial. Initially appointed as Deputy Director in 1964, Hall becomes Acting Director from 1968 through 1972 and then Director through 1979. During this stage, two other ideological angles have an impact on the Centre: feminism and race. With the third stage come diversification, internationalization, and institutionalization: ideological expansion into such areas as sexuality, postcolonialism, and postmodernism; geographical expansion beyond Britain; and academic expansion in every respect. In 1987, in response to economic pressures, the Centre is turned into a university department. The process is clear: the concern with contemporary popular culture remains evident throughout; ideological analysis enters the scene with the second stage, becoming ever more expansive thereafter; and work across disciplines and objects of study increase in the second stage, becoming thereafter ever more comprehensive, as well.

In the light of such reach and breadth, Moore's findings, as he writes in the mid 1990s, are indeed striking: minimal work on the use and interpretation of the Bible. In surveying biblical studies, he does uncover various lines of development that reveal points of contact with the distinctive features of cultural studies: a growing body of work on the representation of the Bible in the arts, visual and literary; my deployment of the term as a synonym for ideological criticism; and a variety of works having to do with the Bible in the contemporary world. However, Moore's findings in this regard are noteworthy: minimal interaction with the discourse of cultural studies. In effect, all variations fall way short of his call for properly informed interchange.

Regarding my proposal, three observations are made. First, I had not pursued the task of "'translating' extra-biblical cultural studies into a biblical studies idiom" (21), relying instead on the history of biblical criticism as theoretical framework for my deployment of the term. Second, toward this end, I had used the problematic of reading in biblical criticism as angle of vision, taking it to "its logical conclusion" through my emphasis on the constructive role of real readers, situated and pespectival, in interpretation. Lastly, as a result, I had equated cultural studies with ideological criticism, thus matching to a degree the ideological impulse of cultural studies. Summing up, while aware of cultural discourse, I had not engaged in critical interchange. The other variations, while not as thoroughly dissected, fared no better in the end. Moore's judgment was unambiguous: these were all worthwhile lines of development for his vision of "biblical cultural studies," but they fell way short of the informed interaction called for by his vision and program. At the same time, the pursuit of the Bible as a cultural icon in the contemporary world emerged as the "real promise of cultural studies for biblical studies" (23).

Theoretical-Institutional Limitations: Schüssler Fiorenza

A year later, in 1999, Schüssler Fiorenza's engagement appeared in a collection of essays titled *Rhetoric and Ethic: The Politics of Biblical Studies*. The aim of the volume was to elaborate, both theoretically and practically, a new way of doing biblical studies. Toward this end, most specifically in the study on "Changing the Paradigms: The Ethos of Biblical Studies," Schüssler Fiorenza invoked the concept of paradigm and traced the path of biblical studies in terms of "paradigm criticism" (37), identifying a number of paradigms and characterizing the new approach envisioned as rhetorical-emancipatory.[4] This move was accompanied by a definition of the notion of paradigm, the identification of the major paradigms at work in the history of biblical studies, and a rationale for the proposed shift toward one grounded in rhetoric-ethics-politics as the future of interpretation.

Within this project, my proposal received a mixed reaction. On the one hand, it was found to be on point in two regards: first, the process of analysis by way of paradigms was endorsed; and second, the ideological thrust of the paradigm of cultural studies was found to be in agreement with her proposed rhetorical-emancipatory shift. On the other hand, my proposal was found wanting. The set of paradigms outlined was deemed as too restrictive, amounting to variations of only one dimension of the religio-theological interpretation of the biblical texts. To understand this evaluation and its ramifications for the present proposal, it is necessary to expand on Schüssler Fiorenza's vision and project.

With regard to definition, she notes, invoking the work of Thomas Kuhn as guiding theoretical framework (Kuhn 1962), a paradigm involves a "common ethos," marking and binding a "community of scholars" through a network of

---

4. Although other designations were regarded as equally applicable—rhetorical-ethical; rhetorical-political; feminist-postcolonial emancipatory—this one was chosen because of its explicit reference to the method and goal of the new approach.

"institutions and systems of knowledge" (38). Consequently, a change in paradigm, in the common ethos among scholars in place, requires a change in the institutional structures that underlie the production of epistemic systems. Further, paradigms need not exclude one another but can exist beside and offer correction to one another. With respect to identification, she posits four in all: doctrinal-fundamentalist, scientific-historical, hermeneutic-(post)modern, and rhetorical-emancipatory. Their mutual relation is laid out chronologically. Writ large, the sequence proceeds as follows: At first, from Christian antiquity through the Enlightenment, the doctrinal-fundamentalist paradigm functioned as the norm; it also remains vibrant today, especially in the public realm. Then, with the Enlightenment and through most of the twentieth century, this first paradigm was displaced by the scientific-historical, which became the center in the academy. Lastly, with the advent of postmodernity and during the last quarter of the twentieth century, this second paradigm was called into question by two others, the hermeneutic-postmodern and the rhetorical-emancipatory, but without success in decentering it. The overall relation is, therefore, one of conflict, and indeed one in which the various paradigms in question are described as mutually exclusive. With regard to rationale, she presents the rhetorical-emancipatory as the path to follow for the future on the basis of the context and task of criticism: fostering a "public, radical democratic ethos" in the face of geopolitical colonialism and worldwide injustice (33).

Further amplification of the sequence is in order. A twofold point of departure for contemporary developments is evident. To begin with, the ethos of the doctrinal-fundamentalist paradigm involves a view of the biblical texts as divinely revealed, hence sacred Scripture, and as conveying unitary meaning "beyond ideology and particularity" (40). In its contemporary version, as espoused by the multiple ranks of "neoconservative Christians," the paradigm insists on a literal reading of the Scriptures, presented as the sole Christian way of interpretation (39). Its institutional foundation is placed among "fundamentalist movements" with a vision of a biblical religion (39). In the face of domination and injustice, this ethos adopts a twofold position: it opts for a strategy of spiritualization, either directing the gaze toward an otherworldly realm of God or claiming a this-worldly realm of righteousness; and it offers certainty through the demarcation of clear doctrines, group boundaries, and rigid identities. Subsequently, in reaction to dogmatic and ecclesial control of interpretation, the scientific-positivist paradigm emerges in the nineteenth century. Its ethos calls for a view of the biblical texts as historically distant and as bearing a single meaning. The paradigm espouses an objective method of retrieval through contextualization. Its institutional location lies in the Eurocentric world of the academy and the discipline of scientific historiography. Before domination and injustice, this ethos opts for rejection of all religious-theological or social-cultural engagement and offers the promise of historical certitude.

Both foundational paradigms, Schüssler Fiorenza argues, conceal their theological and ideological interests through their respective claims. In reaction, two paradigms surface in the late twentieth century. The first of these is the (post) modern-hermeneutical (or -cultural). Its ethos involves a view of the biblical texts as perspectival constructions of "symbolic universes" and as multidimensional in meaning (43). The paradigm stresses the linguistic character of all interpretation as well as the pluralism of approaches, leading to a vision of competing interpretations of texts. Its institutional foundation is the academy and postmodern discursive frameworks in particular. In the face of domination and injustice, this ethos remains ideologically and theologically removed, and thus unable to address the situation of struggle behind texts and interpretations. The second, the rhetorical-emancipatory, moves to fill this critical lacuna. Its ethos demands a view of the biblical texts as rhetorical constructions forged in specific historical and cultural contexts, thus as ethical and political constructions as well, and as deriving meaning from their respective rhetorical aims and strategies as mobilized in given sociocultural contexts. The paradigm foregrounds the rhetorical dimension of all interpretations, their construction as ethical and political projects in context, calling, therefore, for analysis of aims and strategies as well as ethics and politics. Its institutional placement is characterized as still in the making although, as rhetorical-ethical-political, it must attend to the public sphere as a whole. Faced with domination and injustice, this ethos is openly committed to liberation, over all structures of domination and with the ideal of well-being for all.

In sharp contrast to the other paradigms, Schüssler Fiorenza advances a view of the biblical critic as a "public ... intellectual" (44): first and foremost, seeking transformation through liberation and justice; second, engaging texts and interpretations in a rhetorical key, bringing out and passing judgment on their emancipatory or oppressive stances and ramifications; third, doing so in the public realm and thus dealing with biblical interpretation of all sorts. For such a critic, biblical texts and interpretations constitute a "site of struggle," for which a "radical democratic imperative" is crucial (45–46).

In the light of this vision and project, my proposal is found wanting in three respects. First, the paradigms in question have been drawn in terms of "method." Such configuration confines itself to the readings of the academy and passes over the readings of religious communities, whose goal lies primarily in "spiritual nourishment and motivation" (38). Indeed, from both a feminist and a postcolonial perspective, such self-confinement exposes itself to critique, given its removal from social-political movements for change. Second, while paradigms classified by method do interact with one another, paradigms classified by theory ultimately cannot—it is impossible to mix "religious dogmaticism, historical positivism, cultural relativism, and emancipatory ... commitment" (38). Finally, paradigms of method, unlike paradigms of theory, fail to take into consideration institutional formations; the accompanying "languages and cultures" of paradigms are bypassed (39).

Cultural Formations Limitations: Smith

Ten years later, in 2009, Smith's engagement appeared as part of an edited collection of essays on the Gospel of Mark from the point of view of method and theory (Anderson and Moore 2009). The volume is designed to serve as a multi-lens introduction to Mark through a variety of prominent critical approaches: narrative; reader response; deconstruction; feminism; social studies; postcolonial. Smith's contribution, which bears the subtitle of "Making Mark," was a reading of the gospel from the perspective of cultural studies (Smith 2009). Following standard procedure in such studies with an overriding focus on method and theory, Smith provides a description of the approach in general—what cultural studies implies and entails (origins and development, dynamics and mechanics), followed by an application to the text in question—Mark, in this case, both generally (the gospel as a whole) and concretely (Mark 15:1–15, the unit involving the death of the Baptist).

A brief introduction situates the advent and impact of cultural studies in biblical criticism and the place of his own project therein. For Smith, cultural studies marks a key turn in biblical studies, signified by multiplicity of readers and perspectives—inclusion of readings of all sorts, as well as a view of all readings as constructed and ideological. Mark emerges as a site involving the conjunction of many other sites or, as he puts it, a "website with links to other sites" (183). The result is a "making of Mark" in many contexts and from many angles (183).

Within this framework, my proposal is cited approvingly on three counts: (1) its analysis of criticism in three stages, with cultural studies as the final stage, characterized by growing attention to real readers; (2) its conception of cultural studies as crisscrossed by diversity of critics and methods; and (3) its portrayal of all such methods and critics as ideological in character. At the same time, a move beyond my proposal is evident, though implicit, through a view of cultural studies as encompassing not only the realm of biblical scholarship but also any number of other such realms of interpretation. Such a move does convey a critique. To grasp this evaluation and its repercussions for the present proposal, a keener sense of Smith's vision and program for biblical criticism is in order.

Cultural studies, he argues, calls for a broadly defined analysis of culture, on both scores—that of analysis and that of culture. On the one hand, a most expansive concept of culture is required: encompassing all dimensions, central or marginalized; extending to all formations, across time and space; and including practices and products of all sorts. On the other hand, an equally expansive model of analysis is also demanded: approaching practices and products not as givens but as constructs, and, toward this end, having recourse to a variety of methods. Given this call, a move beyond academic criticism is imperative: reaching out beyond the interpretive center, the world of professional scholars, to marginalized readers; doing so in all formations, across historical periods and spatial contexts; and taking into consideration practices as well as products, in all directions. Such a move embodies what Smith identifies as the key element in cultural studies, namely, the "democratization" of culture (182). For biblical criticism, therefore, the adoption of cultural studies entails the exploration of cultural products and practices "from ancient times to the present" (186). The goal behind such exploration is "to pay close attention to the 'other'" at all times (207), including a radical sense of the critic's own otherness within such diversity.

Smith's analysis of Mark serves as an example of such exploration, as he examines the fate of the gospel in a variety of cultural formations, foregrounding throughout the ideological import of the practices and products in question. On the one hand, he takes up the reception of Mark, showing its making at work in various practices and products: the transmission of the text and the significance of textual variations, with particular attention to the influence of dogmatic issues of contention; the translation of the text and the importance of word choice in vernacular renderings, with reference to the presence of ecclesial conflicts in William Tyndale's translation into English; the framework of interpretation, by way of established conventions both in professional societies and in scholarly literature; and the representation of the text in visual art, with artistic renderings of the Harlem Renaissance in mind. On the other hand, he addresses the construction of the text, advancing a postcolonial interpretation of its making in context: a text that, while resisting the imperial framework of Rome, reproduces this framework in its own representation of Jesus' identity and role.

In the light of such a vision and program, my proposal regarding grand models of interpretation in biblical criticism cannot but come across as too circumscribed. In this he would stand in agreement with Schüssler Fiorenza. The proposal also comes across, given the lack of overt critique, as readily expandable, through a continuing multiplication of readers and perspectives via cultural practices and products. In this he proceeds in a different direction than Schüssler Fiorenza, taking into consideration the religious-theological tradition of interpretation certainly, as the incorporation of textual criticism and vernacular translations makes clear, but also integrating any number of other such traditions, cultural formations, such as the visual arts. From the point of view of the democratization of culture, Smith would see my proposal as favoring the interpretive center but also as not ruling out in principle marginalized practices and products.

CRITICAL RECEPTION: DIALOGICAL ENCOUNTER

Having outlined these pointed representations and evaluations of my proposal for a cultural studies model, I proceed to engage them in critical dialogue. I do so in two steps: first, by responding to the critique tendered as a whole; then, by high-lighting the major limitation noted and granted, and hence the main element in need of reconsideration and reformulation. In so doing, I lay out the foundations of a vision and program of my own, properly calibrated within the spectrum of proposals in place. The result is a clear need for expansion on several fronts.

Disciplinary Expansion: Engaging Moore

Moore's assessment of the proposal I find mostly on target. To begin with, I did use as working framework the history of biblical criticism. It was my aim to chart its path and to do so *from within*, showing how internal and external pressures, discursive and material alike, combined to bring about the proposed succession of interpretive models, up to and including what I called "cultural stud-ies." Further, in pursuing this aim, I did deploy as an angle of inquiry—among others—that of reading strategy. My purpose was to expose the identity and role of the critic assumed by the various models: from "scientific" reader, informed and universal, to "real" reader, contextual and perspectival. This latter construct I des-ignated as central to "cultural studies." Lastly, in line with such identification, I did harp on all interpretation as construction on the part of such readers. My aim was to highlight the need for ideological analysis of all readers and readings, with a view of such analysis as broad-based, encompassing any number of differential constructions and relations of power in society and culture.

At the same time, as the adverb "mostly" intimates above, Moore's assess-ment does contain a couple of comments with which I would not agree. For example, he describes my bibliographical reference to cultural studies as seem-ingly an "afterthought" (21). Actually, my invocation of the term "cultural" was the result of interchange with such work, though this did not find its way into the study. My stress on construction and ideology in interpretation certainly owed much to this tradition. Similarly, Moore argues that, for me, the model was sig-nified by the emergence of critics from the Third World and among minority scholars in the First World. To be sure, I did argue that the advent of these Others had radically changed the character of the field, especially given their concern with real readers. Such stress on internationalization I also owe to the tradition. Actually, however, my use of the term "cultural" was grounded on the contextuality and partiality of all critics, regardless of geopolitical or racial-ethnic origin. It was this insistence on construction and ideology that accounted for my use of the term as a synonym for ideological criticism.

In sum, I did not advance the cultural studies model out of critical engagement with the tradition of cultural studies. Given the context, such interaction would have been thoroughly out of place. There is no question, certainly, that such a critical vision of the confluence of the two fields in general, and of any proposed interdisciplinary focalization in particular, is indispensable. This is especially true in a field of studies that is, as Moore has shown, as broad and ever-broadening as cultural studies. To my mind, Moore is pointing in this direction but not yet there. No reason is given, for example, for the decided tilt toward analysis of the Bible as "cultural icon" in the contemporary world, relegating the other dimensions of ideology, interdisciplinary exploration, and critical mission.

To conclude, the equation of cultural studies and ideological criticism is not one that I would advance today. I would now refer to the fourth grand model of interpretation as ideological criticism. All such grand models apply solely to criticism and its history. For biblical criticism to be characterized as "cultural," consequently, an additional component is needed.

Theoretical-Institutional Expansion: Engaging Schüssler Fiorenza

Schüssler Fiorenza's assessment of the proposal I find on the whole, but not altogether, to the point. First, in advancing the various paradigms of interpretation, I did work with the history of criticism as frame of reference, and thus within the ambit of the academy. My purpose was to show how fundamental and long-held tenets of academic criticism, largely operative in three of the paradigms in question, had come undone, both from within and from without, by the advent of "cultural studies," understood as ideological criticism. I sought to expose, therefore, how radically the field had changed, in theory and in practice. Second, in approaching the spectrum of paradigms, I did argue that, while such models were in competition with one another in the field, they were not mutually exclusive and that, in effect, "cultural studies" called for critical dialogue in all directions. I sought to present the boundaries of such models not as rigid and exclusivist in every respect but rather as porous and relational in many respects. Finally, in unpacking each paradigm, I did not bring out the institutional foundation behind them, the context of the academy, its languages and cultures, nor did I address the question of ethos in light of domination and injustice. My purpose was to surface other principles of interpretation in comparative fashion: epistemic, theological, pedagogical.

Yet, as suggested above by the phrase "but not altogether so," I do not find myself in agreement with a number of comments. I do not, for instance, find it quite accurate to say that the proposed grand models were constructed in terms of method rather than theory. Each paradigm I presented as encompassing a broad variety of methods, all of which could be brought together on the basis of an overall theoretical framework, as delineated by a set of fundamental principles. In addition, I also do not quite agree with the view that such paradigms, qua academic, can readily interact with one another. Despite my call for critical dialogue throughout, emerging out of "cultural studies," I did describe such paradigms as complex and conflicted, so that interaction across them can prove quite difficult, even between approaches within a single paradigm. Finally, I do not think it quite accurate to say self-restriction to the realm of the academy removed me from social movements for change. In the development toward "cultural studies," which I characterized as one of decolonization, I foregrounded the impact that a radically changing demographic portrait among critics had signified for the field, through the infusion of new faces and voices, all products and conveyors of social movements—women, non-Western, and minority scholars. With them, the causes and concerns of such movements entered the academy and the field and changed them.

In sum, in advancing the fourfold set of paradigms for biblical interpretation, I confined myself to the world of the academy, leaving out of consideration approaches to and readings of the Bible operative in the world of religious communities. Given the context, including them would have been quite out of place. Without doubt, careful attention to religious and theological readings of the Bible in the Christian community, as well as to the religious and theological dimensions of all readings of the biblical texts, is indispensable. In this regard Schüssler Fiorenza points the way by identifying four such paradigms in the history of interpretation: from antiquity; through the Enlightenment and modernity; to the contemporary era signified by the turn of the twentieth century. This way must be pursued, expanded both in terms of traditions and communities.

To conclude, the given restriction in scope of biblical criticism, actually a working confinement rather than a formal one, to the world of scholarship is not one that I would continue today. I would now include the world of religious-theological interpretation as part and parcel of the task of criticism. For biblical criticism to undertake such a task, therefore, an additional layer of meaning is needed for its proposed characterization as cultural.

Cultural Formations Expansion: Engaging Smith

Smith's assessment of the proposal, both explicit and implicit, is very much on target. I did focus exclusively on biblical interpretation as the learned criticism of the academy, its major theoretical frameworks and their corresponding panoplies of methodological approaches at work. I also did place such discursive developments within the framework of the academic world as a whole, yielding

a view of criticism as a tradition of cultural production alongside other traditions, influenced by their trajectories and by the times, as well. In so doing, I
did concentrate on the center rather than on the peripheries, examining biblical interpretation as carried out by only the few who have the rigorous and
sophisticated training, as well as the social and cultural privileges, that such
interpretation presupposes. At the same time, I did leave the door wide open in
principle for expansion, since I foregrounded the significance of real readers in
all interpretation, situated and perspectival, and for analysis of all texts, all readings of texts, and all readers in terms of social-cultural location and ideological
stance within such locations.

It is worth pointing out, moreover, that, in addressing the academy, the
center of the interpretation, I actually did so with the peripheries in mind. It
was my purpose to show how, through the phenomenon of cultural studies, the
center, its disciplining tenets, and controls, had been severely impacted by the
arrival of faces and voices from a variety of marginalized positions, bringing with
them novel and pressing concerns from such locations and agendas. This impact
was not only in terms of numbers and problematics, but also in terms of reconceptualization and reformulation of the center as center, whereby other lines of
research could be pursued on secure theoretical and methodological grounds.

In sum, in advancing cultural studies as a paradigm within the unfolding
path and present repertoire of biblical interpretation, I limited myself to the world
of criticism, leaving out of consideration approaches to and readings of the Bible
operative in other worlds of interpretation. Given the context, such incorporation
would have been entirely out of place. To be sure, attention to the reading of the
Bible outside the context of scholarship is a must. For such an enterprise, Smith
points the way in a firm direction.

To conclude, the given restriction in scope of biblical criticism, again more
of a confinement in practice than in principle, to the world of the academy is
not one that I would preserve today. I would now include the whole realm of
interpretation as part and parcel of the task of criticism. For biblical criticism to
undertake such a task, an additional layer of meaning is needed for its proposed
characterization as cultural.

CULTURAL BIBLICAL CRITICISM:
A FUTURE FOR THE BIBLICAL PAST

With the foundations for a vision and program of my own duly outlined, I
conclude by unpacking the various elements in question toward a full-fledged
proposal. In so doing, I proceed logically rather than chronologically, moving

from the more focused to the more panoramic limitation noted and expansion entertained. The result amounts to a fifth paradigm or grand model of interpretation, embodying a radical re-visioning of the task of criticism itself. In effect, the proposal entails a view of biblical interpretation in terms of major traditions of reading, each presupposing a material matrix of its own and constituting a cultural production of its own. Within the proposal, therefore, academic-scholarly criticism represents one such tradition of reading among others. At the same time, however, the proposal imposes a weighty demand on this tradition: a call to amplify its object of analysis by bringing under its angle of vision not only its own path as a tradition of reading but also all other traditions of reading. Needless to say, the ramifications of such a turn and its corresponding demand for criticism are enormous. Indeed, the proposal moves way beyond attention to paradigms of interpretation within the academic-scholarly tradition by multiplying the "texts" in question. As a result, it can be properly designated as a different paradigm or grand model of interpretation. In what follows, I trace this expansion in terms of reading traditions step by step, following the preceding critical engagement with other mappings.

INTEGRATING RELIGIOUS-THEOLOGICAL TRADITIONS OF READING

In response to the critique of Schüssler Fiorenza, I have already stated that I would no longer subscribe to a confinement of biblical criticism to analysis of the academic-scholarly tradition of reading. Such a decision, while certainly of fundamental importance for the conception and practice of the discipline, is, when taken in context, not as novel a move as it would at first appear. Its roots can be readily traced to the initial proposal itself.

Such a restriction in scope was not adopted as a matter of principle. It was not the result of a formal, theorized delimitation regarding the proper object of criticism. There was no explicit or reasoned commitment to the traditional conception of this object: the texts and contexts of antiquity plus the history of their interpretation in the academy insofar as such interpretation sought to establish antiquity—to recreate the meaning of such texts and to reconstruct the nature of such contexts. The restriction was taken over, rather, as a point of strategy. It was an established, working demarcation used with a specific purpose in mind, namely, to explain how the mode of criticism toward its traditional object of inquiry had changed, swiftly and profoundly, in the recent history of interpretation and how such a change had brought about a corresponding development in its received configuration. The result, I argued, was the inclusion of other texts and contexts in their own right, alongside those of antiquity itself: the academic readings of modernity and postmodernity as exercises in the representation of antiquity, as re-*constructions* of texts and re-*creations* of contexts, plus the readers behind such representations. As such, I had opened the door *de facto* for an extension in scope within the same tradition of reading. At the same time, I had also left the door wide open for a *de iure* extension to other traditions of reading, insofar as they too constituted exercises in re-presenting antiquity.

In the light of this response to Schüssler Fiorenza, I have further ventured, in reflecting upon a vision and program for the future, that biblical criticism should encompass the analysis of other reading traditions, beyond the academic-scholarly one, in the world of religious-theological interpretation. This proposal on my part thus represents a further and highly significant extension in the scope of the discipline, but one that follows deliberately and logically upon earlier foundations.

In such a move, terms like "confinement" and "extension" are to be emphasized. The question is not one of leaving behind but of going beyond the traditional parameters of biblical criticism. In fact, I would still hold that close attention to the academic-scholarly tradition of reading should remain at the forefront of criticism, both in terms of looking back or historical re-reading and looking around or contemporary re-viewing. To my mind, what takes place in the discursive framework of scholarship, within the material matrix of the academy, is extremely important, given its power and its reach, and should continue to be foregrounded. This is, after all, the context in which—for better and/or for worse—the task of criticism is carried out, and thus the context in which critics conceptualize and formulate such a task. As such, attention to historical trajectories and grand models of interpretation, to the spectrum of theoretical frameworks and critical approaches within such models or paradigms, and to the relations between these formations and others areas of studies in the academy, remains a fundamental mission of criticism. Indeed, it could be readily argued in this regard that such attention is more pressing now than ever, given the far-reaching and broad-ranging discursive changes brought upon scholarly interpretation by similarly far-reaching and broad-ranging material changes taking place in the academic matrix—and vice-versa, in ongoing dialogical fashion.

Within this tradition, I would still uphold the cartographic validity and heuristic fruitfulness of approaching its trajectory in terms of four major paradigms of interpretation, each quite comprehensive and complex. At the same time, much work remains to be done throughout. To begin with, close analysis of modern and postmodern interpreters and interpretations has barely begun. Similarly, analysis into and from the angle of the various formations of ideological criticism, both those long-established and those of more recent vintage (health-disability), stands in need of greater development and sophistication. Further, analysis in terms of intersectionality, bringing together at once all formations and relations of differential power in culture and society, finds itself at a stage of gestation.

To be sure, the focus of such critical work would remain on what has always been a rather limited tradition of interpretation in terms of both venue and audience. On the one hand, this is work from the academy, on the academy, and to the academy. Its venue is the rarefied world of scholarship. On the other hand, this is work produced, distributed among, and consumed by a small number of individuals. Its audience is quite reduced. The time and expertise required for critical production and consumption prove forbidding for all but a few specialists and students. Nonetheless, given its home in scholarship and the academy, its formations and relations in universities across the world, such work remains sharply influential and consequential.

At the same time, I would now argue for the expansion of biblical criticism to other realms of religious-theological interpretation. Such a project would call for similar analysis of how biblical texts and contexts are invoked and deployed by other reading traditions within the religious-theological realm. Here I have in mind such other traditions of reading as the following:

- the academic-theological: the appeal to and use of the Bible in other disciplines of Christian studies—historical studies, theological studies, ethical studies, and practical studies.
- the ecclesial-normative: the appeal to and use of the Bible in the life of the church as institution—doctrinal statements, institutional stipulations, liturgical applications, and spiritual practices.
- the ecclesial-relational: the appeal to and use of the Bible in the mission of the church toward the world—social-cultural projections, missionary enterprises, inter-religious dialogue, social-cultural critique.
- the popular-devotional: the appeal to and use of the Bible in the daily lives of individuals and communities, outside or beside official institutional usage—group readings, communitarian appropriations, and personal practices.

Such analysis would move biblical criticism beyond its traditional object, expanded within criticism itself, to a broad variety of other religious-theological contexts: the academy, the institutional church, the people at large.

Such a vision and program for the future would affirm, in ringing fashion, Schüssler Fiorenza's call for a focus on religious communities. It would also expand and complicate this call beyond its view of four paradigms of interpretation: doctrinal-fundamentalist (church as foundation); scientific-positivist (academy as foundation); (post)modern-hermeneutical (academy as foundation); and rhetorical-emancipatory (foundation in process). The analytical focus would be on other traditions of reading the Bible within the overall world of religious-theological interpretation—academic, ecclesial, or popular—and on the whole range of variations within such traditions. The mode of analysis would be both formalist, attentive to the mechanics and dynamics of interpretation, and ideological in character, attentive to social-cultural location and agenda. For such work, I would argue, the biblical critic is particularly well-suited, given extensive training in theory and method—provided, of course, that such training is properly expansive.

A final point is worth raising here: the implicit categorization of biblical criticism as a particular tradition of reading within the religious-theological spectrum of interpretation. So does Schüssler Fiorenza pursue it, and so have I done as well in my own response to her vision-program for the future. We have both approached it, in our different ways, as a constitutive discipline of Christian studies. Not everyone would, and not everyone does. It has been argued that biblical criticism could be pursued not only in a non-theological vein—a position that could actually be advanced as well from within Christian studies from the perspective of scientific analysis, but also outside of the framework of Christian studies and within the framework of the human sciences or the liberal arts as one field of study among others or as a subset of another such field, like classical studies or comparative religions—a stance that could be readily taken from a position of liberal humanism.

Were one to follow this path, two comments would be in order. On the one hand, both approaches presuppose theological decisions in their own right, the claim that religious-theological formations and relations can be surmounted through scientific methodology and the embedding of biblical criticism in a non-theological discursive framework. Both claim embedding would be open to and demand critical analysis. On the other hand, one could still argue that the use of biblical texts and contexts in the various disciplines of Christian studies is worth studying as part of their reception history and would constitute a valid extension of scope for a non-theological and humanist approach.

INTEGRATING SOCIAL-CULTURAL TRADITIONS OF READING

In addressing the implicit critique signaled by Smith, I have already affirmed that I would no longer restrict myself to academic-scholarly criticism and thus to what he characterizes, within a dialectic of center-margins, as the center of biblical interpretation. The description of this tradition as central is one that I find to the point. It is certainly a world highly privileged by elite education, with all the ramifications that such training and expertise bring in society and culture. It is thus a world marked by power formations and relations involving set criteria of professional expertise, reading, and evaluation and leading to a view of other ways of reading as inferior and peripheral. As decisive as this decision of mine proves for the conception and exercise of the discipline, it is, when taken in context, not as radical as it would seem at first sight. Its roots may be found already in the initial proposal.

To begin with, in adopting such a delimited focus, my aim was, in part, to show how the irruption of a number of peripheral Others had brought about a de-centering of learned criticism, materially as well as discursively. In so doing, I had expanded the scope of the discipline to the margins, although only insofar as the margins had joined and were active within the academic center. Similarly, in deploying such a demarcated focus, I espoused a key twofold development in criticism: the constructed and pointed character of all readings and the role of real readers, contextualized and perspectival, in such constructions. Thereby I had allowed in principle for a twofold expansion in scope: analytical, inclusive of approaches of all sorts, academic and otherwise; and cultural, inclusive of flesh-and-blood readers of all types.

In keeping with this reaction to Smith, I have also argued, in contemplating a vision and program for the future, that biblical criticism should incorporate the analysis of reading traditions across the whole range of social and cultural interpretation, thus beyond not only the academic-scholarly tradition as such but also the realm of religious-theological interpretation in general. The present proposal represents, therefore, yet a further, and even more significant, expansion in the object of inquiry for the discipline, but one that also builds intentionally and logically upon earlier foundations.

In such a move, terms like "restriction" and "extension" should be emphasized. The question is of amplifying rather than downplaying the broadened parameters signified by the integration of religious-theological interpretation as a whole in biblical criticism. Indeed, I would argue that sustained scrutiny of this tradition of reading in general should remain paramount, both in terms of past re-reading and present re-viewing. What transpires at the discursive level of the theological, broadly understood, within a variety of religious matrices (academy, church, people) is crucial. This is a tradition of reading in which the biblical texts and contexts have figured prominently, given their acceptance—howsoever understood and expressed—as a foundation for Christian beliefs and practices. Consequently, attention to the role of the Bible across the constitutive disciplines of Christian studies, throughout all institutional channels of the churches, and across the realm of popular appropriation, must remain a driving aspect of the mission of criticism. This is especially the case insofar as this is a tradition of reading that remains thoroughly under-analyzed, regardless of level. The work to be done in this regard is enormous.

Nevertheless, I would press for expansion of biblical criticism to the entire spectrum of social and cultural interpretation. This project would entail analysis of the way in which biblical texts and contexts are invoked and deployed by reading traditions throughout society and culture. Such traditions of reading could be summarized as follows:

- the cultural-discursive: the appeal to and use of the Bible across the whole of cultural production—e.g., the realm of the arts, literary and visual and musical; and the realm of the academy, the whole range of field of studies other than Christian studies.

- the social-material: the appeal to and use of the Bible across the spectrum of material matrices—e.g., economic, political and geopolitical, military systems.

Such a vision and program for the future unreservedly endorses Smith's call for a focus on biblical interpretation traditionally viewed as peripheral by the center of academic criticism. They would multiply in multiple directions the foray taken by Smith into pictorial representation by African American artists of the Harlem Renaissance. The mode of analysis would again involve a formalist dimension, attentive to the dynamics and mechanics of interpretation, and an ideological dimension, attentive to social-cultural location and agenda. For such work, again, the biblical critic is well-positioned, given theoretical and methodological training, especially if such training is appropriately inclusive.

Integrating Interdisciplinary Engagement

In response to the critique lodged by Moore, I have already indicated that I would no longer identify the fourth paradigm of interpretation as cultural studies but rather as ideological criticism. A word about both object and mode of analysis is in order. The object would remain—as in the case of the other grand models—on the academic-scholarly tradition of reading, as expanded: the texts and contexts of antiquity; the interpretations of these texts and contexts in modernity and postmodernity, and the contexts of such interpretations; the interpreters behind these interpretations and the contexts of such interpreters. The mode would highlight the differential formations and relations of power, involving domination and subordination, across the various dimensions of identity in society and culture—whether in antiquity, modernity, or postmodernity. As a result, I have suggested that the designation of cultural studies be taken to signify a fifth paradigm of interpretation, one markedly different in the object rather than the mode of analysis. This grand model would comprehend the traditions of reading the biblical texts and contexts beyond the academic-scholarly, both those within the more circumscribed religious-theological realm and those within the comprehensive social-cultural world. I have further argued that such analysis should be pursued in close critical engagement with the field of cultural studies as such. This decision bears significant ramifications for the conception and practice of the discipline, although it is once again, when taken in context, not as ground-breaking a move as it would seem at first sight. Its roots lie, I would suggest, in the initial proposal.

In my original delineation of the various grand models at work in the discipline, I pointed out how the emergence and consolidation of the new paradigms had taken place by way of direct and sustained interaction with other general areas and particular fields of study, beyond the long-standing anchor of historical studies. This discursive shift was largely due, in my opinion, to failure on the part of traditional historical criticism to engage in critical interchange with the field of historiography, where important critical developments and discussions were taking place. The result was twofold: on the part of historical criticism, a continuing commitment to a mode of analysis firmly rooted in classical philology, with empiricism, linearity, and objectivism as underlying pillars; on the part of the emerging criticisms, a turn away from historiography at a time when the latter found itself in a profound situation of flux.

Such was certainly the case with the first two models, literary and socio-cultural biblical criticisms, which looked for grounding and orientation in the human and social sciences respectively. As a result, acquaintance with literary, rhetorical, and psychological theory, on the one hand, and with anthropological or sociological theory, on the other hand, became *de rigueur*. Such was the case, as well, with the third model, ideological criticism, which looked for grounding and orientation in feminist and materialist studies, racial-ethnic and sexuality studies, postcolonial studies, and in areas such as disability studies. Consequently, familiarity with such frameworks and approaches became a sine qua non as well. This discursive shift need not have been as sharp as it was, since within historiography itself the same problematics were having an impact and were being addressed. In any case, the present call for anchoring and direction in cultural studies with respect to cultural biblical criticism simply extends this logic and practice of interdisciplinary engagement a step further.

In the light of this response to Moore, I would further specify the need for explicit and careful mapping of the proposed conjunction between biblical studies and cultural studies. I have in mind both general and detailed mapping, along the lines of what I have urged and undertaken elsewhere with regard to other such interdisciplinary engagements.

Let me begin with a word about general mapping. In a recent attempt to identify and theorize the poetics of minority biblical criticism (Segovia 2009), I argued that such a study constituted a variation within the conjunction of two long-established and broad-ranging fields of study, biblical studies and racial-ethnic studies. Such a study, I further pointed out, represented a tall order indeed, given the character of each field as highly complex, constantly changing, and sharply conflicted in terms of discursive framework and disciplinary parameters. For any such confluence to take place in properly informed fashion, I added, a manageable sense of the overall layout of each field and a clear vision of the proposed interdisciplinary focalization are in order. This, in turn, calls for a mapping of the constitutive components of each field and the relations among them, as well as a blueprint identifying the specific components from each field to be brought together and explanation of why and how to do so. In espousing cultural biblical criticism, therefore, I find a similar sense of overall layout and specific interaction between biblical studies and cultural studies imperative. Needless to say, any exercise along these lines represents no less a tall order.

Let me continue with a word about detailed mapping. In an earlier effort to clarify the conjunction between biblical studies and postcolonial studies, another well-established and broad-ranging field, at work in postcolonial biblical criticism, I set out to examine the definition and practice of postcolonial analysis (Segovia 2005). This I pursued by way of a review of the literature—from overviews of the field in general introductions to criticism, through a general introduction to the field as such, to mappings of the field in detailed introductions. My aim was to secure a measure of clarity and consistency in the use of terms and concepts, with proper application to biblical criticism in mind. The analysis revolved around two fundamental questions: the proposed meaning of postcolonial criticism and the envisioned scope for such criticism. The inquiry yielded, first of all, a variety of recurring topics of discussion in each area of concern. The inquiry further revealed, across each and every topic under each area, profound complexity, ongoing change, and keen disagreement. In promoting cultural biblical criticism, consequently, I regard a similar review of the literature and command of the terrain of cultural studies as indispensable. Such a review, as Moore's own overview shows, will yield just as highly convoluted, shifting, and controverted a discursive framework.

Such mapping is meant to avoid any type of soft interchange in interdisciplinary study, in which recourse to a different field of studies can take place without a proper sense of historical trajectory, its present set of problematics, and the range of critical options within such problematics. In such efforts the conjunction comes across as lopsided in favor of the host field, and the interchange gives the appearance of dabbling or unreflective intervention in the other field. Likewise, an appeal to particular theorists or theories in the other field of studies can take place without a proper sense of the context and agenda of such stances and critics within the discursive framework as a whole. Such procedure makes the conjunction appear much too localized, while the interchange comes across as rather simplistic. Lastly, the use of the other field of studies can be carried out without a proper sense of critical sifting and engagement, appropriating terms and concepts toward indiscriminate funneling or resorting to unreflective prooftexting. In such a course of action, the conjunction comes across as ready-at-hand, and the interchange gives the appearance of unquestioned appropriation.

Such a vision and program for the future would endorse, in every respect, Moore's call for greater attention to the interdisciplinary character of the project. It would expand in various directions his grounding work in tracing the path of cultural studies and highlighting its various main stages of development: comparative analysis of the range of proposals regarding the definition and practice of cultural studies, with a focus on the questions of meaning and scope; identification of the key topics of discussion operative in both areas of concern and outlining of the spectrum of opinions present in each case; pursuing at all levels of the interchange critical sifting and engagement; finally, identifying, charting, and critiquing lines of contact already at work in the exercise of cultural biblical criticism. Much work remains to be done therefore, especially if one takes seriously, as one must, the global nature of cultural studies today. In such work, once again, the mode of analysis would involve a formalist as well as an ideological dimension, attentive to dynamics and mechanics as much as to locations and agendas. For such work, the biblical critic emerges as well-equipped, in the light of broad training in theory and method, provided that such training has followed the increasing focus of recent years on interdisciplinary interaction.

Cultural Biblical Criticism: To What End?

The vision and program I have in mind for the future of the biblical past in and through the model of cultural biblical criticism should now be clear. The proposal constitutes a constructive response to the critiques offered of my initial assessment of the biblical present and a fruitful conversation with the programs offered for the future of biblical criticism. What remains is a sense of the why: what end(s) does such a project serve? This question presupposes a more fundamental one: what is the role envisioned for and assigned to biblical criticism? Given its magnitude and importance, and given the need to pursue it in comparative fashion by reference to criticism in general, it must remain a question for another time and venue. What I would like to offer here, by way of conclusion, is a critical summary of the role of the critic that underlies the critiques and programs advanced by my three interlocutors. I shall then conclude with a brief anticipation of my own.

Smith offers pointers in this direction at the beginning and the end of his exposition of cultural studies, but without a comprehensive driving vision (181–83, 208–209). Three features for contemporary criticism come to the fore: democratization, deconstruction, scrutinization. First, a critic is to break through any distinction between high and low culture and attend to cultural formations of any sort. For the biblical critic, this means going beyond academic-scholarly criticism and addressing the range of uses of the Bible in any period or context. In so doing, the critic practices democratization by bringing marginalized cultural formations under the lens of analysis. Second, a critic is to cut through any view of cultural formations as givens and to approach them instead as signifiers of enveloping "historical cultural forces." For the biblical critic this entails looking upon texts and interpretations alike as reflecting and conveying the exercise of power in any number of ways. In this way, the critic moves toward deconstruction by way of ideological unmasking. Lastly, a critic is to examine the "other" intensely: all others, as "sites" of multiple practices and products driven by underlying "patterns of thought," in multidimensional fashion. For the biblical critic this means seeing texts and interpretations as websites in which many cultural formations, in themselves sustained by grounding ideologies, crisscross in complex and conflicted fashion. In so doing, the critic scrutinizes by casting an unrelenting gaze upon the other.

Moore touches on the question of critical mission at the end of his exposition of biblical cultural criticism (1998b, 23), but only briefly and indirectly. The postmodern critic, for whom cultural criticism constitutes an essential task, is to examine the Bible as a cultural icon in the contemporary world. In so doing, postmodern criticism takes up the spirit of modern criticism, but in a different realm: while the latter revealed the "unutterable strangeness of antiquity," the former exposes the alienness and eeriness that often characterizes the use of the Bible today. At the heart of criticism, therefore, lies the goal of "shocking," of rendering "otherness" palpable to the point of astonishment and discomfort, indeed estrangement. This the modern critic did by way of the "unfamiliar," the biblical past, and the postmodern critic does by way of the "familiar," the interpretive present. Such a display of "otherness," of difference, would seem to constitute the primary mission of the biblical critic.

For Schüssler Fiorenza, the sense of critical mission is present throughout her proposal for a rhetorical-emancipatory paradigm, in sustained and systematic fashion. In a world marked by structural domination and injustice, the critic is to embody the ideal of liberation, through appropriation of a rhetorical-emancipatory paradigm of interpretation and the adoption of an ethical-political vision and perspective. Within such a vision, texts and interpretations constitute sites of struggle that side with emancipation or oppression within the global structures of domination and injustice. The critic is always to ask, therefore, the *cui bono* question of past and present alike: "What kind of values and visions do biblical texts and their contemporary interpretations advocate? Do they value theological visions that contribute to the well-being of everyone in the global *cosmopolis*, or do they reinforce the languages of domination and hate as theological?" (54). In so doing, the critic is to go beyond exposé to action, taking up the struggle for liberation in the public sphere. This struggle entails the promotion of a more just and radical democratic ethos, cosmopolitan in vision, through a critique of religion, its stances and practices, in the "global polis" (54). Ultimately, the struggle goes beyond the boundaries imposed by traditional biblical criticism: beyond *biblical*, by encompassing the Scriptures and traditions of other religions; beyond *criticism*, by including readers of all sorts, who are viewed as capable of engaging in engaged and transformative reading.

To begin with, I stand in agreement with Smith's implicit vision of the critic as democratizing, deconstructive, and scrutinizing. It is imperative to look at all traditions of reading the Bible, to do so always in the light of the broader material and discursive frameworks at work, and to do so unrelentingly. At the same time, I note the lack of a grounding rationale: why, exactly, take on and display such features as a biblical critic? A broader religious-theological and social-cultural framework for such a mission is in order. Further, I sympathize with Moore's conception of the critic. I do agree with the task of laying bare the other, in all its difference, although I wonder why the other is perceived or described only as radically or shockingly different. I am intrigued by such an underlying dialectic of otherness. At the same time, I find the goal of displaying otherness and bringing about estrangement wanting. Such a stance, it seems to me, needs unpacking. It calls for a broader framework, both religious-theological and social-cultural, that would inform and guide such a project.

Lastly, I find Schüssler Fiorenza's vision of the critic entirely on target. Here the sense of a broader framework is unmistakable, and it is one of social-cultural conflict worldwide. A struggle prevails, at all times and in all places, between domination and emancipation, and in this struggle religion, its stances and practices, plays a role, yielding religious-theological conflict as well. Consequently, the critic has no option but to cast her/his lot in the struggle and do so publicly. At the same time, I would argue for amplification. First, while the struggle is certainly vertical, involving global structures, it is also horizontal and interlayered, involving a web of local structures. Domination and injustice take place in many ways and from many angles, and these cannot all be brought under the same tent. Second, while the *cui bono* question is indeed indispensable, it should also be open to multiplicity of meaning and diversity of readings. Texts and interpreta-tions do exhibit emancipatory or oppressive tendencies, but the reading of such tendencies may yield a wide range of opinion, which positions must be subjected to critical analysis as well.

In the end, I would argue, *in nuce*, for a vision of the critic as a voice for freedom and justice, dignity, and well-being, in religion and theology as well as in society and culture. This voice, I would add, the critic exercises in a world in conflict, crisscrossed by discourses and matrices of oppression and injustice, degradation and dis-ease—now, in the past, and in the future. In this exercise, I propose the Bible might be used as an instrument that addresses society and culture in many and conflicted ways—in antiquity, modernity, and postmoder-nity. As such, the Bible might be viewed as providing a theoretical framework for Christian conviction and praxis, with the sense that the Scriptures might prove of assistance—both positively and negatively—in pointing to and conjuring up a different world, globally as well as locally. The unpacking of this vision remains, alas, a task for the future.

21

Signifying on the Fetish:
Mapping a New Critical Orientation

Vincent L. Wimbush

This essay makes the case for a new critical orientation that has as its focus not historical criticism and its ever increasing razzle-dazzle offshoots, but a critical history (Nora 1994, 300) involving engagement and fathoming of forms of representations and expressivity (including artifacts), modes of performativity, structures of social-cultural-psychological dynamics and power relations—in effect, the phenomenon most often referred to with the English shorthand "Scriptures." In this essay about the future of a discourse about Scriptures that has been complexly oriented to the study of the past, I arrogate to myself the right and privilege to think with that fluid and haunting modern formation now called the Black Atlantic, with particular focus on the history of the people now called African Americans.

I begin with a number of illuminating and provocative statements that help make the case for a different starting point and orientation to critical inquiry:

> ... [T]hrough conquest, trade, and colonialism, [the West] made contact with every part of the globe ... religion and cultures and peoples throughout the world were created anew through academic disciplinary orientations—they were signified ... names [were] given to realities and peoples.... ; this naming is at the same time an objectification through categories and concepts of those realities which appear as novel and 'other' to the cultures of conquest. There is of course the element of power in this process of naming and objectification ... the power is obscured and the political, economic, and military situation that forms the context of the confrontation is masked by the intellectual desire for knowledge of the other. The actual situation of cultural contact is never brought to the fore within the context of intellectual formulations ... (Long 1986, 3–5)

> ... [In the transition from] from First Contact time ... to Reverse Contact now-time ... the Western study of the Third and Fourth World Other gives way to the unsettling confrontation of the West with itself as portrayed in the eyes and handiwork of its Others. Such an encounter disorients the earlier occidental sympathies which kept the magical economy of mimesis and alterity in some sort of imperial balance. (Taussig 1999, xv)

Rather than worry about its epistemology we ought to acknowledge the role of fetish as pragmatic application.... Modernity ... is a perspective that distinguished fact from fetish and truth from error.... [Following the theory and challenge of Bruno Latour, we should instead orient ourselves] in favor of a perspective from *amodernity* ... [that] tracks the subject's capacity to make do (*fait faire*) with the fetish, a process that dispenses with questions concerning belief and instead concentrates on those oriented around practice. (Aravamudan 1999, 274)

> ... I was very much affrighted at some things I saw ... any object I saw filled me with new surprise. I ... asked ... the use of it, and who made it.... (Equiano 1789, 62, 67)

By challenging us to revisit with more honesty and courage the situation that they are convinced is most determinative of the structuring and politics of our modern and contemporary worlds, including our thinking about our thinking—the first contact/confrontation between the West and the Rest (of the World)—the writers quoted above, in different ways, to be sure, have opened a wide window onto some of the issues and problems that are compelling for our consideration of the theme that collects the essays of this volume. Among such issues should surely be the making and ongoing uses of Scriptures as fetish, the effects and artifacts of a type of uncritical transference.

I am concerned in this essay with a focus on a complex group among the world of the Other, the peoples who constitute the Black Atlantic. Beyond what may be my personal interests, I argue this focus to be important because such peoples' experiences can help us to see things we would not otherwise see about the history and shape of the world we share, including the ramifications of our basic world-maintaining ideologies and practices. Focus on such a people's experiences may help us see how Scriptures—far beyond interest in the lexical and indexical—mean in society and culture. Sensitive but deep excavations of social textures and critical histories are needed that will map and model a different critical orientation to what is called biblical studies.

Olaudah Equiano as Point of Entry

I have chosen the late eighteenth-century Black Atlantic figure Olaudah Equiano and his self-described "interesting narrative" as the historical-discursive site to serve as entry point for the needed excavation and mapping. *The Interesting Narrative of the Life of Olaudah Equiano or Gustavus Vassa, the African. Written by Himself* (1789) has since its publication been read and interpreted for many different purposes and publics—in literary and cultural criticism; in eighteenth-century English social-cultural history; in the history of abolitionism on both sides of the Atlantic; and in African diaspora and slavery studies. Some have attempted to explain (away) Equiano's spirituality, but there are no extensive efforts to interpret him and his story in terms of the history of religions, much less in terms of the problematics of Scriptures. The narrative is particularly important for interest in the dynamics of fetishization and vernacularization, because of the manner in which Equiano figures himself as focal point of contemporary moral and political-economic crises brought on by violent conquest, disruption, and enslavement.

In his story he figures himself as a qualified insider ("almost an Englishman") who has been an outsider ("stranger"=slave) looking in: one to whom initially the English books did not "speak," yet one who is complexly in possession of—and becomes self-possessed in complex relationship to—the supreme (English) Book. Through his initial involuntary but later shrewd, strategic, voluntary travels by ship and through his associations with other nonwhite "strangers" ("Indians") and white eccentrics (religious dissenters and politicians), Equiano was able— through struggles, luck, trickery, and hard work—to make the books "speak" to him and eventually, through his own writing, "speak" back to the constraining structure of English-inflected scripturalization. His story can be understood both as an "epic"—a *script-ur[e]-alizing*—of life in the Black Atlantic diaspora and as a "founding text" of a more poignantly expansive and pluralistic modern Britain and United States. Although Equiano was in many respects somewhat unusual in some of his experiences, his "making do" with the Bible (understood by him as nationalist-cultural fetish) was and remains fairly typical of black folks' "making do" with the North Atlantic worlds they had been made to undergo, whether slave or "free" (the latter status always and everywhere in the eighteenth century throughout the Atlantic worlds understood in highly qualified terms). Metonymic of the black-inflected vernacularization of Scriptures, Equiano's story provides the outline for a layered history of Black Atlantic representations, gestures, and mimetic practices.

The entire story behind Equiano's narrative cannot be told here. I have chosen to focus on what is arguably the story that captures much of the poignancy of his crafting of his life—the one having to do with what is often referred to as the "talking book." Here is the little story within the larger life story:

I had often seen my master and Dick employed in reading; and I had a great curiosity to talk to the books, as I thought they did; and so to learn how all things had a beginning; for that purpose I have often taken up a book, and have talked to it; and then put my ears to it, when alone, in hopes it would answer me; and I have been very much concerned when I found it remained silent. (Equiano 1995, 68)

The story of the "talking book" was made quite significant as motif and trope for some of the earliest North Atlantic black writers. Thus, in addition to Equiano, the trope appears in the life stories of James Albert Ukawsaw Gronniosaw (1770), John Marrant (1785), Quobna Ottobah Cugoano (1787), and John Jea (1815). The story was made to serve some mostly shared and overlapping functions having to do with observation about black life in the eighteenth and early nineteenth centuries of the North Atlantic worlds (Gates 1988, 127–69).

Far from being a forgettable minor incident in the remembrance and recording of the "facts" about his life, the trope of the talking book is significant as part of Equiano's construction of an "interesting" life. It is part of his attempt to write what may be called a "fiction" of "self-creation" (Bland 2000). This little story within Equiano's life story is made into a figure or trope signifying (the young) Equiano's status and situation as "stranger"—as one who is ignorant of and outside the ways and orientations of the dominant white world (Carretta 2005, 286–87; also Kristeva 1991).

The ironically named "talking book" scene occurs within the larger narrative context in which the young Equiano is seen to be fascinated and confused about the names, functions, and imports of different strange objects—among them a "watch" or clock hanging above the chimney; a portrait; snow; and a book. The clock the boy Equiano thinks of as a sort of machine that records and reports all he does to (white) authorities. The eyes on the face of the hanging portrait he assumes to watch his every move. Seeing snow for the first time, he assumes it to be salt (63–68).

And the book? It was the last of the list of strange objects and phenomena associated with the world of the whites, the uses of which the young boy of the narrative had to ponder over. He thought the book to be a special object—one with which he thought he, like others, could communicate. He observed that a person could speak to, be spoken to, and be acknowledged by, the thing that is called by the whites "the book." The clock and the portrait seemed to represent the severest of gazes. They afforded little or no opportunity for engagement or interaction, serious or playful. They did not acknowledge his humanity. They were only recorders of his presence as interloper, stranger, as though he were dangerous and threatening. They were to him quite threatening, fear-inducing, oppressive. With such objects, what could one do? One could only be seen and reported by, or try not to be seen and reported by, them.

What was called the book, however, seemed to mean more, require more, and promise more. Not only did the book require attention and engagement on the part of the one holding it, it also held the promise of providing valuable information and perspective—about "how all things had a beginning" (68). This promise of the book reveals rather poignantly the mature story-telling Equiano's baseline interest: not in literacy for its own sake or in narrow terms, but in that which literacy opened up in terms of freedoms and identity. In this story is found instead the book-reading, book-writing, book-selling Equiano's registration of ardent curiosity about and interest in the depths, the mysteries, the secrets, the social and political power that books may represent or communicate. The young Equiano senses dimly but pointedly the iconic, fetishizing status of the book and the corresponding operations and politics in the dominant culture.

Given the societies and cultures Equiano was forced to negotiate, and given the attention to it throughout his story, clearly the book that was of interest to Equiano, even if other books are in mind, was the Bible. That this book did not "speak" to him, did not acknowledge him, but "remained silent" is clearly very disturbing to Equiano, rendering him silent, seemingly distraught, vulnerable, powerless, paralyzed. Yet his state of being disturbed was reflected not so much in what he records within the immediate narrative context about the book. He actually says far less than the other early black writers who drew upon the story: Gronniosaw (to reflect his ardent frustrated desire to be accepted into white dominant culture); Marrant (to provide evidence of his inside and superior status relative to the Indian); Cugoano (to castigate modern-world slavery, racism, and colonialism based upon twisted exegetical treatments); or Jea (to indicate the spiritual power involved in the reading of the book that is the Bible and how, relative to such, he assumed freedom; Gates 1988, 132–69). His state is made clear in what he does with the story in the immediate narrative context and throughout the larger narrative. Equiano preferred to say little more than that he was (within narrative time)—and remained at the time of writing the narrative—"very much concerned."

This reaction, however, is something of a clever understatement and reflective of a rather particular narratological interest and strategy. Even if Equiano as narrator does not say much about the situation in the immediate narrative context, the "silence" of the book within the narrative speaks volumes—and rather loudly. The silence of the book in the hands of the young Equiano should not be taken lightly; it is not comic relief. It is meant to point out a serious problem and challenge. It is an indication of the basic difference and conflict between the world that shaped Equiano and the dominant world of the peoples of the book.

I say "basic" because the young Equiano within the narrative seems to represent for the mature narrative-writing Equiano the epitome of that part of Africa that he claims is his homeland. (This notwithstanding questions now being raised—most notably by Carretta [2005, xi, xvi, 319–20, 350–53]—regarding Equiano's birthplace. That Equiano may not have been born in Africa does not affect the argument I make in this essay.) So the silence of the book seems to symbolize the chasm between the two worlds brought into contact and determinative of the structuring of Equiano's experience. There are in the narrative other instances and experiences in which the differences between the worlds are made clear. With the silent book episode, the reader of Equiano's narrative is made to understand that who the young Equiano is, what he represents, is not consonant with the world that is symbolized by the book, including book talking and reading.

The silence is met with silence. The latter must cover up for the young and the mature Equiano a mix of strong emotions—awe, fear, suspicion, bemusement, humiliation, hesitation, reservation, resistance. Only such a mix of responses can explain what the mature Equiano was doing with the story he writes: he writes/talks back—against his youthful self's experience of the silence of the book. The writing of the narrative on the part of the *mature* Equiano belies the paralysis and silence of the *young* Equiano. Through the *(non)*talking book scene, a fundamental instance of cultural "contact" or clash between worlds is set up: more than any other object-symbol, the book—and the relationship to it—is made to represent the dominant white world into which Equiano has been thrust. Like (mis)identifying and (mis)understanding the import of snow or a clock or a portrait, being engaged by and knowing how to engage a book signifies deeply (Bloom 1975). Only with the book it is much more the case: being able to "talk" to it and being addressed by it is the mark of belonging to and participating in the worlds of the whites, the type of worlds defined by the dominants Equiano was made to serve. Here the book is the fetish—the door, the window, the key to the other dominant world. Not being able to "talk" to the book and not being addressed by it is *the* sign of being a "stranger."

Since the onset of the modern world, with its attendant cultural contacts and discoveries (otherwise known as invasions and conquests), relationships to the book have figured prominently in self-definitions and the contours and dynamics of power (Gundaker 1998, 15–32; Ong 1982; Street 1993). Although the discourses about such matters have taken place largely on terms set by white dominants, Equiano, as one among the newly "discovered" made a "stranger" and slave, provides some rare and valuable perspectives on the issue. Although he was likely encouraged by religious dissenters to write his life story, there should be little doubt that he was under considerable psychological pressure, if not also political restraints, at the time of the writing of his narrative. Yet Equiano does manage to articulate sentiments about the book that are reflective of the major sensibilities and orientations of the worlds of the peoples of the Black Atlantic. On the surface these sentiments appear simply to represent in relationship to the book and to literacy the negative or absence. But must we assume that the "very much concerned" mature Equiano thinks only about his deficit in relationship to the book, his inferiority in relationship to the culture of the book? I think something different is registered here.

It needs to be remembered that neither the young nor the maturing Equiano is characterized as a pathetic figure. To be sure, through the course of his life, Equiano goes through many negative and heartbreaking experiences and losses. He acknowledges these experiences and seems often to sigh in discouragement, loneliness, and near resignation; however, he does not allow such experiences to be his unraveling or undoing. He is nothing if not remarkably resilient and somewhat wily. Especially in the first two chapters of his narrative, Equiano engages in comparative description and analysis: he pointedly compares his tribal traditions and mores to those of Europeans, the English in particular (on a lesser plane and in different points throughout the narrative, Indian tribes and others are brought into the comparison framework). As the mature Equiano engages in such critical cultural analysis, there is not a whiff of a sense of inferiority on his part. In fact, he seems quite comfortable comparing aspects of his tribal traditions—as he is able to remember them, or as the older Equiano prefers to remember them— to the dominant cultures with which he makes contact. It is striking and rather ironic that, in several respects, Equiano's tribal home traditions are boldly argued to have as much if not more affinity with ancient biblical traditions than the contemporary traditions of the dominant whites (chap 1).

Although clearly not happy about being snubbed by the book, Equiano is not thrown back upon himself in shock and dejection. He does not view himself as somehow pathetic for not being talked to by the book. He does not become angry at the refusal of the book to acknowledge him, nor does he hold forth about it as a reflection of antiblack racism and colonialism. He does not appear to react as though the situation had anything to do with where he comes from, or by claiming that he was made a slave by the fact that he was black. His silence in the face of the (book's) silence is not pathetic; it is profound. It is one of those rare moments in which Equiano the writer has little to say.

Another way of reading Equiano's seemingly muted immediate response to the book's (ongoing, repeated) failure to acknowledge him is to look at how he looks at his own story as published book, that is, his development into a reading and writing figure of some renown. In this story of his development into a famous writer, he not only "talks back" to the book, he makes the book "talk" to him with a vengeance. Because he makes the subtle but powerful connection between his writing and the silence of the books of his youth, he does not feel the need to hold forth through his youthful self at any length about the meaning of the incident. In the nature of the fabrication and construal of the story about the (non)talking book, the mature story-telling Equiano was signifying upon the book and upon literacy. That it was a youthful Equiano who has the experiences with the book is most important. The mature story-telling Equiano had in mind the construction of his life story in relationship to this phenomenon of the (non)talking book that for obvious reasons has to prefigure the development of Equiano into a famous writer and citizen-activist. In other words, everything in Equiano's story turns around the (non)talking book, even as, or precisely because, the writer does not make anything of the trope in immediate narrative context. How could the youthful Equiano, who is rejected by the book, be associated with the mature Equiano, who is the well-known well-received writer? The incident was intended to be full of irony, meant to force the reader to see that the silence of the book was not only not the end of the matter, but that it represents the beginning of Equiano's negotiation with the dominant white world.

So the (non)talking book incident is a prefiguring—it hints that the major divide between the world that Equiano constructs as his original formative world and the dominant white world into which he has been thrust is literacy, represented by the book. It is assumed that no one can successfully participate in and negotiate the dominant white world without the ability to handle books, to read and write. That there were illiterate whites was always evident (Cavallo and Chartier 1999, 213–83). Yet the marker that seemed most dramatically to set apart blacks (and other nonwhites) from whites, and to justify the continued subjugation of the former in relationship to the latter, was literacy—at least literacy in relationship to the scripts and related practices of European cultures.

For reasons that may be obvious (including his location), Equiano makes the major difference between the two different worlds, as he understands and remembers and experiences them, revolve chiefly and poignantly around the issue of European-styled literacy. The identification of such an issue is also acknowledgement that the two worlds represent two different sets of sensibilities, different epistemologies, different orientations. It is significant that the youthful Equiano is the one who experiences the repeated silence and snubbing of the book: in terms of the narrative timelines, he is the one who is closer to (the memory of) African tribal customs, sensibilities, and practices. The mature story-telling Equiano seems to want to make the interaction between his youthful self and English books a matter of actual pointed conflict. This conflict is important to the story-telling Equiano not so much in order to inveigh against the evils of the dominant white world, and certainly not so that he might somehow establish his and his kindreds' incapacity and inferiority. It was important in order to make his story "interesting," that is, poignant, ironic, in this immediate narrative context, to be sure, but also throughout the story, through the emphases on the silence of the book.

This repeated emphasis, in turn, became the basis of conveying Equiano's remarkable development and progress. The silence and snubbing of the book was made to represent for Equiano the point of radical difference and conflict between who he was in relationship to his African homeland and who he was becoming in relationship to the world he eventually successfully negotiated. It was in Equiano's narratological-political interests to include the story about the non-talking book, because Equiano's version and placement of the story make the point of the little story and the big story clear: less about a contrast between evil deeds, hypocrisy, and moral corruption on the part of the white world and weaknesses, shortcomings, and deficits on the part of the black world, and more about the sheer stark difference between the two worlds that the book reveals and what heroics it took for him to overcome that difference. Finding himself unable to negotiate English letters, how could Equiano be seen or see himself as anyone other than "stranger," as someone standing on foreign cultural-ideological grounds? How could the youthful Equiano, made to be so ignorant about the major issues involved, respond except with concern?

The challenge for Equiano the writer was to make clear to readers the terms on which negotiation with the white world could be realized. The talking book story also pinpointed the issue around which Equiano (along with some others, to be sure) thought the issue of black integration and negotiation revolved—literacy, engagement of western (in this case, English) letters.

The issue of literacy here masks what is usually the issue behind the issue—power. Yet precisely because power is almost always at issue, it is important to be as specific as possible about how power is at issue here. In Equiano's story, power is at issue in the use of literacy as a marker that erects and maintains cultural boundaries, that identifies and keeps in place insiders and outsiders. This is what the young Equiano was confronted with: he was established in the little story as outsider, stranger—not first strictly on account of his origins, his "race," but on account of his lack of social power, his facility with the book. The racialization of his status as stranger was not named as an explanatory factor. Equiano's racial/ethnic identity was sometimes seen in the story as part of a belated rationalization or grudging explanation for being the stranger. Refusing quickly and explicitly to name racism as the decisive factor for the exclusion allowed Equiano the opportunity to develop his story as an "interesting" story, acceptable to white readers, about his struggle to acquire the skills of literacy and become "almost an Englishman."

THE FUTURE OF THE BIBLICAL PAST

The social psychology of Equiano's "use" of literacy, an understanding of the work it was made to do for him, can shed light on the larger phenomenon of reading in society and culture, including the reading of the Bible. Equiano's construal of the talking book story did not concern itself with revelation of the great evil or recalcitrance of individual whites. With some notable exceptions, whites in Equiano's life story are characterized as being sometimes fair-minded, sometimes evil, sometimes ignorant, and so forth. What was at issue for Equiano was the unmasking and accounting of the chief differences in orientation to the world between the world he partly "invented" (Morrison 1995) and called his own and the world of the whites as he construed and experienced it. He had also to address the stated assumptions about the superiority of the orientation associated with the world of the whites. It is the orientation of the dominant white world and its registrations of a certain kind of power in association with literacy that Equiano's construal of the talking book story signifies on.

Equiano's life story points to the basis for his successful negotiation of the North Atlantic worlds, namely, his recognition that such worlds were built around the fetishization of the book (including the Book) and correlative assumptions: that humanity is recognized and certified through the engagement of (western) letters in the book; that black peoples, on account of what they must be made to represent, insofar as they are made to be slaves, could not/should not engage such letters; and that, because of their incapacities in terms of letters, they could not be considered part of the civilized world or "great chain of being" (Gates 1988, 130, 167).

The most important point Equiano seemed to want to make in his storytelling, especially the talking book story as its core, is that he went on to live and thrive—that is to say, to learn to read, to experience talking to the book and making the book talk back to him. These experiences were the seeds of a great story, of his story—a story that "spoke" to different publics: to those royals and political and other elites who had power to still the trafficking in slaves and to unchain those who remained enslaved in Britain; and to those circles across the English-speaking North Atlantic worlds, of sympathizers and potential sympathizers, convicted abolitionists, whether religiously or otherwise inspired. These contemporary publics were importuned, challenged, inspired, entertained, and accommodated in explicit terms throughout the story.

Yet I also detect another public—perhaps the most important public—that, ironically, Equiano did not identify, because he could not. He could only identify in veiled or indirect terms or in terms that were flat and stereotypical, the public he actually represented and mirrored: enslaved and freed black peoples of the North Atlantic worlds. It may even have been the case that he was not with every word and expression addressing or always aware of the weight of this "public." He certainly knew that this far-flung and humiliated "public" could hardly be addressed directly in writing—not by the sort unofficially encouraged and made licit and feasible, if not commissioned, by whites, notwithstanding their abolitionist commitments. He was also doubtless aware that the folk who constituted such a conceptualized "public" *qua* public could hardly be expected to "speak" back to him or to read him. Yet the most basic and poignant point of the story—about the very difficult but successful construction of a black life—I am convinced is not intended so much for the entertainment, enlightenment, or appeasement of potential white sympathizers, but for other "strangers" who are also black. It was intended to represent a black self-writing to a collective black self, or perhaps, reflective of a "school" of black readers (of the text[ure]s of the world as experienced by black peoples). It was intended to entertain, to challenge, to inspire—yes. But on different terms and for reasons that are different from those associated merely with the interests and sentiments of white abolitionists. It was a story that may reflect awareness of such readers, but it is heavier, reflecting far more concern about far more serious consequences. Equiano as writer very likely was aware of the importance of pointing out that he understood how the dominant world was constituted, or had been woven, and the terms on which it continued to justify itself. More precisely, his story reflected—I think intentionally—his understanding that what underpinned this dominant world was its orientation to and its use of the Book. This orientation, Equiano discovered, presumed that only its own book(s) and traditions and practices mattered, that all things important pivoted around it, including individual freedom, survival, and the capacity to thrive and succeed in the society.

Coming to such recognition was not, for Equiano, capitulation or assent or defeat. He understood it to be a realistic view born of his experiences at sea and in the many societies seafaring afforded him opportunity to experience. These experiences led him to the view that black existence, in spite of some minor differences in arrangements and styles, was everywhere in the North Atlantic worlds a matter of struggle, opposition, humiliation, challenge, "oppugnancy" (Long 1986, 177–78, 197). Black survival and negotiation of the white world required critical analysis and strategic responses. Negotiation was thought possible only insofar as the western structure and arrangement of dominance was seen realistically and honestly for what it was.

Toward A New Critical Orientation in the Academic Study of the Bible

Equiano's life story is a dramatic window onto the North Atlantic worlds' humiliation of the black self. However, with the talking book story more is signified:

Scriptures are signified on, insofar as Equiano understood that the structure in place was built on the Bible and so proceeded to construct his life story in signifying/mimetic relationship to such structuring. The black struggle for survival and freedom and acquisition of power was understood by Equiano to turn around awareness of and response to the dominant culture's festishizing of the book, the Bible.

This awareness inspired Equiano to structure his story as a scriptural/biblical story that signified on the very use of Scriptures in North Atlantic societies, Britain in particular. His signifying practice is at the same time an example of vernacularization—for the sake of resistance, survival, freedom, and thriving—in complex response to the dominants' uses of the book. Equiano's story does not represent a fully explicit theory about such a phenomenon. It really only names the problem and drops some hints regarding the needed strategic response on the part of the black self, represented as the outsider looking in. Equiano's story can be used as a window onto the phenomenon and dynamics of the western fetishization of the book as well as a laying of tracks for vernaculars of North Atlantic blacks in response.

There are major implications of Equiano's work for a different critical orientation in the academic study of the Bible. This involves orienting the discourse to that past that has (over)determined the structural power relations of the modern world by placing focus not on texts but on the social textures of the peoples and their consciousness of and responses to such structures. The peoples' responses in the form of practices of signifying (on) Scriptures provide the road maps for a more compelling and meaningful future for critical work.

List of Contributors

Yong-Sung Ahn, Presbyterian College and Theological Seminary, Seoul, Korea

George Aichele, Adrian College, Michigan, U.S.A.

Pablo R. Andiñach, Instituto Universitario ISEDET, Buenos Aires, Argentina

Roland Boer, University of Newcastle, Australia

Fiona C. Black, Department of Religious Studies, Mount Allison University, Sackville, New Brunswick, Canada

Philip Chia, Chinese University of Hong Kong, Hong Kong

Nancy Cardoso Pereira, Universidade Severino Sombra, Rio de Janeiro, Brazil

Jione Havea, United Theological College and School of Theology, Charles Sturt University, New South Wales, Australia

Israel Kamudzandu, St. Paul School of Theology, Kansas City, Missouri, U.S.A.

Milena Kirova, University of Sofia, Sofia, Bulgaria

Tat-Siong Benny Liew, Pacific School of Religion and the Graduate Theological Union, Berkeley, California, U.S.A.

Monica Jyotsna Melancthon, United Faculty of Theology, MCD University of Divinity, Melbourne

Judith McKinlay, Department of Theology and Religious Studies, Otago University, New Zealand

Sarojini Nadar, School of Religion, Philosophy and Classics, University of KwaZulu Nala, Pietermaritzburg, South Africa

Jorge Pixley, Seminario Teológico Bautista-Managua, Managua, Nicaragua

Jeremy Punt, Faculty of Theology, University of Stellenbosch, South Africa

Elisabeth Schüssler Fiorenza, Harvard Divinity School, Harvard University, Cambridge, Massachusetts, U.S.A.

Fernando F. Segovia, The Divinity School, Vanderbilt University, Nashville, Tennessee, U.S.A.

Hanna Stenström, University of Uppsala, Uppsala, Sweden

Vincent L. Wimbush, Institute for Signifying Scriptures, Claremont Graduate University, Claremont, California, U.S.A.

Gosnell Yorke, School of Religion, Philosophy and Classics, University of KwaZulu Nala, Pietermaritzburg, South Africa and Northern Caribbean University, Mandeville, Jamaica

Bibliography

Adam, A. K. M., Stephen E. Fowl, Kevin J. Vanhoozer, and Francis Watson. 2006. *Reading Scripture with the Church: Toward a Hermeneutic for Theological Interpretation.* Grand Rapids: Baker Academic.

Adam, Ian, and Helen Tiffin, eds. 1991. *Past the Last Post: Theorizing Post-Colonialism and Post-Modernism.* New York: Harvester Wheatsheaf.

Aejmelaeus, Lars, and Antti Mustikallio. 2008. *The Nordic Paul: Finnish Approaches to Pauline Theology.* London: T&T Clark.

Ahn, Byung Mu. 1981. Jesus and the Minjung in the Gospel of Mark. Pages 138–52 in *Minjung Theology: People as Subjects of History.* Edited by Commission on Theological Concerns of the Christian Conferene of Asia. Maryknoll, N.Y.: Orbis.

Ahn, Yong-sung. 2006. *The Reign of God and Rome in Luke's Passion Narrative: An East Asian Global Perspective.* Leiden: Brill

Aichele, George, ed. 2000. *Culture, Entertainment, and the Bible.* Sheffield: Sheffield Academic Press.

———. 2001. *The Control of Biblical Meaning: Canon as Semiotic Mechanism.* Harrisburg, Pa.: Trinity.

Aichele, George, and Richard Walsh, eds. 2002. *Screening Scripture: Intertextual Connections between Scripture and Film.* Harrisburg, Pa.: Trinity.

Alexander, M. Jacqui. 2005. *Pedagogies of Crossing: Meditations on Feminism, Sexual Politics, Memory and the Sacred.* Durham, NC: Duke University Press.

Almalech, Moni. 2006. *The Colours in the Pentateuch: Linguistic Picture of the World.* Sofia, Bulgaria: Sofia University Press.

Alves, Rubem. 1970. *Religión: ¿Opio o instrumento de liberación?* Montevideo, Uruguay: Tierra Nueva.

Andersen, Francis I. 1959–1960. The Early Sumerian City-State in Recent Soviet Historiography. *Abr-Nahrain* 1:56–61.

———. 1970. *The Hebrew Verbless Clause in the Pentateuch.* Nashville: Abingdon.

Andersen, Francis I., and David Noel Freedman. 1989. *Amos: A New Translation with Introduction and Commentary.* AB 24A. New York: Doubleday.

Anderson, G. W. 1990. Scandinavian Old Testament Scholarship. Pages 609–13 in *A Dictionary of Biblical Interpretation.* Edited by R. J. Coggins and J. L. Houlden. London: SCM.

Andreev, Emil. 2005. *The Glass River.* Veliko Turnovo, Bulgaria: Faber.

Andrew, Maurice E. 1982. *The Old Testament and New Zealand Theology.* Dunedin, New Zealand: Faculty of Theology, University of Otago.

———. 1990. *Treaty Land Covenant.* Dunedin, New Zealand: Andrew.

———. 1999a. *The Old Testament in Aotearoa New Zealand.* Wellington, New Zealand: Deft.

——. 1999b. *Set in a Long Place: A Life from North to South.* Christchurch, New Zealand: Hazard.

Ang, Ien. 2001. *On Not Speaking Chinese: Living between Asia and the West.* New York: Routledge.

Angus, Samuel. 1914. *The Environment of Early Christianity.* London: Duckworth.

——. 1929. *The Religious Quests of the Graeco-Roman World: A Study in the Historical Background of Early Christianity.* London: Murray.

——. 1933. *Christianity and Dogma.* Sydney: Angus & Robertson.

——. 1939. *Essential Christianity.* Sydney: Angus & Robertson.

Appavoo, J. T. 1993. *Communication for Dalit Liberation: A Search for an Appropriate Communication Model.* Edinburgh: University of Edinburgh Press.

Archie, Nola J., George Rosendale, and Rainbow Spirit Elders. 1997. *Rainbow Spirit Theology: Towards an Australian Aboriginal Theology.* Sydney: HarperCollins.

Arul Raja, S. J., A. Maria. 1996. Towards a Dalit Reading of the Bible: Some Hermeneutical Reflections. *Jeevadhara* 26/151:29–34.

——. 1997. Some Reflections on a Dalit Reading of the Bible. Pages 336–45 in *Frontiers of Dalit Theology.* Edited by V. Devasahayam. Chennai: Gurukul; New Delhi: ISPCK.

——. 2002. Breaking Hegemonic Boundaries: An Intertextual Reading of the Madurai Veeran Legend and Mark's Story of Jesus. Pages 251–60 in *Scripture, Community and Mission: Essays in Honor of D. Preman Niles.* Edited by Philip L. Wickeri. Hong Kong: CCA.

Asante, Molefe Kete. 2007. *The History of Africa: The Quest for Eternal Harmony.* New York: Routledge.

Ásgeirsson, Jon Ma. 2008. Biblical Scholarship in Iceland during the Twentieth Century and Beyond. Unpublished document now kept by Hanna Stenström and available on request.

Assman, Hugo. 1971. *Opresión-liberación: Desafío a los cristianos.* Montevideo, Uruguay: Tierra Nueva.

Aravamudan, Srinivas. 1999. *Tropicopolitans: Colonialism and Agency, 1688–1804.* Durham, N.C.: Duke University Press.

Baasland, Ernst. 1995. Neutestamentliche Forschung in Skandinavien (und Finnland). *BThZ* 12:146–66.

Bailey, Randall C. 2009. That's Why They Didn't Call the Book Hadassah! The Interse(ct)/(x)ionality of Race/Ethnicity, Gender, and Sexuality in the Book of Esther. Pages 227–50 in *They Were All Together in One Place? Toward Minority Biblical Criticism.* Edited by Randall C. Bailey, Tat-siong Benny Liew, and Fernando F. Segovia. SemeiaSt 57. Atlanta: Society of Biblical Literature.

Banana, Canaan S. 1991. The Case for a New Bible. Pages 69–82 in *Voices from the Margin: Interpreting the Bible in the Third World.* Edited by R. S. Sugirtharajah. Maryknoll, N.Y.: Orbis.

Barstad, Hans, and Magnus Ottoson, eds. 1988. *The Life and Work of Sigmund Mowinckel.* SJOT 2.

Barstad, Hans, and Arvid Tångberg, eds. 1994. *History and Ideology in the Old Testament.* SJOT 8.

Barthes, Roland. 1974. *S/Z.* Translated by Richard Miller. New York: Hill & Wang.

——. 1986. *The Rustle of Language.* Translated by Richard Howard. Berkeley: University of California Press.

———. 1988. *The Semiotic Challenge*. Translated by Richard Howard. New York: Hill and Wang.

Barton, John. 1998a. Historical-Critical Approaches. Pages 9–20 in *The Cambridge Companion to Biblical Interpretation*. Edited by J. Barton. Cambridge: Cambridge University Press.

Barton, John, ed. 1998b. *The Cambridge Companion to Biblical Interpretation*. Cambridge: Cambridge University Press.

Beal, Timothy. 2002. *Religion and Its Monsters*. New York: Routledge.

———. 2008. *The End of the Word as We Know It*. Orlando: Harcourt Brace.

Beaman, Lori G. 2006. *Religion and Canadian Society: Tradition, Transitions, and Innovations*. Toronto: Canadian Scholars Press.

Belich, James. 1996. *Making Peoples: A History of the New Zealanders From Polynesian Settlement to the End of the Nineteenth Century*. Auckland: Penguin Books (NZ).

Bengtsson, Håkan. 2006. "De sakna den rätta insikten"–svensk bibelteologi om judendom. Pages 49–69 in *Forskning pågår ... Från Svenska kyrkans forskardagar 2005*. Edited by Björn Ryman. Stockholm: Svenska kyrkans enhet för forskning och kultur, Svenska kyrkan.

Benjamin, Walter. 1968. *Illuminations*. Translated by Harry Zohn. New York: Schocken Books.

Bentzen, Aage. 1949. Skandinavische Literatur zum Alten Testament 1939–1948. *TRu* N.F. 17:273–328.

Berns-McGown, Rima. 2008. Asking the Right and Wrong Questions: Is Our Diverse Population Changing Canada's Relationship to the World? *Literary Review of Canada* 16/3:24–25.

Berquist, Jon L. 1996. Postcolonialism and Imperial Motives for Canonization. *Semeia* 75:15–35.

Beteille, Andre. 1981. *The Backward Classes and the New Social Order*. New Delhi: Oxford University Press.

Bhabha, Homi. 1994. *The Location of Culture*. London: Routledge.

Binney, Judith. 1995. *Redemption Songs: A Life of Te Kooti Arikirangi Te Turuki*. Auckland: Auckland University Press with Bridget Williams Books.

Bisoondath, Neil. 1994. *Selling Illusions: The Cult of Multiculturalism in Canada*. Toronto: Penguin.

Bland, Sterling L. 2000. *Voices of the Fugitives: Runaway Slave Stories and Their Fictions of Self-Creation*. Westport: Greenwood.

Bloom, Harold. 1975. *A Map of Misreading*. New York: Oxford University Press.

Blount, Brian K. 1995. *Cultural Interpretation: Reorienting New Testament Criticism*. Minneapolis: Fortress.

Blount, Brian K., ed. 2007. *True to Our Native Land: An African American New Testament Commentary*. Minneapolis: Fortress.

Bockmuehl, Markus N. A. 2006. *Seeing the Word: Refocusing New Testament Study*. Grand Rapids: Baker Academic.

Boer, Roland. 1998. Remembering Babylon: Postcolonialism and Biblical Studies in Australia. Pages 24–48 in R. S. Sugirtharajah *Asian Biblical Hermeneutics and Postcolonialism. Contesting the Interpretations*. Maryknoll, N.Y.: Orbis.

———. 2004. Editorial. *The Bible and Critical Theory* 1:1–6. http://bibleandcriticaltheory. org/index.php/bct/article/viewFile/14/2.

------. 2003. *Marxist Criticism of the Bible*. London: Continuum.

------. 2007a. *Criticism of Heaven: On Marxism and Theology*. Leiden: Brill.

------. 2007b. *Rescuing the Bible*. Oxford: Blackwell.

------. 2007c. *Symposia: Dialogues Concerning the History of Biblical Interpretation*. London: Equinox.

------. 2008. *Last Stop Before Antarctica: The Bible and Postcolonialism in Australia*. SemeiaSt. Atlanta: Society of Biblical Literature.

------. ed. 2006. Dossier on the Seminar. *The Bible and Critical Theory Journal* 2/2. Melbourne: Monash University ePress.

Boer, Roland, and Edgar W. Conrad, eds. 2003. *Redirected Travel: Alternative Journeys and Places in Biblical Studies*. London: T&T Clark.

Boff, Leonardo. 1996. *Ecología: grito de la tierra, grito de los pobres*. Buenos Aires: Lumen.

Bonilla-Silva, Eduardo. 2003. *Racism Without Racists: Color-Blind Racism and the Persistence of Racial Inequality in the United States*. Lanham: Rowman & Littlefield.

Boudillion, M. F. C. 1977. Traditional Religion and an Independent Church. Pages 61–79 in *Christianity South of the Zambezi*. Edited by D. N. Beach. Vol. 2 of *Christianity South of the Zambezi*. Edited by D. N. Beach. Zimbabwe: Mambo Press.

Bowlby, Paul. 2003. Diasporic Religions in Canada: Opportunities and Challenges. *Canadian Issues/Thèmes Canadiens* April:45–46.

Bowlby, Paul, and Tom Faulkner. 2001. *Religious Studies in Atlantic Canada: A State of the Art Review*. Waterloo: Wilfred Laurier Press.

Boyarin, Daniel. 1994. *A Radical Jew: Paul and the Politics of Identity*. Berkeley: University of California Press.

Boyd, Robin. 1973. The Use of the Bible in Indian Christian Theology. *IJT* 22:141–62.

Bramadat, Paul. 2005. Beyond Christian Canada: Religion and Ethnicity in Multicultural Canada. Pages 1–29 in *Religion and Ethnicity in Canada*. Edited by Paul Bramadat and David Seljak. Toronto: Pearson Longman.

Brenner, A. 2000. Foreword. Pages 7–12 in *Culture, Entertainment and the Bible*. Edited by George Aichele. JSOT 309. Sheffield: Sheffield Academic Press.

Brett, Mark. 2000. *Genesis: Procreation and the Politics of Identity*. London: Routledge.

------. 2008. *Decolonizing God: The Bible in the Tides of Empire*. Sheffield: Sheffield Phoenix.

Breward, Ian. 1975. *Grace and Truth: A History of Theological Hall Knox College, Dunedin 1876–1975*. Dunedin: Theological Education Committee, Presbyterian Church of New Zealand.

Brown, Michael Joseph. 2004. *Blackening of the Bible: The Aims of African American Biblical Scholarship*. Harrisburg, Pa.: Trinity.

Bryan, Christopher. 2005. *Render to Caesar: Jesus, the Early Church and the Roman Superpower*. Oxford: Oxford University Press.

Buck-Morss, Susan. 2000. Hegel and Haiti. *Critical Inquiry* 26:821–62.

Buell, Denise K., and Caroline Johnson Hodge. 2004. The Politics of Interpretation: The Rhetoric of Race and Ethnicity in Paul. *JBL* 123:235–51.

Bulkeley, Tim. 2005. *Amos: Hypertext Bible Commentary*. Auckland: Hypertext Bible [CD].

Byron, Gay L. 2009. Ancient Ethiopian and the New Testament: Ethnic (Con)texts and Racialized (Sub)texts. Pages 161–90 in *They Were All Together in One Place? Toward Minority Biblical Criticism*. Edited by Randall C. Bailey, Tat-siong Benny Liew, and Fernando F. Segovia. Atlanta: Society of Biblical Literature.

Byron, John. 2008. *Recent Research on Paul and Slavery*. Sheffield: Sheffield Phoenix.

Byrskog, Samuel. 2005. Bibelvetenskap i Sverige. *Tro&Liv* 5:15–21.

Cadwallader, Alan. 2008. *Beyond the Word of a Woman: Recovering the Bodies of the Syrophoenician Women*. Adelaide: ATF Press.

Caldwell, L. W. 1987. Third Horizon Ethnohermeneutics: Re-Evaluating New Testament Hermeneutical Models for Intercultural Bible Interpreters Today. *AJT* 1:314–33.

Callahan, Allen Dwight. 2006. *The Talking Book: African Americans and the Bible*. New Haven: Yale University Press.

Campbell, Antony F. 2005. *Rethinking the Pentateuch: Prolegomena to the Theology of Ancient Israel*. Louisville: Westminster John Knox.

———. 2008. *The Whisper of the Spirit: A Believable God Today*. Grand Rapids: Eerdmans.

Canevacci, M. 1996. *Sincretismos—uma exploração das hibridações culturais*. São Paulo: Studio Nobel.

Carden, Michael. 2004. *Sodomy: A History of a Christian Biblical Myth*. London: Equinox.

Cardoso Pereira, Nancy, ed. 1997. *¡Pero nosotras decimos!* RIBLA 25. San José: Departamento Ecuménico de Investigaciones.

Carley, Keith. 2001. Ezekiel's Formula of Desolation: Harsh Justice for the Land/Earth. Pages 143–57 in *The Earth Story in the Psalms and the Prophets*. Edited by Norman C. Habel. The Earth Bible 4. Sheffield: Sheffield Academic.

Carr, Dyanchand. n.d. Dalit Theology is Biblical and It Makes the Gospel Relevant. Pages 71–84 in *A Reader in Dalit Theology*. Edited by A. P. Nirmal. Chennai: Gurukul.

Carrasco, Victoria. 1997. Antropología andina y bíblica—"Chaquiñan" andino y Biblia. Pages 24–44 in *La palabra se hizo India. RIBLA* 26. Edited by Luz Jiménez. San José: Departamento Ecuménico de Investigaciones.

Carretta, Vincent. 2005. *Equiano the African: Biography of a Self-Made Man*. Athens: University of Georgia Press.

Carroll, Robert P. 1998a. Lower Case Bibles: Commodity Culture and the Bible. Pages 46–69 in *Biblical Studies/Cultural Studies: The Third Sheffield Colloquium*. Edited by Cheryl J. Exum and Stephen D. Moore. JSOTSup 266. Sheffield: Sheffield Academic.

———. 1998b. Poststructuralist Approaches: New Historicism and Postmodernism. Pages 50–66 in *The Cambridge Companion to Biblical Interpretation*. Edited by J. Barton. Cambridge: Cambridge University Press.

Carter, Tomeiko Ashford, ed. 2010. *Virginia Broughton: The Life and Writings of a National Baptist Missionary*. Knoxville: University of Tennessee.

Cavalcanti, Tereza, ed. 1993. *From manos de mujer. RIBLA* 15. San José: Departamento Ecuménico de Investigaciones.

Cavallo, Guglielmo and Roger Chartier, eds. 1999 [1995, 1997]. *A History of Reading in the West*. Translated by Lydia G. Cochrane. Amherst: University of Massachusetts Press.

Charsley, Simon. 2004. Interpreting Untouchability: The Performance of Caste in Andhra Pradesh, South India. *Asian Folklore Studies* 63:267–90.

Cheng, Patrick S. 2002. Multiplicity and Judges 19: Constructing a Queer Asian Pacific American Biblical Hermeneutic. *Semeia* 90/91:119–33.

Chuh, Kandice. 2003. *Imagine Otherwise: On Asian American Critique*. Durham: Duke University Press.

Clarke, Sathianathan. 1998. Paraiyars Ellaiyamman as an Iconic Symbol of Collective Resistance and Emancipatory Mythography. Pages 35–53 in *Religions of the Mar-*

ginalised: Towards a Phenomenology and the Methodology of Study. Edited by Gnana Robinson. Bangalore/Delhi: UTC/ISPCK.

———. 1998b. *Dalits and Christianity: Subaltern Religion & Liberation Theology in India.* Delhi: Oxford University Press.

———. 2002a. Viewing the Bible through the Eyes and Ears of Subalterns in India. *BibInt* 10/3:245–66.

———. 2002b. Dalits Overcoming Violation and Violence: A Contest Between Overpowering and Empowering Identities in Changing India. *The Ecumenical Review* 54/3:278–97.

Clough, Patricia Ticineto, ed. 2007. *The Affective Turn: Theorizing the Social.* Durham: Duke University Press.

Cochrane, James R. 1999. *Circles of Dignity: Community Wisdom and Theological Reflection.* Minneapolis: Fortress.

Cohen, Abraham. 2008. *Everyman's Talmud.* Sofia: Cybea.

Collins, J. J. 2004. The Politics of Biblical Interpretation. Pages 195–211 in *Biblical and Near Eastern Essays. Studies in Honour of Kevin J Cathcart.* Edited by C. McCarthy and J. F. Healey. London-New York: T&T Clark.

———. 2005. *The Bible after Babel. Historical Criticism in a Postmodern Age.* Grand Rapids: Eerdmans.

Comblin, José. 1985. *Introdução Geral ao Comentario Bíblico: Leitura da Biblia na Perspectiva dos Pobres.* Petrópolis: Vozes and Impressa Metodista Editoral Sinodal.

Cone, James H. 1969. *Black Theology and Black Power.* New York: Seabury.

———. 1970. A Black Theology of Liberation. Philadelphia: Lippincott.

Conrad, Edgar W. 2002. *Reading Isaiah.* Eugene, Oregon: Wipf and Stock.

———. 2004. *Reading the Latter Prophets: Toward a New Canonical Criticism.* London: T&T Clark.

Copher, Charles B. 1989. Three Thousand Years of Biblical Interpretation with Reference to Black Peoples. Pages 105–28 in *African American Religious Studies: An Interdisciplinary Anthology.* Edited by Gayraud Wilmore. Durham: Duke University Press.

———. 1991. The Black Presence in the Old Testament. Pages 146–64 in *Stony the Road We Trod: African American Biblical Interpretation.* Edited by Cain Hope Felder. Minneapolis: Fortress.

Crawshaw, John, and Chris Marshall. 2007. Re-engaging with the Bible in a Postmodern World: A Discussion. *Stimulus* 15:17–20.

Croatto, J. Severino. 1981. *Liberación y Libertad.* Lima: CEP. English trans: *Exodus, A Hermeneutics of Freedom.* Maryknoll, N.Y.: Orbis.

———. 1986. *El hombre en el mundo: estudio del Génesis 1,1–2,3 y 2,4–3,24.* Buenos Aires: La Aurora.

———. 1989. *Isaías 1–39.* Buenos Aires: La Aurora.

———. 1994a. *Hermenéutica bíblica: para una teoría de la lectura como producción de sentido.* Buenos Aires: Lumen.

———. 1994b. *Isaías 40–55. La palabra profética y su relectura hermenéutica.* Buenos Aires: Lumen.

———. 1997a. *Exilio y sobrevivencia: tradiciones contraculturales en el Pentateuco: Comentario de Génesis 4,1–12,9.* Buenos Aires: Lumen.

———. 1997b. Simbólica cultural y hermenéutica bíblica. Pages 67–77 in *La palabra se hizo India*. *RIBLA* 26. Edited by Luz Jiménez. San José: Departamento Ecuménico de Investigaciones.

———. 2001. *Isaías 56–66. Imaginar el futuro. Estructura retórica y querigma del Tercer Isaías*. Buenos Aires: Lumen.

———. 2002. *Hermenéutica práctica*. Quito: Centro Bíblico Verbo Divino.

Curtin, Philip D. 1990. *The Rise and Fall of the Plantation Complex: Essays in Atlantic History*. New York: Cambridge University Press.

Cvetkovich, Ann. 2003. *An Archive of Feelings: Trauma, Sexuality, and Lesbian Public Cultures*. Durham: Duke University Press.

Cvornyek, R. L. 1999. The Hidden History: African-American Contributions to the Bible Cause. Pages 203–11 in *The Holy Bible (CEV): The African-American Jubilee Edition*. New York: American Bible Society.

Dabydeen, David. 1991. On Cultural Diversity. Pages 97–106 in *Whose Cities?* Edited by Mark Fisher and Ursula Owen. New York: Penguin.

Darragh, Neil. 2004. The Future of Christian Thought in the South. Pages 207–14 in *The Future of Christianity: Historical, Sociological, Political, and Theological Perspectives from New Zealand*. Edited by John Stenhouse, Brett Knowles, and G. A. Wood. ATF Series 12. Adelaide: ATF Press.

Davaney, S. G. 2001. Theology and the Turn to Cultural Analysis. Pages 3–16 in *Converging on Culture: Theologians in Dialogue with Cultural Analysis and Criticism*. Edited by D. Brown, S. G. Davaney, and K. Tanner. Oxford: Oxford University Press.

Davidsen, Ole, ed. 2005. *Litteraturen og det hellige. Urtekst-Intertekst-Kontekst*. Aarhus: Aarhus universitetsforlag.

Davidson, Allan K. 1991. *Christianity in Aotearoa: A History of Church and Society in New Zealand*. Wellington: Education for Ministry.

———. 2000. New Zealand History and Religious Myopia. Pages 205–21 in *Mapping the Landscape: Essays in Australian and New Zealand Christianity*. Edited by Susan Emilsen and William W. Emilsen. New York: Peter Lang.

———. 2004. Christianity and National Identity: The Role of the Churches in "the Construction of Nationhood." Pages 16–35 in *The Future of Christianity: Historical, Sociological, Political, and Theological Perspectives from New Zealand*. Edited by John Stenhouse, Brett Knowles, and G. A. Wood. ATF Series 12. Adelaide: ATF Press.

Davidson, Allan K., and Peter J. Lineham. 1995. *Transplanted Christianity: Documents Illustrating Aspects of New Zealand Church History*. 3rd. ed. Palmerston North, New Zealand: Department of History, Massey University.

Davidson, Robert. 2002. The Bible in Church and Academy. Pages 161–73 in *Sense and Sensitivity: Essays on Reading the Bible in Memory of Robert Carroll*. Edited by Alastair G. Hunter and Philip R. Davies. JSOTSup 328. London: Sheffield Academic Press.

Davis, Kortright. 1990. *Emancipation Still Comin': Explorations in Caribbean Emancipatory Theology*. New York: Orbis.

De Gruchy, Steve M. n.d. *See–Judge–Act: Putting Faith into Action. A Handbook for Christian Groups Engaged in Social Transformation*. Unpublished Training Manual. University of KwaZulu-Natal.

De Gruchy, Steve M., and Willem Ellis. 2008. Christian Leadership in "Another Country": Contributing to an Ethical Development Agenda in South Africa Today. Pages 9–20 in *From Our Side: Emerging Perspectives on Development and Ethics.* Edited by Steve S. M. De Gruchy, N. Koopman, and S. Strijbos. Amsterdam: Rozenburg Publishers.

de Man, Paul. 1979. *Allegories of Reading.* New Haven: Yale University Press.

Debray, Régis. 1996. The Book as Symbolic Object. Pages 139–52 in *The Future of the Book.* Edited by Geoffrey Nunberg. Berkeley: University of California Press.

Deleuze, Gilles. 1988. *Bergsonism.* Translated by Hugh Tomlinson and Barbara Habberjam. New York: Zone Books.

———. 1990. *The Logic of Sense.* Translated by Mark Lester and Charles Stivale. New York: Columbia University Press.

———. 1994. *Difference and Repetition.* Translated by Paul Patton. New York: Columbia University Press.

Deleuze, Gilles, and Claire Parnet. 2007. *Dialogues II.* Translated by Hugh Tomlinson and Barbara Habberjam. New York: Columbia University Press.

Deleuze, Gilles, and Félix Guattari. 1994. *What Is Philosophy?* Translated by Hugh Tomlinson and Graham Burchell. New York: Columbia University Press.

DeLoughrey, Elizabeth M. 2007. *Routes and Roots: Navigating Caribbean and Pacific Island Literatures.* Honolulu: University of Hawai'i Press.

Derrida, Jacques. 1973. *Speech and Phenomena.* Translated by David B. Allison. Evanston: Northwestern University Press.

———. 1976. *Of Grammatology.* Translated by Gayatri Chakravorty Spivak. Baltimore: The Johns Hopkins University Press.

———. 1978. *Edmund Husserl's Origin of Geometry: an Introduction.* Translated by John P. Leavey, Jr. Lincoln: University of Nebraska Press.

———. 1981. *Dissemination.* Translated by Barbara Johnson. Chicago: University of Chicago Press.

Devasahayam, Veeramani. 1992. *Outside the Camp: Bible Studies in Dalit Perspective.* Madras: Gurukul.

Devonish, Hubert. 2007. *Language and Liberation: Creole Language Politics in the Caribbean.* Kingston: University of the West Indies Press.

Dick, Devon. 2010. *The Cross and the Machete.* Kingston: Ian Randle Publishers.

Dietrich, Gabriele. 2001. *A New Thing on Earth: Hopes and Fears facing Feminist Theology.* New Delhi: ISPCK.

Dietrich, Walter, and Ulrich Luz, eds. 2002. *The Bible in a World Context: An Experiment in Contextual Hermeneutics.* Grand Rapids: Eerdmans.

Dimova, Theodora. 2007. *Adriana.* Sofia: Ciella.

Donaldson, Laura. 1999. The Sign of Orpah: Reading Ruth through Native Eyes. Pages 20–36 in *Vernacular Hermeneutics.* Edited by R. S. Surgirtharajah. Sheffield: Sheffield Academic.

Donchev, Anton. 1998. *The Peculiar Knight of the Holy Book.* Sofia: Library 48.

Donfried, K. P. 2006. *Who Owns the Bible? Toward the Recovery of a Christian Hermeneutic.* Companions to the New Testament. New York: Crossroad (Herder and Herder).

Douglas, Kelly Brown. 2001. Marginalized People, Liberating Perspectives: A Womanist Approach to Biblical Interpretation. *AThR* 83:25–40.

Draper, Jonathan A. 1996. Great and Little Traditions: Challenges to the Dominant Western Paradigm of Biblical Interpretation. *Bulletin for Contextual Theology* 3:1–2.

Du Bois, W. E. B. 1903. *The Souls of Black Folk: Essays and Sketches.* Chicago: A. C. McClurg.

———. 1995. To the Nations of the World. Pages 639–41 in *W. E. B. Du Bois: A Reader.* Edited by David Levering Lewis. New York: Henry Holt [1900].

Dube, Musa W. 1996. Readings of Semoya: Batswana Women's Interpretations of Matt. 15:21–28. *Semeia* 73:111–29.

Dussel, Enrique. 1985. *Caminhos de Libertação Latino-Americana.* Volume 4. São Paulo: Paulinas.

DuttaAhmed, Shantanu. 1996. Border Crossings: Retrieval and Erasure of the Self as Other. Pages 337–50 in *Between the Lines: South Asians and Postcoloniality.* Edited by Deepika Bahri and Mary Vasudeva. Philadelphia: Temple University Press.

Dvoryanova, Emilia. 1992. *The Aesthetic Nature of Christianity.* Sofia: Sofia University Press.

———. Emilia. 2006. *The Earthly Gardens of the Holy Mother.* Sofia: Obsidian.

Eagleton, Terry. 1991. *Ideology.* London: Verso.

Eco, Umberto. 1976. *A Theory of Semiotics.* Bloomington: Indiana University Press.

———. 1979. *The Role of the Reader.* Bloomington: Indiana University Press.

Edwards, Brent Hayes. 2003. *The Practice of Diaspora: Literature, Translation, and the Rise of Black Internationalism.* Cambridge: Harvard University Press.

Ehrman, Bart D. 1993. *The Orthodox Corruption of Scripture.* Oxford: Oxford University Press.

Einspahr, Jennifer. 2010. Structural Domination and Structural Freedom: A Feminist Perspective. *Feminist Review* 94: 1–19.

Eisenstein, Elizabeth L. 1979. *The Printing Press as an Agent of Change.* 2 vols. Cambridge: Cambridge University Press.

Elvey, Anne. 2005. *An Ecological Feminist Reading of the Gospel of Luke: A Gestational Paradigm.* Lewiston, N.Y.: Edwin Mellen.

Engberg-Pedersen, Troels. 2003a. Indledning. Pages 9–28 in *Den nye Paulus og hans betydning.* Edited by Troels Engberg-Pedersen. Copenhagen: Gyldendal.

Engberg-Pedersen, Troels, ed. 2003b. *Den nye Paulus og hans betydning.* Copenhagen: Gyldendal.

Engberg-Pedersen, Troels, et al., eds. 2006. *Kanon. Bibelens tilblivelse og normative status. Festskrift til Mogens Müller i anledning af 60-års-fødelsedagen den 25. januar 2006.* Forum for Bibelsk Eksegese 15. København: Museum Tusculanums Forlag.

Engnell, Ivan. 1943. *Studies in Divine Kingship in the Ancient Near East.* Uppsala: Almqvist & Wiksell.

———. 1969. *A Rigid Scrutiny: Critical essays on the Old Testament.* 2nd. ed. Translated from Swedish and edited by John T. Willis in cooperation with Helmer Ringgren. Nashville: Vanderbilt University Press.

Epp, Eldon Jay, and George W. MacRae., eds. 1989. *The New Testament and Its Modern Interpreters.* Philadelphia: Fortress; Atlanta: Society of Biblical Literature.

Equiano, Olaudah. 1995. *The Interesting Narrative and Other Writings.* Edited with an introduction by Vincent Carretta. New York: Penguin Books.

Erskine, Noel L. 2000. Biblical Hermeneutics in Modern Caribbean Experience: Paradigms and Prospects. Pages 209–25 in *Religion, Culture, and Tradition in the Caribbean.* Edited by Hemchand Gossai and Nathaniel S. Murrell. New York: St. Martin's Press.

Esman, Milton J. 2005. Canada and the United States: Diaspora Nations. Pages 13–16 in *Canadian Issues* (Fall).

Estermann, Josef, et al. 2006. *Teología andina: el tejido diverso de la fe indígena*. La Paz: ISEAT.

Exum, J. Cheryl, and Stephen D. Moore. 1998a. Biblical Studies/Cultural Studies. Pages 19–45 in *Biblical Studies/Cultural Studies. The Third Sheffield Colloquium*. Edited by Cheryl J. Exum and Stephen D. Moore. JSOTSup 266. Gender, Culture, Theory 7. Sheffield: Sheffield Academic Press.

———, eds. 1998b. *Biblical Studies/Cultural Studies. The Third Sheffield Colloquium*. JSOTSup 266. Gender, Culture, Theory 7. Sheffield: Sheffield Academic Press.

Fanon, Frantz. 1963. *The Wretched of the Earth*. Translated by Constance Farrington. New York: Grove.

———. 1967. *Black Skin, White Masks*. Translated by Charles Lam Markmann. New York: Grove.

Farndon, John. 2007. *China Rises: How China's Astonishing Growth will Change the World*. New York: Virgin Books.

Fasholé-Luke, E. W. 1975. The Quest for African Christian Theology. *JRT* 32:69–89.

Fatum, Lone. 1991. Image of God and Glory of Man: Women in the Pauline Congregations. Pages 56–137 in *Image of God and Gender Models in the Judaeo-Christian Tradition*. Edited by Kari Elisabeth Børresen. Oslo: Solum.

———. 2003. Tro, håb og gode gerninger. Kristusfællesskabet som social konstruktion. Pages 120–55 in *Den nye Paulus og hans betydning*. Edited by Troels Engberg-Pedersen. Copenhagen: Gyldendal.

———. 2006. Bedrevidende Bibel. Fra skriftautoritet til kanonisk kontrol. Pages 242–55 in *Kanon. Bibelens tilblivelse og normative status. Festskrift til Mogens Müller i anledning af 60-års-fødselsedagen den 25. januar 2006*. Edited by Troels Engberg-Pedersen et al. Forum for Bibelsk Eksegese 15. København: Museum Tusculanums Forlag.

Fejo, Wali. 2000. The Voice of the Earth: An Indigenous Reading of Genesis 9. Pages 140–46 in *The Earth Story in Genesis*. The Earth Bible, 2. Edited by Norman C. Habel and Shirley Wurst. Sheffield: Sheffield Academic.

Felder, Cain Hope. 1989. *Troubling Biblical Waters: Race, Class, and Family*. Maryknoll, N.Y.: Orbis.

———. 1991. Race, Racism, and the Biblical Narratives. Pages 127–45 in *Stony the Road We Trod African American Biblical Interpretation*. Edited by Cain Hope Felder. Minneapolis: Fortress.

———. 1993. Cultural Ideology, Afrocentrism and Biblical Interpretation. Pages 184–95 in *Black Theology: A Documentary History. Volume Two: 1980–1992*. Edited by James H. Cone and Gayraud Wilmore. 2 vols. Maryknoll, N.Y.: Orbis.

Felder, Cain Hope, ed. 1991. *Stony the Road We Trod African American Biblical Interpretation*. Minneapolis: Fortress.

Feldman, Shelley. 2001. Exploring Theories of Patriarchy: A Perspective from Contemporary Bangladesh. *Signs* 26/4:1097–1127.

Ferens, Dominika. 2002. *Edith and Winnifred Eaton: Chinatown Missions and Japanese Romances*. Urbana: University of Illinois Press.

Fitzmyer, Joseph A. S.J. 2008. *The Interpretation of Scripture: In Defense of the Historical-Critical Method*. Mahwah: Paulist.

Ford, Richard Thompson. 2008. *The Race Card: How Bluffing about Bias Makes Race Relations Worse*. New York: Farrar.

Foskett, Mary F. 2002. The Accidents of Being and the Politics of Identity: Biblical Images of Adoption and Asian Adoptees in America. *Semeia* 90/91:135–44.

Foskett, Mary F. and Jeffrey Kah-Jin Kuan, eds. 2006. *Ways of Being, Ways of Reading: Asian American Biblical Interpretation*. St. Louis: Chalice.

Fowler, Robert M., E, Blumhofer, and Fernando F. Segovia, eds. 2004. *New Paradigms for Bible Study: The Bible in the Third Millennium*. New York: T&T Clark.

Franchetto, Bruna. n.d. Línguas indígenas e comprometimento lingüístico no Brasil: situação, necessidades e soluções. *Cadernos de Educação Escolar Indígena* 3:9–26.

Franzmann, Majella. 2004. *Jesus in the Nag Hammadi Writings*. London: Continuum.

Freire Paulo. 1996. *Pedagogy of the Oppressed*. rev. ed. Translated by M. Ramos. Harmondsworth: Penguin.

Fridrichsen, Anton. 1972. *The Problem of Miracle in Primitive Christianity*. Minneapolis: Augsburg. (ET of *Le Problème du Miracle dans le Christianisme Primitif* published by the Faculty of Protestant Theology at the University of Strasbourg 1925).

———. 1994. *Exegetical Writings: A Selection*. Translated and edited by Chrys C. Caragounis and Tord Fornberg. Tübingen: Mohr-Siebeck.

Frisotti, Heitor. 1994. Pueblo Negro y Biblia: reconquista histórica. *RIBLA* 19:47–62. See: http://www.claiweb.org/ribla/ribla19/pueblo%20negro.html.

Frye, Northrop. 1971. *The Bush Garden: Essays on the Canadian Imagination*. Toronto: House of Anansi.

———. 1982. *The Great Code: The Bible and Literature*. London: Ark.

Gamble, Harry Y. 1995. *Books and Readers in the Early Church*. New Haven: Yale University Press.

García-Treto, Francisco. 2000. Hyphenating Joseph: A View of Genesis 39–41 from the Cuban Diaspora. Pages 134–45 in *Decolonizing Biblical Studies: A View from the Margins*. Fernando F. Segovia. New York: Orbis.

Garry, Ann. 2011 Intersectionality, Metaphors and the Multiplicity of Gender, *Hypatia* 26/4:826–50.

Gates, Henry Louis, Jr. 1988. *The Signifying Monkey: A Theory of Afro-American Literary Criticism*. New York: Oxford University Press.

Gebara, Ivone. 2002. *El rostro oculto del mal: una teología desde la experiencia de las mujeres*. Madrid: Trotta.

———. 2004. Teología de la liberación y género: ensayo crítico feminista. Pages 107–36 in *Religión y género*. Edited by S. Marcos et al. Madrid: Trotta.

———. 2005. Bible et communautés croyantes: interactions fécondes et conflits. Presentation at "Lire la Bible" Colloque Omnes Gentes, Louvain-la-Neuve. See: www.lumenonline.net/.../8._Bible_et_communaut%E9s_croyantes.doc?cidReq= lumen_+LV.

Gerhardsson, Birger. 1994. *Fridrichsen, Odeberg, Aulén, Nygren, Fyra teologer*. Lund: Novapress.

———. 2005. Uppsalaexegetiken. Pages 392–95 in *Sveriges kyrkohistoria 8. Religionsfrihetens och ekumenikens tid*. Edited by Ingmar Brohed. Stockholm: Verbum.

Gibson, Mel (director). 2004. *The Passion of the Christ*. Newmarket Films.

Gillmayr-Bucher, Susanne. 2004. Body Images in the Psalms. *JSOT* 28/3:301–26.

Gilmore, Alec. 2000. *A Dictionary of the English Bible and its Origin*. Sheffield: Sheffield Academic.

Glancy, Jennifer A. 1998. House Reading and Field Readings: The Discourse of Slavery and Biblical/Cultural Studies. Pages 460–77 in Exum and Moore 1998b.

Gluckman, Max. 1954. *Rituals of Rebellion in South-East Africa*. Manchester: Manchester University Press.

Gnanavaram, M. 1997. Some Reflections on Dalit Hermeneutics. Pages 329–35 in *Frontiers of Dalit Theology*. Edited by V. Devasahayam. Chennai: Gurukul; New Delhi: ISPCK.

Gooder, P. 2008. *Searching for Meaning. An Introduction to Interpreting the New Testament*. London: SPCK.

Goodhart, David. 2008. Has Multiculturalism had its Day? A Leading British Critic Finds Canada's Approach Outdated. *Literary Review of Canada* 16/3:3–4.

Gossai, Hemchand. 1988. The Old Testament: A Heresy Continued? *WW* 8:150–57.

Grant, Robert M., with David Tracy. 1984. *A Short History of the Interpretation of the Bible*. 2nd. ed. Minneapolis: Fortress.

Green, J. B. 1995. The Challenge of Hearing the New Testament. Pages 1–9 in *Hearing the New Testament. Strategies for Interpretation*. Edited by J. B. Green. Grand Rapids: Eerdmans.

———. 2005. Learning Theological Interpretation From Luke. Pages 55–78 in *Reading Luke: Interpretation, Reflection, Formation*. Edited by C. Bartholomew, J. B. Green, and A. C. Thiselton. Grand Rapids: Paternoster.

Gregory, Howard, ed. 1995. *Caribbean Theology: Preparing for the Challenges Ahead*. Kingston: Canoe Press.

Gresser, Edward. 2007. Is "Free Trade" Working? Testimony before the Senate Commerce Committee, Subcommittee on Interstate Commerce, Trade and Tourism, 18 April. http://www.ppionline.org/ppi_ci.cfm?knlgAreaID=108&subsecid=206&contentid=254256.

Gugelberger, G. M. 1994. Postcolonial Cultural Studies. Pages 581–85 in *The Johns Hopkins Guide to Literary Theory & Criticism*. Edited by M. Groden and M. Kreiswirth. Baltimore: Johns Hopkins University Press.

Gundaker, Grey. 1998. *Signs of Diaspora, Diaspora of Signs: Literacies, Creolization, and Vernacular Practice in African America*. New York: Oxford University Press.

Gunn, David M. 1998. Colonialism and the Vagaries of Scripture: Te Kooti in Canaan. Pages 127–42 in *God in the Fray: A Tribute to Walter Brueggemann*. Edited by Tod Linafelt and Timothy K. Beal. Minneapolis: Fortress.

Gutiérrez, Gustavo. 1971. *Notas para una teología de la liberación*. Lima: Centro de Estudios y Publicaciones.

———. 1973. *A Theology of Liberation: History, Politics, and Salvation*. Translated by Sister Caridad Inda and John Eagleson. Maryknoll, N.Y.: Orbis.

———. 1986. *Hablar de Dios desde el sufrimiento del inocente: una reflexión sobre el libro de Job*. Salamanca: Sígueme.

Gyllenberg, Rafael. 1944. Den exegetiska forskningen i Finland under det senaste halvseklet. *SEÅ* 9:5–34.

Habel, Norman, ed. 2000–2002, *The Earth Bible*. 5 vols. Sheffield: Sheffield Academic Press.

——— ed. 2004. *Seven Songs of Creation: Liturgies for Celebrating and Healing Earth: An Earth Bible Resource*. Cleveland: Pilgrim Press.

Habel, Norman, and Peter Trudinger, eds. 2008. *Exploring Ecological Hermeneutics*. Atlanta: Society of Biblical Literature.

Haddad, Beverley G. 2000. African Women's Theologies of Survival: Intersecting Faith,

Feminisms, and Development. Ph.D. diss., University of Natal.

Halapua, Winston. 2008. Moana Methodology of Leadership. Paper presented at Talanoa Oceania 2008: Mana, Vanua, Talanoa. Centre for Ministry, North Parramatta, NSW, Australia (September 30).

Hall, Kenneth O., ed. 2006. *Rex N: Rex Nettleford—Selected Speeches*. Kingston: Ian Randle Publishers.

Harrill, J. Albert. 2006. *Slaves in the New Testament: Literary, Social, and Moral Dimensions*. Minneapolis: Fortress.

Harrisville, R. A. 1995. A Critique of Current Biblical Criticism. *WW* 15:206–13.

Hartman, Lars. 1976. New Testament Exegesis. Pages 51–65 in *Uppsala University 500 years. 1, Faculty of Theology at Uppsala University*. Edited by Helmer Ringgren. Uppsala: Uppsala University.

———. 1986. *Uppsala Exegetiska Sällskap 1936–1986*. Uppsala: Pro Veritate.

———. 1992. Scandinavian School: NT Studies. Pages 1002–4 in *ABD* Vol 5. Edited by David Noel Freedman et al. New York: Doubleday.

Haug, Wolfgang Fritz. 2000. O projeto do Dicionário Histórico-Crítico do Marxismo. *Crítica Marxista* 10:139–48. See: http//www.unicamp.br/cemarx/criticamarxista/C_Haug.pdf.

Havea, Jione. 2003. *Elusions of Control: Biblical Law on the Words Of Women*. Atlanta: Society of Biblical Literature.

———. 2007. Is There a Home for the Bible in the Postmodern World? *JES* 42:547–59.

———. 2008. Telling as If a Local: Toward Homing the Bible Outside Western [Main] streams. *JOSKIRAN: Journal of Religion and Thought* 5:80–95.

———. forthcoming. Bare Feet Welcome: Redeemer Xs Moses @ Enaim, in *Bible, Borders, Belongings*. Edited by Elaine Wainwright, David Neville, and Jione Havea.

Hayes, J. H., and C. R. Holladay. 1987. *Biblical Exegesis: A Beginner's Handbook*. rev ed. Atlanta: John Knox.

Hayles, N. Katherine. 1999. *How We Became Posthuman: Virtual Bodies in Cybernetics, Literature, and Informatics*. Chicago: University of Chicago Press.

Heine, Gunnar. 2000. Theology and Spirituality. Pages 122–48 in *Nordic Folk Churches. A Contemporary Church History*. Edited by Björn Ryman et al. Grand Rapids: Eerdmans.

Hens-Piazza, G. 2002. *The New Historicism*. Minneapolis: Fortress.

Hess, M. E. 2004. The Bible and Popular Culture. Engaging Sacred Text in a World of Others. Pages 207–24 in Fowler, Blumhofer, and Segovia 2004.

Hill Collins, Patricia. 1998. *Fighting Words: Black Wo/men & the Search for Justice*. Minnesota: University of Minnesota Press.

Hjelde, Sigurd. 2006. *Sigmund Mowinckel und seine Zeit: Leben und Werk eines norwegischen Alttestamentlers*. FAT 50. Tübingen: Mohr Siebeck.

Hoffman, John W., and Michael J. Enright, eds. 2008. *China Into the Future: Making Sense of the World's Most Dynamic Economy*. Singapore: John Wiley.

Holmberg, Bengt, and Mikael Winninge, eds. 2008. *Identity Formation in the New Testament*. WUNT 227. Tübingen: Mohr Siebeck.

Horsley, Richard A. 1995. Innovation in Search of Reorientation. New Testament Studies Rediscovering its Subject Matter. *JAAR* 62:1127–66.

Hristova, Boriana Vladimirova, trans. and ed. 1994. *The Book of Enoch* [Bulgarian]. Sofia: Silhuette-33.

———, trans. and ed. 2008. *Queen Mab* [Bulgarian]. Sofia: Queen Mab.

Huie-Jolly, Mary. 2002. Maori "Jews" and a Resistant Reading of John 5:10–47. Pages 94–110 in *John and Postcolonialism: Travel, Space and Power*. Edited by Musa W. Dube and Jeffrey L. Staley. London: Sheffield Academic Press.

Husserl, Edmund. 1978. *The Origin of Geometry*. Translated by David Carr. Pages 157–80 in Jacques Derrida, *Edmund Husserl's Origin of Geometry: an Introduction*. Lincoln: University of Nebraska Press.

Hylton, Patrick C. 2002. *The Role of Religion in Caribbean History: From Amerindian Shamanism to Rastafarianism*. Edited by Klaus May. Washington D.C.: Billpops.

Ihimaera, Witi. 1986. *The Matriarch*. Auckland: Heinemann.

James, Leslie R. 2000. Bible and Decolonization in Post-World War II Caribbean Political Discourse. Pages 143–66 in *Religion, Culture and Tradition in the Caribbean*. Edited by N. S. Murrell and H. Gossai. New York: Palgrave.

Jennings, S. C. A. 2007. "Ordinary" Reading in "Extraordinary Times": A Jamaican Love Story. Pages 49–62 in *Reading Other-Wise: Socially Engaged Biblical Scholars Reading with Their Local Communities*. Edited by Gerald O. West. Atlanta: Society of Biblical Literature.

Jeppesen, Knud, and Benedikt Otzen, eds. 1984. *The Productions of Time: Tradition History in Old Testament Scholarship*. Sheffield: Almond.

Jesurathnam, K. June 2002. Towards a Dalit Liberative Hermeneutic: Re-reading the Psalms of Lament. *Bangalore Theological Forum* 34/1:2–3.

Jiménez, Luz, ed. 1997. *La palabra se hizo india*. RIBLA 26. San José: Departamento Ecuménico de Investigaciones.

Jobling, Jánnine. 2002. *Feminist Biblical Interpretation in Theological Context: Restless Readings*. Burlington: Ashgate.

John, M. P. 1965. The Use of the Bible by Indian Christian Theologians. *IJT* 14/2:43–51.

Johnson, Sylverster A. 2004. *The Myth of Ham in Nineteenth-Century American Christianity: Race, Heathens, and the People of God*. New York: Palgrave Macmillan.

———. 2010. The Bible, Slavery, and the Problem of Slavery. Pages 231–48 in *Beyond Slavery: Overcoming Its Religious and Sexual Legacies*. Edited by Bernadette Brooten. New York: Palgrave.

Kaeppler, Adrienne. 1993. *Poetry in Motion: Studies of Tongan Dance*. Nuku'alofa: Vava'u.

Käsemann, Ernst. 1972/73. The Problem of a New Testament Theology. *NTS* 19:235–45.

Kearney, Michael. 1984. *World View*. Novato: Chandler & Sharp.

Keegan, Terence J. 1995. Biblical Criticism and the Challenge of Postmodernism. *BibInt* 3:1–14.

Kelber, Werner. 1983. *The Oral and the Written Gospel*. Philadelphia: Fortress.

Kelley, Shawn. 2002. *Racializing Jesus: Race, Ideology and the Formation of Modern Biblical Scholarship*. New York: Routledge.

Keown, Mark J. 2008. *Congregational Evangelism in Philippians: The Centrality of an Appeal for Gospel Proclamation to the Fabric of Philippians*. Milton Keyes: Paternoster.

Kieffer, René, and Birger Olsson, eds. 1993. *Exegetik idag. Nya frågor till gamla texter* (Religio 11). Lund: Teologiska Institutionen.

Kim, Chan-Hie. 1995. Reading the Cornelius Story from an Asian Immigrant Perspective. Pages 165–74 in Segovia and Tolbert 1995a.

Kim, Chang-Rak. 1997. Giro-e Seo-it-neun Minjung Shin-hak (Minjung Theology Standing at the Crossroad). *Shin-hak Sa-sang* (*Theological Thought*) 96:54–98.

Kim, Uriah (Yong-Hwan). 2002. Uriah the Hittite: A (Con)Text of Struggle for Identity. *Semeia* 90/91:69–85.

King, Ursula, ed. 1994. *Feminist Theology from the Third World: A Reader*. Maryknoll, N.Y.: Orbis.

Kirova, Milena. 2005. *Biblical Femininity: Mechanisms of Construction, Politics of Representation*. Sofia: Stigmati & Sofia University Press.

Kelso, Julie. 2007. *O Mother, Where Art Thou? An Irigarayan Reading of the Book of Chronicles*. London: Equinox.

Knight, Douglas, and Gene M. Tucker., eds. 1985. *The Hebrew Bible and Its Modern Interpreters*. Philadelphia: Fortress; Atlanta: Society of Biblical Literature.

Koshy, Susan. 2008. Why the Humanities Matter for Race Studies Today. *PMLA* 123:1542–49.

Kraft, Robert A. 2007. Para-Mania: Beside, Before and Beyond Bible Studies. *JBL* 126:5–27.

Kraft, Robert A., and George W. E. Nickelsburg Jr., eds. 1986. *Early Judaism and Its Modern Interpreters*. Philadelphia: Fortress; Atlanta: Society of Biblical Literature.

Kreitzer, Larry J. 2002. *Gospel Images in Fiction and Film*. Sheffield: Sheffield Academic.

Kristeva, Julia. 1984. *Revolution in Poetic Language*. Translated by Margaret Waller. New York: Columbia University Press.

———. *Strangers to Ourselves*. Translated by Leon S. Roudiez. New York: Columbia University Press.

Kuck, David. 2007. *Preaching in the Caribbean: Building up a People for Mission*. Kingston: Faith Works.

Kurewa, John Wesley Z. 1997. *The Church in Mission: A Short History of The United Methodist Church in Zimbabwe, 1897–1997*. Nashville: Abingdon.

———. 2000. *Preaching & Cultural Identity: Proclaiming the Gospel in Africa*. Nashville: Abingdon.

Kwok, Pui Lan. 1998. Jesus/the Native: Biblical Studies from a Postcolonial Perspective. Pages 69–85 in Segovia and Tolbert 1998.

———. 1998. Reflection on Women's Sacred Scriptures. *Concilium* 1998 (3): 105–12.

———. 2004. Finding a Home for Ruth: Gender, Sexuality, and the Politics of Otherness. Pages 135–54 in Fowler, Blumhofer, and Segovia 2004.

———. 2005. *Postcolonial Imagination and Feminist Theology*. Louisville: Westminster John Knox.

Kysar, R. 2005. *Voyages with John: Charting the Fourth Gospel*. Waco: Baylor University Press.

Lanner, Laurel. 2006. *"Who Will Lament Her?" The Feminine and the Fantastic in the Book of Nahum*. LHBOTS 434. New York: T&T Clark.

Lategan, B. C. 1988. Why So Few Converts to New Paradigms in Theology? Pages 65–78 in *Paradigms and Progress in Theology*. Edited by J. Mouton, A. Van Aarde, and W. Vorster. Pretoria: HSRC.

Lategan, B. C, and W. S. Vorster, eds. 1985. *Text and Reality. Aspects of Reference in Biblical Text*. Atlanta: Scholars Press.

Laughton, J. G. 1961. *From Forest Trail to City Street: The Story of the Presbyterian Church among the Maori People*. Christchurch: The Presbyterian Bookroom.

Lawrence, Louise J. 2007. Being "Hefted": Reflections on Place, Stories and Contextual Bible Study. *ExpTim* 118/11:530–35.

Lee, Myung-Bak. 2008. We Must Guard against Infodemics. Address to the National Assembly. http://www.koreatimes.co.kr/www/news/nation/2008/07/116_27445.html

Levenson, Alan. Missionary Protestants as Defenders and Detractors of Judaism: Franz Delitzsch and Hermann Strack. 2002. *JQR* 92:383–420.

Liew, Tat-siong Benny. 2002. More Than Personal Encounters: Identity, Community, and Interpretation. *USQR* 56:41–44.

Liew, Tat-siong Benny and Vincent L. Wimbush. 2002. Contact Zones and Zoning Contexts: From the Los Angeles 'Riot' to a New York Symposium. *USQR* 56:21–40.

Lindeskog, Gösta. 1950a. Nordische Literatur zum Neuen Testament 1939–1949. *TRu N.F.* 18:217–38.

———. 1950b. Nordische Literatur zum Neuen Testament 1939–1949 (Fortsetzung). *TRu N.F.* 18:288–317.

Ling, Amy and Annette White-Parks, eds. 1995. *Mrs. Spring Fragrance and Other Writings.* Urbana: University of Illinois Press.

Lodberg, Peter, and Björn Ryman. 2000. Church and Society. Pages 99–121 in *Nordic Folk Churches: A Contemporary Church History.* Edited by Björn Ryman et al. Grand Rapids: Eerdmans.

Long, Charles H. 1986. *Significations: Signs, Symbols, and Images in the Interpretation of Religion.* Philadelphia: Fortress.

Lowe, Lisa. 2006. The Intimacies of Four Continents. Pages 191–212 in *Haunted by Empire: Geographies of Intimacy in North American History.* Edited by Ann Laura Stoler. Durham: Duke University Press.

Lugones, Maria. 2007. Heterosexualism and the Colonial/ Modern Gender System. *Hypatia* 22:186–209

———. 2010. Toward a Decolonial Feminism. *Hypatia* 25:742–59.

Lutteman, Ester. 1959. *Kyrkan-mitt öde: fragment ur en själs historia.* Stockholm: Wahlström och Widstrand.

Luz, U. 1994. *Matthew in History: Interpretation, Influence, and Effects.* Minneapolis: Fortress.

Lyons, William John. 2005. A Man of Honour, A Man of Strength, A Man of Will? A Canonical Approach to Psalm 137. *Didaskalia* 16:41–68.

McDonald, Lee Martin. 2011. *Origin of the Bible: A Guide for the Perplexed.* New York: T&T Clark.

McFague, Sallie. 2008. *A New Climate for Theology: God, the World, and Global Warming.* Minneapolis: Fortress.

McKean, John. 1994. *The Church in a Special Colony: A History of the Presbyterian Synod of Otago & Southland 1866–1991.* Dunedin: Synod of Otago Southland, Presbyterian Church of Aotearoa New Zealand.

McKenzie, N. R. 1942. *The Gael Fares Forth.* 2nd. ed. Wellington: Whitcombe & Tombs.

McKinlay, Judith. 2006. *Reframing Her: Biblical Women in Postcolonial Focus.* Sheffield: Phoenix.

McKinney, Larry. 1998. The Growth of the Bible College Movement in Canada. *Did* 9:31–48.

McKnight, S., and G. R. Osborne, eds. 2004. *The Face of New Testament Studies: A Survey of Recent Research.* Grand Rapids: Baker Academic.

McQueen, Cilla. 1982. *Homing In.* Dunedin: John McIndoe.

Magalhães, A.C. Mello. 200 anos de Bíblia no Brasil. See: http://victorhfm.multiply.com/reviews/item/6.

Mahbubani, Kishore. 2008. *The New Asian Hemisphere: The Irresistible Shift of Global Power to the East.* New York: Public Affairs.

Maeda, Daryl J. 2009. *Chains of Babylon: The Rise of Asian America.* Minneapolis: University of Minnesota Press.

Maier, Harry O. 2002. *Apocalypse Recalled: The Book of Revelation after Christendom.* Minneapolis: Fortress.

———. Coming out of Babylon: A First-World reading of Revelation among Immigrants. 2005. Pages 62–81 in *From Every People and Nation: The Book of Revelation in Intercultural Perspective.* Edited by David Rhoads. Minneapolis: Fortress.

———. 2007. The Familiar Made Strange: An Orientation to Biblical Study in Vancouver. *Teaching Theology and Religion* 10:80–86.

Maluleke, Tinyiko S. 1996. Theological Interest in AIC's and other Grass-root Communities in South Africa. Part 1 and Part 2. *Journal of Black Theology in South Africa* 10:18–29.

———. 2001. African Ruths in Ruthless Africa: Reflections of an African Mordecai. Pages 237–51 in *Other Ways of Reading: African Women and the Bible.* Geneva: WCC Publications.

Maluleke, Tinyiko S., and Sarojini Nadar. 2004. Alien Fraudsters in the White Academy: Agency in Gendered Colour. *JTSA* 120:5–17.

Manchala, Deenabandhu. n.d. *Reading together with the Dalits: An Exploration for Common Hermeneutical Directions amidst Plurality of Interpretations.* Unpublished.

Manson, Ian. 2005. R. B. Y. Scott: A Force for Personal and Social Regeneration. *Touchstone* 23:32–42.

Marshall, Christopher D. 2007. Re-engaging with the Bible in a Postmodern World. *Stimulus* 15:5–16.

Marshall, I. Howard. 2004. *New Testament Theology: Many Witnesses, One Gospel.* Downers Grove, Ill: InterVarsity Press.

Massey, Doreen. 2001. *Space, Place, and Gender.* Minneapolis: University of Minnesota Press.

Massey, James. 1994. *Towards Dalit Hermeneutics.* New Delhi: ISPCK.

———. 1995. *Dalits in India: Religion as a Source of Bondage or Liberation with Special Reference to Christians.* New Delhi: Manohar.

Mathur, Colette, Frank-Jürgen Richter, and Tarun Das. 2005. *India Rising: Emergence of a New World Power.* Singapore: Marshall Cavendish.

Mazrui, Ali. 1990. *Cultural Forces in World Politics.* London: James Curry.

Mbiti, John S. 1969. *African Religions & Philosophy.* New York: Frederick A. Praeger.

Meadowcroft, Tim. 2000. Some Questions for the Earth Bible. Unpublished paper presented to ANZATS Conference, Christchurch.

———. 2006. *Haggai. Readings: A New Biblical Commentary.* Sheffield: Sheffield Phoenix.

———. 2007. The Subtle Temptations of State Sponsored Theological Education: A New Zealand Perspective. *Teaching Theology and Religion* 10:25–33.

Meek, Theophile J. 1958. Near Eastern Studies. *Encyclopedia Canadiana* 7:259–60.

Melanchthon, Monica J. 2005. Dalit Readers of the Word: The Quest for Hermeneutics and Method. Pages 45–64 in *Frontiers in Dalit Hermeneutics.* Edited by James Massey and Samson Prabhakar. Bangalore/New Delhi: BTESSC/CDSS.

———. November 2005b. Dalits, Bible and Method. *SBL Forum.* Online: www.sbl-site.org/publications/article.aspx?articleId=459.

———. 2007. Akkamahadevi and the Samaritan Woman: Paradigms of Resistance and Spirituality. Pages 35–54 in *Border Crossings: Cross-Cultural Hermeneutics.* Essays in Honor of Prof. R. S. Sugirtharajah. Edited by D. N. Premnath. Maryknoll, N.Y.: Orbis.

Mesters, Carlos. 1983. *Flor sin defensa. Una explicación de la Biblia a partir del pueblo.* Bogotá: CLAR.

Mesters, Carlos and Francisco Rodrigues Orofino. 2007. Sobre a Leitura Popular da Bíblia. *Adital: Notícias da América Latina e Caribe.* Online: http://www.adital.com.br/site/noticia.asp?lang=PT&cod=30207.

Michaylov, Kalin. 2007. *Shed in Your Name: Poems and Fragments.* Sofia: Sofia-S.A.

Míguez, Néstor. 2004. Reading John 4 in the Interface between Ordinary and Scholarly Interpretation. Pages 334–47 in *Through the Eyes of Another: Intercultural Reading of the Bible.* Edited by Hans de Wit, Louis Jonker, Marleen Kool, and Daniel Schipani. Amsterdam: Institute of Mennonite Studies–Vriej Universiteit.

———. Latin American Reading of the Bible: Experiences, Challenges, and its Practice. 2006. *ExpTim* 118:120–29.

Miller, Patrick D. 1986. *Interpreting the Psalms.* Minneapolis: Augsburg Fortress.

Miranda, José Porfirio. 1971. *Marx y la Biblia.* México: Río Hondo.

Mitchell, Christine. 2007. Temperance, Temples and Colonies: Reading the Book of Haggai in Saskatoon. *SR* 36:261–77.

Moir, John S. 1982. *A History of Biblical Studies in Canada: A Sense of Proportion* Chico: Scholars Press.

Moore, Albert C. n.d. The Religious Significance of Modern Maori Artists: Traditional Religions and New Mixtures. Pages 31–45 in *The Catholic Presbyterian.* Dunedin: Theological Hall, Knox College.

Moore, Stephen D. 1992. *Mark & Luke in Poststructuralist Perspectives: Jesus Begins to Write.* New Haven: Yale University Press.

———. 1994. *Poststructuralism and the New Testament.* Minneapolis: Fortress.

———. 1998b. Between Birmingham and Jerusalem: Cultural Studies and Biblical Studies. Pages 1–32 in Moore (ed) 1998a.

——— ed. 1998a. *In Search of the Present: The Bible through Cultural Studies. Semeia* 82. Atlanta: Society of Biblical Literature.

Morisada Rietz, Henry W. 2002. My Father Has No Children: Reflections on a *Hapa* Identity: Toward a Hermeneutic of Particularity. *Semeia* 90/91:145–57.

———. 2006. Living Past: A *Hapa* Identifying with the Exodus, the Exile, and the Internment. Pages 192–203 in Foskett and Kuan 2006.

Morris, Meaghan. 1988. *The Pirate's Fiancée: Feminism, Reading, Postmodernism.* London: Verso.

———. 1990. Metamorphoses at Sydney Tower. *New Formations* 11:5–18.

Morris, Paul, Harry Ricketts, and Mike Grimshaw, eds. 2002. *Spirit in a Strange Land: A Selection of New Zealand Spiritual Verse.* Auckland: Godwit.

Morrison, Toni. 1995. Site of Memory. In *Inventing the Truth: The Art and Craft of Memoir.* Edited by William Zinsser. Boston: Houghton and Mifflin.

Mostert, Christiaan. 2002. *God and the Future: Wolfhardt Pannenberg's Eschatological Doctrine of God.* London: T&T Clark.

Mowinckel, Sigmund. 1921–1924. *Psalmenstudien I–IV.* Oslo: SNVAO.

———. 1951. *Han som kommer. Messiasforventningen i det Gamle Testament og på Jesu tid.* Copenhagen: Gad. (ET 1956: *He That Cometh.* Oxford: Blackwell).

Moxnes, Halvor, Turid Karlsen Seim, and Reidar Aasgaard. Fortolkning og forkynnelse. Det nye testamente ved Universitetet i Oslo i det 20. århundre. *NTT* 101:33–51.

Mugambi, J. N. K. 1997. The Bible and ecumenism in African Christianity. Pages 68–85 in *The Bible in African Christianity: Essays in Biblical Theology.* Edited by H. W. Kinoti and J. M. Waliggo. Nairobi: Acton.

Murrell, Nathaniel Samuel. 1991. Wresting the Message from the Messenger: The Rastafarai as a Case Study in the Caribbean Indigenization of the Bible. Pages 169–88 in *Voices from the Margin: Interpreting the Bible in the Third World.* Edited by R. S. Sugirtharajah. Maryknoll, N.Y.: Orbis.

———. 2000. Dangerous Memories, Underdevelopment and the Bible in Colonial Caribbean Experience. Pages 9–35 in *Religion, Culture and Tradition in the Caribbean.* Edited by N.S. Murrell and H. Gossai. New York: Palgrave.

———. 2009. *Afro-Caribbean Religions: An Introduction to Their Historical, Cultural, and Sacred Traditions.* Philadelphia: Temple University Press.

Nadar, Sarojini. 2000. Emerging From Muddy Waters. Pages 15–32 in *Claiming Our Footprints: South African Women Reflect on Context, Identity and Spirituality.* Edited by D. M. Ackermann, E. J .Getman, H. Kotze, and J. Tobler. Stellenbosch: Ecumenical Foundation of South Africa.

———. 2003. Power, Ideology and Interpretation/s: Womanist and Literary Perspectives on the Book of Esther as Resources for Gender-Social Transformation. Ph.D. diss., University of Natal.

———. 2009. Toward a Feminist Missiological Agenda: A Case Study of the Jacob Zuma Rape Trial. *Missionalia* 37:85–102.

———. forthcoming. Who's Afraid of the Bible Believing Christian? Reading the Bible in Relation to Neo-Pentecostal Challenges. *JTSA* 132.

Naidenov, Ivaylo. 2008. *The Biblical Jonas.* Sofia: Biblical Collegium.

Nash, Jennifer. 2008. Rethinking Intersectionality. *Feminist Review* 89/1:1–15.

Nath, Kamal. 2008. *India's Century.* New York: McGraw-Hill.

Naudé, P. 2005. Can We Still Hear Paul on the Agora? An Outsider Perspective on South African New Testament Scholarship. *Neot* 39:339–58.

Nedelchev, Michail, ed. 1999. *The Savior.* Sofia: Citizen Association.

Needham, D. E. 1984. *From Iron Age to Independence: A History of Central Africa.* Zimbabwe: Longmans.

Nelavala, Surekha. 2006. Smart Syrophoenician Woman: A Dalit Feminist Reading of Mark 7:24–31. *ExpTim* 118/2:64–69.

Nelson, Alissa Jones. 2009. Job in Conversation with Edward Said. SBL Forum, n.p. Online: http://sbl-site.org/Article.aspx?ArticleID=797

New Biblical Dictionary. 2007. Sofia: New Person. Translation of *New Biblical Dictionary.* 1996. 3rd. ed. Nottingham: Inter-Varsity Press.

Ngai, Sianne. 2005. *Ugly Feelings.* Cambridge: Harvard University Press.

Nirmal, Arvind P. 1990. *Heuristic Explorations.* Madras: CLS/Gurukul.

Noll, Mark A. 1987. Review Essay: Bible in America. *JBL* 106:493–509.

Nora, Pierre. 1994. Between Memory and History: *Les Lieux de Memoire.* Pages 284–300 in *History and Memory in African-American Culture.* Edited by Genevieve Fabre and Robert O'Meally. New York: Oxford University Press.

Norget, Kristin. 1997. Progressive Theology and Popular Religiosity in Oaxaca, Mexico. *Ethnology* 36:67–83.

Norris, Peter Joseph. 1999. *Southernmost Seminary: The Story of Holy Cross College, Mosgiel 1900–97.* Auckland: Holy Cross Seminary.

Nunberg, Geoffrey, ed. 1996. *The Future of the Book.* Berkeley and Los Angeles: University of California Press.

O'Brien Wicker, Kathleen, Althea Spencer Miller, and Musa W. Dube, eds. 2005. *Feminist New Testament Studies: Global and Future Perspectives.* New York: Palgrave.

Økland, Jorunn. 2004. *Women in Their Place. Paul and the Corinthian Discourse of Gender and Sanctuary Space.* JSNTSup 269. London: T&T Clark.

Olsson, Birger. 1985. A Decade of Text-Linguistic Analyses of Biblical Texts at Uppsala. *ST* 39:107–26.

———. 1999. Förändringar inom svensk bibelforskning under 1900-talet. Pages 68–135 in *Modern svensk teologi.* Edited by in Håkan Eilert et al. Stockholm: Verbum.

———. 2008. Att läsa Bibeln tillsammans med de döda: Om svensk receptionskritik på 2000-talet. *SEÅ* 73:143–59.

O'Neill, John. 1961. *The Theology of Acts in Its Historical Setting.* London: SPCK.

———. 1972. *The Recovery of Paul's Letter to the Galatians.* London: SPCK.

———. 1975. *Paul's Letter to the Romans.* Harmondsworth: Penguin.

Ong, Walter J., S.J. 1967. *The Presence of the Word.* New Haven: Yale University Press.

———. 1982. *Orality and Literacy.* New York: Methuen.

Oredsson, Sverker. 1997. Svenska teologer under naziteiden. *STK* 73:167–78.

Painter, John. 1979. *John: Witness and Theologian.* London: SPCK.

———. 2002. *1, 2 and 3 John.* Collegeville, Minn.: Liturgical Press.

Palmer, Delano. 2010. *Messianic "I" and Rastafari in Dialogue: Bio-Narratives, The Apocalypse, and Paul's Letter to the Romans.* Lanham: University Press of America.

Palumbo-Liu, David. 1995. Theory and the Subject of Asian America Studies. *Amerasia Journal* 21:55–65.

Partner, N. F. 2008. Historiography (Concordia University, Wisconsin). Online: http://www.cuw.edu/Academics/programs/history/historiography.

Patte, Daniel. 1995. *The Ethics of Biblical Interpretation: A Reevaluation.* Louisville, Kentucky: Westminster.

Pattel-Gray, Anne. 1998. *The Great White Flood: Racism in Australia; Critically Appraised from an Aboriginal Historico-Theological Viewpoint.* Atlanta: Scholars Press.

Pattemore, Stephen. 2004. *The People of God in the Apocalypse: Discourse, Structure and Exegesis.* SNTSMS 128. Cambridge: Cambridge University Press.

Paulson, Graham. 2006. Towards an Aboriginal Theology. *Pacifica* 19/3:310–20.

Peacock, Philip V. 2005. Methodological Issues in Dalit Biblical Hermeneutics. A paper presented to a seminar on "Biblical Hermeneutics" held at the Bishop's College, Kolkata. Unpublished.

———. September 2007. Untouchability is the Key. *In God's Image: Journal of Asian Women's Resource Centre for Culture and Theology* 26/3:56–58.

Peebles, J. W. 1993. Preface. Pages 1–11 in *The Original African Heritage Study Bible: The King James Version.* Edited by Cain Hope Felder. Nashville: James C. Winston.

Pessoa, Jadir de Morais, and Madeleine Félix. 2007. *As Viagens dos Reis Magos.* Goiania: Editora da UCG.

Petersen, Robin. 1995. Time, Resistance and Reconstruction: Rethinking Kairos Theology. Ph.D. diss., University of Chicago.

Phillipson, G. A. 2004. Missionary Printer: William Colenso at Paihia 1834–52. Pages 127–38 in *Building God's Own Country: Historical Essays on Religions in New Zealand.* Edited by John Stenhouse and Jane Thomson. Dunedin: University of Otago Press.

Philpott, Graham. 1993. *Jesus is Tricky and God is Undemocratic: The Kin-Dom of God in Amawoti.* Pietermaritzburg: Cluster Publications.

Pixley, Jorge. 1982. *El libro de Job.* San José, Costa Rica: SEBILA.

———. 1983. *Éxodo: una lectura evangélica y popular.* México: CUPSA. Eng. trans.: 1987. *On Exodus: A Liberation Perspective.* New York: Orbis Books.

Pixley, Jorge, and Clodovis Boff. 1986 *Opçión por los Pobres.* Buenos Aires: Paulinas.

———. 1990. *Historia sagrada, historia popular.* San José: DEI.

Plank, Karl A. 2008. By the Waters of a Death Camp: An Intertextual reading of Psalm 137. *Literature and Theology* 22:180–94.

Porter, Frances, and Charlotte Macdonald. 1996. *"My Hand Will Write What My Heart Dictates": The Unsettled Lives of Women in Nineteenth-Century New Zealand as Revealed to Sisters, Family and Friends.* Auckland: Auckland University Press with Bridget Williams Books.

Premnath, Devadasan N. 2007. Biblical Interpretation in India: History and Issues. Pages 1–16 in *Ways of Being, Ways of Reading: Asian American Biblical Interpretation.* Edited by Mary F. Foskett and Jeffrey Kah-Jin Kuan. St. Louis: Chalice.

Prenter, Regin. 1964. Dansk teologi av idag. *STK* 40:1–10.

Pullman, Philip. 1995. *The Golden Compass.* New York: Random House.

———. 1997. *The Subtle Knife.* New York: Random House.

———. 2000. *The Amber Spyglass.* New York: Random House.

Punt, Jeremy. 1998. New Testament Interpretation, Interpretive Interests, and Ideology: Methodological Deficits amidst South African Methodolomania. *Scriptura* 65:123–52.

———. 2004. Whose Bible, Mine or Yours? Contested Ownership and Bible Translation in Southern Africa. *HvTSt* 60:307–28.

———. 2006. Using the Bible in post-Apartheid South Africa: Its Influence and Impact amidst the Gay Debate. *HvTSt* 62:885–907.

———. 2007. Popularising the Prophet Isaiah in Parliament: The Bible in post-Apartheid, South African Public Discourse. *Religion & Theology* 14:206–23.

———. 2009. Post-Apartheid Racism in South Africa. The Bible, Social Identity and Stereotyping. *Religion & Theology* 16:246–72.

———. forthcoming. Empire as Material Setting and Heuristic Grid for New Testament Interpretation. Comments on the Value of Postcolonial Criticism. *HvTSt.*

Pyle, Kenneth B. 2007. *Japan Rising: The Resurgence of Japanese Power and Purpose.* New York: Public Affairs.

Pyper, Hugh S. 2005. *An Unsuitable Book: the Bible as Scandalous Text.* Sheffield: Sheffield Phoenix.

Räisänen, Heikki. 2000a. *Beyond New Testament Theology: A Story and A Programme.* 2nd. ed. London: SCM.

———. 2000b. Biblical Critics in the Global Village. Pages 9–28 in Räisänen et al. 2000.

Räisänen, Heikki., Elisabeth Schüssler Fiorenza, R. S. Sugirtharajah, Krister Stendahl and

James Barr, eds. *Reading the Bible in the Global Village: Helsinki*. Atlanta: Society of Biblical Literature.

Ramos Salazar, Humberto. 1997. *Hacia una teología Aymara: desde la identidad cultural y la vida cotidiana*. La Paz: CTP-CMI.

Reid-Salmon, Delroy A. 2008. *Home Away from Home. The Caribbean Diasporan Church in the Black Atlantic Tradition*. London: Equinox.

Reinken, Judy. 2004. Responses. Pages 233–37 in *Land and Place: He Whenua, He Wahi: Spiritualities from Aotearoa New Zealand*. Edited by Helen Bergin and Susan Smith. Auckland: Accent Publications.

Reumann, John. 1966. Editor's Introduction. Pages iii–xiv in *The Bible and the Role of Women: A Case Study in Hermeneutics*. Krister Stendahl. FBBS 15. Philadelphia: Fortress.

Reyes Archila, Francisco, ed. 1997a. *Hermenéutica y exégesis a propósito de la Carta de Filemón. RIBLA* 28. San José: Departamento Ecuménico de Investigaciones.

———. 1997b. Hermenéutica y exégesis: Un diálogo necesario. Pages 9–36 in *Hermenéutica y exégesis a propósito de la Carta de Filemón. RIBLA* 28. Edited by Francisco Reyes Arcilla. San José: Departamento Ecuménico de Investigaciones.

Rhodes, Erroll F., and Liana Lupas. 1997. *The Translators to the Reader: The Original Preface to the King James Version of 1611 Revisited*. New York: American Bible Society.

Richter, Frank-Jürgen, and Pamela C. M. Mar, *Asia's New Crisis: Renewal Through Total Ethical Management*. Singapore: Wiley.

Ricoeur, Paul. 1975. Biblical Hermeneutics. *Semeia* 4:27–148.

———. 1991. Response to Josef Blank. Pages 283–86 in *Paradigm Change in Theology. A Symposium for the Future*. Edited by H. Küng and D Tracy. Translated by M Köhl. New York: Crossroads.

Riesenfeld, Harald. 1968. Varmed sysslar Nya testamentets exegetik? *SEÅ* 33:179–84.

———. 1953. The Ministry in the New Testament. Pages 96–127 in *The Root of the Vine: Essays in Biblical Theology*. Edited by Anton Fridrichsen et al. London: Dacre.

Ringgren, Helmer. 1968. Mål och uppgifter i Gamla testamentets exegetik. *SEÅ* 33:175–78.

———. 1976. Old Testament Exegesis. Pages 41–49 in *Uppsala University 500 years. 1, Faculty of Theology at Uppsala University*. Edited by Helmer Ringgren. Uppsala: Uppsala University.

Ringgren, Helmer, and Lars Hartman. 1992. Scandinavian School. OT Studies. Pages 1001–2 in *ABD* Vol. 5. Edited by David Noel Freedman et al. New York: Doubleday.

Roach, Joseph. 1996. *Cities of the Dead: Circum-Atlantic Performance*. New York: Columbia University Press.

Rohrbaugh, Richard, ed. 1996. *The Social Sciences and New Testament Interpretation*. Massachusetts: Hendrickson.

Rose, Deborah Bird. 2005. *Reports From A Wild Country: Ethics for Decolonisation*. Sydney: University of New South Wales Press.

Rowland, Christopher. 1993. "Open Thy Mouth for the Dumb": A Task for the Exegete of Holy Scripture. *BibInt* 1:228–45.

Rowley, H.H., ed. 1951. *The Old Testament and Modern Study*. Oxford: Clarendon.

Runions, Erin. 2000. Hysterical Phalli: Numbers 16, Two Contemporary Parallels, and the Logic of Colonization. Pages 182–205 in *Culture, Entertainment and the Bible*. Edited by George Aichele. Sheffield: Sheffield Academic.

———. 2009. Disco-Reggae at Abu Ghraib: Music, the Bible and Torture. *Religion Dis-*

patches June 22. http://www.religiondispatches.org/archive/humanrights/1560/disco-reggae_at_abu_ghraib:_music,_the_bible_and_torture. Accessed June 30 2009.

Rupert, Greenberry G. 1911. *The Yellow Peril: Or, The Orient Vs. the Occident as Viewed by Modern Statesmen and Ancient Prophets*. Britton: Union Publishing.

Rushton, Kathleen P. forthcoming. On the Crossroads between Life and Death: Reading Birth Imagery in John in the Earthquake Changed Regions of Otautahi Christchurch, in *Bible, Borders, Belongings*. Edited by Elaine Wainwright, David Neville, and Jione Havea.

Rutledge, David. 1996. *Reading Marginally: Feminism, Deconstruction and the Bible*. Leiden: Brill.

Rydstedt, Anna. 1994. Utan betyg i exegetik. Pages 11–12 in *Dikter*. Edited by Göran Sonnevi and Jan Olov Ullén. First published in *Bannlyst prästinna*. Stockholm: Bonnier 1953.

Ryman, Björn. 2000. Church of Sweden, 1940–2000. Pages 49–61 in Ryman, Björn et al. 2000.

Ryman, Björn, et al. 2000. *Nordic Folk Churches. A Contemporary Church History*. Grand Rapids: Eerdmans.

Sadler, Rodney A. Jr. 2007. The Place and Role of Africa and African Imagery. Pages 23–30 in Blount (ed) 2007.

Said, Edward. 1979. *Orientalism*. New York: Vintage.

———. 1983. *The World, the Text and the Critic*. Cambridge: Harvard University Press.

———. 1993. *Culture and Imperialism*. New York: Vintage.

Salevao, Iutisone. 2000. "Burning the Land": An Ecojustice Reading of Hebrews 6:7–8. Pages 221–31 in *Readings from the Perspective of Earth*. The Earth Bible, 1. Edited by Norman C. Habel. Sheffield: Sheffield Academic.

Samartha S. J., Stanley. 1991. The Asian Context: Sources and Trends. Pages 36–49 in *Voices from the Margin: Interpreting the Bible in the Third World*. Edited by R. S. Sugirtharajah. Maryknoll, N.Y.: Orbis.

Sandoval, Chela. 2000. *Methodology of the Oppressed*. Minneapolis: University of Minnesota Press.

Santos, Lucimeire. Tradição Revigorada. Caderno de Cultura. *Jornal Tribuna do Planalto* (January 13, 2008). See: http:www.tribunadoplanalto.com.br/modules.php?name=News&file=article&sid=2761&mode=thread&order=0&thold=0.

Schaaf, Y 1994. *On Their Way Rejoicing: The History and the Role of the Bible in Africa*. Translated by P Ellingworth. Carlisle: Paternoster.

Schinelo, Edmilson and Nancy Cardoso Pereira. 2007. *Teología da Libertação e Educação Popular-Partilhando e Avaliando Práticas de Educação Libertadora*. São Leopoldo, R.S: Ceca/Cebi.

Schnabel, Eckhard J. 2002. *Early Christian Mission*. 2 vols. Downers Grove, Ill: InterVarsity Press.

Schneiders, S. M. 1999. *The Revelatory Text: Interpreting the New Testament as Sacred Scripture*. 2nd. ed. Collegeville: Liturgical Press.

Schreiner, Thomas R. 2008. *New Testament Theology: Magnifying God in Christ*. Grand Rapids: Baker Academic.

Schüssler Fiorenza, Elisabeth. 1964. *Der vergessene Partner: Grundlagen, Tatsachen und Möglichkeiten der beruflichen Mitarbeit der Frau in der Heilsorge der Kirche*. Düsseldorf: Patmos.

———. 1975. Feminist Theology as a Critical Theology of Liberation. *TS* 36/4:606–36.

———. 1983. *In Memory of Her: A Feminist Theological Reconstruction of Christian Origins.* New York: Crossroad.

———. 1989. Text and Reality-Reality as Text: The Problem of a Feminist Historical and Social Reconstruction Based on Texts. *ST* 43:19–34.

———. 1985. *Bread Not Stone: The Challenge of Feminist Biblical Interpretation.* Boston: Beacon.

———. 1991a. Changing the Paradigms. Pages 75–87 in *How my Mind Has Changed.* Edited by James M. Wall and David Heim. Grand Rapids: Eerdmans.

———. 1991b. The Crisis of Hermeneutics and Christian Theology. Pages 117–40 in *Theology at the End of Modernity. Essays in Honor of Gordon D Kaufman.* Edited by S. G. Davaney. Philadelphia: Trinity.

———. 1992. *But She Said: Feminist Practices of Biblical Interpretation.* Boston: Beacon.

———. 1993. *Discipleship of Equals: A Critical Feminist Ekklesia-logy of Liberation.* New York: Crossroad.

———. 1994. *Jesus: Miriam's Child, Sophia's Prophet: Critical Issues in Feminist Christology.* New York: Continuum.

———. 1998. *Sharing Her Word: Feminist Biblical Interpretation in Context.* Boston: Beacon.

———. 1999. *Rhetoric and Ethic: The Politics of Biblical Studies.* Minneapolis: Fortress.

———. 2000a. *Jesus and the Politics of Interpretation.* New York: Continuum.

———. 2000b. Defending the Center, Trivializing the Margins. Pages 29–48 in Räisänen et al. 2000.

———. 2000c. The Ethics of Biblical Interpretation: Decentering Biblical Scholarship. Pages 107–23 in Räisänen et al. 2000.

———. 2001. *Wisdom Ways: Introducing Feminist Biblical Interpretation.* Maryknoll, N.Y.: Orbis.

———. 2003. *Grenzen überschreiten. Der theoretische Anspruch feministischer Theologie. Ausgewählte Aufsätze.* Münster: LIT Verlag.

———. 2007. *The Power of the Word: Scripture and the Rhetoric of Empire.* Minneapolis: Fortress.

———. 2008. Reading Scripture in the Context of Empire. Pages 157–71 in *The Bible in the Public Square. Reading the Signs of the Times.* Edited by C. B. Kittredge, E. B. Aitken, and J. A. Draper. Minneapolis: Fortress.

———. 2009a. *Democratizing Biblical Studies: Toward an Emancipatory Pedagogical Space.* Louisville: Westminster John Knox.

———. 2009b. Toward an Intersectional Analytic: Race, Gender, Ethnicity, and Empire in Early Christian Studies. Pages 1–24 in *Prejudice and Christian Beginnings.* Edited by Laura Nasrallah and Elisabeth Schüssler Fiorenza. Minneapolis: Fortress.

———. 2010. Rethinking the Educational Practices of Biblical Doctoral Studies. Pages 373–93 in *Transforming Graduate Biblical Education: Ethos and Discipline.* Edited by Elisabeth Schüssler Fiorenza. Atlanta: Society of Biblical Literature.

———. 2011. *Transforming Vision: Explorations in Feminist The*logy.* Minneapolis: Fortress.

Schwantes, Milton. 1989. Jacob el pequeño. Visiones de Amos 9–7. Homenaje al pastor Werner Fuchs. *RIBLA* 1:87–99.

———. 2008. Anotações sobre a Teologia de Libertação. *Pós-Escrito. Revista eletrônica da Faculdade Batista do Rio de Janeiro* 1.1:1–18. See: http://www.fabat.com.br/pos-escrito/pdf/revista01/1schwantesartigoanotacoes.pdf.

Schwantes, Milton and Pablo Richard, eds. 1992. Editorial. *Biblia 500 Años:¿Conquista o Evangelización? RIBLA* 11. See: http://www.claiweb.org/ribla/ribla11/editorial.htm.

Scott, James S. 2002. Religion, Literature, and Canadian Cultural Issues. *Literature & Theology* 16:113–26.

Segovia, Fernando F. 1995a. "And They Began to Speak in Other Tongues": Competing Modes of Discourse in Contemporary Biblical Criticism. Pages 1–32 in Segovia and Tolbert 1995a.

———. 1995b. Cultural Studies and Contemporary Biblical Criticism: Ideological Criticism as Mode of Discourse. Pages 1–19 in Segovia and Tolbert 1995b.

———. 1995c. The Text as Other: Towards a Hispanic American Hermeneutic. Pages 276–98 in *Text & Experience: towards a Cultural Exegesis of the Bible*. Edited by D. Smith-Christopher. Sheffield: Sheffield Academic Press.

———. 1998a. Pedagogical Discourse and Practices in Cultural Studies. Pages 137–67 in Segovia and Tolbert 1998.

———. 1998b. Biblical Criticism and Postcolonial Studies: Toward a Postcolonial Optic. Pages 49–65 in *Asian Biblical Hermeneutics and Postcolonialism: Contesting the Interpretations*. R. S. Sugirtharajah. Maryknoll, N.Y.: Orbis.

———. 1999. Notes Towards Refining the Postcolonial Optic. *JSNT* 75:103–14.

———. 2000. *Decolonizing Biblical Studies: A View from the Margins*. New York: Orbis.

———. 2000a. Interpreting Beyond Borders: Postcolonial Studies and Diasporic Studies in Biblical Criticism. Pages 11–35 in Segovia 2000.

———. 2000b. Reading-Across: Intercultural Criticism and Textual Posture. Pages 59–83 in Segovia 2000.

———. 2005. Mapping the Postcolonial Optic in Biblical Criticism: Meaning and Scope. Pages 23–78 in *Postcolonial Biblical Criticism: Interdisciplinary Intersections*. Edited by Stephen D. Moore and Fernando F. Segovia. London: T&T Clark.

———. 2008. Postcolonial Biblical Criticism: Taking Stock and Looking Ahead. *JSNT* 30:489–502.

———. 2009. Toward Latino/a American Biblical Criticism: Latin(o/a)ness as Problematic. Pages 193–223 in Bailey, Liew, and Segovia 2009.

Fernando F. Segovia., ed. 2000. *Interpreting Beyond Borders*. Sheffield: Sheffield Academic.

Segovia, Fernando F. and Mary Ann Tolbert, eds. 1995a. *Reading from This Place*. Vol. 1 of *Social Location and Biblical Interpretation in the United States*. Minneapolis: Fortress.

———. 1995b. *Reading from This Place*. Volume 2 of *Social Location and Biblical Interpretation in the Global Scene*. Minneapolis: Fortress.

———. *Teaching the Bible: The Discourse and Politics of Biblical Pedagogy*. Eugene: Wipf & Stock.

Segovia, Fernando F., and R. S. Sugirtharajah, eds. 2007. *A Postcolonial Commentary on the New Testament Writings*. The Bible and Postcolonialism 13. London: T&T Clark.

Segundo, Juan Luis. 1975. Buenos Aires: Lohlé. English trans: *Liberation of Theology*. Maryknoll, N.Y.: Orbis.

Sharma, R. S. 1993. Toying with History. *Indian Express* (13 January): 8.

Shaull, Richard. 1996. Foreword. In *Pedagogy of the Oppressed*. Paulo Freire. rev. ed. Translated by M. Ramos. Harmondsworth: Penguin.

Sherwood, Yvonne. 2000. *A Biblical Text and its Afterlives: The Survival of Jonah in Western Culture.* Cambridge: Cambridge University Press.

Shih, David. 2005. The Seduction of Origins: Sui Sin Far and the Race for Tradition. Pages 48–76 in *Form and Transformation in Asian American Literature.* Edited by Zhou Xiaojing and Samina Najmi. Seattle: University of Seattle Press.

Shih, Shu-mei. 2008. Comparative Racialization: An Introduction. *PMLA* 123:1347–62.

Shirk, Susan L. 2007. *China: Fragile Superpower.* Oxford: Oxford University Press.

Shohat, Elia. 2001. Area Studies, Transnationalism and the Feminist Production of Knowledge. *Signs* 26/4:1269–72.

———. 2002. Area Studies, Gender Studies, and the Geographies of Knowledge. *Social Text* 20/3:67–78.

Simpson, Peter. 2001. *Answering Hark: McCahon/Caselberg Painter/Poet.* Nelson: Craig Potton.

Sinnott, Alice M. 2001. Job 12: Cosmic Devastation and Social Turmoil. Pages 78–91 in *The Earth Story in Wisdom Traditions.* Edited by Norman C. Habel and Shirley Wurst. The Earth Bible 3. Sheffield: Sheffield Academic.

Sissons, Jeffrey. 1991. *Te Waimana The Spring of Mana: Tuhoe History and the Colonial Encounter.* Te Whenua Series 6. Dunedin, New Zealand: University of Otago Press.

Slater, Peter. 1997. *Religion and Culture in Canada/Religion et culture au Canada.* Waterloo: Canadian Corporation for Studies in Religion.

Smith, Abraham. 2010. Taking Space Seriously: The Politics of Space and the Future of Western Biblical Studies. Pages 59–92 in Schüssler Fiorensa and Richards 2010.

Smith, Andrea. 2010. Indigeneity, Settler Colonialism, White Supremacy. *Global Dialogue* 12. Online: http://www.worlddialogue.org/content.php?id=488.

Smith, Anna Deavere. 2000. *Talk to Me: Listening Between the Lines.* New York: Random.

Smith, Abraham. 2008. Cultural Studies: Making Mark. Pages 181–209 in *Mark & Method: New Approaches in Biblical Studies.* 2nd. ed. Edited by Janice Capel Anderson and Stephen D. Moore. Minneapolis: Fortress.

Soares Prabhu, George M. 1980. Towards an Indian Interpretation of the Bible. *BiBh* 6:151–70.

———. 1996. Towards an Indian Interpretation of the Bible. *Indian Theological Studies* 33/3:249–59.

Solberg, S.E. 1981. Sui Sin Far/Edith Eaton: First Chinese-American Fictionist. *MELUS* 8 (1981):27–39.

Sollamo, Raija. 1996. The Origins of LXX Studies in Finland. *SJOT* 10:159–68.

Song, Choan-Seng. 1979. *Third-Eye Theology: Theology in Formation in Asian Settings.* Maryknoll, N.Y.: Orbis.

———. 1984. *Tell Us Our Names: Story Theology from an Asian Perspective.* Maryknoll, N.Y.: Orbis.

Soards, M. L. 1996. Key Issues in Biblical Studies and Their Bearing on Mission Studies. *Missiology* 24:93–106.

Souza, João Carlos de. 2004. O caráter religioso e profano das Festas Populares: Corumbá, Passagem do Século XIX para o XX. *Revista Brasileria de História* 24/48:331–51.

Spickard, Paul R., and Kevin M. Cragg. 1994. *A Global History of Christians: How Everyday Believers Experienced Their World.* Grand Rapids: Baker Academic.

Spillers, Hortense J. 2003. *Black, White, and in Color: Essays on American Literature and Culture.* Chicago: University of Chicago Press.

Stanton, Elizabeth Cady. 1898. *The Woman's Bible: A Classic Feminist Perspective.* New York: European Pub. Co.; repr., Mineola: Dover, 2002.

St. Clair, Raquel Annette. 2008. *Call and Consequences: A Womanist Reading of Mark.* Minneapolis: Fortress.

Staiger, Janet, Ann Cvetkovich, and Ann Reynolds, eds. 2010. *Political Emotions: New Agendas in Communication.* New York: Routledge.

Stendahl, Krister. 1962. Biblical Theology, Contemporary. Pages 418–32 in *IDB* Vol. 1. Nashville: Abingdon.

———. 1966. *The Bible and the Role of Women. A Case Study in Hermeneutics.* FBBS 15. Philadelphia: Fortress.

———. 2002. Zur Situation der neutestamentlichen Exegese um 1930. Erinnerungen und Reflexionen. *TZ* 57:207–15.

Street, Brian., ed. 1993. *Cross-Cultural Approaches to Literacy.* Cambridge: Cambridge University Press.

Sugirtharajah, R. S. 1994. Introduction and Some Thoughts on Asian Biblical Hermeneutics. *BibInt* 2:251–63.

———. 1998a. Biblical Studies in India: From Imperialistic Scholarship to Postcolonial Interpretation. Pages 283–89 in Segovia and Tolbert 1998.

———. 1998b. *Asian Biblical Hermeneutics and Postcolonialism. Contesting the Interpretations.* Maryknoll, N.Y.: Orbis.

———. 2000. Critics, Tools and the Global Arena. Pages 49–60 in Räisänen et al. 2000.

———. 2001. *The Bible and the Third world: Precolonial, Colonial and Postcolonial Encounters.* Cambridge: Cambridge University Press.

———. 2002. *Postcolonial Criticism and Biblical Interpretation.* New York: Oxford University Press.

———. 2003a. Loitering With Intent: Biblical Texts in Public Places. *BibInt* 11:566–78.

———. 2003b. *Postcolonial Reconfigurations: An Alternative Way of Reading the Bible and Doing Theology.* St. Louis: Chalice.

———. 2005a. Postcolonial Criticism and Asian Biblical Studies. Pages 73–84 in *Critical Engagement in the Asian Context. Implications for Theological Education and Christian Studies.* Edited by Preman Niles. Hong Kong: ACHEI/UBCHEA.

———. 2005b. *The Bible and Empire: Postcolonial Explorations.* Cambridge: Cambridge University Press.

Sugirtharajah, R. S., ed. 1991. *Voices from the Margin: Interpreting the Bible in the Third World.* 1st ed. Maryknoll, N.Y.: Orbis.

———, ed. 1998. *The Postcolonial Bible.* The Bible and Postcolonialism 1. Sheffield: Sheffield Academic Press.

Sugirtharajah, R. S., and Cecil Hargreaves, eds. 1993. *Readings in Indian Christian Theology.* Vol 1. London: SPCK.

Sunshine, Cathy A. 1985. *The Caribbean: Survival, Struggle and Sovereignty.* Boston: South End Press.

Surburg, Raymond. 1983. The Influence of the Two *Delitzsches* on Biblical and Near Eastern Studies. *CTQ* 47:225–40.

Syren, Roger. 1995. Before the Text and After: The Scandinavian School and the Formation of Scripture. Pages 225–37 in *Text and Experience: Towards a Cultural Exegesis of the Bible.* Edited by Daniel Smith-Christopher. Sheffield: Sheffield Academic.

Tate, R. W. 2008. *Biblical Interpretation. An Integrated Approach.* 3rd. ed. Peabody: Hendrickson.

Taussig, Michael. 1993. *Mimesis and Alterity: A Particular History of the Senses.* New York: Routledge.

Taylor, B. 2006. *Saying No to Babylon: A Reading of the Book of Daniel.* Kingston: Self-published.

Thangaraj, Thomas. 1999. The Bible as Veda: Biblical Hermeneutics in Tamil Christianity. Pages 133–43 in *Vernacular Hermeneutics.* Edited by R. S. Sugirtharajah, Sheffield: Sheffield Academic.

Thelle, Rannfrid I. 2000. Historiens utfordringer. Gammaltestamentlig forskning ved Det teologiske fakultet i det 20. århundre. *NTT* 101:17–32.

Thomas, Oral. 2010. *Biblical Resistance Hermeneutics in a Caribbean Context.* London: Equinox.

Thompson, Pat. 1994. Europe 1992: Implications for the Caribbean. Pages 111–24 in *Crossroads of Empire: The European Caribbean Connection 1492–1992.* Edited by A. Cobley. Cave Hill, Barbados: University of the West Indies Press.

Thompson, William D. 1981. *Preaching Biblically: Exegesis and Interpretation.* Nashville: Abingdon.

Titus, N. 2010. Toward a Unified and Contextual Program in Theological Education in the Caribbean. Pages 488–93 in *Handbook of Theological Education in World Christianity: Theological Perspectives—Regional Surveys—Ecumenical Trends.* Edited by D. Werner et al. Pietermaritzburg: Cluster Publications.

Townsley, Gillian. forthcoming. *The Straight Mind in Corinth: Queer Readings Across 1 Cor 11:2–16.* Semeia Studies. Atlanta: Society of Biblical Literature.

Trebilco, Paul R. 2000. The Goodness and Holiness of the Earth and the Whole Creation (1 Tim 4:1–5). Pages 204–20 in *Readings from the Perspective of Earth.* Edited by N. Habel. The Earth Bible, Volume 1. Sheffield: Sheffield Academic Press.

———. 2004. *The Early Christians in Ephesus from Paul to Ignatius.* WUNT 166. Tübingen: Mohr Siebeck.

———. 2006. *"Global" and "Local" in the New Testament and in Earliest Christianity.* Inaugural Professorial Lecture Series. Dunedin: University of Otago.

———. 2012. *Self-Designations and Group Identity in the New Testament.* Cambridge: Cambridge University Press.

Trebilco, Paul, and Simon Rae. 2006. *1 Timothy.* Singapore: Asia Theological Association.

Treco, Ria M. The Haitian Diaspora in the Bahamas. http://lacc.fiu.edu/research_publications/working_papers/WPS_004.pdf Accessed July, 2009.

Treier, Dan J. 2008. *Introducing Theological Interpretation of Scripture: Recovering a Christian Practice.* Grand Rapids: Baker Academic.

Tronier, Henrik. 2003. Kristus som værdiomvendende blik. Pages 156–90 in Engberg-Pedersen 2003.

Trudinger, Paul. 2004. On Reclaiming the Term "Evangelical" for its Rightful Use. *ExpTim* 116/3:79–81.

Tuckett, C. 1987. *Reading the New Testament: Methods of Interpretation.* Philadelphia: Fortress.

Tuwere, Ilaitia. 2008. Sa Meke Tiko na Vanua [The land is now dancing]. Paper presented at Talanoa Oceania 2008: Mana, Vanua, Talanoa. Centre for Ministry, North Parramatta, NSW, Australia (October 1).

Ulloa, A. 2010. The Origins of Ecumenical Theological Education in Latin America and the Caribbean. Pages 476–88 in *Handbook of Theological Education in World Christianity: Theological Perspectives—Regional Surveys—Ecumenical Trends*. Edited by D. Werner et al. Pietermaritzburg: Cluster Publications.

United Bible Societies. 2002. *UBS World Annual Report for 2001*. Reading, UK: United Bible Societies.

Ukpong, Justin S. 1996. The Parable of the Shrewd Manager (Lk. 16:1–13): An Essay in the Inculturation Biblical Hermeneutic. *Semeia* 73:189–212.

———. 2001. New Testament Hermeneutics in Africa: Challenges and Possibilities. *Neot* 35:147–68.

Vaka'uta, Nasili. 2005. Reading beyond the Reefs: A Sketch of an Oceanic Hermeneutics. Unpublished paper presented to ANZABS Conference, Christchurch.

———. 2008. Myth of (Im)purity and the Peoples of the (Is)lands: A Tongan Reading of Ezra 9–10. Paper presented at International Society of Biblical Literature 2008. University of Auckland, Auckland, Aotearoa/New Zealand (July 2007).

———. 2009. "Tālanga: Theorizing a Tongan Mode of Interpretation." *AlterNative: An International Journal for Indigenous Peoples* 5:1: 26–39.

———. 2011. *Reading Ezra 9–10 Tu'a-Wise: Rethinking Biblical interpretation in Oceania*. International Voices in Biblical Studies 3. Atlanta: Society of Biblical Literature.

Vander Stichele, Caroline, and Todd Penner, eds. 2005. *Her Master's Tools? Feminist and Postcolonial Engagement of Historical-Critical Discourse*. Atlanta: Society of Biblical Literature.

Vidales, Raúl. 1982. *Volveré ... y seré millones*. Lima, Peru: CELADEC.

Villalobos, Manuel. 2011. Bodies *Del Otro Lado* Finding Life and Hope in the Borderland: Gloria Anzaldúa, the Ethiopian Eunuch of Acts 8:26–40, *y Yo*. Pages 191–221 in *Bible Trouble: Queer Reading at the Boundaries of Biblical Scholarship*. Atlanta: Society of Biblical Literature.

Wainwright, Elaine. 2005. Looking Both Ways or in Multiple Directions: Doing/Teaching Theology in Context into the Twenty-First Century. *Pacifica* 18:123–40.

———. 2006. *Women Healing/Healing Women: The Genderization of Healing in Early Christianity*. London: Equinox.

Walsh, Richard. 2003. *Reading the Gospels in the Dark: Portrayals of Jesus in Film*. Harrisburg, Pa.: Trinity.

———. 2005. *Finding St. Paul in Film*. New York: T&T Clark.

Wan, Sze-Kar. 2000. Does Diaspora Identity Imply Some Sort of Universality? An Asian-American Reading of Galatians. Pages 107–31 in Segovia 2000.

———. 2006. Betwixt and Between: Toward a Hermeneutics of Hyphenation. Pages 137–51 in Foskett and Kuan 2006.

Wardhaugh, Ronald. 1992. *An Introduction to Sociolinguistics*. Blackwell Textbooks in Linguistics. Oxford: Blackwell.

Warrior, Robert Allen. 1991. A Native American Perspective: Canaanites, Cowboys, and Indians. Pages 287–95 in *Voices from the Margin: Interpreting the Bible in the Third World*. Edited by R. S. Sugirtharajah. Maryknoll, N.Y.: Orbis.

Webster, John C.B. 1992. *The Dalit Christians: A History*. Delhi: ISPCK.

West, Gerald. O. 1995. *Contextual Bible Study*. Pietermaritzburg: Cluster Publication.

———. 1996. Reading the Bible Differently: Giving Shape to the Discourse of the Dominated. *Semeia* 73:21–42.

———. 1999a. Being Partially Constituted by Work with Others. *JTSA* 104:44–54.

———. 1999b. Contextual Bible Study: Creating Sacred and Safe Place for Social Transformation. *Grace and Truth* 2:51–63.

———. 1999c. *The Academy of the Poor: Towards a Dialogical Reading of the Bible.* Sheffield: Sheffield Academic.

———. 2001. Contextual Bible Study in South Africa: A Resource for Reclaiming and Regaining Land, Dignity and Identity. Pages 169–84 in *Towards an Agenda for Contextual Theology: Essays in Honour of Albert Nolan.* Edited by McGlory T. Speckman and Larry T. Kaufmann. Pietermaritzburg: Cluster Publications.

———. 2007a. *Reading Other-wise: Socially Engaged Biblical Scholars Reading with their Own Communities.* Atlanta: Society of Biblical Literature.

———. 2007b. The Bible and the Female Body in Ibandla lamaNazaretha: Isaiah Shembe and Jephthah's Daughter. *OTE* 20/2: 489–509.

———. 2008. Hearing the (Theological) Voice of the Other in the City Mission: A South African Perspective (Discussion paper). http://www.tf.uio.no/arkiv/citymission/doc/city_mission_abstract.pdf.

West, Gerald O., and Muse W. Dube. 1996. An Introduction: How We Have Come to "Read With." *Semeia* 73:7–20.

Westphal, M. 1997. Post-Kantian Reflections on the Importance of Hermeneutics. Pages 57–66 in *Disciplining Hermeneutics: Interpretation in Christian Perspective.* Edited by Roger Lundin. Grand Rapids: Eerdmans.

Wharton, Thomas. 2001. *Salamander.* New York: Washington Square Press.

White-Parks, Annette. 1995. *Sui Sin Far/Edith Maude Eaton: A Literary Biography.* Urbana: University of Illinois Press.

Wilfred, Felix. 1996. Towards a Subaltern Hermeneutics: Beyond the Contemporary Polarities in the Interpretation of Religious Traditions. *Jeevadhara* 26/151:45–62.

———. 2005. *The Sling of Utopia: Struggles for a Different Society.* New Delhi: ISPCK.

———. 2008. *Margins: Site of Asian Theologies.* New Delhi: ISPCK.

Williams, Demetrius K. 2004. *An End to This Strife: The Politics of Gender in African American Churches.* Minneapolis: Fortress.

———. 2009. 'Upon All Flesh': Acts 2, African Americans, and Intersectional Realities. Pages 289–310 in Bailey, Liew, and Segovia 2009.

Williams, James. 2003. *Gilles Deleuze's Difference and Repetition.* Edinburgh: Edinburgh University Press.

Williams, Lewin L. 1994. *Caribbean Theology.* Research in Religion and Family: Black Perspectives. New York: Peter Lang.

Wimbush, Vincent L. 1991. African Americans and the Bible: Outline of An Interpretive History. Pages 81–97 in *Stony the Road We Trod: African American Biblical Hermeneutics.* Edited by Cain Felder. Minneapolis: Fortress.

———. 1993. Reading Texts through Worlds, Worlds through Texts. *Semeia* 62:129–39.

———. 2000. Introduction: Reading Darkness, Reading Scriptures. Pages 1–43 in Wimbush (ed) 2000.

———. 2007. We Will Make Our own Future Text: An Alternate Orientation to Interpretation. Pages 43–53 in Blount (ed) 2007.

———. 2009a. Scriptures for Strangers: the Making of an Africanized Bible. Pages 162–77 in *Postcolonial Interventions: Essays in Honor of R. S. Sugirtharajah.* Edited by Tatsiong Benny Liew. Sheffield: Sheffield Phoenix.

———. 2009b. "No Modern Joshua": Nationalization, Scriptures, and Race. Pages 259–78 in *Prejudice and Christian Beginnings: Investigating Race, Gender, and Ethnicity in Early Christian Studies*. Edited by Laura Nasrallah and Elisabeth Schüssler Fiorenza. Minneapolis: Fortress.

———. 2010. The Work We Make Scriptures Do for Us: An Argument for Signifying (on) Scriptures as Intellectual Project. Pages 355–66 in Schüssler Fiorensa and Richards 2010.

Wimbush, Vincent L., ed. 2000. *African Americans and the Bible: Sacred Texts and Social Textures*. New York: Continuum.

———, ed. 2008. *Theorizing Scriptures. New Critical Orientations to a Cultural Phenomenon*. Signifying (on) Scriptures. New Brunswick: Rutgers University Press.

———, ed. forthcoming. *Interruptions, Mimetics, and Orientations: Reading Scriptures, Reading America Among U.S. Communities of Color*.

Yamaguchi, Satoko. Father Image of G*d and Inclusive Language. A Reflection in Japan. 2003. Pages 199–224 in *Toward a New Heaven and a New Earth: Essays in Honor of Elisabeth Schüssler Fiorenza*. Edited by Fernando F. Segovia. Maryknoll, N.Y.: Orbis Books.

Yee, Gale A. 1995. The Author/Text/Reader and Power: Suggestions for a Critical Framework. Pages 109–18 in *Reading from this Place* in Segovia and Tolbert 1995a.

———. 2006. Yin/Yang is Not Me: An Exploration into an Asian American Biblical Hermeneutics. Pages 152–63 in Foskett and Kuan 2006.

Yieh, John Yueh-Han. 2007. Chinese Biblical Interpretation: History and Issues. Pages 17–30 in *Ways of Being, Ways of Reading: Asian American Biblical Interpretation*. Edited by Mary F. Foskett and Jeffrey Kah-Jin Kuan. St. Louis: Chalice.

Yorke, Gosnell. 1991. *The Church as the Body of Christ in the Pauline Corpus: A Re-examination*. Lanham: University Press of America.

———. 2004. Bible Translation in Anglophone Africa and her Diaspora: A Postcolonialist Agenda. *Black Theology: An International Journal* 2:153–66.

———. 2007. Hearing the Politics of Peace in Ephesians: A Proposal from an African Postcolonial Pespective. *JSNT* 30:113–27.

———. forthcoming. The United Bible Societies and Bible Translation in the Caribbean: A Postcolonial Phenomenon. *The Encyclopedia of Caribbean Religions*. Edited by Patrick Taylor and Frederick Case. Illinois: Illinois University Press.

Yorke, Gosnell, J. Ukpong, and S. Davidson. 2010. The Bible and Africana Life: A Problematic Relationship. Pages 39–44 in *The Africana Bible: Reading Israel's Scriptures from Africa and the African Diaspora*. Edited by Hugh Page et al. Minneapolis: Fortress.

Zabatiero, Júlio. 1998. A Bíblia e o Pensamento Teológico na América Latina. *Boletim Teológico/FTL - B* 10(29):7–13. See: http://www.scribd.com/doc/17054007/A-Biblia-e-o-Pensamento-Teologico-na-America-Latina-Julio-Zabatiero.

Zachariah, Anshi. September 2007. Understanding Christ beyond Boundaries: Voices from beyond the Boundaries. *In God's Image: Journal of Asian Women's Resource Centre for Culture and Theology* 26/3:59–61.

Zachariah, George. September 2007. The Parable of the not so Prodigal Daughters: A Postcolonial Dalit Womanist Reading. *In God's Image: Journal of Asian Women's Resource Centre for Culture and Theology* 26/3:65–72.

Zakaria, Fareed. 2008. The Rise of the Rest. Pages 1–5 in *The Post-American World*. New York/London: Norton.

Zarev, Vladimir. 1998. *Four Passionaries for Father Bogomil and for the Perfection of Fear*. Sofia: Development Foundation.

CPSIA information can be obtained at www.ICGtesting.com
Printed in the USA
BVOW08s2114110316

440088BV00001B/23/P

9 781589 837034